The publisher gratefully acknowledges the generous support of the Humanities Endowment Fund of the University of California Press Foundation.

Barolo and Barbaresco

Barolo and Barbaresco

THE KING AND QUEEN OF ITALIAN WINE

Kerin O'Keefe

UNIVERSITY OF CALIFORNIA PRESS

University of California Press, one of the most distinguished university presses in the United States, enriches lives around the world by advancing scholarship in the humanities, social sciences, and natural sciences. Its activities are supported by the UC Press Foundation and by philanthropic contributions from individuals and institutions. For more information, visit www.ucpress.edu.

University of California Press
Oakland, California

Library of Congress Cataloging-in-Publication Data
O'Keefe, Kerin, author.
   Barolo and Barbaresco : the king and queen of Italian wine / Kerin O'Keefe.
      p.   cm.
   Includes bibliographical references and index.
   ISBN 978-0-520-27326-9 (cloth, alk. paper) —
   ISBN 978-0-520-95923-1 (electronic)
   1. Barolo (Wine)—Italy.   2. Barbaresco (Wine)—Italy.   I. Title.
TP559.I8O378   2014
338.4′766320945—dc23   2014020012

Manufactured in the United States of America

23 22 21 20 19 18 17 16 15 14
10 9 8 7 6 5 4 3 2 1

In keeping with a commitment to support environmentally responsible and sustainable printing practices, UC Press has printed this book on Natures Natural, a fiber that contains 30% post-consumer waste and meets the minimum requirements of ANSI/NISO Z39.48-1992 (R 1997) (*Permanence of Paper*).

For Paolo, Barolo lover and love of my life

CONTENTS

ILLUSTRATIONS

MAPS

FIGURES

After publishing *Brunello di Montalcino: Understanding and Appreciating One of Italy's Greatest Wines,* a book on Barolo and Barbaresco was the natural progression, given that these wines, together with Brunello, make up the trinity of Italy's top wines—and no, I'm not ranking them necessarily in that order. I believe that all three share and deserve their lofty reputations as part of the trio of Italy's finest wines.

Like my book on Brunello, this book will take an in-depth look at all aspects of Barolo and Barbaresco, two of Italy's most fascinating and storied wines. It will discuss the stunning side-by-side growing areas of these two wines, separated only by the city of Alba, and profile a number of the fiercely individualistic winemakers who create structured yet elegant and complex wines of remarkable depth from Italy's noblest grape, Nebbiolo. Although Nebbiolo can yield good—sometimes even great—wines in other select areas of Piedmont and in other limited areas of neighboring regions, including a narrow slice of Lombardy, the grape excels in Barolo and Barbaresco as nowhere else. Its success rate in the rest of Italy and the world on the other hand is actually dismal, proving the unique relationship between Barolo, Barbaresco and Nebbiolo.

Like most lovers of these two aristocratic wines, I discovered Barolo first, which is not unusual, since this is the more famous and larger of the two denominations. I have to thank my husband, Paolo, a true Barolophile, as well as my late father-in-law, Ubaldo, for introducing me to the wine. Ubaldo collected but didn't regularly drink fine wine, and his well-stocked wine cellar included Barolos from the late 1950s, 1960s, and 1970s including Kiola, Marchesi di Barolo, Fontanafredda, and Luigi Bosca as well as several bottles of 1964 Barbaresco from a certain little producer in Barbaresco by the name of Gaja; and Brunellos from Biondi Santi and Lisini from the 1970s and 1980s. When I moved to Italy in 1991, after several lengthy stays in the late 1980s, Paolo and I began our regular raids on the cellar (with Ubaldo's generous approval). These wines allowed me the unique experience of tasting aged Barolo and Barbaresco, often at the height of their glory, and at other times starting their inevitable decline, but even the latter still demonstrated that they had aged with dignity. I can remember thinking at first that Barolo was like a Fellini film: with my first sip, I wasn't quite sure what was going on but I knew I liked it, by the next sip it was starting to make sense, and by the time I finished the glass I was hooked.

In the early 1990s my husband and I also began what has become a regular routine of spending many weekends throughout the year in Barolo—a mere two hours away from our home—to enjoy steaming plates of tajerin topped with fresh funghi porcini, rich plates of Uova al Tegamino con Tartufo Bianco (Fried Eggs with Alba White Truffle) and Brasato al Barolo, all paired with Barolo. These feasts have always been followed by visits to the area's many small wineries. Later, when I began writing full-time, I would spend the best part of my visits to producers walking the vineyards, some of the most hallowed in Italy, and getting to know the winemakers and growers first in Barolo, and then later in Barbaresco, an unsung jewel in the world of fine wines.

One of my most vivid memories of these early weekend visits is from 1994, even if the circumstances were very grave, and it is one of the events that encouraged me to write it all down and seriously consider a career in wine writing. We left early in the morning of November 5 in a steady rain that by the time we reached the Langhe hills around Alba had become a ferocious downpour, although no one realized that we were soon to be caught up in the middle of what has since become known as La Grande Alluvione or the Great Flood of 1994, when the Tanaro River overflowed its banks. The flood swept away roads and bridges in and around Alba and in parts of Barolo and Barbaresco, and the torrential rains caused mudslides that damaged or carried away more than a few hilltop vineyards, and in a couple of instances, even entire hillsides.

Undeterred at first by the deluge, that afternoon we had a long lunch in the village of Barolo and then went to see legendary winemaker Bartolo Mascarello to purchase a case of his just-released 1990 Barolo. While we were talking with Mascarello, the lights went out, and Signora Mascarello came in with a candle. As Paolo and I sipped a glass of Barolo, Bartolo continued to draw his iconic labels—two of which he gave us—and recounted his days as a partisan. He also talked about the many changes, not all of them welcome, that were occurring in the insular world of Barolodom. We were entranced, and thoroughly disappointed when an hour later the lights returned, and it was time to make our way back to the hotel. The next day we were among the last to cross the Tanaro in Alba before all the bridges and roads in and out of the city were closed.

During my frequent travels to Barolo and Barbaresco over the last two decades, I've tried thousands of wines and visited hundreds of producers, not only as a wine lover but as wine writer, and have written on the areas and their wines in *Wine News, Decanter, World of Fine Wine,* and most recently, *Wine Enthusiast*. After I began writing this book in 2011, I visited every producer profiled as well as many who are not in the book. With more than 500 local wineries making and bottling Barolo and Barbaresco, I could not visit every producer and am sure that there are more unknown gems waiting to be discovered.

Besides spending much of the last three years on lengthy visits to Langhe, and my previous groundwork for specific articles on the areas' wines and wineries, I also attend many organized tasting events, including Nebbiolo Prima, which annually showcases the latest releases from the Langhe and Roero, and lately Le Loro Maestà in Pollenzo, a comparative tasting of Piedmont and Burgundy—all of which have proven invaluable research for this book.

I would like to address any concerns over possible conflicts of interests: there aren't any. I do not consult for or have any business or commercial relationship with any wineries or their importers. I have chosen producers solely on the merits of their Barolos and Barbarescos. Regarding quotations, the vast majority are from field interviews I've conducted as research for this book or on occasion from interviews undertaken for my previous articles on Barolo and Barbaresco. Otherwise, quotations are documented in a note. And unless otherwise noted, I've translated all material from Italian into English myself.

I suggest pouring yourself a glass of Barolo or Barbaresco to sip while you delve into Italy's most noble denominations—the very best way to truly discover these fascinating wines. Enjoy!

Introduction

BAROLO AND BARBARESCO,
THE PRIDE OF PIEDMONT

LOCATED IN THE NORTHWEST, PIEDMONT, which means "foot of the mountain," is Italy's second largest region and borders Switzerland and France as well as the Italian regions of Lombardy, Valle d'Aosta, and Liguria. True to its name, Piedmont is the most mountainous region in Italy, and not only do mountains cover more than 43 percent of its surface area while hills make up another 30 percent, but the region is also surrounded on three sides by mountains. On clear autumn days, somewhat rare, since much of the region is often shrouded in autumnal mists and fog, the sight of these snow-capped mountains towering in the distance behind extensive networks of undulating vineyards that have turned blazing gold and red mesmerizes the many wine and food lovers who descend on southern Piedmont every October and November to taste the area's prized white truffles and celebrated wines. On those clear days one can also make out the pyramid-shaped Monviso. According to locals, Monviso, one of the highest and most picturesque peaks in Italy, is the real-life inspiration for Paramount Pictures' iconic logo, and from a spring beneath its majestic slopes rises the river Po, Italy's largest river.

The entire region is considered one of the most important in Italy in terms of quality wine production, and Piedmont prides itself on not producing any IGT (Indicazione Geografica Tipica) wines, which are less strictly controlled than the country's DOC (Denominazione di Origine Controllata) and DOCG (Denominazione di Origine Controllata e Garantita) designations. Piedmont boasts a whopping forty-five DOC wines and fifteen DOCGs, including Barolo and Barbaresco, widely known as Italy's most noble wines.

Barolo and Barbaresco both hail from a hilly area known as the Langhe. Located in southern Piedmont, the Langhe (also sometimes referred to as

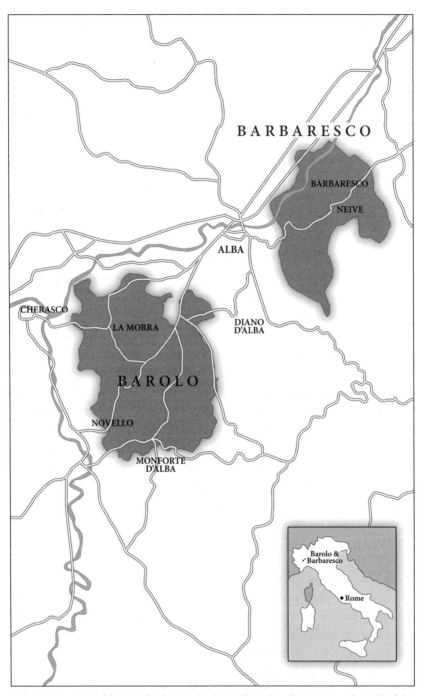

MAP 1. Overview of the Langhe showing both Barolo and Barbaresco on either side of the city of Alba. In June 2014 Langhe became a UNESCO World Heritage Site, along with Roero and Monferrato.

simply Langhe and also Langa) spreads out around the town of Alba. The Langhe hills reportedly take their name from a Celtic word meaning "tongues of land," which, with a bit of imagination, describe the shape of the area's steep, extended hills that run parallel to each other and are divided by deep, narrow valleys. It is here, in the Barolo denomination to the southwest of Alba and in the Barbaresco growing zone northeast and east of the city, that native grape Nebbiolo yields world-class wines of renowned structure and complexity. The best Barolos and Barbarescos are on par with the finest bottlings from Burgundy, Bordeaux, and Montalcino, and are among the elite wines of the world.

Nebbiolo is also planted in tiny amounts in other select areas of Piedmont, including in Roero, just on the other side of the Tanaro River from the Langhe, but the zone's highly sandy top soils produce wines that mature early, and in general they possess less perfume, structure, and complexity than their cousins over in Barolo and Barbaresco. However, Nebbiolo planted in one particular area in Roero, in the Valmaggiore site located in the Vezza d'Alba township, can yield wines with lovely floral aromas, bright red fruit flavors, and elegant tannins. Even a few top Barolo producers, including Bruno Giacosa and Luciano Sandrone, make Nebbiolo d'Alba Valmaggiore, and these wines have a growing fan base. The grape is also cultivated in Ghemme, Gattinara, Lessona, and Carema, all in Piedmont, as well as in the Valtellina area of Lombardy and in parts of Valle d'Aosta.

Even though Nebbiolo can yield very good and great wines from these areas, they rarely match the complexity and sheer majesty of the best Barolos and Barbarescos. It is therefore no coincidence that none of these other wines are obliged under their production regulations to be made solely with 100 percent Nebbiolo, although to be fair, a number of producers in these areas, especially in Roero, Valtellina, and Carema (where only two producers turn out Carema Doc's entire annual production of 50,000 bottles), use exclusively Nebbiolo even if their production codes allow them to add other grapes. Barolo and Barbaresco on the other hand are obliged by their production codes, rigidly controlled under Italy's DOCG system, to be made exclusively with Nebbiolo.

Brave producers in other parts of the world, including California, Washington, Australia, South America, and even Baja California, Mexico, with few exceptions, have met with little success with the variety. Having said that, I would like to note two wineries in the United States, Palmina in California's Santa Barbara County and Barboursville in Virginia, that are making Nebbiolos that show surprising varietal typicity alongside the grape's intriguing combination of structure and finesse. Wines from both producers also demonstrate aging potential that should allow them to develop even more complexity with cellaring. However, these two wineries are among a handful of exceptions, and of all the noble grape varieties, Nebbiolo remains one of the least planted in the world—and with good reason.

Nebbiolo, like Pinot Noir and Sangiovese, is a notoriously demanding and finicky grape that truly excels—on what is for Nebbiolo a relatively large scale—only in the very specific growing conditions found in the Langhe. However, this is not to say that every Barolo and Barbaresco is an exceptional wine. Even though the number of excellent wines across the board is indeed impressive, finding them can be a monumental challenge. Not only are there a number of large bottlers that still prefer quantity over quality, but one of the biggest obstacles for wine lovers is making sense of the dizzying number of labels available today from the myriad of small and very small producers that have emerged since the 1990s. Many if not most of these firms make a range of Barolos and Barbarescos from nearly 250 officially recognized vineyard areas between the two denominations, and there are also notable stylistic differences between producers and their wines—all of which has created widespread consumer confusion. An explosion in production over the last two decades has only exasperated the situation.

Since the mid-1990s, following profound cultural, agricultural, and technical changes that were set in motion some years earlier and turned Barolo and Barbaresco into two of the most sought-after wines from Italy, production in both denominations has soared. A look at annual bottle numbers shows that overall production of Barolo more than doubled between 1996 and 2013: from 6,192,267 bottles in 1996 to a potential of 13,902,404 bottles in 2013. Barbaresco, which is about a third the size of Barolo in terms of both hectares under vine and bottle numbers, increased from 2,406,800 bottles to potentially 4,681,737 bottles in the same period. One of the biggest changes in this period is that many small farmers in both denominations stopped selling grapes to the handful of large producers and bottlers that dominated Langhe's wine scene for decades. Today there are more than one thousand growers between the two areas and more than five hundred producers who make and bottle Barolo and Barbaresco as well as companies that just bottle and sell the wines. And over the past twenty years, zealous growers and producers have cut down woods, fruit trees, and hazelnut groves to make way for Nebbiolo, and to this end many have also pulled up vines that were previously planted with other grape varieties in order to plant Barolo and Barbaresco vineyards in their respective areas.

Because Nebbiolo is extremely site sensitive, it yields different results depending on where in the growing zone it is planted. Producers in Barolo and Barbaresco have long understood that some vineyards and even entire vineyard areas, known locally by the French term *crus,* are superior to others, and as far back as the late nineteenth century, Lorenzo Fantini, in his *Monograph of Viticulture and Enology in the Province of Cuneo,* published in 1895, classified certain vineyards, such as Barbaresco's Rio Sordo, as "first-rate." Yet it wasn't until the 1980s that producers in both denominations began adding cru names to labels on a wide scale. Seeing, however, that these crus were unofficial until 2007 for Barbaresco and late 2009 for Barolo, before this, producers outside the historical cru borders claimed to be inside, while others began using their own made-up fantasy names to adorn labels. As a result, and to the ire of those producers with holdings in the heart of the Langhe's top vineyard sites, the historical cru names started to lose significance.

To combat the problem, after more than a decade of delimiting the growing zones that generated bitter disputes and infighting among producers and authorities, in 2007 Italy's Minister of Agriculture officially recognized 65 distinct vineyard areas (defined by the extraordinarily languid term *menzioni geografiche aggiuntive* or "additional geographic mentions") in Barbaresco, with another added later bringing the total to 66, and in December 2009, it sanctioned 170 vineyard areas in Barolo (that came into effect starting with the 2010 vintage), although only a fraction of these defined areas are truly remarkable. On top of this, Barolo producers can also produce Barolo designated by the eleven villages that make up the denomination. As if having over five hundred individual producers and 247 microzones did not already bewilder even the most determined Barolo and Barbaresco lover, producers are also allowed to add their individual vineyard name to the more general cru area shared by numerous producers. And, lest we forget, estates that had the foresight to register their own invented names before the geographic mentions became official—and who could prove they had been actively using the name on the labels—are allowed to use these "fantasy names" in lieu of one of the geographic mentions—for example, Gaja's Sorì Tildin.

This is where this book comes into play. *Barolo and Barbaresco* will guide wine lovers through the daunting array of labels, crus, and vineyards, village by village. The chapters dedicated to the individual villages will give readers information on the geography, geology, and microclimate of each, and what these impart to Barolo and Barbaresco. Each of these chapters will also list detailed producer profiles of those estates making excellent Barolos and Barbarescos of authenticity that best express Nebbiolo and their individual terroir.

As readers of my previous book, *Brunello di Montalcino: Understanding and Appreciating One of the Italy's Greatest Wines,* already know, I strongly prefer terroir-driven wines, which are not always the top scorers in mainstream wine and food magazines. I could care less about how famous a wine or winery is, so don't be surprised if those Barolos and Barbarescos annually bestowed the highest scores by critics who reward only dense concentration and pungent oak sensations of vanilla and espresso are missing. While these wines—which are a throwback to the opulence-craving world of the 1990s (think big hair, *Dallas* reruns, and women's shoulder pads) and reflect the Jurassic taste buds of certain wine critics—have thankfully decreased in number, there are still too many as far as I'm concerned.

I do not hate barriques per se, and have in fact included a number, albeit small, of producers who employ these small barrels if their wines express terroir and finesse. On the other hand, I have no appreciation in general for wines strangled by new oak, but have even less tolerance when it comes to Barolo and Barbaresco, whose unique characters are easily destroyed by the toast, espresso, and vanilla sensations of new wood. I have therefore not included wines that seem more 1990s Napa or Australian than Piedmontese. In those few cases where I have included a winery that adheres to this style, entirely or in part, it is only because of a major historical role the winery has played, and this will be duly noted. There will be more about the various styles of Barolos and Barbarescos in chapter 4, "The Barolo Wars."

I would like to note that there has been a marked step away from the overoaked and overextracted wines that widely marred the denomination for most of the 1990s and for much of the first decade of this century, and that the choice of fantastic wines to pick from was, very happily, an immensely difficult chore but one that I thoroughly enjoyed.

PART ONE

The Place, the Grape, the History, and the Wine

ONE

The Ancient Origins of the Langhe Hills

ONE OF THE KEYS TO UNDERSTANDING BAROLO and Barbaresco lies beneath the surface of the Langhe, home to both wines. The Langhe hills, which rise up on the right bank of the Tanaro River, are composed of sedimentary rock from the Oligocene and Miocene epochs, although the area's original formation began earlier, some thirty-six million years ago, with the collision of the European and African plates. The Langhe is located within the Internal Western Alpine Arc, at the junction of the Alpine and Apennine thrust belts that formed the eponymous mountain chains. Yet the most fundamental geological event for the area was the formation of the Piedmont Tertiary Basin, which has fascinated geologists for well over a century: many of the geological ages, used internationally, are named after areas within the perimeters of the Basin, including Tortonian after Tortona, Serravallian after Serravalle, and Langhian after Langhe.[1]

This basin of deep water started forming in the Early Oligocene, and continued through the Serravallian and Tortonian ages, collecting a succession of sediments over 4,000 meters (13,123 feet) thick, consisting of mudstones and fine grain particles. From the Oligocene to the early Messinian (a time interval of twenty-eight million years) the basin was filled by normal marine waters, as is testified by the existence of marine fossils (both micro and macro). Then, some six million years ago, still during the Messinian age, the basin was disconnected from the Atlantic Ocean and exceedingly high salinity in the water was caused by fast evaporation, as the presence of fossils of marine protists, insects, and fauna suggests. This event "left a significant amount of marls (fine grained clay and carbonate sediment) and gypsum before eventually filling up again very fast at the closing of the Messinian (5.33 million years ago), when the connection with the Atlantic ocean was re-established," explains Francesca Lozar, a micropalaeontologist at the University of Turin whom I interviewed for this book along with her colleagues Marco Giardino and Eleonora Bonifacio.

Eventually, the submerged land was pushed above the water. According to Marco Giardino, associate professor of applied geomorphology at the University of Turin, "About five million years ago, strong seismic activity beneath the Langhe Basin, as the western part of the Piedmont Tertiary Basin is known, thrust the submerged land upwards, causing the trapped water to escape and forming the Langhe hills." Giardino, who also consults for Nuoverealtà, a small a group of united Barolo and Barbaresco producers, explains that the Langhe hills are technically defined as *cuestas*, ridges formed by tilted sedimentary rock. The tectonic activity that created the hills was followed by severe erosion that swept the younger sediment, rock, and debris from the top of the slopes to the bottom, creating different deposits of varied sediments between the highest and lowest areas, and may be one reason why certain grape varieties do better than others on different parts of the same hill, although altitude and sun exposure also play crucial roles.

Giardino adds that another decisive factor in the makeup of the Langhe occurred just sixty thousand years ago, when the Tanaro River, the Langhe's major waterway, changed its course from north, heading toward Turin, to present-day east, toward Asti and Alessandria. "The Tanaro's eastern course accelerated erosion, enhancing the cuesta formations of the Langhe hills and at the same time separating Langhe from the Roero area, which remains lower. It also meant that the water eroded the hills down to the much older substratum below. Much of the eroded sediment in the upper areas of the Langhe washed down to the Roero, which did not experience the same violent uplifting as the Langhe, and hence the Roero has younger, sandier soils," explains Giardino. This chronic erosion on Langhe's steep slopes remains a major challenge in the area, and many growers today plant grass between the vines or let it grow spontaneously to help stop deterioration and above all landslides, which sometimes occur in the area after torrential rains.

GEOLOGY IN A GLASS

In terms of viticultural performance, the Langhe's soils and geology were already being lauded as far back as two thousand years ago, starting with Pliny the Elder in the first century A.D. In his celebrated tome, *Natural*

History, Pliny wrote, "The cretaceous earth that is found in the territory of Alba Pompeia, and an argillaceous soil, are preferred to all others for the vine."[2] Starting at the end of the nineteenth century, contemporary chroniclers began defining the area in strictly geological terms, which, because of persistent erosion that limits the amount of topsoil that forms, are still widely used today to define the Langhe's terrain. The first attempt to dissect the Langhe's growing areas came in 1879 when Lorenzo Fantini began writing his monograph, "Viticoltura ed Enologia nella provincia di Cuneo," which he completed in 1895. He was perhaps the first to write on the Langhe's Miocene origins and to indicate the best vineyard sites in Barolo and Barbaresco, but in 1930, Ferdinando Vignolo-Lutati, a professor at the University of Turin, fellow at Turin's Academy of Sciences, and honorary president of the Piedmont section of Italy's Botanical Society, published what would become the benchmark work on the geological makeup of the Barolo growing zone, with a particular focus on Castiglione Falletto.

Vignolo-Lutati, a native of Castiglione Falletto in the heart of the Barolo denomination, divided the Barolo growing zone into three ages: Helvetian (now replaced by the term Serravallian), Tortonian, and Messinian. According to Lutati, "Almost all of Castiglione Falletto, Monforte d'Alba, Castelletto and Perno [the latter are hamlets of Monforte d'Alba], Serralunga d'Alba and parts of Barolo and Grinzane" were of Helvetian origin comprised of "alternating layers of beds of sand, sandstone layered with marls and sandy marls" that were "generally gray or yellowish sporadically interspersed with layers of bluish gray marls." Lutati went on to write that much of Barolo, a small portion of Castiglione Falletto, most of La Morra, and Verduno were instead Tortonian, "formed principally of gray and bluish gray marls." Lutati also maintained that the nature of the terrain in La Morra and Verduno was more complex, being formed in both the Tortonian and the Messinian ages, and that these villages have calcareous and chalky formations,[3] which echoes the description of Verduno given decades earlier by Fantini.

Generally speaking, the Langhe is composed of marine sediments characterized by a substratum of alternating layers of marls (consisting of clay and calcium carbonate) and sandstone, and besides being formed in three geological ages, the area also has three principal geological formations. The oldest in the Barolo growing zone is the Lequio formation, from the Serravallian and Tortonian ages, and is found predominantly in Serralunga d'Alba and in parts of Monforte d'Alba, home to the more structured and long-lived Barolos. The Lequio formation consists of silty marls, made up of clay and calcium carbonate, and sandstone, ranging from light yellow, almost white, tending to gray. The second formation, Sant'Agata Fossili Marls—predominantly from the Tortonian age and part of the Messinian—consists mainly of calcareous clay and marls that are bluish-gray. It is typically found in the villages of Barolo and La Morra, which generally produce the most perfumed and elegant Barolos, and in Barbaresco. The third formation, Arenarie di Diano d'Alba from the Serravallian and Tortonian ages, is particularly rich in sand (for the denomination)—especially in the subsoils. This formation is found primarily in parts of Castiglione Falletto,[4] known for producing Barolos with both structure and elegance.

These geological formations are fundamental in the Langhe, even more so than in other areas, according to Eleonora Bonifacio, soil scientist and professor at the University of Turin. "To put it in context, the most developed soils in the world are in the Tropics, where it is difficult to identify the original material that broke down to create the soil there. Soils in the Langhe on the other hand are not very developed due to continuous erosion and the consequential reshaping of the surface that sweeps away the topsoil and hinders its transformation. This is why we can use geological formations to divide the Langhe growing area; if the soil is not very developed it maintains the particle size distribution of the rock. On the other hand, this makes it more difficult to really study the wide variability among actual soils, which exist even if the rocks are the same," explains Bonifacio. She adds that because identifying the diverse soils found throughout the Langhe requires physical and chemical analysis, the area's soils have not been mapped out on a wide scale.

One of the few studies done on the area's soils was funded by the Piedmont Region and published in 2000. The study, coordinated by lead researcher Moreno Soster, analyzed various aspects of the Barolo growing area in the first half of the 1990s, and one of the most interesting outcomes is the pedological table the researchers compiled between 1991 and 1993 of fifteen test sites. According to this pedological table, the soil with the highest percentage of sand in the growing zone is found in Castiglione Falletto, followed by Serralunga, then Novello, Barolo, and finally La Morra, which has the least amount of sand and sandstone in the denomination but the highest amount of clay. However, this data is not wholly confirmed by the region's impressive data bank, Banca Dati Regionale dei Terreni Agrari—Laboratorio Agrochimico Regione Piemonte, whose data has been compiled by numerous soil studies conducted at the request of individual growers on their respective holdings in municipalities throughout the region.

According to the data bank's statistics, in terms of the major Barolo villages, parts of Monforte d'Alba have the most sand followed by Barolo, Castiglione Falletto, Serralunga d'Alba, La Morra, and Verduno. To keep this argument in context, I'd like to point out that the percentage of sand found in the soils and subsoils in the Langhe is far lower than the amount found in the Roero: an average of 22.9 percent in the major Barolo villages as opposed to an average of 32 percent in Roero, with some villages in the latter denomination, such as Vezza d'Alba and Montà, having soils that consist of 44 percent and 50 percent sand respectively according to the region's data banks.

In general, soils and subsoils with a high percentage of sand and sandstone drain quickly, meaning that vineyards located in sandy terrain, such as those found in certain areas of Monforte d'Alba, Barolo, and Castiglione Falletto, perform better in rainy years, while in drought years they suffer from water stress more than those vineyards that have a higher percentage of clay, which retains moisture. Vice versa, areas with more clay, like La Morra, tend to perform better in years in which there is less precipitation, while they suffer more in rainy years. However, Igor Boni, the lead soil researcher in the Soster Barolo study, points out, "In normal climatic years, vines in sandier soils generally perform better because they produce less, accumulating more sugar in the grapes." Beds of sand in the subsoils are also crucial, since they allow roots to easily grow far beneath the surface, where they can have access to more water and nutrients, and this may partially explain why healthy, old vines are not uncommon in the denomination when compared to other wine-producing areas in Italy, although there are other reasons for this that will be discussed in chapter 2 on Nebbiolo.

One of the fundamental components of the Langhe's soils is calcium carbonate (the principal component of limestone). It is generally agreed that the higher the amount of calcium carbonate in the soil, the more structure the wine will have. It was therefore unsurprising to see in Soster's Barolo study that out of the fifteen test sites, the four from the village of Serralunga d'Alba, the village most associated with powerfully structured Barolos of great longevity, had the highest amounts of calcium carbonate, while vineyards in La Morra, which produce among the most elegant Barolos, tend to have the least amount of calcium carbonate. This data was backed up by the region's aforementioned data bank, Banca Dati Regionale dei Terreni Agrari. Once again, to put this aspect of the area's soils into perspective, the average amount of calcium carbonate was far lower in Roero: an average of 16 percent compared to Barolo's average of over 23 percent, with some Roero villages like

Vezza d'Alba having only 11.6 percent calcium carbonate overall. When compared to Serralunga's 28.9 percent calcium carbonate, La Morra's 19.9 percent, or the village of Barbaresco's 18.6 percent or Neive's 23.2 percent, one can understand why Roero Nebbiolos have a more delicate structure than their Langhe counterparts. But, as Igor Boni points out, the region's Barolo study also revealed that, based on calcium carbonate alone, two vineyards within the same village and even lying side by side can have "soils with different characteristics," and that there are often "different rock sediments within just meters from the crest further down," proving the wide variety of soil conditions in Barolo that have not, or perhaps cannot, be defined by mere statistics regarding certain components.

It's important to note at this point that while the region's data banks on agricultural land can give averages, the data banks represent basically a collection of fragmented studies carried out by individual producers over numerous years. At the same time, the Barolo study funded by the Piedmont Region looked at only fifteen test sites, which makes it difficult to make sweeping judgments about the entire denomination, yet it is still a valuable guide to understanding the area. Sadly, and rather shockingly, no such in-depth study has been repeated, and one has never been performed in Barbaresco, where the main geological formation is Sant'Agata Fossili Marls. As geologists point out, one feature of the Barbaresco zone, also found in the Barolo denomination, is that the topsoil is very thin and in some places lacking entirely.[5] This fact is confirmed by Barbaresco producers themselves, and according to Italo Sobrino of Cascina delle Rose, "Having a very thin topsoil means that the roots of my vines go straight down to the much older soil beneath the surface, where there is more water and nutrients."

On one final note, the Barolo study headed by Soster discouraged further such studies when it declared in its conclusions: "Even the soils, which are found on sites with different exposures and that present very different particle sizes, seem to have no real influence on the musts and wines."[6]

For more on the soils of individual villages in Barolo and Barbaresco, please see their respective chapters in parts 2 and 3.

CLIMATE IN THE LANGHE

Wedged between the Maritime Alps and the Apennines of the Italian Riviera, the lower area of the Langhe, where the Barolo and Barbaresco denominations lie, has a temperate continental climate with hot summers and cold winters. However, the Apennines protect the area from storms and cold air currents arriving from the sea, while the warmer Mediterranean air tempers the colder air coming down off the Alps. Because of the many different hills and ridges, both the Barolo and the Barbaresco growing zones boast a number of different microclimates, which have a crucial effect on Nebbiolo's ripening. Both denominations also benefit from significant differences between day and night temperature changes during the summer months, prolonging the growing season that in turn generates wines with more intense aromas and complexity. Barolo, where the best vineyards lie between 200 and 450 meters (656 feet and 1,476 feet) above sea level, has a longer growing season than Barbaresco.

Barbaresco, which has approximately the same vineyard altitudes as Barolo, has a milder climate thanks to its closer proximity to the Tanaro River. Breezes generated by the river give much needed ventilation in the summer time while creating cooling mists in the early autumn—ideal conditions for Nebbiolo. Generally speaking, these conditions allow the grape to reach more uniform and earlier maturation in Barbaresco than in Barolo.

For more on climate and how climate change is affecting Nebbiolo, see chapter 2.

LANGHE'S EARLY HISTORY

Artifacts collected at the Federico Eusebio Civic Museum in Alba show that the Langhe was inhabited in Neolithic times, but the first permanent settlers in the Langhe are presumed to have been tribes of Celtic-Ligurian origin who populated the area in the fifth century B.C. Seeing that these tribes migrated from the Ligurian coast, where the ancient Greeks had already introduced viticulture, there is speculation that these tribes introduced grape growing and winemaking in the Langhe. In the first century B.C. Alba was founded as the Roman town of Alba Pompeia, and as the Romans were infamous consumers and connoisseurs of wine, we can be sure that they were growing grapes for wine production. Pliny the Elder confirms this supposition a century later when he extolled the suitability of Alba's soils for growing vines. Other proof is found in Alba's Civic Museum, where an ancient gravestone found in Pollenzo is inscribed to Marcus Lucretius Crestus, Merkator Vinarius, or "wine merchant."

After the fall of Rome, barbarian invaders took over the area, and lent their name to the village of Barbaresco, which derives from Barbarica Silva, meaning "woods of the barbarians." From shortly after the fall of Rome until the late Middle Ages, during the rule of the Lombards and later when the area was annexed to Alba during Charlemagne's rule, the Langhe hills were subjected to numerous raids carried out by bandits, and it is believed the area was sparsely inhabited. According to historical chronicles, in the tenth century, King Berengarius allowed for a fortification in Barolo, a precursor to the castle standing there today, to deter nearly a century of Saracen raids. In the early thirteenth century, land ownership and territorial divisions became more peaceful, and the areas around Barolo and its surrounding villages changed hands numerous times.

The fortunes of the village of Barolo and the rest of the lower Langhe changed forever in 1250 when the Falletti family acquired Barolo and the surrounding areas from the Commune of Alba. In the thirteenth century, the Fallettis were a wealthy family but not of noble origins, and they peacefully gained control over much of the land around the village of Barolo, counting some fifty large holdings by the year 1300. In 1486 Barolo became part of the State of Monferrato, and in 1631, as part of the Treaty of Cherasco signed by Duke Vittorio Amedeo I, the village and surrounding areas went under the control of the House of Savoy. During these tumultuous times, Barolo and its environs, which had been granted the status of county, suffered greatly at the hands of the French during France's struggle for power with Spain. In 1730, the Falletti's Barolo properties were transformed into a marquisate, or territory ruled by a marquis, and Gerolamo Falletti IV became its first marquis, or *marchese* in Italian.

The last Marchese di Barolo, Carlo Tancredi Falletti, married French-born Juliette Colbert de Maulévrier in 1807. The two lived in Turin but summered in Barolo, where the family still possessed extensive holdings, and where, by the 1830s, they played a fundamental role in the birth of Barolo (the wine), but more on this in chapter 3.

Noble Nebbiolo

WHILE THE LANGHE'S UNIQUE GROWING conditions are fundamental in producing beguiling Barolos and Barbarescos, an equally important factor (others may well argue *the* most important factor) is of course Nebbiolo, the sole grape allowed in both wines and which finds its maximum expression in select parts of the two growing zones. Nebbiolo is one of the world's most alluring yet infuriating grapes and can cause winemakers both joy and heartbreak. It is often compared to Pinot Noir, not only because both are extremely site sensitive, but also because like Pinot Noir, Nebbiolo yields complex, long-lived wines that are not deeply colored but are stunningly luminous. Perhaps Nebbiolo's most wonderful trait, however, is its intense aromatics, which change as the wine ages —going from wild cherry and fresh rose petals to forest floor, leather, tar, and balsamic notes.

Nebbiolo has long been dubbed Italy's most noble grape. It was already defined by Lorenzo Fantini as "the Prince of grapes" in his late nineteenth-century monograph on viticulture and enology,[1] and as the "King of Vines" by countless other writers after him. And like most royals, Nebbiolo is notoriously fickle and demanding. Or as Nick Belfrage aptly remarked in his wonderful book, *Barolo to Valpolicella*, "It is a temperamental creature, not to say neurotic."[2] It is one of the most challenging grapes in the world and truly excels only in certain areas with very specific growing conditions—namely, the calcareous marls of the Langhe hills. Nebbiolo has one of the longest growing cycles of any grape in the world, and the longest in Piedmont, where it is the first to bud and the last to ripen. For this reason, growers still favor south, southwestern, and southeastern exposures, which guarantee more sunshine to help with ripening, although rising temperatures and frequently torrid growing seasons since 2003 are putting this philosophy to the test. While some producers are now debating what constitutes optimum exposure given the change in climate, nearly all growers still agree that Nebbiolo's ideal altitudes range between 250 and 450 meters (820 and 1,476 feet)—lower altitudes put the vines at risk for spring frosts, while higher may impede ripening.

Seeing that this demanding grape needs such precise growing conditions in order to perform, it's unsurprising that Nebbiolo isn't a globe-trotter and is also one of the least planted varieties in all of Italy. According to Unione Italiana Vini, based on the most recent official statistics available from an international agricultural census in 2010, of the 5,992 hectares (14,806 acres) of Nebbiolo planted in the world, 4,477 hectares (11,063 acres) are planted in Piedmont, 811 hectares (2,004 acres) are in Lombardy's Valtellina, and 44 hectares (109 acres) are cultivated in Valle d'Aosta, demonstrating the grape's predilection for the Alpine foothills and a continental climate. It is also planted—albeit in minute and ever-decreasing amounts—in Lombardy's Franciacorta, where a few producers still add it as part of the blend to make Curtefranca Rosso. In Sardinia, many vines once thought to be Nebbiolo actually turned out to be Dolcetto, although there are now 84 hectares (208 acres) of Nebbiolo planted on the island. Only about 456 hectares (1,127 acres) of Nebbiolo are planted in the rest of the world, including 75 hectares (185 acres) in the United States, 180 hectares (445 acres) in Mexico, 48 hectares (119 acres) in Argentina, 98 hectares (242 acres) in Australia, and 26 hectares (64 acres) in Uruguay.[3] As the figures above suggest, Nebbiolo is most associated with Piedmont, which accounts for 80 percent of the world's total plantings of Nebbiolo. Even in Piedmont, Nebbiolo accounts for only 9 percent of the region's total wine production, and most of it is in the Langhe, which together with Roero counts 3,879 hectares (9,585 acres) of the grape. Of that, the lion's share, over 2,600 hectares (6,425 acres), is cultivated for the production of Barolo and Barbaresco.

There are several theories regarding Nebbiolo's name, and the most accepted is the grape's association with the Italian word *nebbia*, meaning "fog." It is generally believed that the grape was so named because it was traditionally harvested at the end of October when thick autumn fogs engulf the Langhe, although it should be noted that since about 2003, rising summertime temperatures accompanied by frequent droughts have pushed the harvest date forward by two to three weeks according to producers. Other theories claim that Nebbiolo's name derives instead from the fog-like veil that forms on the skins of the dark berries during ripening. Still another theory speculates Nebbiolo derives from word *nobile*—meaning "noble" in Italian—in honor of the aristocrats and kings who grew Nebbiolo and who were among the first to produce Barolo at their country estates as well as serve the wine at court in the late 1800s. Nebbiolo also has several synonyms, including Chiavennasca in Valtellina, Spanna in Piedmont's Novara province, and Picotendro or Picotener in Valle d'Aosta and in the Canavese area in northern Piedmont.

Nebbiolo is one of the oldest recorded grapes in Italy, and its first written mention dates to 1266, when the lord of the castle of Rivoli refers to the "Nibiol" grape in his list of wines.[4] Another early derivation of Nebbiolo appears in a 1287 contract between a certain Otto Milo and Enrico Lequio, which was recovered in the medieval building of the S. Spirito Hospital in Alba. Lequio was leasing land from Milo in "the place between the two bridges" of the Tanaro where he wanted to plant rows of "vitibus neblori."[5] Other citations for Nebbiolo appear in the early 1300s, most famously in one of the first ever treatises on agriculture, *Ruralium Commodorum,* written by Pietro de' Crescenzi in 1309, where the author writes, "Nubiola . . . is wonderfully vinous . . . and makes excellent wine and one to conserve, it's very powerful."[6] There are several other mentions of Nebbiolo in modern literature based on references found in obscure documents from fourteenth-century landholders, which although credible have not always been confirmed. However, the first official mention of Nebbiolo within what is now the Barolo denomination hails from town records in the Barolo village of La Morra. In 1431 a notary public added a new chapter to the town's statutes that originally dated back to 1402 regarding the grape *nebiolium* as well as *pignolium*—a grape that has since disappeared from the area. The revised laws governing La Morra stipulated that anyone caught cutting a vine of either grape would be fined five lire—a substantial sum for the times. As if this punishment didn't already demonstrate an almost ferocious respect and appreciation for the two varieties, yet another chapter of the same statutes suggested cutting off the right hand of anyone caught a second time.[7]

Even if we know that Nebbiolo has been in Piedmont for at least seven centuries and perhaps far longer, and while experts consider the hills around Alba to be the grape's spiritual home, we still don't know for sure where the grape originated. And according to Anna Schneider, a professor of ampelography at the University of Turin, we may never know. However, Schneider, one of the world's most dynamic and respected experts on Italian grape varieties, whom I first interviewed in 2004 and again for this book, isn't convinced the grape was originally introduced by the Greeks—one of the most commonly purported myths regarding the grape's provenance. "Until we discover Nebbiolo's parents, we can't say for sure where the grape originated. However, the ancient Greeks influenced viticulture much more in southern Italy than northern Italy, and I think it's a mistake to assume that the Greeks brought in most of our grape varieties. But it's a very complex issue," says Schneider.

Schneider and her colleagues have performed groundbreaking research on Nebbiolo—including DNA analysis—and although they still haven't found the grape's parents, they have found very close relatives and cousins. "We're following a trail to hunt down Nebbiolo's parents, but still haven't found them for sure. We don't know if we ever will or even if they still exist because they could be extinct, or mutated by evolution," says Schneider. "There are about a dozen varieties that are close relatives, ten of which are first-degree relatives—parents or offspring. All of these are varieties found in Piedmont or in Valtellina, where Nebbiolo has a number of blood relatives. Two of the best-known of these close relatives are Freisa and Vespolina while lesser-known varieties include Brugnola, Rossolino and Neretto di Bairo. We also discovered that Bubbierasco, a rare grape from the Saluzzo area that's almost extinct, is unquestionably an offspring of Nebbiolo. And we also know that Nebbiolo doesn't have any first-degree relatives in any cultivated vineyards in other areas of Europe, only in Piedmont and Valtellina."

In 2000 Schneider and her colleagues, R. Botta, N. S. Scott, and M. R. Thomas, also identified another blood relative of Nebbiolo, Rosé. This came as a shock because until they published a scientific paper that same year revealing their conclusions, Rosé had always been considered a subvariety of Nebbiolo, along with Michet and Lampia. It was even sanctioned in the production codes of both Barbaresco and Barolo until the regulations were revised in 2007 and 2010, respectively, at which time the wording was changed to accommodate the latest scientific findings on Nebbiolo and Rosé. So instead of listing the three subvarieties, the latest production codes for both wines now state simply "Nebbiolo" as the only grape allowed in Barolo and Barbaresco. "While studying Nebbiolo's intravarietal variability, first by the morphology of the plants and then their genetics, we realized that the grape known as Nebbiolo Rosé isn't a subvariety of Nebbiolo but is instead a distinct variety. In other words, Rosé derives from a different seedling, but it is without a doubt a very close relative of Nebbiolo and most likely has a first-degree relationship with Nebbiolo, such as a father, son, or brother," explains Schneider.

So far Italy's National Register of Grapevines has not registered Rosé as a separate variety, and there are more than a few Barolo and Barbaresco producers who hope it never does. Although only a very few Barolo and Barbaresco producers still have a limited amount of Rosé in their vineyards, including Castello di Neive in the eponymous Barbaresco village and Elvio Cogno in the Barolo township of Novello, they feel it gives their wines more intense perfume and elegance. For now, and until Rosé is officially registered as a distinct grape, these estates and others are free to use the variety if it is already in their vineyards.

Excluding Rosé, which because of its very light color had already fallen out of fashion decades ago, the two subvarieties of Nebbiolo planted in Barolo and Barbaresco are Michet and Lampia. According to Professor Vicenzo Gerbi, who teaches enology at the University of Turin, Michet is the superior of the two because "it has smaller bunches, smaller berries, and yields more structured wines." He also told me the afternoon I interviewed him at Ampeleon, Alba's Enological School, that "Michet, which is a genetic mutation of Lampia caused by a virus, is more resistant to disease." However, although Michet produces higher quality, it also produces low quantity, and today Lampia, which growers and winemakers generally say is the most reliable in terms of production, is the most diffused subvariety of Nebbiolo in the Langhe.

Clonal research, which started in the late 1970s and 1980s, has now yielded thirty-six approved clones according to Professor Silvia Guidoni, who teaches at the University of Turin's Department of Agriculture, Forest and Food Sciences. Of these, CVT CN 142, CVT CN 230, CVT 71, CVT 423, and CVT 185 have been the most popular in the Langhe for new plantings since the early 2000s. As Guidoni told me during one of our interviews in 2013, the best new clones "offer reduced productivity, and more open bunches," which she says is crucial because Nebbiolo generally has very compact clusters. Having less compact bunches reduces the risk of fungal diseases, which in turn means less need for chemical or copper-sulfur treatments and healthier grapes overall.

Despite the availability of new clones, a number of growers in the Langhe, including Mauro Mascarello of Giuseppe Mascarello and Franco Massolino among others, still prefer to carry out massal selections of the best-performing plants in their vineyards to propagate new generations of Nebbiolo with the estate's own genetic stock. According to the growers, besides being the offspring of hearty vines that have had decades to adapt to their growing conditions, plants resulting from massal selections offer genetic diversity that reduces the risks that an entire vineyard can be subject to a certain disease or perform badly during adverse climatic conditions, as can happen when a vineyard is populated by a single clone.

VINEYARD MANAGEMENT

Because of the steep incline of the majority of Nebbiolo vineyards in both Barolo and Barbaresco, much of the vineyard management is still performed by hand, including pruning, tying back the canes and grape thinning, and, above all, harvesting, which is rigorously manual. The only jobs performed using tractors are generally spraying fungicides, cutting the grass between the rows or turning the soil, as well as trimming the shoots on top of the vines. These days almost all producers in the Langhe grow grass between the rows, not only to create competition that should encourage vines to produce less grapes (and hence more concentrated fruit), but mostly as a way to help stop erosion, one of the biggest challenges in the Langhe, thanks to the vertical slopes and thin soil. In the last decade, grass between the rows also keeps the soil cool during excessive heat and drought.

When compared to other major Italian winemaking regions, producers in the Langhe have a healthy respect for old vines, and a surprising number of producers make Barolo and Barbaresco from thirty-, forty- and fifty-year-old vines, while a small but still significant number of Langhe's growers lovingly tend even older Nebbiolo plants. While the majority of producers in other regions, such as Tuscany, focused more on quantity in the 1960s and 1970s and often planted more productive clones, and many still prefer to replant every twenty to twenty-five years, since younger plants produce more grapes, the majority of Nebbiolo growers have always been too small to have even considered the expense of replanting, especially given the minute size of their holdings. Instead, Langhe producers have long opted to replace individual vines when plants died or when they could no longer produce even a minimum number of bunches. And only when absolutely necessary do growers replant their entire vineyards of Nebbiolo. Some producers have also told me that one reason for the advanced age of the vines could be that since the early 1990s, the region has given economic incentives to growers who adhere to sustainable viticultural practices. The incentives encouraged a number of growers to eschew harsh chemicals and use more organic vineyard practices, and this has kept vines healthy and productive. Although I believe this is in fact a viable explanation, there is no hard evidence to prove it.

As we have seen, Nebbiolo is notoriously site sensitive, and even in the optimal growing conditions of the Langhe, one of the main challenges for growers is the vine's excess vigor, which manifests in the length of the shoots (also known as canes). "Nebbiolo is extraordinarily vigorous, and produces incredibly long canes," says Professor Guidoni. These canes are trained upward, and in the summer create a very high leaf canopy, much higher than other local varieties. For anyone visiting the Langhe's vineyards during summer and before the harvest, this unusual height—normally between 2 to 2.5 meters (6.5 to 8.2 feet) and even up to nearly 3 meters (9.8 feet) in older vineyards—makes it easy to distinguish Nebbiolo from other local varieties such as Barbera and Dolcetto, which grow lower to the ground. (After the harvest, however, it's easier to spot the Nebbiolo vines, since the leaves turn yellow, while the leaves of the other local red varieties turn red.)

Yet the real difficulty with the length of the canes is the space between individual buds, or internodes, which is also very long. This unusual distance between buds—15 to 20 centimeters (6 to 8 inches)—is exacerbated by the fact that on Nebbiolo vines, the basal bud, the first bud closest to the plant, is sterile. According to grape grower and Barolo producer Alfio Cavallotto, "Actually, it can be the first three or four buds that are sterile, so you generally have to leave eight to ten buds on fruiting canes to have adequate production and balance." For this reason, nearly all producers employ long pruning methods and the classic Guyot training system, whereby one fruit bearing cane is trellised horizontally along a wire. Each winter, growers will leave one fruit-bearing cane that produces the grape bunches that year, and one "wood cane" is held over for the following year. Guyot training is also considered one of the best training systems for controlling yields, especially in thin, infertile soil. Spurred cordon on the other hand, the training system used in Montalcino for Sangiovese, for example, doesn't work with Nebbiolo, as that training system shortens the cane down to the first two nodes, which, as explained above, are generally nonproductive on Nebbiolo vines.

Controlling this excess vigor of the canes is fundamental in today's vineyard management. "The shoots have to be trimmed with a shearing machine mounted on top of a tractor to keep the canes and vines at a healthy level for ideal grape production," says Aldo Vacca, the director at Produttori del Barbaresco co-op cellar. Other ways to control vigor include drastically reducing or even eliminating fertilizer, planting grass or even better, cereal crops between the rows (as the farmers traditionally did up until the early

1960s during the days of mixed-crop agriculture), using vigor-controlling rootstocks, such as 420 A, and selecting new clones that are less vigorous. Regarding clones, Guidoni points out, however, that "while new clones have been chosen because they're less vigorous, as of today, there aren't any clones that in absolute terms can be defined as being low vigor." Guidoni adds that cultivating 4,000–5,000 plants per hectare is crucial for Nebbiolo to control the growth of both leaves and fruit production.

Aldo Vacca feels that 4,000 plants per hectare is ideal: "Higher densities of plants per hectare of Nebbiolo can create excessive leaf canopies that in turn can generate constant humidity. It can also create problems performing manual maintenance of the leaves." Managing the leaf canopy is another key component to having healthy and ripe Nebbiolo. "The leaf canopies are trained vertically to avoid shading the bunches, and in summer we have to spend a lot of time eliminating the sterile lateral shoots. Great care is taken to preserve the main shoots and to allow bunches exposure to both sun and air to reduce humidity. Leaves on the main shoots are also crucial because they contribute to grape maturation (through photosynthesis), above all in terms of aroma evolution and tannin development in the final phases of the growing season," explains Vacca. Vacca also warns that for Nebbiolo cultivation "it's generally unadvisable to defoliate the bottom part of the vines where the bunches are in the last weeks leading up to the harvest, the way you normally do for other varieties." A number of producers learned this the hard way in 2003 when they eliminated leaves near the bunches and ended up with cooked grapes by harvest time.

Bunch thinning, or green harvesting, is also crucial and in August most producers cut off excess bunches, leaving a single bunch per grapevine, normally four to six bunches per plant. However, if up until the 1980s eliminating any bunches was still taboo in Langhe and seen as a waste of perfectly good grapes, these days a number of producers carry out excessive green harvests that yield overly concentrated wines with significant alcohol levels. A steady rise in summer temperatures has producers debating the practice, with some producers insisting that grape thinning should now be reined in given that the cool and sometimes damp growing seasons of the past that often led to poor and uneven maturation have been surpassed by scorching temperatures and droughts that leave grapes higher in sugar. On the other side of the debate are producers that feel grape thinning is now more important than ever because the hotter, drier conditions can easily send plants loaded with bunches into heat and water stress.

Nearly all local producers agree that summertime temperatures have notice-ably risen over the last few decades and that precipitation during the critical periods of the growing season in the Langhe has gone down. Most producers also cite the scorching 2003 vintage as the turning point, but according to Professor Federico Spanna, the head of agrometeorology for Piedmont's Department of Agriculture, the trend toward warmer, drier growing seasons actually began toward the last half of the 1980s. Spanna also warns, "Global warming isn't the appropriate term here. Climate change in this area mani-fests itself in erratic weather patterns and in climate anomalies and extremes that are often polar opposites." Spanna, whom I interviewed for this book in 2013, explains that "the Langhe still gets the same amount of rain, for exam-ple, but rather than dispersed throughout the year, there are now periods of very high precipitation generated by intense rain or snow falling in shorter periods throughout the year, accompanied by longer hot and dry spells."

He argues that numerical data alone regarding temperature change and precipitation does not tell the whole picture. "It's crucial not to base an analy-sis on any given year on straight numerical data. Crunching numbers alone could make it appear that two years that were actually very different in terms of climate and distribution of heat and rain were similar. It's key to under-stand how and when weather patterns and anomalies are distributed during the year, as this will have a drastic effect on the growing cycle and perform-ance of crops."

Even though Spanna feels the real effects of climate change in the Langhe are unstable and abnormal weather patterns, he agrees that there is an overall warming trend, but he challenges the popular notion that the torrid 2003 vintage was the turning point: "Don't forget that 2002 was an unusually cold and wet year, while 2004 was perfectly normal for the Langhe." According to Spanna, temperature records registered in Castiglione Falletto since 1981 show that overall temperatures have gone up by one degree Celsius in the last three decades: "From 1981 to 1990, the average annual temperature was 12.4 degrees Centigrade, with a warming trend starting at the end of the 1980s. The average temperature rose to 12.7 from 1991 to 2001, but between 2002 and 2012 it jumped to 13.5 degrees Centigrade." He adds that yearly precipitation, recorded in La Morra since 1929, has only dropped by a few millimeters.

"And then we have a spring season like we just had in 2013, which has been the coolest and wettest registered since we began collecting climate data in the area," says Spanna. He also points out that until the beginning of the twentieth century, some hilly areas of Piedmont were home to a thriving population of olive trees, which have succumbed to the thermal aberrations in the most recent winter seasons, in particular the rigid winters of 2012 and 2013. However, Spanna also feels that the changes in the Langhe's climate have generally been beneficial to Nebbiolo production: "If you look at overall quality since the late 1980s, there are about seven or eight very good to outstanding vintages every decade and only two or three mediocre or poor vintages. Before this, and in particular during the 1970s, cooler, wetter weather in the summer and during the harvest led to the opposite, offering up only two or three very good or outstanding harvests every ten years."

While the last few decades have certainly seen many good and great vintages, such as 1988, 1989, 1996, the undervalued but excellent 1998, 1999, 2001, the phenomenal 2004, the excellent 2006, and the outstanding 2010, there have been a number of vintages showing cooked fruit and high alcohol, such as the overrated 1997, the disastrous 2003, the overhyped and forward 2007, and the overall lackluster and uneven 2009. While there are of course some notable exceptions—Barolos and Barbarescos made by the best mid- and small-sized producers whose limited production of estate grapes allows them to better control quality in tough vintages—many wines from the scorching 2003, 2007, and 2009 vintages also suffered from excruciatingly bitter, green tannins. This is because the plants shut down as a defensive measure against the extreme heat and drought, and even though the grapes continued to accumulate sugar levels, the seeds often didn't reach ideal maturation. As a result, I've found a number of unbalanced and astringent wines from these vintages along with wines that were dominated by alcohol sensations. In fact, a number of Barolos and even a few Barbarescos from the 2007 and 2009 vintages declare 15 percent alcohol on their labels, although many of these are likely closer to 15.5 percent (in Italy declared alcohol levels can be up to a half degree less than the actual alcohol level). Although some bottlings have the structure to support the high alcohol, others don't.

The extreme heat during the growing season now has some growers and producers debating the sacred *sorì,* those hilltop vineyards with full southern exposure that have long been considered the very best for Nebbiolo maturation. These vineyards are easily identifiable after a snowfall because the snow melts first in the celebrated *sorì,* and growers have long used this natural phenomenon as the benchmark to distinguish vineyards with optimum growing conditions for fickle Nebbiolo, which still has its reputation as being notoriously difficult when it comes to reaching ideal maturation. Although the jury is still out, a number of producers (obviously those that don't have *sorì*) say that full southern exposures in today's hotter growing seasons produce unbalanced Barolos and Barbarescos with elevated alcohol levels that may necessitate blending in some Barbera to add back fresh acidity (strictly forbidden under the regulations that govern production of both Barolo and Barbaresco). Other producers—yes, those owning vineyards with full southern exposures—say that Nebbiolo still benefits from the intense and long hours of sunlight offered only by perfect southern exposures, and that vineyard management is key to controlling low acidity and high alcohol.

At this point, only time will tell, but it does appear that the long-held views of what constitutes ideal conditions for Nebbiolo are being put to the test. A prime example is the Barbaresco village of Treiso, where Dolcetto reigned supreme until the 1990s. While this is in part due to the fact that until the late 1990s there was actually more demand for Dolcetto than Barbaresco, producers there also admit that Nebbiolo now performs better than it traditionally did in Treiso's higher, cooler altitudes, making the case that perhaps what have long been considered ideal conditions for Nebbiolo are indeed changing to include higher altitudes and more varied exposures, although all producers say full northern exposures should still be avoided at all costs.

Increased temperatures during the growing season have shortened Nebbiolo's infamously long growing cycle by an average of two weeks, with the harvest now commencing on the first few days of October as opposed to mid- to late October, the traditional start of the Nebbiolo harvest until just a decade ago. According to Professor Guidoni, who feels that 2003 actually marks the starting point of the Langhe's hotter, drier growing seasons, the increased temperatures during the summer are "reducing day and night temperature differentials," which are crucial for Nebbiolo's aromatic development and complexity.

It should be noted, however, that Piedmont is not alone in the battle against rising temperatures and erratic, extreme weather patterns. To help combat the problem, on April 19, 2013, Italy's Ministry of Agriculture passed an unprecedented decree to allow vines—even those in denominations like Barolo and Barbaresco that are by law dry-farmed—the possibility of emergency irrigation in cases of water stress. As a motive for this radical change of policy, the decree cites "the climate all over Italy . . . [which] for the last few years has been characterized by a constant rise in temperatures in spring, summer, and autumn, aggravated by a scarcity of rain." Even though I have been against such a measure in the past because of the possibility that indiscriminate irrigation could compromise quality, recent vintages of Barolo, Barbaresco, and also Brunello have convinced me the measure is now necessary.

DISEASES

Nebbiolo is susceptible to several fungus diseases, namely, peronospora, which is very active in spring at about the same time that Nebbiolo flowers. Nebbiolo is also prone to oidium (also known as powdery mildew) and botrytis, although to a lesser extent. The latest danger to Nebbiolo vines, and perhaps the most serious, is flavescence dorée, part of the family of diseases known as grapevine yellows, caused by phytoplasmas. It is an epidemic disease characterized by its rapid spread from one vine to another via a cicadellidae leafhopper. Although parties don't agree on just when the disease was first detected in the Langhe's vineyards, it appears to have arrived around 2009, and many growers I spoke with are convinced the disease has been widely spread through contaminated plants acquired at grapevine nurseries.

Although many producers in the Langhe prefer to spray copper-sulfur mixtures against fungus diseases as opposed to harsher chemicals, most producers use chemical insecticides against flavescence dorée. However, some producers do indeed use the organic alternative, pyrethrin, to combat the disease, although they admit that it is far less convenient, since it breaks down in sunlight and can be sprayed only in the evening.

THREE

The King of Wines, the Wine of Kings

WHILE WE KNOW THAT THE FIRST WINE called Barbaresco hails from the 1894 vintage (see chapter 14), decades after Barolo first made its appearance, it is difficult to say exactly when the latter, as we know it today, was created. However, based on contemporary accounts, most historians agree that a dry version of Nebbiolo has been around since at least the mid-1800s. Before this, Nebbiolo-based wines made in and around the hills of Barolo appear to have been sweet wines and sometimes even sparkling, but even these precursors to today's Barolo apparently had admirers, among them the English elite and Thomas Jefferson.

In *Barolo, the Jewel of the Langa,* Barolo producer and historian Maurizio Rosso writes that in 1751 a group of Italian diplomats with contacts in London created a company to import wines from Piedmont into England. Later that year the first shipment of "Barol" arrived, and "was judged on par with Bordeaux." This marks the first time Barolo, albeit a derivative of the name, appears in a written document as the name of the wine, which before this and well into the nineteenth century was still called Nebbiolo or Nebbiolo da Barolo. The House of Savoy's Carlo Emanuele III, the king of Sardinia, whose distant descendant eventually became the first king of Italy in 1861, financed the next shipment to England, which, however, arrived spoiled thanks to a cargo of oranges that had rotted during the voyage, and had been placed on top of the barrels. Another attempt, this time financed by two Englishmen, was also unsuccessful, as it seems the wine became spoiled on the first leg of the journey in mule trains from Cuneo to Nice. After these foiled attempts, exporting Barolo to the United Kingdom was eventually abandoned.[1]

In 1787, while U.S. minister to France, Thomas Jefferson traveled to Turin, where he tasted what was a precursor to Barolo and Barbaresco, made partly or wholly from what is presumably the Nebbiolo grape. Jefferson wrote in his journal that he found the wine, "Nebiule," "about as sweet as the silky Madeira, as astringent on the palate as Bordeaux and as brisk as Champagne. It is a pleasing wine."[2] Just a few years later, when serving as secretary of state (1790–93), Jefferson put in a standing order with his trusted wine merchant from Europe for "five or six dozen of the best Nebiule wine should it become available." Later, as president of the United States, "he served 250 bottles of Nebbiolo."[3]

As Jefferson's account demonstrates, before 1800, wines made with Nebbiolo, including the wine we now know as Barolo, were simply called Nebbiolo or Nebbiolo da Barolo, meaning Nebbiolo from Barolo in reference to the town. It's important to note that most of the wine from this period was sold in demijohns, and there are no surviving bottles from this era, with one famous exception: a wine labeled simply "Cannubi 1752," the oldest Langhe bottling in existence and owned by the Manzone family. We assume that this ancient bottle was made with Nebbiolo, and it aptly demonstrates that whoever bottled the wine thought the vineyard name was more important than the name of the grape or the village.

Jefferson's account is one of many that describe the Nebbiolo-based wines from the eighteenth century as sweet, presumably because winemakers were not able to carry out complete fermentation, with the result that some residual sugar remained in the wine, or perhaps winemakers purposely stopped fermentation before all the sugar had been turned into alcohol, to cater to consumers' preference for sweeter wines. Given the lack of winemaking knowledge and the primitive equipment as well as colder air temperatures that could have blocked fermentation shortly after Nebbiolo was harvested at the end of October, I tend to agree with the former theory.

OUDART AND BAROLO—FACT OR MYTH?

At some point around the mid-1800s, dry versions of Barolo appeared, but exactly who is responsible for this transformation is a matter of debate among twenty-first-century historians. Based on recent documents and publications, it now appears this aspect of Barolo history was rewritten over the years to offer a more romanticized version of events. Nearly all written accounts before 2004 give credit for creating Barolo as we know it today to Louis Oudart, a Frenchman whom history describes as an enologist and friend of the French-born Juliette Colbert de Maulévrier, known in Italy as Giulia Falletti, the Marchesa di Barolo. While it is unanimously agreed that Giulia Falletti played a major role in the story of modern-day Barolo, some critics question Oudart's role.

Giulia Falletti and her husband, the Marchese di Barolo, Carlo Tancredi Falletti, were married in 1807 and moved to Turin in 1814. The couple summered at the Barolo castle where the Falletti family had a vast estate with holdings throughout what is now the Barolo denomination. Sometime after moving to Piedmont, the marchesa took an interest in producing the local wine, which she evidently thought had great potential but needed a drastic overhaul. According to the most widely circulated legend regarding Barolo, at this point Giulia Falletti called on her "friend" Oudart and asked him to leave France to come oversee the Falletti's winery in Barolo. Once he arrived, within no time at all, or so the legend has it, Oudart applied his in-depth knowledge of quality winemaking that was already well-known and practiced in France. Oudart soon began turning out dry Barolo, single-handedly transforming Barolo from a sweet wine that easily spoiled during transportation into a world-class wine that was soon being enjoyed at royal courts all over Europe.

Still another version of the tale, even recounted by Arturo Marescalchi and Giovanni Dalmasso, two of the early twentieth century's most esteemed Italian experts in viticulture and enology, in their 1937 publication, *Storia della vite e del vino in Italia,* maintains that the marchesa discovered Oudart through her friend Camillo Benso Cavour, an Italian nobleman and later the first prime minister of a unified Italy. According to this rendering, it was Cavour who summoned Oudart from the latter's hometown of Reims to come to Piedmont to oversee winemaking at Cavour's Grinzane Cavour estate. While both these accounts make nice reading, and they do offer a plausible French connection to Barolo's quality transformation, in the last decade a number of publications have surfaced that debunk what many critics now consider myths surrounding Barolo.

One of these, *Il vino piemontese nell'Ottocento,* a 2004 collection of extracts from a series of conferences held in Turin from 2002 to 2004, maintains that an Italian general, Paolo Francesco Staglieno, is responsible for the creation of dry Nebbiolo. Even though Staglieno's name has appeared in some nineteenth- and early twentieth-century chronicles, for the most part his role in perfecting Barolo has been greatly diminished in some accounts while others have maintained—wrongly say Staglieno's fans, which include contemporary historians and academics—that the Italian wine expert actually advocated sweet wines. For the most part, however, history has ignored Staglieno.

According to Piedmont historian Giusi Mainardi, who contributed to and edited the above-mentioned book, Staglieno, who authored a benchmark manual on winemaking, *Istruzione intorno al miglior modo di fare e conservare i vini in Piemonte*, published in 1835, "was called upon by Camillo Benso, Count of Cavour to follow winemaking at his Grinzane Cavour estate where he was the enologist from 1836 until the early 1840s. In 1845, Grinzane still produced wine 'using the Staglieno method.'"[4] This method was geared toward making quality wines destined for aging that could also withstand travel for export and that Mainardi's research demonstrates were vinified dry.

Mainardi goes on to write that from 1836 until 1846, Staglieno worked directly for the House of Savoy's Carlo Alberto, the king of Sardinia, whose royal court was in Turin and whose son would become the first king of Italy in 1861, to oversee all aspects of winemaking at the Royal Agenzia di Pollenzo estate and winery. Staglieno left the position only when he retired at the age of seventy-three because of health problems.[5] In 2003, Mainardi and her colleague Pierstefano Berta republished Staglieno's 1835 winemaking handbook, in which the general unequivocally writes on the importance of completely fermenting the local red wines so that they are dry as opposed to sweet, and on the necessity of using closed fermenting vats that not only stopped flies and dirt from entering the must but also limited air contact and hence were better for carrying out complete fermentation. Staglieno's insistence that cellar hygiene was crucial further proves he was way ahead of his time: while this may seem like a no-brainer today, cellar hygiene—or the lack of it—would remain a problem well into the twentieth century.

Oudart on the other hand was a French-born grape and wine merchant (not from Reims by the way) who had moved to Genoa in the early 1800s and later set up a winery there, Maison Oudart et Bruché, with his cousin. By the time Oudart showed up in the Alba area, King Carlo Alberto and Cavour had already improved Barolo under Staglieno's guidance and were evidently producing dry versions of it. This version of events is backed up by letters to the king from Staglieno, including one written in 1841 in which the enologist apologizes to the king, saying, "I'm sorry that the wine isn't mature, it still has a vein of sweetness and therefore I cannot let it be served yet at the Royal dinners, but the lot of wine marked with the letter C is already ready and has absolutely no sweetness."[6] Staglieno's winemaking handbook makes several other references to the importance of wines being dry.

A recent biography of Louis Oudart written by Anna Riccardi Candiani backs up Mainardi's findings that Staglieno, and not Oudart, played the major role in perfecting Barolo in the 1830s and 1840s. After years of thorough research, Candiani writes that it was actually Oudart who sought employment from Camillo Benso Cavour, and not the other way around, as the popular legends have always stated. Cavour hired the Frenchman for a short period to follow an experiment with French grapes but apparently only after Staglieno left. Letters demonstrate that in 1845 Oudart was vinifying some wines in Pollenzo, apparently as an experiment to make sparkling wines from Piedmont grapes using the Champenois method, but this joint venture also appears to have been fleeting according to Candiani. Perhaps one of the most surprising results of Candiani's research, however, is that despite all the digging through historical documents and letters, the author was unable to find any written evidence whatsoever of a connection between Giulia Falletti and Louis Oudart. For that matter, however, there has never been any confirmation that Staglieno worked for the Marchesa di Barolo either, but given the close relationships among the Piedmont nobility, it is safe to assume that they shared information on their winemaking progress.

BAROLO AND THE HOUSE OF SAVOY

Pundits still agree, however, that the Piedmont nobility was fundamental in making, improving, and distributing Barolo in the mid-nineteenth century, regardless of which winemaker was actually in the cellar. This connection to the aristocrats and to the House of Savoy, who not only served the wine at court but also made it at their royal estates, earned Barolo its famed moniker "the King of Wines, the Wine of Kings."

Even though it does indeed seem that Giulia Falletti first introduced King Carlo Alberto to Barolo sometime in the early 1830s and inspired him to start his own Barolo production, no one truly believes the tale that after he famously asked the marchesa during one of her frequent visits to his court when he could taste the celebrated wine she made at her Barolo estates, she answered by sending 325 ox-drawn carts, each loaded with a large barrel of wine—one for every day of the year minus the forty days of Lent—to the royal palace in Turin.

FIGURE 1. Castello di Barolo. The former summer residence of the Falletti family, the Marchesi di Barolo. Giulia Falletti played a fundamental role in the transformation of Barolo into a quality wine in the first half of the nineteenth century. Photograph by Paolo Tenti.

Giulia Falletti was a pious woman who founded many charities, her most famous being her charities for orphans, young unwed mothers, and women in prison. While no one knows for sure if the marchesa actually had any passion for wine, she certainly was business minded enough to understand that making and selling quality wine would greatly help fund her philanthropy. King Carlo Alberto on the other hand seemed to take a keen interest in winemaking from the point of view of someone who appreciated and indulged in good wine. Not only did he acquire wine from the Marchesi di Barolo to serve at his royal court, but he also invested in winemaking at his own estate, the Agenzia di Pollenzo. Construction of the royal agricultural estate began in 1833, and winemaking was a major part of the complex. In 1838, the king also acquired the Castello di Verduno, and at both estates he hired Staglieno to oversee winemaking.

During the 1830s and 1840s, Camillo Benso, the Count of Cavour, was also making radical changes to agriculture at his Grinzane Cavour estate that included more rational methods for viticulture and better conditions for farmers. As already mentioned, he too hired Staglieno to improve winemaking and also hired Oudart for a period, during which time the two experimented with international grape varieties.

King Carlo Alberto passed his passion for wine down to his son, Vittorio Emanuele, who became king of Sardinia in 1849 after his father abdicated the throne and would become the first king of Italy in 1861. After years of stopping at a hunting lodge at the Fontanafredda estate in Serralunga on frequent hunting trips, to change horses at the estate's stables, Vittorio Emanuele decided the property would be an ideal place to cultivate Nebbiolo for Barolo, as well as provide the perfect residence and future business venture for the two illegitimate children he had with his mistress, Rosa Vercellana, known as "La Béla Rosin." The king acquired the estate in 1858 and in 1864 began planting new vineyards at Fontanafredda, which he had already put in the name of the couple's two natural children, Maria Vittoria and Emanuele Alberto.

According to the estate's chronicles, a document in the Turin State Archives records the first reference to a wine hailing from the property: a "Barbera Fontanafredda 1867." The same document also mentions a "Nebiolo [*sic*] Barolo 1868" and "Barolo 1865," and it is assumed the latter two refer to wines made from grapes grown in the vineyards at Fontanafredda in Serralunga or from vineyards in the village of Barolo. However, Fontanafredda wines from this period were still being vinified and aged in the royal cellars in nearby Pollenzo.

Royal accounts show the first specific mention of a Barolo vineyard acquired by the king in 1866, and this seems to be the origin of the brand Tenimenti di Barolo e Fontanafredda. The royal accounts also attest to the presence of vineyards and a wine cellar on the property in 1870, as well as the planting of more vineyards and the construction of new buildings and cellars. By all indications, Vittorio Emanuele was gearing up wine production at Fontanafredda, including of his prized Barolo, which he made for his own consumption and was supplied to all the residences and estates of his royal family. After Vittorio Emanuele died in 1878, Fontanafredda was no longer funded by the king's estate, and his natural son, Emanuele di Mirafiore, by now an expert winemaker who had a flair for business, created the E. Mirafiore winery, which not only produced but also sold wine, with particular focus on Barolo.

This business venture changed the fortunes of Barolo by allowing connoisseurs—and not just members of the royal family and European elites—access to the wine by bringing it to the open market. Price lists currently on display at Fontanafredda show Mirafiore was already selling Barolos from the 1891 and 1892 vintages both in barrels and in cases of twelve bottles. Emanuele di Mirafiore, who traveled extensively around Europe's famed wine regions to better understand winemaking, was also way ahead of his time in terms of promoting his wines. In 1887 he became the first producer to open up his estate cellars to the public, and entered his Barolo in major national and international wine competitions, winning gold medals in 1888 at the Brussels World's Fair and in 1892 in Berlin, just to cite a few from that period. Other Barolo houses, many of which are still in existence today, also made their appearance in the latter half of the 1800s. They include Comm. G.B. Burlotto in Verduno, Pio Cesare in Alba, Oddero in La Morra, Giacomo Ascheri in Bra, and Marchesi di Barolo in Barolo. After Giulia Falletti, the last Marchesa di Barolo, died in 1864, the trust she had created to continue funding her charitable institutions, the Opera Pia Barolo, continued winemaking at the Falletti's Barolo property, but it eventually sold the winery in Barolo to the Abbona family, who still own it today. The trust also sold off other holdings in the area, and the resulting land division greatly shaped the future of Barolo, but more on that later.

To reflect the increasing importance of quality winemaking in the area, in 1881 the city of Alba founded the city's enological school, the Scuola Enologica d'Alba, headed by a brilliant twenty-six-year-old named Domizio Cavazza. Cavazza, a graduate in agricultural sciences at Milan's university, had continued his studies at the renowned institutions in Versailles and Montpellier before coming to Alba. After his arrival, he soon realized the great potential of winemaking in Barbaresco, just on the other side of the city of Alba. Before Cavazza established a cooperative cellar in the village in 1894, grapes from Barbaresco had generally been sold to the Barolo houses and were most likely vinified for Barolo production. After 1894, Barbaresco estates made their own wine, and Barbaresco became a prestigious wine in its own right, although production was nearly thwarted in the first half of the twentieth century.

MEZZADRIA AND SMALL LANDOWNERS

One of the unusual aspects of winemaking in the Langhe, when compared to other important winemaking areas of Italy, is the number of small farmers who have owned land, albeit tiny surface areas, since the late 1800s or the early 1900s. By contrast, in most wine-producing areas of Italy, including Tuscany, farms and land were owned almost exclusively by a class of landed gentry who had sharecroppers known as *mezzadri* work their land until sweeping land reforms reshaped agriculture after the Second World War. This sharecropping system, the *mezzadria*, had a negative effect on quality winemaking, as there was very little incentive for the sharecroppers to make quality wines because the landlords encouraged them to produce quantity.

This is a complex issue, and an entire book could be dedicated to the subject. Since it is also fundamental to understanding the history of Barolo and Barbaresco, it deserves mention here, although this is by no means an exhaustive explanation.

As already explained, decades before Italy became a unified country in 1861, Piedmont was part of the Kingdom of Sardinia and was the power center of the ruling House of Savoy, whose royal court was in Turin, the capital of the Savoy empire. The House of Savoy's rule was interrupted between 1796 and 1815 when Piedmont and eventually the rest of the Italian Peninsula were invaded by the French and fell under Napoleonic rule. During his rule, the French leader introduced the ideals that had fueled the French Revolution, and thus, Napoleon got rid of the established dynasties as well as those privileges enjoyed by aristocrats and the church. Napoleon's republican government confiscated and sold church property, and Jews received equal rights for the first time. Most crucially, in the context of this book, Napoleon proclaimed the end to feudal practices, revoking feudal titles and ended primogeniture rights, all of which stimulated land sales. This in turn created a new class of landholders, who bought and sold land as a commodity. Although Napoleon's reforms were not completely implemented before his government was toppled, and Piedmont returned to Savoy rule, they stimulated great social changes and helped set the stage for Italian unification decades later. Napoleon's rule spread throughout the peninsula, but the impact of French domination was particularly strong in Piedmont, the first region to be conquered. Case in point: if in Tuscany, in the first half of the twentieth century, land was owned almost entirely by the ruling classes and aristocracy whose large holdings were farmed by a peasant class of sharecroppers, in nineteenth-century Piedmont, land was owned not only by the ruling classes like the Fallettis (who had sharecroppers) but also by wealthy entrepreneurs, and in some cases, even by peasants. According to Daniel Zibalatt's book, *Structuring the State*, in the post-1815 period in Piedmont, "the phenomenon of property-owning peasantry had developed the furthest among Italy's regions as a result of the Napoleonic commercializing reforms." And if in other parts of Italy, well into the twentieth century, many landholders still passed their holdings down to the oldest son, in Piedmont both male and female offspring were inheriting land long before this. This constant division among generations of siblings and heirs has led to the tiny holdings distributed over a large number of growers in the Langhe.

Land became a crucial indicator of wealth in the first half of the nineteenth century, and the French doctrines of the right to own land and private property, along with legal equality for all, were fundamental principles of Napoleon's regime, and took root in northern Italy. When Piedmont became the cradle of Italian unification in the mid-1800s, these ideals were—to a certain extent—maintained in the region, although less so in central and southern Italy, where Napoleonic rule had less lasting influence. One group that particularly benefited from Napoleonic rule was Piedmont's Jewish population, which enjoyed equality under Napoleon until the regime was toppled in 1815, and again after the king passed a Royal Decree in 1848 to emancipate the Jews. This allowed Jewish people to acquire land, and their landholdings would become significant toward the last half of the century.

Once Italy was unified in 1861, the monarchy and its government continued the practice of confiscating and selling church property. A number of older grape growers-turned-producers told me during interviews held for the writing of this book that their grandfathers acquired land at the end of the 1800s or early 1900s from Jewish landholders. According to these veteran growers, since much of this land had originally been confiscated from the church, Catholics feared excommunication if they bought the land directly, so a lot of property was purchased at some point by Piedmont's Jews, who eventually sold it to local peasants under long-term payment plans.

Still other property was sold off by the Marchesa di Barolo's charitable foundation, the Opera Pia Barolo. While much of the land was sold to Piedmont's newly established nineteenth-century entrepreneurs (Piedmont was one of the first industrialized regions thanks to firms like Fiat, founded in 1899, and Olivetti, founded in 1908), during economic hard times following World War I, and later in the aftermath of the global economic crises after the 1929 stock market crash, these same entrepreneurs sold off slices of land to save their empires, and eventually simply in order to survive.

For all of these reasons, although sharecropping existed in Piedmont until the 1950s, it did not define agriculture to the extent that it did in central Italy, thanks to the surprising number of peasants who ended up owning small parcels of land throughout Piedmont, and especially in the Langhe, where it was hoped that grape growing and farming could sustain a family. This is not to say, however, that owning tiny plots of land increased the fortunes of the area's peasants—far from it. Most of the new class of landowning farmers had been and remained poverty stricken, and then had to pay back debts for the land they had somehow acquired. The Langhe remained a backward and economically depressed area until well after the Second World War. However, the enormous sacrifices that were made in order to own property instilled in the growers and farmers a fierce devotion to the land they had struggled so hard to acquire and maintain. If outside industrialists swept into Tuscany in the 1970s and 1980s to buy land that farmers were only too happy to sell, the Langhe's vast network of small farmers rarely sold their holdings, and even today growers almost never sell their property. Producers often recount the following politically incorrect but poignant analogy to highlight how important land is to them: If a man from the Langa finds out that his neighbor has had an affair with his wife, he'll be furious, but he'll get over it. If a man from the Langa finds out that a neighbor has trespassed on his land, he'll kill him.

THE FIRST CHALLENGES AND
THE FIRST REGULATIONS

Not long after production of the new and improved Barolo got off the ground, growers and producers of the fledging wine were faced with unprecedented challenges. The first was oidium, a fungal disease that arrived in the Langhe in 1850. Also known as powdery mildew, oidium was the first of three devastating vine diseases that were inadvertently brought into the region from the United States on vine cuttings imported by avid botanists during the last half of the nineteenth century. By the late 1850s, Piedmont's growers were using sulfur treatments to combat the disease thanks to the bishop of Biella, who first experimented with his own vineyards and then shared his findings with local priests, who in turn introduced them to parishioners.[7] The second scourge was peronospora, another fungal disease, which arrived in 1879. Nebbiolo is particularly susceptible to peronospora, since the disease is most active in the spring at about the time Nebbiolo has bud break and is very delicate; growers eventually discovered that copper sulfate treatments greatly helped. The third disease, phylloxera, was the most dangerous. This deadly, root-eating louse, which made its debut in France's Rhône region in 1863 and proceeded to destroy the *Vitis vinifera* vines across Europe, arrived in Piedmont in 1886. Fortunately, experiments in France had by then discovered that grafting European grapevines onto resistant North American rootstocks stopped the aphid. In the Langhe, strict measures were put in place to quarantine and destroy vineyards at the first sign of infection, and a committee had already been formed to teach growers how to graft their vines onto American rootstocks.

Despite the solution, phylloxera would be a menace well into the first decades of the twentieth century, as most Langhe growers were too poor to carry out the remedy and/or too isolated to have been updated on the technique of regrafting their vines, and the pest devastated local winemaking.

By the first years of the twentieth century, despite the significant challenges of the times, both Barolo and Barbaresco had become so famous that they were being imitated outside of their growing areas. In 1908, an association was founded to protect both wines from fraudulent imitations, followed in 1926 by the first delimitation of both wine zones. These two associations culminated in the founding of the first Consorzio di Tutela in 1934 to protect Barolo and Barbaresco from fraud and to guarantee their authenticity for consumers.

As in other areas of Italy, the outbreak of World War I hit the Langhe hills hard. Farmers were called to arms, and women and children, and even political prisoners, maintained the vineyards, carried out the local harvests, and made wine, though with dubious results. Uncontrolled outbreaks of peronospora and above all phylloxera nearly thwarted production.

By the time the First World War was over, vineyards in Barolo and Barbaresco lay in ruins. Many producers replanted with varieties they felt, rightly or wrongly, to be more resistant to both peronospora and phylloxera—namely, Barbera, Dolcetto, and even Freisa—and planted less Nebbiolo. Wine production increased overall, creating a glut that pushed prices down. At about the same time, Italy's Fascist regime discouraged grape production but greatly encouraged the cultivation of wheat and other food crops. The post–World War I period was one of the darkest times for Italian winemaking, and when the stock market crash forced many of Turin's entrepreneurs into bankruptcy, the demand for local wines also crashed. To further compound matters, investors who had recently acquired the area's largest producer, Fontanafredda, went into bankruptcy in 1930, creating a domino effect as many growers who had always sold their grapes to the estate lost their primary source of income.

By the time things had improved somewhat, Italy soon became engulfed in the Second World War. Once again, production generally ground to a standstill during the conflict, and when farmers returned from the war, the countryside and their farms lay in ruin. Social unrest also marked this post-war period; the monarchy was dissolved as a Republican government was voted in, and a number of Italians advocated for communism. Sharecropping was phased out and eventually abolished. Poverty dominated rural Italy, and prices for goods soared as a result of inflation. It is safe to say that quality wine was not a priority in this period, and demand for the fruit of Langhe's vineyards plummeted. Of all the local wines, demand for Barbera and Dolcetto outstripped that for Barolo, and the lack of demand eventually pushed prices for Barolo down to almost the same prices as Dolcetto and Barbera. Production of Barbaresco on the other hand had practically ceased in the 1920s, and would not be resuscitated until the late 1950s.

The 1940s through the 1970s were years of intense hardship and upheaval for the Langhe, resulting in a mass exodus out of the Piedmont countryside as young men and women sought work in the many factories springing up in Turin and other parts of northern Italy.

Although they probably would not have believed it back then, within just a few decades, many would return, thanks to the Renaissance of Barolo and Barbaresco.

FOUR

The Barolo Wars and Their Effect on Both Denominations

FOR MOST SMALL FARMERS IN THE LANGHE, the poverty and deprivation that marked the post–World War II period continued right through the 1970s, compounded by a serious scarcity of water. Since pumping water uphill from the Tanaro River would have been prohibitively expensive, producers in most of the Langhe hills still relied on well water, which often dried up by late summer or early fall, and not all homes and cellars had running water. Household water rationing remained a fundamental part of life in the Langhe until water was finally carried down to the area's many small villages from the surrounding Alps via an ingenious system of tubes and pipes that relied on gravity. The lack of a constant water supply in the most rural areas would last until the mid-1980s, by which time even the most isolated farms finally got hooked up to the water supply. Veteran winemaker and former local politician Giacomo Oddero, one of the true gentlemen of Barolo, was a key player in bringing a constant supply of clean, fresh water to the Langhe.

Oddero worked tirelessly at this crusade for decades and in my opinion has never gotten the full credit he deserves. For without a reliable source of clean, running water, the revamping of Barolo and Barbaresco, including the transformation of many small growers into wine producers, would have been virtually impossible. Undoubtedly this lack of accessible water had a huge impact on cellar hygiene at the many small farms in the area, and on the mentality of previous generations, who obsessively conserved water or simply didn't have access to it. Producer Mauro Veglio recalls, "Using any water at all in the cellars was not only unheard-of, it was downright sacrilegious, right up until the 1980s." Here, however, it is important to note the division in wine production that long defined the Langhe.

Until the 1980s, wine production remained sharply divided between winemakers and grape growers. Most Barolo-producing houses were relatively large-scale operations set up in Alba that made wine from grapes they purchased from local farmers. They were, as you would expect, sprawling affairs with large cellars that were geared toward quantity production. The growers on the other hand sold nearly their entire crop, saving just a little to make a tiny amount of wine for home consumption, although some also vinified wine to sell in demijohns. By all accounts, the vast majority of these growers had primitive cellars even by the standards of the period. There were of course exceptions to this division, although they were few and far between; Bartolo Mascarello and Cavallotto are two examples. These two families have been grower-producers since the 1920s and 1940s and as such were adequately equipped for winemaking, since it was their primary business as opposed to the home winemaking affairs of the vast majority of growers.

Besides generally having unsuitable wine cellars and poor equipment, until the 1980s, the majority of growers in the Langhe also had to grow other crops in addition to grapes in order to survive. These included wheat, fruit, and hazelnuts, and many grape farmers also had at least an ox and a cow as well as chickens. Celebrated boutique producer Elio Altare remembers the 1960s and much of the 1970s as years of immense hardship, and he paints a less than pretty picture of the reality of the times. "I worked the vineyards with an ox-drawn plow until 1970, until I was twenty. In the cellars, the growers had old casks, passed down from generation to generation and the barrels leaked because the wood was old and rotten," says Altare. He also explains one of the major reasons why Nebbiolo underwent marathon-fermenting and postfermentation maceration times back in the days of yore, and it wasn't simply to tame hyperbolic tannins. "Growers who made Barolo for their own consumption or to sell it as a side business left Nebbiolo to ferment and then macerate on the skins for months, but not because the wine needed it. Instead, it was a matter of convenience: right after they got Nebbiolo into the cellars, farmers and their families were busy harvesting wheat and doing countless other chores that needed be done all at the same time," Altare explains.

He also recounts the dealings between growers and grape buyers, which were a far cry from the usual descriptions of the solid, generational "through thick and thin" partnerships that many large firms routinely insist they have always had with the local grape growers. "In 1975, we had the most beautiful, perfect grapes waiting to be picked. I can remember standing around every day before the harvest with hundreds of other growers in Alba's Piazza Savona, outside Caffè Umberto, trying to convince the *négociants* [grape merchants] to buy our grapes. But they waited another two weeks—just as the grapes were about to rot on the vines—before they offered to buy fruit that year, forcing all of us to sell at a loss." Altare also points out that the buyers routinely paid growers an entire year later, which was standard and accepted practice at the time.

The mid-1970s were a turning point in Barolo history. As in the rest of the Western world, young men and women who came of age in Italy in the late 1960s and early 1970s began questioning the status quo, and in the Langhe, this meant questioning the staunchly patriarchal society that for generations had accepted what essentially amounted to a class division that penalized the *contadini,* the farmers and growers who were the lowest rung on the country's social ladder whether they owned land or not. Altare and a group of young twenty-somethings from around the Barolo hills demanded change. They wanted to improve their lot and realized that to do this, they either had to leave farming behind altogether, or if they stayed, they would have to drastically improve the backward conditions and start turning out quality wines in their own right as opposed to selling grapes to the large Barolo houses. At the same time that Altare and his peers were chafing at the bit in Barolo, over in Barbaresco, a charismatic and ambitious young man named Angelo Gaja was already hard at work changing ... just about everything regarding Barbaresco production—from vineyard management to barrel aging.

In 1976, a group of young growers from Barolo, among them Elio Altare and Enrico Scavino, went to Burgundy to see how their counterparts on the other side of the Alps were able to not only grow grapes but make fine wine from which they were also able to earn a living. It proved to be a life-changing experience for the young men, who returned home with a driving ambition to overhaul vineyard management and update their antiquated cellars. They would go back to France numerous times over the next few decades, along with new recruits from the Langhe hills.

By this time, luminaries Beppe Colla at Prunotto, Angelo Gaja, and Bruno Giacosa, all expert winemakers and grape buyers who knew (and still know) the Langhe growing areas better than anyone, had begun bottling single-vineyard versions of Barolo and Barbaresco, sending shock waves through the growing zones when they were first released in the late 1960s and early 1970s. Up until then, producers had made both wines exclusively by blending Nebbiolo from different vineyards in different villages in the respective growing zones. The philosophy behind blended wines was that certain vineyards and villages added distinct characteristics to the wine. For example, an ideal Barolo would have grapes from la Morra for perfume, from Castiglione for finesse, and from Serralunga for structure. Another reason for blending is that the practice can compensate for vineyards or villages that didn't perform well in certain vintages. However, Colla, Gaja, and Giacosa were among the first to appreciate the superiority of certain vineyards over others, and were keen to imitate the French concept of Grands Crus.

Imitating France, and later Napa Valley, was to become a key motivation in the Barolo and Barbaresco Renaissance, even if some of the changes that were about to sweep across the Langhe would prove unsuitable for Nebbiolo.

THE SAW HEARD 'ROUND THE LANGHE

In 1978, after several years of experiments, Angelo Gaja released the first Barbarescos partially aged in barriques. These notoriously expensive wines became an almost overnight sensation, with both Italian and international critics on both sides of the Atlantic lauding the wines for their polish and flair. Gaja's critical—and economic—success set off a series of imitators and imitations, and played a fundamental role in the genesis of the Italian wine revolution that soon engulfed the entire country. And if Gaja's 1978 bottlings can be compared to Paul Revere's midnight ride announcing the British invasion, then the sound of Elio Altare's chain saw first striking against his father's *botti* is the shot heard 'round the world.

By the early 1980s, *botti,* large casks made of Slavonian oak, had become the main point of contention among the new generation of growers-turned-producers who wanted to completely overhaul winemaking in the area. Their reasoning was that what they considered the greatest wines in the world, and those that received the most admiration from critics around the world—namely, Bordeaux and Burgundy as well as cult offerings from Napa Valley—were aged in barriques: 225-liter (or, as in Burgundy, 228-liter) barrels made of French oak. Altare and a growing contingent of other Langhe vintners increasingly despised the leaking, often rancid barrels that were passed down through the families. In 1983, Altare took matters into his own hands.

That year, tensions between Altare and his father reached an explosive point. Just two years earlier, Elio had spent weeks in the hospital as a result of chemical poisoning from products his father used on the crops, especially on the fruit trees. "After he sprayed the fruit trees again that year, I went out and bought a chainsaw and cut them all down. While I was at, I decided it was time to eliminate the old barrels, and cut them to pieces with the chain saw," says Elio, whose infuriated father promptly disinherited him. Undeterred, in 1984, Elio, who was by now renting the cellars and vineyards from his family, purchased his first barriques.

Even though Altare's actions were extreme, to say the least, by the time he hacked up his father's barrels, there was a general revolt against age-old customs in the area, and not just in the cellars. By the early 1980s, a handful of ambitious growers, often encouraged by an equally small but growing contingent of quality-minded Barolo and Barbaresco producers who purchased grapes, began performing another sacrilege: bunch thinning. Also known as green harvesting, this technique reduces yields so that plants can channel their energies into fewer bunches and produce higher-quality grapes with more sugar. Gaja, once again the pioneer when it came to reducing yields, was chastised by his father's shaking head. Altare argued with his father over grape thinning, and eventually won, as did countless other sons. Michele Chiarlo couldn't convince his loyal growers to throw away perfectly good grapes, and first rented, then bought his own vineyards at Cerequio in La Morra. Locals were so distraught over Chiarlo's first green harvest in 1983 that they promptly called in the help of the parish priest, who warned of impending doom and begged the producer to stop tempting fate.

The Barolo Wars were officially under way.

THE CONFLICT

The mid-1980s were marked by the 1986 "Methanol scandal," which killed twenty-three people and blinded dozens more in northern Italy. The scandal involved two-liter bottles of "wine" labeled Barbera that were manufactured by a winery in Piedmont that added methanol in order to increase alcohol levels. The scandal caused exports and national consumption to plummet, and consumers around the world shunned bottlings from Piedmont for the next few years. Now more than ever before, was the time for the region's producers, and in particular those in the Langhe, to embark on a campaign to prove to the world that great change was under way.

Thankfully, the following years yielded a string of outstanding vintages for Barolo and Barbaresco, including the 1988, 1989, and 1990, the latter the first of what was to be hailed as the "vintage of the century" by international and Italian journalists. The 1990 vintage was the culmination of a number of factors. The unusually warm growing season led to more forward Barolos and Barbarescos with rounder, softer tannins. The vintage also marked the denomination's growing use of barriques, which offered more mundane and ubiquitous sensations of toasted oak, vanilla, and chocolate that put many influential critics in their comfort zone. Before this, these same celebrated palates either ignored Barolo and Barbaresco or slammed it, finding the wine hostile and incomprehensible upon its release. Since the vast majority of Langhe wineries never kept back any old vintages (and still don't) to hold vertical tastings of older wines that could demonstrate the beauty, power, depth, and complexity of aged Barolo and Barbaresco, one can perhaps begin to understand the allure of this new generation of easy-to-understand, instant-gratification wines that soon flooded the Langhe. By the early 1990s, more and more growers had begun making wines themselves, and many opted for increasingly lower yields, rotary fermenters and barriques, all of which virtually guaranteed high scores from critics, which in turn increased sales.

This period was marked by what were often contentious debates between those who were dubbed the "Modernists"—a now ridiculously outdated term still hung onto by some journalists and producers even though there is no longer anything remotely modern or even vaguely exciting about barriques or overoaked and overextracted wines—and the "Traditionalists." The "Modernists" not only revamped what was wrong in their crude cellars, but most spoke out sharply against anything that could be called "traditional"—both a term and a concept that had by then become a slur in the area. The "Traditionalists" on the other hand were a small and diminishing number by the early 1990s. They were led by Barolo icon and philosopher Bartolo Mascarello; his outspoken cousin and expert in local history, Beppe Rinaldi, nicknamed Citrico because of his scathing, no-holds-barred comments; and the late, great Teobaldo Cappellano, whose sharp wit and unparalleled combination of common sense and adventure are sorely missed to this day. The division between the two camps was as solid as a wall, and tensions in the area ran high for years.

While the so-called Modernists advocated concentrated wines with more fruit sensations and barrique aging they thought softened Nebbiolo's fierce tannins, and wanted wines that would be approachable upon release, the Traditionalists argued that excessive grape thinning, short, violent fermentations in rotary fermenters, sorting tables and barriques destroy Barolo's and

Barbaresco's unique characteristics of leather, tar, and rose, replacing the latter with espresso, chocolate, and vanilla notes, while Nebbiolo's nervous acidity and bracing tannins were exchanged for extracted but enervated wines with lower acidity and bitter wood tannins that don't soften with time as do Nebbiolo's innate tannins. While the "Modernists" wanted power and concentration, the "Traditionalists" desired complexity, and most of the latter strived for elegance over raw muscle.

The critics agreed with the Antitraditionalists, as can be seen from the former's scores in publications from the day. In its October 31, 1994, edition, *Wine Spectator* gave the 1989 Barolo from Bartolo Mascarello, a fabulous, gorgeous wine of complexity and elegance, a lowly and insulting 76 points, while it awarded far higher scores to barrique-aged wines from the same vintage. In the same issue, the tasting editor "retried Bruno Giacosa's wines," which it had initially tasted a year earlier as barrel samples, and scored them in the mid-70s and below; the latter "fared considerably better" just a year later, although Giacosa's 1989 Barolo Collina Rionda—now one of the true cult bottlings from the Langhe—still received a miserly and misplaced 78 points.

Throughout the 1990s and the first years of the New Millennium, U.S. and U.K. critics couldn't get enough of the dense, overly extracted, and over-oaked Barolos and Barbarescos. Neither could Italy's wine guides, including Gambero Rosso's *Guide to Italian Wines,* which bestowed countless Three Glasses—its highest award—to many of the most un-Nebbiolo-like Barolos and Barbarescos.

Although it is one of the most taboo subjects in both denominations, the unnaturally dark color of many of the bottlings hailing from the Langhe from the 1990s until the first part of this century certainly back up rumors of illicit blending of Nebbiolo with other grapes, such as Cabernet and Merlot, to soften tannins and darken Nebbiolo's naturally lighter color. A blind panel tasting of 2001 Barolos that I organized in 2011 in Alba for *Decanter* magazine certainly had the panel asking "Where's the Nebbiolo here?" in comments tasters wrote in their notes and reiterated during the post-tasting discussion. However, fear generated by the 2008 Brunello grape blending scandal in Montalcino, combined with a change in consumer preferences away from sheer power and evident oak and toward more authentic wines, seem to have given producers new respect for Nebbiolo and dampened any enthusiasm for blending, which has never been proven and is rarely brought up in the denomination. Only a few producers have commented, usually off record, on this issue, one in particular asking where I think fruit from the five thousand vines of Cabernet and Merlot planted in his village ends up, since so little of it actually ends up bottled as Langhe Rosso DOC according to the same producer.

TRUCE IN BAROLO AND BARBARESCO

Before the first decade of the New Millennium was over, an unofficial cease-fire gradually took hold in Barolo and Barbaresco, helped along by the emergence of a middle-of-the-road style that is now widespread in both denominations—so much so, in fact, that a number of recently arrived wine writers even question if the Barolo Wars ever actually took place. But yes, the wars most certainly did take place, and based on the numerous tastings I do every year in both denominations, the two distinct styles that battled for survival for decades are both alive and well, although the producers themselves are much more at ease with this coexistence, and most no longer insist that one style should dominate.

In fact, a number of producers who used to be part of the warring factions have helped create this more recent in-between style. These producers combine methods from the two schools of thought, such as a conventional alcoholic fermentation lasting about ten days followed by another two weeks of skin maceration, followed by aging one year in barriques (usually a mix of new and used) and one year in large Slavonian casks. Others are utilizing mostly used barriques that impart little in the way of new wood sensations, or are using *tonneaux,* 500-liter barrels. When done well, this moderated approach to winemaking can generate Barolo and Barbaresco that are often almost ready to drink upon release but that can still age moderately well, and while they are smooth and round and have lightly toasted and vanilla notes, they also retain their Nebbiolo character of black cherry, leather, rose, and truffle.

There is still a cadre of producers who use all new barriques, or mostly new along with used ones, for malolactic fermentation and/or aging, which I feel can strangle Nebbiolo's vibrant personality and unique aromatic and flavor profile. Many producers in La Morra, for example, continue to rely on new barriques, presumably to beef up their more delicately structured Barolos with wood tannins. While the village as a whole performed well with the 2008 vintage, many wines from the scorching 2009 vintage showed dominant wood sensations, cooked fruit and markedly bitter wood tannins, proving that not only can barriques change the *tipicità* or authenticity of the wines, but, when used inappropriately or during especially difficult vintages, they can also obliterate Nebbiolo's natural beauty.

And before readers think I'm prejudiced against barriques, I can honestly say that I don't have anything against these small French barrels—as long as I don't smell or taste the dominant wood sensations they easily impart. Some producers from the Langhe have become masters with barriques, including Elio Altare over in La Morra and rising star Andrea Sottimano over in Neive, and with 500-liter tonneaux, like Luciano Sandrone in Barolo. And of course there are iconic producers like Gaja in Barbaresco and Scavino in Castiglione Falletto who have long used a mix of new and used barriques the first year and botti the second. All of these producers make magnificent wines. However, some winemakers still have not grasped the fine art of aging in small French barrels, and as recently as 2013 during a particularly grueling session of Nebbiolo Prima, the segment on La Morra to be exact, there was so much new oak wafting out of the glasses that at one point I wrote in my notes, "Wonder if all this wood poses a fire hazard." I also contest the concept that barriques soften Nebbiolo's tannins; while the best producers, like those cited above, go to extremes to ensure quality barrels, like Gaja, who, as recounted in the book *Sorì San Lorenzo*, spent years going to France to choose the wood and bring it back to Barbaresco where he would carefully follow the seasoning process before sending it to the cooperage, others are using lower-quality or poor-quality barrels that impart green, astringent tannins. Still other producers use barriques to hide mediocre wine under vanilla, toast, and coffee notes in the hopes of pumping up bland, one-dimensional wines with no character.

I readily admit that most of my favorite Barolos and Barbarescos—the ones I find most fascinating thanks to their inimitable character and Nebbiolo purity—are generally those made with traditional methods. By that I mean those wines that have undergone slow fermentation (usually without using selected yeasts) followed by lengthy postfermentation maceration with the skins—often made with the customary submerged cap method the locals call *steccatura*, whereby wooden boards hold down the cap. This method slowly and gently extracts aromas, noble tannins, and complexity from Nebbiolo. And I usually prefer wines aged in large casks. Among my favorite Barolos are those from Giacomo Conterno, Bartolo Mascarello, Giacomo Fenocchio, Burlotto and Cavallotto (the latter actually uses rotary fermenters with exceptionally slow rotations for prolonged, gentle extraction with fantastic results). Among my favorite Barbarescos are Roagna, Cascina delle Rose, Rizzi, and Olek Bondonio, along with Adriano Marco e Vittorio.

Overall, quality across the board has never been higher in Barolo and Barbaresco. And while many producers who once used only new barriques have taken a step back—Albino Rocca, for instance, has switched over to Austrian casks, and Mauro Veglio uses far less new wood than before—even the once die-hard traditionalists have borrowed ideas from the other side. Dirty cellars are now an exception, and if years ago large Slavonian casks were handed down through the generations, these days they are changed every ten to fifteen years or regenerated by shaving a thin layer inside, and most casks are smaller in size than in the days of yore. Other enlightened Traditionalists, such as Bruno Giacosa, have large casks, but made of untoasted French oak. And while some still prefer extended fermentation and maceration times, most now keep the total process down to about twenty-five days.

FROM THE CELLAR TO THE VINEYARD

If the Barolo Wars began in the cellar, they ended in the vineyard. Despite all the upheaval regarding cellar practices and the focus on barriques versus botti that dominated the late 1990s and much of the first decade of this century, the biggest change in the last decade has been an increased focus on farming. As growers became winemakers, many initially took advantage of chemical products that helped them save time, such as herbicides and industrially made fertilizers. Fast-forward twenty years, and growers recount that they witnessed the soil turn sterile and the proliferation of harmful pests like the red spider mite, which began to thrive as predator insects disappeared.

An impressive number of producers across Barolo and Barbaresco have stopped using these chemical products and are opting for a more natural approach to vineyard management. The changes in the vineyards have led to changes in the cellar, as Barbaresco producer Andrea Sottimano pointed out to me in 2013: "In 2004 I cut down on chemical herbicides and pesticides, and totally banned them in 2005. I noticed right away that after eliminating these chemical products, my wine had more depth and personality than before. I also noticed changes during vinification, so the next year I started experimenting with spontaneous fermentation, which I could never success-fully do before. Since 2009, after four years of no chemical products in the vineyards, I've fermented with wild yeasts only. My wines are completely different than they were just a few years ago, and I think they're far better." Sottimano still ages his wines in 228-liter Burgundy barrels, but now uses them for multiple vintages so as not to mask the sense of place and the unique personalities his wines now boast by aging in new barrels that impart pronounced wood sensations. "I'd never use new oak like I used to. My wines don't need it," declares the young winemaker.

Although it seemed impossible even a decade ago, the contentious Barolo Wars that shook up the Langhe for over twenty years and enticed growers to become producers have eventually brought matters full circle. The most enlightened producers are returning to the healthier farming methods practiced by their grandfathers, but combine these natural methods with vastly improved knowledge of vineyard management. Using less extreme and invasive cellar practices, a higher than ever number of Barolo and Barbaresco producers now make what are some of the most tantalizing and fascinating wines on earth.

As Pietro Ratti, winemaker and president of the Consorzio told me during one of our recent interviews for this book, "The Barolo Wars not only generated a push in Barolo and Barbaresco to make higher-quality wines, but they had journalists and consumers buzzing about the wines for practically two decades. From a marketing perspective, this was better than any PR-organized campaign imaginable." Unfortunately, there's been a catch to this success, but then again, isn't there always?

FIVE

Expansion, Subzones, and the Future of Barolo and Barbaresco

BOTH BAROLO AND BARBARESCO HAVE ENJOYED great critical and commercial success since the early 1990s. It's almost impossible to imagine that just a decade before this, many producers would often give away a bottle or two of Barolo to their loyal customers who came to the Langhe to stock up on Dolcetto and Barbera, as a way to generate interest in what the producers themselves always considered their flagship wine. The situation is of course inverted now, and as critics started raving about Barolo and Barbaresco, encouraging wine lovers around the world to seek out the best bottlings, two things naturally occurred: prices soared, as did Nebbiolo plantings. To the growers, long used to tough times and sacrifice, it suddenly seemed that the world could not get enough of their wines. Sales were booming, and grape farmers-turned-producers in both denominations—but especially in the better-known Barolo zone—frantically tried to make more Barolo, not just to satisfy the market, but to pay off debts they incurred from renovating or building new cellars, renewing old vineyards, and in many cases, acquiring more vineyard land.

For decades before this, production had been stable in both denominations. In Barolo in 1980, there were 1,111 hectares (2,745 acres) dedicated to production, and this figure nudged up to 1,163 hectares (2,874 acres) in 1990. By 2000, the number had climbed to 1,338 hectares (3,306 acres), and by 2013, the latest statistics available, the acreage had soared to 1,984 hectares (4,902 acres) of Nebbiolo registered to Barolo production. Increases in Barbaresco production, which covers a far smaller surface area than its more famous neighbor, took longer to take off, and while the figures themselves may seem less impressive, plantings here also increased substantially in the last decade. In 1980, there were 472 hectares registered to Barbaresco that by 1998 had grown to just 480 hectares. However, this figure increased to 530 hectares just two years later, and by 2013, there were 684 hectares (1,690 acres) registered as Barbaresco vineyards.

Bottle numbers are more dramatic. In 1980, Barolo production turned out 7.2 million bottles. Bottle production fluctuated in this decade, in part no doubt because of the climatic conditions of various vintages, and presumably because as more growers transitioned into producers, the focus turned from quantity to quality production. By 1990 bottle production actually shifted down to 6.1 million units, but by 2005, this figure had soared to 10.6 million bottles. By 2010, Barolo bottle numbers escalated to over 13 million, and this increased to 13.9 million with the 2013 harvest. In Barbaresco, total output for the denomination fluctuated significantly in the 1980s, but in 1990, total bottle production was 2.3 million. This figure climbed to 3.36 million by 2005, and based on the 2013 harvest, total output was over 4.68 million bottles of Barbaresco.

So just where did growers in the Langhe hills find the space for new plantings in an area already heavily cultivated with vines? Apparently, any place they could. Many of the last hazelnut groves and fruit trees dotting the hills were ripped out and replaced with vines, as were the lowest parts of hills that hitherto had been deemed inadequate for Nebbiolo production. Slopes with less than ideal exposure and soil were also cultivated. However, the most common explanation given by many producers is that Dolcetto and Barbera vineyards, especially those that were planted in areas that were actually ideal for Nebbiolo back when the former wines were more popular, were grubbed up and replanted with Nebbiolo, since the growing conditions were perfect. But for every Dolcetto and Barbera vineyard with perfect Nebbiolo altitude and exposure that was ripped out to make room for Barolo and Barbaresco vines, it is safe to say that far many more less suitable vineyards have also been replanted with Nebbiolo in the last two decades, and even some areas never before under vine.

"These days there are way too many Barolo vineyards in places our grandfathers would never have planted," says cult producer Giuseppe Rinaldi. Countless others, including Franco Anselma of the Giacomo Anselma winery in Serralunga, agree, saying that areas with less than ideal exposure, altitude, and soil are now crammed with site-sensitive Nebbiolo vines. "Before, when anyone wanted to plant a Barolo vineyard, the local chamber of commerce would send out a technician to check exposures, because if there wasn't sufficient southern exposure, you couldn't plant Nebbiolo. Now, no one checks," says Franco. He adds that in the last fifteen years, even trees that have sustained the steep slopes for centuries have been cleared away and replaced with vineyards. "Right here in Serralunga, a producer cleared out the trees just beneath the top part of the hill and planted vines. But not just any vines—Nebbiolo! And every rainy year since then, there's been landslides that carry away part of his vineyard and the slope."

According to the first two production codes for Barolo and Barbaresco, which hail from 1966 and 1980, when both wines became DOC and DOCG, respectively, vineyards were obliged simply to be "those traditional ones for the zone and must be however only those that can give specific quality characteristics to the grapes and wines made from these grapes. Therefore suitable vineyards will be exclusively on hillsides with adequate orientation and predominantly clayey-calcareous soil."

Evidently, what constituted "hillsides" and suitable "orientation" or exposure was open to interpretation, and while these rules seems lax today, producers tell me that until the 1990s, it simply was not even conceivable that anyone would ever plant Nebbiolo on valley floors or in areas with a northern exposure. And while the powers that be maintain this is still the case, recent modifications to the production codes of both wines tell a different story.

In response to rampant planting of Nebbiolo vineyards in unsuitable locations, when Barbaresco modified its production code in 2007 to sanction the newly delimited subzones, known as "geographic mentions," the Consorzio took the opportunity to lay down stricter rules regarding vineyard location. While it still mandates that vineyards must be exclusively on hillsides, the new production code specifically prohibits planting vines on valley floors, in humid or damp terrain, on flatlands, or in areas without sufficient sunlight. It also categorically excludes any northern exposures, and while it does not impose a minimum altitude, Barbaresco vineyards cannot be over 550 meters (1,804 feet) above sea level. In 2010, Barolo followed suit after delimiting its own growing area, and adopted essentially the same rules for vineyard location as in Barbaresco but with some deviations: altitude for Barolo vineyards must be no lower than 170 meters (558 feet) but no higher than 540 meters (1,771 feet), while new plantings are not allowed in zones with northern exposures that fall "from -45° a +45° sexagesimal"—in other words, full-on northern exposures are excluded. Hopefully these measures will help new plantings, but already existing vineyards are presumably grandfathered in.

Until 2010, expansion in the denominations had not been controlled, and the vineyard registers had always been open. This changed after the global economic collapse in late 2008; the fallout from the global crisis had an impact on Barolo and Barbaresco about a year and a half later. "In 2010, there was an economic crises here and in all of Italy that halted sales, just when many young vineyards were producing to their full potential and many newly established producers were debuting their wines," according to Pietro Ratti. In other words, just when more Barolo and Barbaresco bottlings than ever before were ready to hit the market, demand screeched to a stop. Prices dropped, and the reality that Barolo and Barbaresco sales don't just go up crashed down on producers.

"In the face of this crisis, in 2011 we took action by limiting expansion in the two denominations, for the first time ever," says Ratti. "Now we allow only 10 hectares (24.7 acres) of new plantings each year in all of Barolo, and 3 (7.4 acres) in Barbaresco, with a limit of 0.4 hectares (0.98 acres) per year for individual wineries," explains Ratti. Each year, producers who want to expand production must petition the Consorzio, which studies each request on a case-by-case basis, giving precedence to young growers who have only marginal holdings and are trying to increase production. "We can't close the vineyard registers completely because Barolo and Barbaresco are still in evolution, and there are still vineyards that can be converted from other vines that would be suitable for Nebbiolo should producers want to do that," says Ratti.

According to Ratti, during our last interview in January 2013, the economic crisis that started in 2010 has abated, and sales and exports in both denominations had recovered well by late 2012.

SUBZONES

Growers in the Langhe have always shown an obsessive attachment to and devout respect for their vineyards, and even in the past, the most lauded vineyard names were often more important than the name of the wine or the name of the grape, as the oldest known bottling from the Langhe, a bottle labeled simply "Cannubi 1752" demonstrates. Growers and producers in Barolo and Barbaresco were among the first in Italy, many would argue *the* first, to release single-vineyard editions of DOC and later DOCG wines, and to proudly add the specific vineyard name to the label.

Despite this tremendous respect for certain vineyard areas, however, the local custom until the 1970s was to make Barolo and Barbaresco exclusively by blending various vineyards together (obviously within their respective

FIGURE 2. Example of vineyard exposure in Barbaresco. According to local growers, the best vineyards in both the Barolo and the Barbaresco growing zones have always been those where freshly fallen snow melts first, since this demonstrates that the vineyard has warmer, sunnier exposures that encourage ideal ripening for Nebbiolo. Photograph by Paolo Tenti.

denominations) to create natural balance and to have both perfume and structure. And, I would like to point out, many producers today still prefer to make blended Barolos and Barbarescos. However, as mentioned previously, single-vineyard versions play a major role in both denominations. Beppe Colla was the first to vinify and bottle separate vineyards of Barolo and Barbaresco in 1961 under his Prunotto label, but at the time he was highly criticized by other growers and producers. By the late 1960s, others had taken up the challenge—namely, Gaja and Giacosa, both of whom made single-vineyard bottlings of Barbaresco in 1967. It took a few years before the trend caught on, but little by little more producers began turning out single-vineyard bottlings; and they were highly encouraged by Italy's most celebrated wine critic, the late Luigi Veronelli. They were also motivated by Renato Ratti, who in 1975, after extensive interviews with growers and grape merchants, drew up his first map of Barolo's historic vineyards, and indicated those with "special characteristics." A year later, he did the same for Barbaresco, and then in 1985, Ratti revised his Barolo vineyard map, dividing the crus into a first and second category, which became a benchmark for the denomination. By the 1980s, the single-vineyard trend had taken off. By this time, growers throughout the denominations claimed to own slices of the best vineyard areas, or crus, as the locals refer to them—a term obviously adopted from the French.

Almost immediately, these single-vineyard Barolos and Barbarescos commanded higher retail prices, since they clearly implied higher quality, even though this was not always the case. By the early 1990s so many labels were adorned with the names of the most celebrated crus, such as Bussia and Cannubi, that it appeared these vineyards magically expanded every year. Producers with holdings in the heart of these lauded crus began to question the validity of the wines produced on the fringes or beyond the borders of these hallowed vineyards.

While some producers in, near, or relatively near the most famous vineyard areas added the cru name to their labels, those nowhere near the best vineyards were not going to miss out on what was turning out to be a great marketing tool to help sell wines. Many estates soon made up their own names, pure fantasy names, which when placed on a label implied a single vineyard. Sometimes, wines labeled with these fantasy names were technically from a single vineyard but one that was so insignificant that it had never been named before. The exception here of course is Angelo Gaja (isn't it always?), who, despite having holdings in some of the best vineyards in both denominations, chose to add his own made-up names to his single-vineyard bottlings, which he promptly registered so that no one else could use them.

As in the case of barriques versus botti, the single-vineyard concept sharply divided producers, with some producers insisting Barolo and Barbaresco should be only a blend of vineyards, while others felt that Nebbiolo grown in outstanding vineyards was unparalleled and should be made and bottled separately. The strongest critics accused the whole single-vineyard concept as nothing but a gimmick that tricked consumers, since so many wines touted as single-vineyard bottlings were either nowhere near the heart of the crus they claimed to be part of, or simply Barolo and Barbaresco with an invented name. To combat the escalating problem of crus and fantasy names, in 1994 the Barolo and Barbaresco Consorzio set out on an ambitious project to delimit the growing areas and divide the vineyards in every village into subzones. Those charged with this daunting task knew that they would meet strong opposition and would end up creating more subzones than those storied areas they were trying to protect, but I doubt anyone could have foreseen the years of fierce resistance, infighting, and debate, or the convoluted results.

Thirteen years later, the Consorzio proudly unveiled Barbaresco's officially delimited zones: a whopping sixty-five authorized vineyard areas with one more in the wings that was eventually approved in 2010, bringing the final number to sixty-six. Although the original idea had been to define these vineyard areas as crus, or at least *sottozone* or subzones, the Italian government would not allow the latter term, insisting that the small areas didn't satisfy certain requirements regarding surface area and number of producers to be called subzones. So the official, and exceedingly unimaginative, term for what are, for all intents and purposes, subzones is *menzioni geografiche aggiuntive,* or additional geographic mentions.

It took producers in Barolo three more years to overcome relentless territorial disputes that enraged many in this far larger denomination, but the additional geographic mentions went into effect with the 2010 vintage. According to the Consorzio, today there are 181 official geographic mentions, 170 vineyard areas, and 11 village designations (Barbaresco by the way does not have these village-only designations on labels). Unsurprisingly, the sheer number of delimited vineyard areas has created consumer confusion, and perhaps even more unsurprisingly, the vast majority of these subzones in Barolo and Barbaresco have absolutely no distinguishing features, nor do they impart any superior quality. To compound the confusion over already-crammed labels, producers also have the option to add the term *Vigna* (vineyard) followed by the name of a specific vineyard (found within the larger official subzone) along with the official geographic mention. To so do, however, producers must first register their individual vineyard name with the Consorzio and lower yields by ten percent in an effort to further increase quality, and not many producers take advantage of this option. And as a final blow to any real clarity, wineries can still use fantasy names if they registered them before the official delimitations went into effect, as long as they have documentation that the wines were labeled and sold with these fantasy names for a certain number of years before the new rules were applied.

Many producers aren't satisfied with the zoning. While producers generally agree that putting official boundaries on the most storied crus to protect them from expansion and exploitation is a step in the right direction, many growers and winemakers say the geographic mentions are too numerous or in other cases that they are too big and have obliterated smaller vineyard sites by merging them into a larger area. Because the individual towns drew up the borders for their vineyard areas, there's a huge discrepancy in the final results. Castiglione Falletto, for example, remained faithful to the original boundaries of the famed crus and other delimited vineyards, but other municipalities, such as Monforte d'Alba, did a horrendous job and blew

Bussia up into unimaginable proportions (more on this in chapter 12). And there are more than a few unsatisfied producers over in Barbaresco. According to Enrico Dellapiana of Rizzi, "Mapping out the vineyard areas is very important, but I think it could have been done much, much better. For one thing, many mapped-out areas include zones where you can't plant Nebbiolo. While Castiglione Falletto and Serralunga were careful to exclude valley floors, riverbanks, and areas with north exposures, in Monforte d'Alba, Treiso, and Neive, the delimited 'crus' include streams, woods, and valley floors. After all the time and effort spent on this, I think the maps should at least realistically reflect where you can and cannot plant Nebbiolo."

Seeing that these sanctioned subzones are simply indications of location but still falsely convey a sense of superior quality to consumers (of course some of the subzones are of superior quality, but personally, I can think of only about forty great vineyard areas between Barolo and Barbaresco that would merit a distinction based on quality), some producers would like to impose certain restrictions on wines using labels with geographic mentions. "Going forward, I'd like to see lower yields become mandatory for Barolos and Barbarescos that use subzones on the labels. This way, they would at least have some real quality merit," says Ratti. He also points out that with the 2010 vintage, only 70 percent of the geographic mentions were used on labels, and he expects this percentage to drop further as time goes on.

A long-raging legal battle over Barolo's most famous cru, Cannubi, and a controversial decision by Italy's High Court, handed down in October of 2013, have threatened the future of subzones in both denominations and cast doubt on the credibility of all the vineyard boundaries delimited in Barolo and Barbaresco. To be brief: during the long and at times tempestuous negotiations over creating official vineyard boundaries that started in the mid-1990s, producers in the heart of historic Cannubi agreed that the name Cannubi could be added to lesser-known vineyard names on different parts of the same large hill, thereby sanctioning names that some producers had already been using for years: Cannubi Boschis, Cannubi Muscatel, Cannubi Valletta, and Cannubi San Lorenzo. However, only growers that had vineyards in the historic heart of the hill—that first area where the sun melts after snowfall according to producers, and an area that has been lauded for centuries for its superior quality—could use the name Cannubi on its own.

The official Barolo vineyard area boundaries, fruit of a process that the individual towns had started in the mid-1990s, were finalized in December 2008, and the name Cannubi was sanctioned for the historical 15-hectare area only. According to Federico Scarzello, a grower-producer in Barolo and a member of the Barolo town council who actively participated in the grueling delimitation negotiations, "The Consorzio asked all the towns to delimit the vineyard sites in their respective communes. And in Barolo, the boundaries were approved by three separate town administrations, and examined by the growers themselves during a period of more than fifteen years, before the final and therefore official results were delivered to the Consorzio to be inserted into the new production code."

Consorzio members approved the additional geographic mentions at a General Assembly in 2009. However, in 2010, the Consorzio called two meetings that had low turnouts and that several Cannubi landholders claim they had not been notified about. During these meetings, a representative of the Marchesi di Barolo winery, which has holdings in Cannubi Muscatel, proposed extending the right to use the straight Cannubi name to the Boschis, Muscatel, Valletta, and San Lorenzo vineyards. The measure was initially beaten down, but attendees voted in favor of it at the second meeting. The Consorzio decided to let the final decision rest with Italy's National Wine Committee, which had to authorize the final production code. To the shock of other producers, the Committee approved Marchesi di Barolo's request, and in the 2010 modification of the Barolo production code, use of the straight Cannubi name was extended to 34 hectares of vineyards. A group of eleven producers, led by Maria Teresa Mascarello, appealed the decision.

Mascarello and her group, which included Enzo Brezza, Poderi Einaudi, Luciano Sandrone, and Giuseppe Rinaldi, won their appeal in 2012. In response, the Ministry of Agriculture and the Marchesi di Barolo appealed, and in October 2013, Rome's High Administrative Court, the Consiglio di Stato, reversed the lower court's decision, once again sanctioning the expanded Cannubi area of 34 hectares. One of the main motivations for the reversal, according to the court's decision, was Marchesi di Barolo's basic argument that the term Muscatel (where they have their holdings on the larger Cannubi hill) created confusion for consumers because "in common jargon [it] is associated with Moscato, which has notoriously different characteristics from Barolo."

While the owners of Marchesi di Barolo expressed joy over the court's decision, as the daily newspaper *Corriere della Sera* reported, other producers across the denomination are outraged. "It's shameful that Italy's Consiglio di Stato and the Ministry of Agriculture have chosen to satisfy the commercial interests of one winery, Marchesi di Barolo, over the collective interests of all the other producers in Barolo. The decision puts one of the Langhe's most historic vineyard sites at risk. It's also unfair to consumers, who assume Barolos labeled as Cannubi are from the celebrated and restricted vineyard," said Maria Teresa Mascarello immediately following the court's decision. In May 2014, eight producers and landholders appealed the latest decision to the *Corte di Cassazione*, Italy's Supreme Court.

Personally, I feel that the court's latest decision has set a dangerous precedent that could pose a serious risk to the officially delimited boundaries across Barolo and Barbaresco. The whole point of drawing up official vineyard borders was to protect the best sites, while just the opposite happened in the case of Cannubi. And I also find it highly unlikely that any consumers could actually confuse Barolo, a red wine, even it had Cannubi Muscatel added to the label, with a white, sparkling Moscato.

More on the delimited subzones appears in the following chapters dedicated to the individual villages. I also list all the additional geographic mentions in Appendix B and have highlighted what I consider the top areas. Other resources to check out include Alessandro Masnaghetti's cru maps as well as the downloadable maps available on the Consorzio's website: www. langhevini.it.

PRESENT AND FUTURE

Today both of these long-established denominations are suffering growing pains, thanks to unchecked expansion, an ever-increasing number of new producers, and hundreds of subzone designations—many in areas that don't yield superior or special wines. However, despite these present-day challenges and the flaws outlined in the previous section, I firmly believe that the delimitation of subzones—as well as the recent measures to control expansion—will improve Barolo and Barbaresco in the long run, though there are bound to be some speed bumps along the way. Limiting expansion and defining suitable vineyard locations in the production code should deter future planting in unsuitable sites, and while it may not abolish vineyards already planted in less-than-ideal terrain, these measures are steps in the right direction, although it remains to be seen how strictly they will be enforced.

Regarding the glut of official subzones, in my opinion consumers will play a fundamental role in their eventual reduction down to a more rational number as over time wine lovers will continue to seek out bottlings they enjoyed while avoiding those wines that just didn't seem worth the money.

These are after all expensive wines, and no one wants to be disappointed twice. It will also greatly help if the subzones per se could be a quality indicator, and I think Ratti's idea of mandatory lower yields for all bottlings labeled as hailing from designated subzones is sound and would give the added geographic mentions more credibility as a whole. But lest we forget, some of the greatest Barolos and Barbarescos—think Bartolo Mascarello and Angelo Gaja, respectively—are still made from blended vineyards. I predict more producers will return to this customary practice over time, especially in light of the changing climate: blending Nebbiolo from different altitudes, different exposures, and different soils may become a more viable way to find natural balance, rather than relying on any single vineyard area.

However, as with all great wines in the world, great terroir is crucial, but not enough. Some growers with the best vineyards can easily make mediocre wines if they aren't careful in the cellars. As the late Luigi Veronelli used to say, "In 1956 a producer from Burgundy told me, 'Italian producers have golden grapes but make silver wines. Here in Burgundy we have silver grapes but make golden wines.'" To combat this widespread sentiment, in the recent past producers in the Langhe and in much of Italy focused too much on the enology side of making wine, leading to invasive cellar techniques that took off in the 1990s and in the first years of this century. With a growing number of producers focusing more on healthy farming practices while adopting a less-is-more approach in the cellars, the result in both denominations is that quality across the board has never been higher, and as more producers adopt this crucial balance, the outlook is bright, despite the challenges that remain.

The most important guarantee to finding exceptional Barolos and Barbarescos is the name of the producer. However, with so many labels to choose from, so many subzones, and so many different styles of Barolo and Barbaresco out there, finding wines from producers with proven track records may seem like daunting task. What follows in part 2 of this book are producer profiles, broken down village by village. I've chosen those producers I feel are making outstanding wines that beautifully express Nebbiolo and their respective village or vineyard area, as well as those that through blending have created quintessential Barolos and Barbarescos that reflect the beauty, complexity, and fascination of Italy's most noble grape and the rolling Langhe hills.

PART TWO

Profiles of Key Barolo Producers by Village

SIX

Barolo and Novello

THE STRIKING VILLAGE OF BAROLO, which accounts for 12 percent of total Barolo production according to the Consorzio, is the birthplace of the eponymously named wine, for it was in this village that Tancredi and Giulia Falletti, the Marchesi di Barolo, began seriously producing fine red wine from Nebbiolo grapes from their vast holdings in Barolo and Serralunga. History also identifies the French-born marchesa (born Juliette Colbert de Maulévrier) as the first person to produce on a large scale the wine we now call Barolo.

While other villages in the Langhe perch on steep hilltops or spread out along crests, Barolo sits instead on a high U-shaped plateau surrounded by an amphitheater of vine-covered slopes. Like many of its neighbors, Barolo, which is entirely located within the denomination's growing zone, also boasts a medieval castle. The castle originated in the tenth century but was greatly expanded over the years once it became the property of the Fallettis in the 1300s. After being badly damaged by the wars that engulfed the area in the sixteenth century, the family rebuilt the castle, and in the early 1800s, it became the country residence of the Marchesi di Barolo. After the last marchesa died, the castle, which became part of the marchesa's charitable foundation, Opera Pia Barolo, was transformed according to her wishes into a school for the children of Barolo and neighboring villages, and remained so until 1958. The castle was abandoned for many years, until the town purchased it. After extensive renovation, the castle reopened to the public in 2010, and now houses a wine museum.

Barolo, whose name reportedly originates from the Celtic term *bas reul,* meaning "low place," presumably describing the plateau on which the village sits, was principally formed in the Tortonian age. Generally speaking, the soil

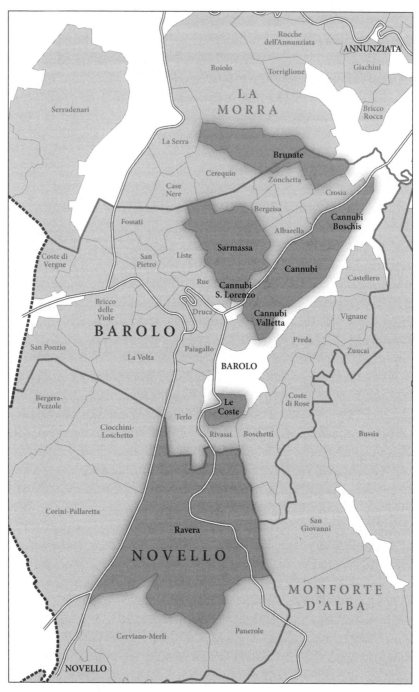

MAP 2. Village of Barolo/Novello.

consists of Sant'Agata Fossili marls, and according to many experts, this grayish-blue soil gives wines from Barolo their elegance, complexity, and perfume. Even though Barolo from its namesake village ages well, most bottlings are usually approachable earlier than more robust wines from villages with Serravallian soil, which has more sandstone and a higher presence of calcium carbonate in the subsoils—namely, Serralunga and Monforte.

Barolo also boasts one of the most recognized names in the denomination: Cannubi, perhaps the most historic cru in all of Barolo, lauded in Lorenzo Fantini's late nineteenth-century work, *Monografia sulla viticoltura ed enologia nella provincia di Cuneo,*[1] and awarded first-category status by Renato Ratti in his cru map of Barolo. Locals have long appreciated the superior quality of grapes hailing from this vineyard area, and the oldest Langhe bottling in existence today is a wine labeled "Cannubi 1752" in the possession of the Manzone family. While it is presumed this ancient Cannubi was made with Nebbiolo, it is significant that whoever bottled the wine thought the vineyard name was more important than the name of the village. According to growers with holdings in the famed site, the denomination's two main soil types—the magnesium rich Tortonian soils, which contain more sand and produce more elegant and fragrant wines; and the heavier, limestone Serravallian soils rich in calcium carbonates, which produce more structured and tannic wines—meet and in some areas overlap in Cannubi. This sandy component allows Cannubi to excel in years with normal climatic conditions; it also performs better than other vineyard areas in wet years thanks to well-draining soil. However, in dry, hot years, it suffers more than many other vineyard sites because its soil does not retain humidity.

As mentioned in the previous chapter, Cannubi has long been the object of fierce debate among producers who have varying and often contentious views about the exact borders of the legendary vineyard area. Veteran growers insist that the real Cannubi, where Nebbiolo truly excels, is limited to a 15-hectare swath (technically an 18-hectare expanse, 15 of which are under vine) of the much larger hillside, and even then only from midhill to the top of this select area, with the lower areas being more suitable for Barbera. Ever since the 1990s, when single-vineyard Barolos became popular, it almost seemed that Cannubi "expanded" each year, as the name appeared on more and more labels, often in conjunction with other vineyard names. The debate over Cannubi and surrounding vineyard areas stretches back at least as far as the late nineteenth century, when Lorenzo Fantini refers not only to Cannubio [*sic*], but also to Cannubio San Lorenzo, Cannubio Boschis (historically also known as Monghisolfo), Cannubio Parrocchiale, and Cannubio Ferri in his *Monografia,* although the latter two vineyard names have since disappeared from use. Almost a century later, Renato Ratti added the name Cannubi to that of Muscatel on his Barolo cru map, and besides defining Cannubi as one of the ten best subzones in all of Barolo, he further indicated both Cannubi Boschis and Cannubi Muscatel as "sub regions with special characteristics." Ratti also encircled the entire Cannubi hill and its adjacent vineyard areas in green to indicate the hill as a "historic sub-region."

By the mid-1990s, the powers that be in the village of Barolo, who had already begun mapping out the commune's approved vineyard boundaries, conceded that four other crus on the same hill as Cannubi could have the option of adding the name Cannubi before the other cru name, thereby validating a decades-long practice already used by many producers while at the same time preserving the classic Cannubi area. The Consorzio and local producers agreed with the town's drawn-up boundaries, and when producers voted in the denomination's final delimitations in 2009, after what had been a grueling process based on historical documents, land registries, and Barolo production information, the name Cannubi on its own was reserved for what has long been considered the historical vineyard site. Producers in the adjacent four areas that had already added the name Cannubi to their other site designations were allowed to continue to do so, thus sanctioning vineyard areas Cannubi Boschis or Boschis, Cannubi San Lorenzo or San Lorenzo, Cannubi Muscatel or Muscatel, and Cannubi Valletta or Valletta. Most if not all producers from the latter four areas opted to include the Cannubi mention on their labels because of its name recognition, its association with exceptional quality, and of course, the higher prices Cannubi Barolos fetch.

But harmony did not last long. In 2010, according to numerous published accounts and according to other local producers, just before Barolo's geographic mentions were to be inserted into the denomination's revised production code, the Marchesi di Barolo company petitioned the Comitato Nazionale Vini (Comitato Nazionale per la Tutela e la Valorizzazione delle Denominazioni di Origne e delle Indicazioni Geografiche Tipiche dei Vini), part of the Ministry of Agriculture, to expand use of the Cannubi name on its own from just the original 15-hectare area to effectively include those four areas that were already adding the name Cannubi to their main geographic mentions. The Ministry of Agriculture agreed and allowed the name Cannubi to encompass what Barolo's town officials had designated as five distinct vineyard areas.

Outrage followed, as did legal action on the part of many growers and producers located in the original Cannubi cru, including Maria Teresa Mascarello and Enzo Brezza, as well others who believe in defending the area's historical crus, like Luciano Sandrone, who has holdings in Cannubi Boschis, and Giuseppe Rinaldi, who has holdings in Cannubi San Lorenzo. The group appealed to the Tribunale Amministrativo Regionale (TAR), asking it to revoke the Ministry of Agriculture's decision. This took two years, and in the meantime, producers in Cannubi and the other four vineyard areas were all allowed to label their Barolos as simply Cannubi. In June 2012, the tribunal in Rome overturned the Ministry of Agriculture's ruling and restored Cannubi to 15 hectares. However, in 2013, the Ministry of Agriculture, joined by Marchesi di Barolo, won an appeal from Italy's high court, which once again extended use of the Cannubi name on its own to the entire hill. In May 2014, Mascarello and seven others appealed to Italy's Supreme Court.

San Lorenzo is another famed vineyard name in the village, but thanks to the intricacies of Italian bureaucracy, which seem bent on creating consumer confusion, the 2010 classification sanctioned two San Lorenzos in the village: Cannubi San Lorenzo and, just across the street, San Lorenzo di Barolo. Other celebrated vineyards include Sarmassa, Castellero, and Ruè, as well as Brunate and Cerequio, although the latter two are more associated with La Morra because the lion's share of these two celebrated vineyard areas is located in that township.

Barolo is also home to some of the most historic and iconic Barolo houses, including Marchesi di Barolo, Bartolo Mascarello, Giuseppe Rinaldi, Brezza, Barale Fratelli, and Borgogno.

Marchesi di Barolo

Via Roma 1
12060 Barolo (CN)
Tel. +39 0173 564400
www.marchesibarolo.com
info@marchesibarolo.com

The Marchesi di Barolo winery, which today is owned by the Abbona family and their partners, produces some 1.5 million bottles of various wines, including seven different Barolos. As its name suggests, the winery, visited by 40,000 tourists a year, originally belonged to the Marchesi di Barolo, Carlo Tancredi and Giulia Falletti, who were the last in line of this noble family. The cellar was the site of the Marchesi's wine production as early as the 1830s, as is demonstrated by the published travel journals of Count Giorgio Gallesio, a notable nineteenth-century botanist. Upon visiting Barolo in 1834, Gallesio writes, "The grapes in Barolo [the area] are Nebbiolo and Neiran [known today as Neretta Cuneese]; with these two grapes the famous wine of Barolo is made, of which however Neiran only ever accounts for about one tenth." Gallesio goes on to write, "The wine of Barolo lasts for many years, and the Marchesi di Barolo conserves it to send to the Court in Turin and others. In this village, it is believed that to have very fine wine, it is essential to make it exclusively with Nebbiolo, or it can be mixed with Neiran to give color, Nebbiolo on its own being too light and too sweet. I visited the Marchese di Barolo's cellar: it is large, half underground with vaulted tunnels, above which is the fermenting area. There were 30 botti, most with aged wine: I tried that from 1833 and it was harsh and unpleasant; the 1832 on the other hand was soft and semisweet."[2]

Tancredi died in 1838, and his wife, Giulia, carried on producing wine from the Falletti's vast holdings in Barolo. The marchesa has long been credited as one of the earliest trailblazers of modern-day Barolo, along with Louis Oudart, the French négociant-turned-winemaker she supposedly hired as a consultant. According to nearly all the histories ever written on Barolo, the Marchesa di Barolo asked her good friend Cavour if she could use "his enologist," Louis Oudart, but there is absolutely no historical proof that the marchesa ever made such a request, or that Oudart ever worked for the Marchesa di Barolo. In his history of Barolo, *Il paese del Barolo*, compiled in 1928 by S. Domenico Massé, the rector of the Barolo College, and authorized by the Società Anonima dei Vini Classici, già Opera Pia Barolo (the name of the Marchesi di Barolo winery after Giulia Falletti's death), the author mentions Oudart but never suggests that the latter worked for the marchesa. Perhaps even more significant is that the author of a recent biography on Louis Oudart concludes, after thorough scrutiny of library archives and contemporary documents, that she "could not find even a single document that linked the enologist to Barolo."[3] I tend to believe evidence that has recently come to light that it was General Paolo Francesco Staglieno who first vinified Barolo as a dry wine (see chapter 3).

Regardless of who was helping with the winemaking, the Marchesi di Barolo's cellars in Barolo were undoubtedly producing Nebbiolo-based wines by the third decade of the 1800s, presumably even before, and based on contemporary accounts, the wines must have been of exceptional quality for the

FIGURE 3. Historic botti at Marchesi di Barolo winery. Although no one knows their exact age, these five 120-hectoliter casks, made from chestnut wood, were already in the cellars when the Abbona family bought the firm in 1929. Known as the Botti della Marchesa, they have been lovingly restored. Photograph by Paolo Tenti.

times. One popular myth states that during one of the marchesa's frequent visits to the royal court, King Carlo Alberto jokingly asked her when he could try her "famous wine, of which he had heard so much," prompting the marchesa to send him over 300 barrels of wine.[4] The tale was embellished over the years, so that most versions even specify that marchesa sent precisely 325 barrels of wine, taking into account the forty days of Lent.[5] While most agree this a nineteenth-century urban legend, it does appear that the Marchesi di Barolo, who were frequent guests at the royal court of Turin, as was the marchesa on her own after she was widowed, introduced King Carlo Alberto and his family to their wine made in Barolo. In 1836, the king hired Staglieno to oversee winemaking at the royal cellars in Pollenzo, and later at Castello di Verduno, which the king acquired in 1838 and where Staglieno began experimenting with dry vinification of red wines.

The Marchesa di Barolo, an extremely pious woman and a philanthropist who had created numerous charities in her lifetime to help the needy in and around Turin, died in 1864 with no heirs. According to her will, upon her death her assets were unified under a single charitable foundation known as Opera Pia Barolo, still in existence today. The Falletti's winery in the center of Barolo and their vineyards throughout the denomination became part of the Opera Pia Barolo, and wine sales helped fund the charity. In 1874, cellar registries compiled by Opera Pia Barolo list the estate's wine as Barolo, including Nebbiolo wines hailing from vineyards in Serralunga, arguably one of the first documents that refers to the wine as Barolo as opposed to "Nebbiolo or wine from Barolo" or as Nebbiolo from other villages.[6]

Yet by the late 1920s, the cellars run by Opera Pia Barolo had run into difficulties. In 1929, a local winemaker, Pietro Abbona, who had been making wines for years at his family's winery in the center of Barolo and whose family owned vineyards in Barolo, acquired the Marchesi di Barolo winery and vineyards from Opera Pia Barolo. Before this, Abbona had already garnered fame for the wines he made at his father's firm, Cavalier Felice Abbona & Figli, winning gold medals at the World's Fair in Vienna in 1873, at Turin's International Exposition in 1884, and at the World's Fair in Brussels in 1910.

Today the firm is run by Ernesto Abbona and his wife, Anna. The sprawling, functional cellars have been renovated over the years, and the Abbonas have carefully restored five enormous chestnut casks dating from the mid-1800s that originally belonged to the Marchesa Giulia Falletti.

Marchesi di Barolo has long been associated with several of Barolo's top crus, and in particular with Cannubi, and as mentioned in the village introduction, Abbona spearheaded efforts to expand use of the Cannubi name from its previously delineated 15 hectares to 34 hectares. The firm owns vineyards throughout the village of Barolo, including Cannubi Muscatel (which now can be called simply Cannubi), Sarmassa, and Costa di Rose. Their single-vineyard Barolos are all made with estate grapes, as is the firm's Barolo del Comune di Barolo and the Riserva, while they source grapes for the straight Barolo. The firm also makes a Barbaresco from Serragrilli vineyards in Neive.

In the cellars, Ernesto Abbona uses different approaches for his various Barolos. He employs more traditional methods for the firm's Barolo Tradizione, the Barolo del Comune di Barolo, and the Barolo Riserva, all of which ferment in stainless steel with temperature control, after which the newly fermented wine is racked into glass-lined concrete tanks that are insulated with a layer of cork. While the Barolo del Comune di Barolo and the Riserva age for two years in large Slavonian casks, the straight Barolo ages for the same amount of time, partly in traditional Slavonian casks and partly in French barrels.

The firm's single-vineyard Barolos have a slightly longer maceration period. All of the crus are aged for two years in wood; part in large casks made of either Slavonian or French oak and part in moderately toasted barriques.

Production

Total surface area: 48 ha (118.6 acres) estate owned + 117 ha (289 acres) owned by growers with whom the winery has worked for years

Barolo: 22 ha (54 acres) estate owned +16 ha (39.5 acres) owned by growers working with the winery; 275,000 bottles

Barbaresco: 2 ha (4.9 acres) estate owned + 10 ha (24.7 acres) owned by growers working with the winery; 87,000 bottles

Barolo Tradizione. A blend of Nebbiolo sourced from various parts of the denomination, this is the mainstay of the firm's Barolo production. Even though it lacks the depth and intensity of the firm's other Barolos, it is still usually a sound, unpretentious offering and a decent value.

Barolo del Comune di Barolo. This is an assembly of the firm's estate Nebbiolo from their vineyard areas in the village of Barolo: Cannubi, Sarmassa, Coste di Rose, Castellero, Boschetti, Preda, Vignane, and Ravera, and every year the percentage of the blend varies depending on the vintage conditions. The 2007, tasted in 2012, is a straightforward Barolo made in a classic style, with sour cherry, rose, and dried prune and balsamic notes. Wild cherry flavors and spice flavors are accompanied by firm but ripe tannins and admirable freshness for the vintage.

Barolo Riserva. Made from estate grapes hailing from various vineyards in the Barolo village, this ages for two years in traditional botti followed by another three years in bottle before being released. The Riservas are classic Barolos, with the fragrance, elegance, and balance one expects from the village that lends its name to the wine. The 2001, tasted in 2012, had the village's trademark bouquet of rose and violet with a hint of leather and a whiff of tar. Still very vibrant and fresh with sour cherry, fig, tea, and sage flavors. Lovely depth and velvety tannins, this will maintain for another decade at least. A hallmark Barolo.

Barolo Cannubi, Barolo Sarmassa, Barolo Coste Le Rose. Aged partly in barriques and partly in a combination of both Slavonian and French casks, past vintages had overwhelming oak sensations of espresso, toast, and vanilla that muffled any obvious vineyard variations and overrode Nebbiolo's varietal character. However, the 2010 Cannubi and Sarmassa display Nebbiolo's floral, red berry, and leather sensations while expressing their individual vineyard areas. Sarmassa showed particularly well, boasting intensity, structure, and juicy fruit.

Barolo 1959. In 2011, the Abbonas graciously opened a bottle of the firm's Barolo 1959, not an outstanding vintage by all accounts. Yet despite its luminous orange-brick hue, the bottle was surprisingly intact, with dried fig, prune, leather, and goudron aromas along with tea, prune, tobacco, and cocoa powder on the palate. While the tannins were almost all smoothed out, the wine still boasted a vein of acidity, but was long past its prime. Great example of the longevity of well-made Barolos produced more than fifty years ago, even from mediocre vintages.

Bartolo Mascarello

Via Roma 15
12060 Barolo (CN)
Tel. +39 0173 56125

For decades, Cantina Bartolo Mascarello has been the flag bearer for classically crafted Barolos of superlative quality. I had the excellent fortune of meeting Bartolo Mascarello on numerous occasions before he passed away in 2005, and over the years I have probably accumulated enough material to write a biography on Barolo's most celebrated elder statesman. Bartolo's sharp wit and courage in the face of the many obstacles he faced, not to mention his soulfully complex and elegant Barolos, have inspired me ever since my husband and I first met him in 1994, during what is now referred to by locals as La Grande Alluvione, or The Great Flood. During our visit, at the height of the storm, the electricity went out, and we continued to talk with Bartolo for hours by candlelight while he drew labels, and we sipped his Barolo 1990. We bought a case of the 1990, of which a single prized bottle remains. For now.

Bartolo learned how to make Barolo from his father, Giulio, who in turn had been trained by his own father, Bartolomeo, who for years had been the cellar master at the Cantina Sociale di Barolo before it closed in the 1920s. In an era when a dozen or so large vinification houses dominated Barolo production and farmers sold their grapes, Giulio Mascarello took the road less traveled when he decided to establish his own winery in 1920 with a loan from family members. His first customers were friends in Genova, where he had worked for several years, who soon spread the word, and by the 1930s Giulio, whose family had possessed a small parcel of vineyards when he started, was able to purchase more vineyards in key Barolo crus Cannubi, San Lorenzo, and Rué, and later in Rocche in La Morra, allowing him to hone his art as a master blender of Nebbiolo for Barolo. And as already mentioned in chapter 4, although many of the growers who became producers in the 1980s still talk about how awful their fathers' Barolos were, being made in rotting casks in unsanitary home cellars and only for family consumption, since they mainly sold grapes to large Barolo-making houses, the Mascarellos, grower-producers since the 1920s, had invested in tanks, barrels, and in the cellars.

Giulio passed away in 1981 at the age of eighty-six, but by then his son Bartolo was firmly at the helm. Bartolo, who joined the firm after the war, had spent the years during the conflict as a partisan fighting against the Germans in the Langhe hills. Upon learning that I was American, Bartolo delightfully recounted how during the liberation of the Langhe he and his friends "saved the Americans"—just the opposite of the usual "how the Americans saved us" stories I've heard over the years from other veteran winemakers. It has nothing to do with wine, but it sheds light on just one of the many experiences that shaped Bartolo Mascarello. As he told it, he and the other partisans, who were still living in the hills at the time, "watched as the Americans came into the Langhe in an assortment of trucks, tanks, and other smaller, open vehicles. We were shocked at these strange cars, which I now know were jeeps but at the time we had never seen anything like it. We asked each other, 'How did they ever win the war in *those?*' A column of the convoy was crossing the Tanaro at one of the shallower points, but it was very slow going. At one point, evidently fed up, one jeep with four young soldiers left the line and drove downriver a few yards and began to cross. We knew right away what could happen, because the river is very deceiving and dangerous. Suddenly, halfway across, the vehicle sunk into a deep hole, and the river was swirling over the soldiers. We got to them quickly and threw out ropes and pulled the men ashore. Afterward, there was a lot of 'Thanks, buddy,' cigarettes, and chocolate."

In yet another of my favorite episodes, on a visit to the cellar in 2002 to buy wine, Paolo and I found Bartolo and a group of ex-partisans, along with a near-empty magnum of his Barolo 1964, reliving the old days just as another member of their group rushed into Bartolo's small office with a large object covered in a towel. When he unwrapped a machine gun, we decided it was time to go, but not before accepting a sip of the 1964, which was breathtaking.

Starting in the 1980s, when critics began their assaults on traditional Barolos in favor of suspiciously dark bottlings with excessive extraction, concentration, and reeking with espresso and oak, Bartolo fought a long battle to defend classically crafted Barolos. Bartolo, the most iconic of Barolo makers, and others with the same philosophy, including Teobaldo Cappellano and Giuseppe Rinaldi, dubbed the Last of the Mohicans for their dogged refusal to make internationally styled Barolos, were branded as has-beens and met with scathing criticism from many journalists and wine guides.

As Bartolo told me in one of our first interviews in the 1990s, after an American importer came to see him and tasted his Barolos, the latter said how much he liked the wines "but what a shame about the color." This was an obvious reference to the luminous ruby garnet hue of Mascarello's Barolos, so much lighter than the inky dark wines the market demanded at the time, and in many export markets still does. To which Bartolo succinctly responded with his trademark irony: "That's like saying the women in Ethiopa are beautiful. Too bad they're black."

Bartolo had long battled illness, and when he had to rely on a wheelchair, his daughter Maria Teresa joined the firm. When she took over the winery, Bartolo demanded that Maria Teresa promise to never use barriques and make what he called "carpenters' wines." To make sure that Maria Teresa would never be tempted to experiment with the small French barrels, in the late 1990s Bartolo bought all new Slavonian casks that filled every possible corner and alcove of the cellar, making it physically impossible to stuff a barrique anywhere. Just in case.

By the first years of the New Millennium, global tastes were changing: seasoned wine lovers began to reject bombastic wines in favor of more authentic wines, while a new generation of wine drinkers rejected the oaky, concentrated style of their parents and looked for unique bottlings. Sensing they were behind the times, the collective wine press started taking a closer look at classically crafted Barolos. Bartolo, whose wines had been scorned or ignored by international and Italian wine publications for most of the 1990s and early 2000s, received the coveted Three Glasses in Gambero Rosso's 2003 edition of *Guide to Italian Wines* (long a supporter of sleek, oaky wines) for his 1998 Barolo—not that this particularly impressed Bartolo or Maria Teresa, whose cadre of loyal customers, including the queen of the Netherlands, had never stopped buying and admiring their Barolos.

FIGURE 4. Maria Teresa Mascarello. Daughter of the iconic Bartolo Mascarello, charismatic Maria Teresa faithfully upholds the traditional vineyard and winemaking practices she learned from her father, who in turn learned from his father. She is also a fierce defender of the historic Cannubi vineyard site. Photograph by Paolo Tenti.

Bartolo spent his last years as Barolo's veteran ambassador, dispensing his philosophy on wine and politics to the cellar's many visitors. To pass the time, he also spent many hours hand drawing labels. His most famous label, the ironic and now iconic "No Barrique No Berlusconi," a protest regarding the double evils facing Barolo and Italy at the time, featured head shots of the infamous prime minister that Bartolo had cut out of Berlusconi campaign flyers his neighbors had thrown away (and were collected by Maria Teresa and his wife at Bartolo's insistence). There are several versions, but the original ones had a flap over the prime minister's face, and as Bartolo said, "When you get sick of looking at him, just pull down the window."

Bartolo passed away in 2005, and since then Maria Teresa, every bit as intense and determined as her father, has done an admirable job following in her father's footsteps. She has also made some necessary changes to the cellars that are attached to the family home in the center of town, including creating a spacious yet homey tasting area next to the cellar. Maria Teresa, a fierce defender of Barolo's historic vineyard sites, inherited her father's no-nonsense attitude about her chosen profession, and while she follows a decidedly non-interventionist approach in the vineyards and the cellar, she shuns the romance of natural wines. As she told me, "Let's not recite poetry, I'm first and foremost a winemaker, and even though I try to intervene as little as possible, if something goes wrong, say with spontaneous fermentation for example, I would resort to selected yeasts if I had to." She also shares her father's unique brand of nonmarketing promotion; just as her father refused to have a phone until 1990, Maria Teresa has no website or e-mail, and rarely leaves her vineyards or cellars to promote her wine. She has also kept the same winemaking methods as her father: fermentation in glass-lined concrete tanks, without selected yeasts or temperature control, with fermentation and maceration lasting anywhere from forty to fifty days, followed by aging in traditional botti.

Production

Total surface area: 5 ha (12.3 acres)

Barolo: 3 ha (7.4 acres), 15,000 bottles

Barolo. Cantina Bartolo Mascarello makes all of the classic Langhe reds, including a richly structured Barbera, but their calling is Barolo. Like her father and grandfather, Maria Teresa makes only one Barolo with blended Nebbiolo from the firm's four crus: Cannubi (the classic heart of the famed growing area), San Lorenzo, and Ruè in the Barolo village and Rocche in La Morra. The firm makes no Riserva. Bartolo Mascarello Barolos are extremely elegant, with great depth that with time develop gripping complexity. The 2008, tasted in 2012, is a quintessential Barolo with earthy, floral aromas and sour cherry and truffle flavors. Bracing but refined tannins are balanced by lovely acidity. Great depth of flavors but needs time to soften. Best 2016 to 2028. Maria Teresa made an outstanding Barolo 2009—no easy feat in this vintage. It has a gorgeous bouquet of rose, with forward notes of leather and a whiff of tar. The palate delivers a hint of carob, spice, and succulent black cherry notes. Impeccably balanced and elegant, this is a textbook Barolo to be enjoyed while 2008 ages. The gorgeous 2010, which underwent fifty-five days of fermentation-maceration, is a textbook Barolo, with vibrant red berry sensations balanced by nervous acidity and a firm tannic backbone. Give this time to develop to its full potential. Drink 2020 to 2045.

————*1999.* Tasted in 2009, this had intense perfume of red rose, truffle, and eucalyptus aromas with a hint of leather. Ripe wild cherry and black tea flavors with still youthful but fine tannins and vibrant acidity. Hallmark Barolo with decades ahead of it. Best through 2029.

————*1971.* This showed beautifully when tasted in 2004. Hallmark tar, rose petal and leather bouquet with carob, truffle, fig, and sweet black tea and tobacco flavors. Silky smooth and impeccably balanced with layers of complexity. Evolved for hours in the glass. A majestic, compelling wine. Should still maintain until 2021.

————*1964.* Tasted most recently in 2008, this is a compelling, stunning Barolo from one of the denomination's most legendary vintages. Fig and carob aromas soon evolved in the glass into dried rose petal, tar, and leather. Surprisingly fresh, with dried cherry, truffle, and clove flavors. Long, linear, and elegant with gripping complexity and fantastic length. Should still maintain for a decade or so.

Giuseppe Rinaldi

Via Monforte 5
12060 Barolo (CN)
Tel. +39 0173 56156. rinaldimarta@libero.it

Giuseppe (Beppe) Rinaldi's soulful, quintessential Barolos are among the best expressions of the floral, earthy, and mineral purity that Nebbiolo can yield when it is planted in prime areas and not forced in the cellar. The firm's bottlings have long been a cult favorite among die-hard Barolophiles and because of the small volume, there is never enough to satisfy everyone.

The family firm was originally founded by Beppe's grandfather, also called Giuseppe, in 1890, and was then taken over by Beppe's father, Battista, in 1947. Battista, by all accounts extremely sharp and serious, graduated with honors from Alba's enological school. He had inherited not only the stone country house on the outskirts of Barolo, beneath which the cellars are still located today, but also prime vineyards in Brunate, Le Coste, and Ravera, all in Barolo, and he went on to acquire small parcels of Cannubi San Lorenzo. As the mayor of Barolo from 1970 to 1975, he was the fundamental force behind the town's acquisition of the Falletti castle, as well as the founding father of the Enoteca Regionale di Barolo. Grower and winemaker Battista's limited number of Brunate Riservas, which he made only in top vintages and released after ten years of bottle aging, have gone down in Barolo folklore as some of the finest Barolos ever made. I've talked to several Barolophiles lucky enough to have tried these rare Barolos, including the outspoken Gianfranco Soldera of Brunello fame, and they consider them among the greatest wines ever made.

Battista's son Beppe, fondly known as "Citrico" (Acidic) among locals on account of his scathing bluntness, now runs the winery, and even though he

FIGURE 5. Giuseppe Rinaldi. One of the denomination's fantastic small producers, outspoken Giuseppe Rinaldi is a defender of classically crafted Barolos and of the area's top vineyard sites. He's also a passionate collector and restorer of Lambretta scooters. Photograph by Paolo Tenti.

continues to make cult Barolos, it appears this single-vineyard bottling, which Beppe stopped producing in 1990, was a point of contention between father and son, with Beppe preferring the hallowed custom of crafting blended Barolos. "I don't believe any individual vineyard can perform well every year, so blending different crus allows me to obtain a natural balance. And blending has become especially important over the last fifteen years as global warming is pushing up summertime temperatures in many of the historical crus, resulting in lower acidity in both the grapes and the wine," declares the winemaker.

Beppe is a beacon of traditional Barolos, but he himself is delightfully nonconformist, as was aptly demonstrated by his large BMW motorcycle, which I saw parked smack in the middle of the living room, in between elegant settees, during my first visit to the cellar several years ago, or the perfectly restored Lambretta scooter parked in the same spot in 2013. Rinaldi is the sole survivor of the trio of Barolo producers that included the late Bartolo Mascarello and Teobaldo Cappellano, dubbed the Last of the Mohicans. As Beppe told me during my visit in 2010, "It was a serious joke, but Barolo producers should defend their denomination, starting with dedicated quality control in the vineyards, and by eliminating the increasing bureaucracy that focuses only on bottle numbers and paperwork and which now takes up too much of our time." Beppe Rinaldi is also an outspoken defender of the much-exploited Langhe hills, saying, "Today Barolo makers have planted vines in areas our grandfathers would never have even dreamed of planting Nebbiolo." In the vineyards, Beppe is firmly against using chemicals of any kind, declaring, "We've never used any chemicals products in our vineyards, ever." Instead, he uses only limited amounts of copper and sulfur against fungus diseases and fertilizes only four or five years and exclusively with manure, just as his father and grandfather did. Rinaldi insists that cellar technology is not the answer to great Barolos but having vines in the right area is key.

Rinaldi, who trained as veterinarian, learned winemaking from his father, and in his cramped cellars dominated by enormous Slavonian casks, Rinaldi turns out traditionally crafted Barolos and believes in guiding rather than forcing the wine. "I don't need selected yeasts. Before selected yeasts were invented, wine fermented spontaneously; I simply let nature takes it course," says Rinaldi. Fermentation takes place in wooden vats, and skin contact lasts on average twenty to thirty days, including during fermentation. And Beppe's opinion regarding aging any of the Langhe wines in barriques? The primitive chair in the corner of the cellar, adorned with the handwritten sign The Best Use for Barriques, says it all.

Until the 2010 vintage, Rinaldi, who is now joined in the cellars by his daughters, Marta, who has a degree in enology from the University of Turin, and Carlotta, who is studying agronomy at the same university and follows the vineyards, made two Barolos. Both wines were vinified and aged in exactly the same way, allowing the different expressions of terroir to shine through. The firm's Cannubi San Lorenzo—Ravera, and Brunate—La Coste, each made from a blend of two of the estate's four vineyards, were quintessential Barolos, and for years have had a cult following around the world, although their extremely limited amounts were never enough to satisfy collectors and wine lovers.

Starting with the 2010 vintage, however, Rinaldi can no longer make these two iconic Barolos as a result of EU regulations that permit only a single-vineyard name to be listed on labels, or none at all. Needless to say, Beppe and his daughters feel they've been let down by their *consorzio* and officials in Rome who should have found ways to protect their producers and their wines. Based on the new rules, Rinaldi will now be bottling a single-vineyard Brunate, as his father had done, and to this they will be adding the maximum of 15 percent allowed by the EU regulations of Le Coste, while the rest of Le Coste, Ravera, and Cannubi San Lorenzo will be blended and labeled as Barolo Tre Tine. I first tried the 2010 Barolos from the tanks in early March 2014, and they are exquisite, so even if the Rinaldis aren't happy with the forced changes to their production, consumers won't mind one bit.

The firm's Barolo vineyards average 300 meters (984 feet) above sea level with the exception of Brunate, which has an average altitude of 350 meters (1,148 feet) above sea level; the average age for Barolo plants wavers between thirty-five and forty years old.

These ultratraditional Barolos are often stunning and always unique, delivering earthy, truffle, leather, floral, and balsamic sensations, and while they are often aggressive in their youth, they soften with age. Beppe is adamant that if some people feel Barolo is too unusual for New World palates, well, tough. Or as he told me, "Barolo is a difficult wine because it isn't like other wines from around the world, making it more difficult to understand at first. But Barolo must remain authentic, and we shouldn't try to imitate other wines from around the world." The firm also makes one of the best Langhe Nebbiolos in the denomination as well as an excellent Barbera.

Production

Total surface area: 6.5 ha (16 acres)

Barolo: 3.8 ha (9.39 acres), 16,000 bottles

Barolo Cannubi San Lorenzo—Ravera.   Of the two Barolos, this is the rounder of the two, with succulent fruit, and it is usually approachable sooner than the Brunate—Le Coste. The 2008 offered Nebbiolo perfume of wild cherry, rose, leather, and nutmeg. Delicious Nebbiolo sweetness with mineral, spice, and truffle. Should develop complexity over the next few years. Drink 2016 to 2028. The 2009 presents a gorgeous bouquet of dried rose petal, violet, and truffle with hints of forest floor and leather. The palate delivers juicy wild cherry and berry flavors, layered with mint and balsamic herbs, and shows depth and balance.

Brunate—Le Coste.   Despite its intense floral notes, this is the more austere of the two Barolos, with bracing tannins and racy acidity that need time to tame. The 2007 is one of the best of the vintage, with a richness of flavors that matched the bracing tannins, all lifted by a vital energy lacking in most 2007s. Wonderful length and balance. Best after 2015. The 2008 has leather, underbrush, and rose aromas along with wild cherry, truffle, balsamic, and tobacco flavors. Still young and aggressive with expected maturity after 2018.

Barolo Tre Tine 2010. The Rinaldis are calling this stunning blend Tre Tine, or Three Vats, in honor of the three separate crus that make up this Barolo. Vibrant and highly perfumed, it's elegant, with crunchy red cherry and spice beautifully balanced by bright acidity and firm tannins. Intense and loaded with finesse.

Brunate 2010. The first time the winery has made this single-vineyard bottling since 1991. It has a gorgeous fragrance of rose, cherry, and balsamic herbs. The palate is intense and full of energy, with rich red berry, vibrant acidity, and firm tannins. A quintessential Barolo with breeding, energy, and impressive structure.

Langhe Nebbiolo. This is one of my favorite Nebbiolos. The 2010 boasts floral, strawberry, and mineral notes. Vibrant, pure fruit flavors and a silky texture. Extreme elegance. Best until 2015 for freshness.

Brezza

Via Lomondo 4
12060 Barolo (CN)
Tel. +39 0173 560921
www.brezza.it
brezza@brezza.it

Located just outside the center of town and surrounded by vineyards, this is another fine maker of classic Barolos. The winery was founded in 1885 by Giacomo Brezza, and the family has owned parcels of Barolo vineyards since the end of the nineteenth century and began bottling at least a portion of their wines in 1910. Today Enzo Brezza and his cousin Giacomo are the fourth generation to run the winery, while Enzo's father, Oreste, a spry octogenarian, greets the many guests who visit the estate's cellars, which are located beneath the family's Hotel Barolo and restaurant.

Brezza now owns vineyards in the village's premier crus, including in the historical part of Cannubi, Sarmassa, and Castellero. Enzo, along with his cousin Maria Teresa Mascarello, was among those who fought to keep the name Cannubi restricted to the historic 15-hectare (37-acre) parcel.

FIGURE 6. Enzo Brezza in the Sarmassa vineyard. Enzo Brezza runs this family winery, which is located in the center of town and has prime vineyard sites in the village of Barolo, including in the heart of Cannubi and Sarmassa. Photograph by Paolo Tenti.

Brezza is in the process of becoming certified organic, and for years has forgone chemical fertilizers, pesticides, and fungicides in the vineyard, and shuns herbicides as well, allowing grass to grow between the rows and turning the earth under the plants. The firm is also switching over to four-wheeled motorcyles or quads for vineyard maintenance because they cause less damage to the Langhe's fragile soil than heavy tractors.

Plant density is kept at a healthy 3,700 plants per hectare, and bunch thinning and green harvests are performed but never excessively. In the cellars, Enzo keeps it very traditional, and while the firm used selected yeasts for fermentation between 1989 and 2009, Enzo stopped using them starting with the 2010 harvest and now allows spontaneous fermentation regulated with keen attention to temperature control. Aging takes place for two years in 30-hectoliter Slavonian oak casks. All of Brezza's crus are vinified and aged the same way, so the differences are solely from terroir.

Production

Total surface area: 22 ha (54.3 acres)

Barolo: 8 ha (19.76 acres), 35,000 bottles

Barolo. Brezza's Barolo is a blend of the various estate Nebbiolo from the firm's holdings throughout Barolo. The 2008, tasted in 2012, is very elegant and enjoyable with classic Nebbiolo nose and flavors and firm but silky tannins and nervous acidity. Pretty, straightforward Barolo with no pretensions. Best 2014 to 2018. The 2010 shows fresh berry, mineral, and bright acidity. It's already showing poise and structure, but give this time to develop fully.

Barolo Cannubi. Cannubi is one of Barolo's most renowned crus and Brezza's is a quintessential bottling from this celebrated hill. Vineyards are situated at 250 meters (820 feet) above sea level, with southeast exposures, both of which encourage ideal ripening. According to Enzo, Cannubi's soil is sandier than that of other famed crus, which lends elegance and refined aromas to its Barolos. The 2008 is stunning, with rose, iris, and violet aromas and a whiff of new leather. Ripe cherry, spice, and mineral palate with bracing but fine tannins and lovely acidity. Gracefully structured, with the finesse of a fine Chambolle-Musigny. Best 2014 to 2028. The 2010 is gorgeous, with an intense fragrance and ripe red fruit flavors that deliver the combination of structure and elegance that has made Cannubi one of the most celebrated vineyards in Barolo.

Barolo Castellero. Before the 2010 vintage, this was last bottled on its own with the 2005 vintage. Located in the village of Barolo at an altitude of 300 meters (984 feet) above sea level, this vineyard site enjoys southern exposures while the soil is a mix of sand, silt, and clay, with a higher percentage of sand. The 2010 was still very young when I tried it in 2014, but already shows blue flower, smoky mineral, and red cherry supported by a tannic structure.

Barolo Sarmassa. This cru sits on the opposite side of the main Barolo ridge from Cannubi, and yet it has a distinct microclimate. According to Enzo, Sarmassa is in a closed valley, and is protected from cold winds and breezes, and its warmer microclimate means that it is the first area where snow melts in the winter. Altitudes range from 250 to 300 meters (820 to 984 feet), and plant ages range from twelve to seventy years old. This is more powerfully structured than Cannubi, with earthier aromas. The 2008 is loaded with underbrush aromas of mushroom and truffle, while the palate boasted rich berry and spice flavors and youthfully gripping tannins that need time to soften. A gripping wine that should develop complexity. Best 2018 to 2030.

The linear 2010 delivers blue flower, black cherry, and black pepper alongside brooding tannins. This possesses an impressive, age-worthy structure. Drink 2020 to 2045. A gripping wine.

Bricco Sarmassa.   Every year Brezza vinifies the highest of its Sarmassa vineyards separately, and in exceptional years bottles Bricco Sarmassa. While this is essentially vinified and aged like the other Barolos, because it has rounder tannins, it does have a longer maceration period to extract more fruit. Bricco Sarmassa is generally approachable earlier thanks to the fine tannins, and while structured, is more elegant than Sarmassa. The 2008 boasts great depth of fruit and spice flavors, with bracing but fine tannins. Its 15 percent alcohol is well integrated thanks to the wine's structure and balance. Best after 2016.

Scarzello Giorgio e Figli

Via Alba 29
12060 Barolo (CN)
Tel. +39 0173 56170
www.scarzellobarolo.com
info@scarzellobarolo.com

Run today by Federico Scarzello, who worked alongside his recently retired father, Giorgio, for years, this small, traditional winery is turning out quintessential Barolos of great breeding and class. Austere in youth, the firm's flagship Barolo, Sarmassa Vigna Merenda, has an age-worthy structure destined to develop layers of complexity with cellaring. Federico's family began bottling Barolo shortly before the end of World War II, and the family owns vineyards in one of the warmest areas of the celebrated Sarmassa cru, bordering on Cerequio. They also make solid Barolos blending Sarmassa with their vineyards in the Terlo subzone.

According to Federico, vineyard management is key to making Barolos of authenticity. "I'm not organic, or biodynamic, but I do limit the use of chemical products in the vineyards while at the same time reducing the use of copper and sulfur," says Federico. To that end, he is in the process of thoroughly analyzing his soils and scrutinizing all aspects of vineyard management: "Conserving the soil and the structure of the terrain is becoming very important, especially now that more producers are abandoning harsh chemicals in a favor of turning the soil." He explains that keeping the ground fresh and avoiding compact layers is fundamental to having healthy vines. To keep the soil healthy, he now plants various crops between the rows every fall, including fava beans and even barley, and is studying alternatives to heavy tractors.

In the cellars, the firm remains refreshingly attached to traditional methods that include eschewing selected yeasts in favor of spontaneous fermentation with ambient yeasts. Scarzello also favors long skin contact, anywhere from twenty-five to fifty-five days depending on the year, including maceration during the actual fermentation period, which Federico says is also a slow and often prolonged process, again depending on the vintage. Aging occurs in 25-hectoliter Slavonian botti where the wine rests for twenty-six to thirty months. The firm generally releases its Barolos about two years after its neighbors, preferring to give the wine more bottle age to soften tannins and develop.

Scarzello also makes a fascinating *metodo classico* sparkling wine from Nebbiolo grapes called Erpacrife.

Production

Total surface area: 5.5 ha (13.6 acres)
Barolo: 3.5 ha (8.7 acres), 10,000–12,000 bottles

Barolo Comune di Barolo.   Made from estate grapes from different parcels in Sarmassa and Terlo where average altitudes reach 250 meters (820 feet) above sea level and soils are calcareous marls with a marked presence of silt. All parcels are vinified separately. The 2007 is a solid Barolo with ripe fruit and surprising freshness for the vintage, but to reach this balance Federico had to discard 50 percent of his grapes.

Barolo Sarmassa Vigna Merenda.   In the best vintages the firm makes a single-vineyard bottling from their Merenda vineyard located in the larger Sarmassa site. Bordering Cerequio, this is one of the warmest areas in Barolo and has long been known for yielding exceptional quality grapes. The 2006, a classic vintage in the Langhe, is a stunning wine, with an archetypical Nebbiolo fragrance of leather, tar, truffle, and balsamic herbs. The palate offers layers of bright sour cherry, cinnamon, and white pepper accented with mint, licorice, and mineral notes. It's impeccably balanced with vibrant acidity and firm tannins and will develop more complexity with time. Drink from 2016 to 2036.

FIGURE 7. Luciano Sandrone. Luciano Sandrone's supple Barolos appeal to many different palates. He ages his wines in 500-liter tonneaux, and while polished, they still demonstrate the complexity and quintessential character of Nebbiolo. He also helped prove the excellent potential of the Cannubi Boschis vineyard site. Photograph by Paolo Tenti.

Luciano Sandrone

Via Pugnane 4
12060 Barolo (CN)
Tel. +39 0173 560023
www.sandroneluciano.com
info@sandroneluciano.com

From his spacious farmhouse and winery facing Cannubi Boschis at the entrance to the village, Luciano Sandrone turns out some of the most sought-after Barolos in the denomination. It is hard to believe that when Sandrone's polished renditions of the local classic first exploded onto the world's fine wine scene, he had only made 1,500 bottles. That was 1981, when Luciano brought his debut Barolo, from the 1978 vintage, to Vinitaly, and an American broker ordered them all.

Luciano, whose father was a carpenter, is one of the few producers who does not hail from generations of growers and winemakers. However, he wanted to make wine, and after graduating from agricultural school in 1973, worked at the Giacomo Borgogno firm for five years and then at Marchesi di Barolo, where he eventually became cellar master and stayed until 1990. In the 1970s, Luciano began acquiring vineyards and vinified his own grapes for the first time in 1978.

From 1990 on, Luciano has dedicated himself full-time to his own winery and has since been joined by his daughter Barbara and his brother Luca, a graduate of Alba's enological school and in charge of the firm's rigidly maintained vineyards. Sandrone judiciously mixes up age-old customs as well as innovation, with the sole goal of making world-class wines that express their grape variety and vineyard origins. For example, he makes both a blended Barolo, Le Vigne, and a single-vineyard bottling, Cannubi Boschis. Rather than engaging in the extended macerations of yesteryear, Sandrone starts off with a one-day warm maceration before fermentation begins, which he feels gently extracts even the most delicate aromas and flavors. After ten days to two weeks of fermentation and maceration, he separates the juice from the solids, and pumps it into smaller tanks to finish fermentation. He also shuns selected yeasts, insisting that each vineyard bestows grapes with their own strain of wild yeast, a crucial factor in making fine, expressive wines. To protect these wild yeasts, the firm avoids pesticides and herbicides in the vineyards. Sandrone does not use either barriques or botti, but instead ages in French tonneaux of 500 liters, which he uses up to five cycles, with only 20 percent to 25 percent of new barrels used for Barolo. Both his Barolos are aged for two years in oak followed by twenty months in bottle.

Production

Total surface area: The firm farms 27 ha (66.7 acres), 75 percent of which are owned.

Barolo Le Vigne.   A blend of Nebbiolo from the estate's Merli, Cerretta, Conterni, and Vignane vineyards all vinified separately, this is Sandrone's nod to the grand tradition of creating balance by blending different vineyards. As he told me, "My blended Barolo becomes the most important bottling in average vintages." Starting with the 2011 harvest, Le Vigne will also include grapes from the firm's recently acquired vineyard in the Baudana area of Serralunga, to add even more complexity and longevity. The 2009 offers intense floral scents of iris, violet, and rose layered with hints of mint and coffee. The palate is rich and vibrant, with a core of black cherry wrapped in cinnamon and spice. This is superbly balanced, elegant, and structured. Enjoyable now, it will also maintain a decade or more.

Barolo Cannubi Boschis. Sandrone's flagship wine, this is made with grapes from the firm's vineyard area on the celebrated Cannubi hill. Situated at 250 meters (820 feet) above sea level, Cannubi Boschis offers particularly advantageous growing conditions, thanks to well-draining soil, its bowl shape, and south-southeast exposure, which benefit from the morning sun that warms up grapes cooled over night. According to Sandrone, "Cannubi Boschis is my best Barolo in outstanding and in difficult years." Structured but extremely elegant, the magnificent 2010 boasts intense sensations, including violet, crushed black cherry, leather, exotic spices, licorice, and sage. It's perfectly balanced and has vibrant energy and gripping depth. It also has great aging potential.

Famiglia Anselma

Loc. Castello della Volta
Via San Pietro 3
12060 Barolo (CN)
Tel. +39 0173 560511
www.anselma.it
info@anselma.it

This winery was founded in 1976, and the Anselma family then began acquiring vineyards throughout the denomination, releasing their first Barolo in 1993. Today the firm is attempting an ambitious project: to focus only on Barolo, and eventually a small amount of Langhe Nebbiolo, from 35 hectares (86 acres) of estate-owned Nebbiolo vineyards in Barolo, Monforte, and Serralunga. In other words, no Dolcetto, Barbera, Arneis, or international varieties. Among their many hectares are holdings in prime areas, including Gianetto and Lazzarito in Serralunga and Gramolere and Bussia in Monforte. The firm's wine is also a result of rigorous selection; it only keeps the best grapes, a fraction of its production potential, and sells the rest to other firms. Along with the Nebbiolo-only philosophy, the family is slowly building what should be one of the most formidable and majestic cellars in the denomination, complete with vaulted archways and ceilings, made entirely with recovered local materials, including old hand-baked bricks, Langhe stones, and oak.

According to Maurizio Anselma, son of the founders and in charge of the winery today, his mother reports that widespread use of chemicals in the 1970s destroyed the vineyard ecosystem, resulting in an invasion of red spiders that attacked the vines. To restore natural equilibrium, the estate stopped using chemical treatments against fungus diseases twenty-five years ago. Seven years after the ban, ladybugs and other predator insects returned, keeping the dreaded red spiders in check. Maurizio, also the firm's enologist, ferments without using selected yeasts, and employs rotary fermenters, which he explains he uses "gently," with very few rotations carried out over a period of forty days. Maurizio maintains that his longer, gentler fermentation-maceration extracts less bitter tannins than do shorter fermentations typically carried out in rotary fermenters, which involve numerous rotations in as little as three or four days and result in a more tumultuous vinification. He also uses Gainmede fermenters—horizontal vats that do not rotate or use pumps, but instead rely on bubbles, a byproduct of the gas naturally formed during the fermentation process—to gently keep the cap submerged. Famiglia Anselma makes five Barolos and in top years a Riserva.

Production

Total surface area: 35 ha (86.48 acres)

Barolo: 35 ha (86.48 acres), 100,000 bottles

Barolo. The firm's Barolo Anselma, a blend of the various vineyard areas, and its Barolo del comune di Barolo and Barolo del comune di Monforte, made from holdings in Barolo and Monforte, respectively, age for two years in 25- and 50-hectoliter botti. This first is usually a solid and structured Barolo that is approachable sooner, while the Barolo del comune di Barolo is fragrant and elegant. The Monforte bottling is the more complex of the three.

Barolo Mosconi and Barolo Le Coste di Monforte. These two single-vineyard bottlings from Monforte are aged for two years in 10- and 25-hectoliter botti. Both are structured Barolos with tannic backbones and good aging potential.

Barolo Riserva ADASI. Made only in top vintages from the family's oldest Monforte vines in Le Coste Monforte and Ravera, this is the firm's signature bottling. Aged for three years in 25- and 50-hectoliter botti, it boasts all the complexity and depth one would expect from a Barolo Riserva. The 2001, tried in 2011, was stunning, and out of sixty wines that I tried from the vintage when I organized a ten-year anniversary tasting for *Decanter*, it came in at number 7. It boasted complex aromas of spice, licorice, and earth and was very well structured with concentrated fruit. Ten years on, this was still very young with plenty of room to evolve further. Best through 2021.

Bric Cenciurio

Via Roma 24
12060 Barolo (CN)
Tel. +39 0173 56317
www.briccenciurio.com
briccenciurio@briccenciurio.com

This small family winery run by Fiorella Sacchetto, her children, and her brother Carlo is making delicious, straightforward Barolos from estate vineyards in the township. Altitudes between 300 and 320 meters (984 and 1,050 feet) above sea level encourage ideal ripening, and plant age, between thirty and forty years old, generates concentrated flavors. The firm uses only ambient yeasts, and aging takes place in both Slavonian casks and used tonneaux.

Barolo.   Aged for two years in 25-hectoliter botti and tonneaux, 20 percent new. The 2008 has pretty Nebbiolo aromas and a bright, floral, berry, and mineral character. Very refined. Drink through 2018.

Barolo Coste di Rose.   Made from the eponymous vineyard, this is aged entirely in 25-hectoliter Slavonian casks. The 2008 offers intense rose, strawberry, and spice sensations with a hint of carob and mineral. Drink through 2022.

Barolo Monrobiolo.   Made from the vineyard of the same name and aged for two years in tonneaux, 20 percent of which are new. The 2008 is less floral than Coste di Rose, with spice, cedar, and tobacco leaf notes. Brawny with aggressive tannins that need time. Drink 2018 to 2028.

Barolo Riserva Coste di Rose.   In top vintages the firm makes a Riserva that it ages for three years in traditional botti. The 2006 has an intriguing balsamic character that delivers eucalyptus, mint, leather, and flint along with crunchy berry sensations. Very austere with impressive depth, this needs time to soften and develop. Drink 2016 to 2036.

To facilitate the accompanying map, Novello has been added here.

Novello is one of the lesser-known Barolo villages, even though it ranks fifth in terms of overall production, having 155 hectares (387 acres) registered to Barolo and accounting for 8.56 percent of the denomination's total output. Yet when compared to Barolo's core villages, simply put, Novello doesn't have as many high-quality vineyard areas and therefore doesn't share the prestige of the more illustrious townships of Barolo, Serralunga, Castiglione Falletto, La Morra, and Monforte.

Yet Novello, which borders the township of Barolo, boasts a handful of very good vineyards and one outstanding cru. Many producers from other villages buy grapes from Novello for their blended Barolos but don't mention the village name on the labels. Novello's top vineyards include Bergera, Sottocastello, and Ravera. Of the three, Ravera (a small portion of which extends into the village of Barolo) is by far the best, and has been recognized for years as a top vineyard area. In his nineteenth-century monograph, Lorenzo Fantini defined Ravera in Novello as a Prime Position, and today the best Barolos from Ravera, like those from Elvio Cogno, can hold their own against top Barolos from throughout the denomination thanks to their complexity, finesse, structure, and aging potential.

Elvio Cogno

Via Ravera 2
12060 Novello (CN)
Tel. +39 0173 744006
www.elviocogno.com
elviocogno@elviocogno.com

Founded by Elvio Cogno in 1991, this is not only Novello's premier estate, but also one of Barolo's rising stars. The winery is located smack in the middle of Ravera and is making superb Barolos from the best parcels in this vineyard.

Yet the history of this estate actually starts in La Morra, when Elvio Cogno founded the Marcarini winery with Giuseppe Marcarini. Marcarini, who was a successful notary (in Italy notaries perform tasks usually reserved for lawyers in the United States), left the running of the estate—including vineyard management and winemaking—almost entirely up to Cogno.

When Marcarini died and his grandchildren came on board in the late 1980s, they made drastic changes and wanted more say in how the winery was run, and they soon bought out Cogno's shares. Cogno returned to his hometown of Novello when he saw that the most important estate in Ravera—an undervalued cru at the time—was for sale.

Elvio bought the farm and invited his daughter Nadia and son-in-law Valter Fissore, who had worked with him at Marcarini for a few years, to join him. After learning the ropes under Elvio, a master Barolo maker, Nadia and Valter now run the estate. Valter—a trained enologist—keeps things very simple and traditional in the cellars. He ferments only with wild yeasts, with long fermentation and maceration times of up to forty days using the hallowed submerged cap method in the presence of perfectly ripe seeds to slowly extract noble tannins. From the mid-1990s until 2004, Valter aged Barolo Ravera for one year in barriques, mostly used, and one year in Slavonian casks, but now ages only in large casks. "The wines aged partly in barriques were good, but have less character than my Barolos aged only in botti," Valter told me in 2013.

According to Valter, keeping things simple in the cellars can be done only when one has perfect grapes, and to this end he is completely focused on his vineyards, eschewing chemical herbicides and pesticides. All of his Barolos come from the Ravera cru, where altitude averages 380 meters (1,247 feet) above sea level, and exposures are south and southeast. What changes among the individual single vineyards are the soils, clones, and vine age.

Production

Total surface area: 11 ha (27 acres)
Barolo: 6 ha (15 acres), 37,000 bottles

Barolo Cascina Nuova. This is a selection of the youngest vines in Ravera, which are generally between twelve and fifteen years old. This is the firm's more approachable and drinkable Barolo, which can be enjoyed young. The 2008 shows Barolo's charming side with delicious but restrained cherry and mineral, soft tannins, and fresh acidity. Lovely and drinkable. Best through 2018.

Barolo Ravera. This is Elvio Cogno's calling card. This section of Ravera is open to refreshing breezes that keep the vineyard cool and humidity and rot at bay. This vineyard performs exceptionally well even in very hot years thanks to the advanced age of the vines, between sixty and seventy years old, that also generate complexity and depth. The extraordinary 2010 opens with intense floral aromas and leather notes, and has persistent strawberry-cherry, spice, and mineral flavors framed in vibrant acidity and firm but fine tannins. A textbook Barolo. Best 2016 to 2028.

Barolo Riserva Vigna Elena. In exceptional years, the firm makes a Barolo Riserva from the Elena vineyard in Ravera. This vineyard, with its southeast exposure and slightly sandier soil, is made entirely with Rosé, which until just a few years ago was called Nebbiolo Rosé, formerly known as one of the three Nebbiolo subvarieties authorized in Barolo production. Now researchers have shown that this grape is a distinct variety, but still a very close relative to Nebbiolo, although the region has yet to register it as an official grape variety. The Elena vineyard tends to perform better in hotter years, and grapes generally take longer to reach full maturity. To tame the bracing tannins, this is aged for three years in botti. The 2006 is an exceptional Barolo with hallmark structure and finesse, compelling depth, and purity of flavors. Lovely balance. Drink 2016 to 2036.

Barolo Bricco Pernice. According to Valter, this is the heart and soul of Ravera. Full southern exposure and protection from winds conspire to create a microclimate that is hotter than the rest of the cru, meaning it excels in cool years like 2008 and 2006. The limestone heavy soil also generates serious tannic structure, necessitating three years' aging in Slavonian casks before release. The 2006 is a quintessential Barolo—all rose, cherry, truffle, and leather. Powerfully structured with bracing tannins that need time, and a long licorice finish. Complex and intense, this is a Barolo-lovers Barolo. Drink through 2036.

SEVEN

Castiglione Falletto

THE SMALL VILLAGE OF CASTIGLIONE Falletto makes what are perhaps the most well-balanced Barolos, noted for their finesse, intense perfume,
and velvety texture combined with impressive structure.

Dominated by its thirteenth-century fortress with its iconic round towers,
Castiglione Falletto was part of the holdings of the Marchese di Saluzzo and
defined as a "castrum et villa," although an ancient inscription discovered on
one of the village's walls gives rise to the theory that Castiglione Falletto may
have already been inhabited in ancient Roman times. In 1225, Saluzzo
awarded what was then essentially a large estate or fief to Bertoldo Falletti,
who built the castle and lent a derivative of his name to the village. Castiglione
Falletto changed hands numerous times over the centuries before becoming
part of the Savoy's holdings in 1601, and the restored castle is still privately
held today.

Located in the very heart of the Barolo denomination, Castiglione Falletto
is one of only three communes that are entirely located within the Barolo
growing zone, and it is the smallest of Barolo's core villages. In terms of
Barolo production, the municipality of just over seven hundred residents has
137 hectares (343 acres) of Barolo vineyards, accounting for just over 7 percent
of the denomination's total output.[1]

Thanks to Castiglione Falletto resident Ferdinando Vignolo-Lutati, a
former professor at the University of Turin and fellow at Turin's Academy of
Sciences, the village is the most studied of all the Barolo zones. In 1929, the
naturalist and academic published what is still the benchmark work on the
Langhe's geological makeup, and although I have already cited major points
of that publication in chapter 1, it's worth repeating the specific references to
Castiglione Falletto again in this chapter. According to Vignolo-Lutati,

FIGURE 8. View of Castiglione Falletto. Dominated by its round tower, Castiglione Falletto is in the very heart of the Barolo denomination. The best vineyard sites in the village make Barolos that combine both structure and finesse. Photograph by Paolo Tenti.

nearly all of Castiglione Falletto is of Helvetian (now called Serravallian) origin, comprised of "alternating layers of beds of sand and sandstone layered with marls and sandy marls" that are "generally gray or yellowish, sporadically interspersed with layers of bluish gray marls." He also maintains that a very small portion of Castiglione Falletto is Tortonian, "formed principally of gray and bluish gray marls."[2]

Vignolo-Lutati's work offers a detailed description of Castiglione Falletto's soils, which he breaks down as follows: "1). Marls—ranging in color from grayish-white to bluish and containing 25–30% calcium carbonate; 2). Clayey, yellow-reddish-brown soils poor in calcium, and 3). Sandy soils with 15% calcium carbonate and 15–20% sandy quartz."[3] He even categorizes the Barolos yielded from each soil type, with Barolos from the first category (the most extensive according to the academic) yielding "the standard Barolo, very fine; from the second soil group—the most infrequent—comes a less-prized Barolo while from third group—also less frequent and yielding lower crops—comes Barolo with lower alcohol perhaps but with an intense perfume that makes it particularly prized even at just one year old."[4]

The complexity of Castiglione Falletto's soil composition is confirmed by the report on Barolo's territory funded by the Piedmont Region, which

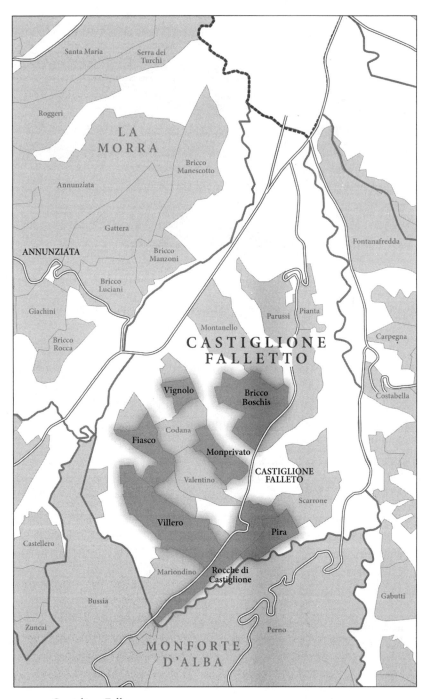

MAP 3. Castiglione Falletto.

describes the village's soil composition as layers of calcareous marls, sandstone, and sand beds interspersed with marls. According to the same study, parts of the village have the overall highest level of sand in Barolo's growing zone. Dr. Stefano Dolzan, who worked on the study, explains: "There are three types of soils in Castiglione Falletto: soils defined as Serralunga d'Alba units—typical of the eponymous village, Barolo units typical of the village of Barolo, and another type called Castiglione Falletto units that occupy the summits of the hills. These last units are Arenarie di Diano d'Alba deposits that are characterized by the higher presence of sand." It is fascinating that this portion of the in-depth study published in 2000 echoes Vignolo-Lutati's findings from seven decades earlier.

Given the undisputed complexity of the soil, it's no surprise that Castiglione Falletto Barolos tend to be among the most multifaceted in the denomination, combining perfume, elegance, and depth. The village, which has twenty geographic mentions, is home to some of Barolo's best crus, including Monprivato, Rocche di Castiglione, Bricco Boschis, Villero, Fiasco, and Pugnane, with the latter along with Paruzzo [sic] singled out as Prime Locations by Lorenzo Fantini at the end of the nineteenth century. Most of the vineyards face southwest and west toward La Morra, while to the south of the village center vineyards face east and southeast toward Monforte d'Alba.

Cavallotto

Tenuta Bricco Boschis
Via Alba—Monforte Bricco Boschis
12060 Castiglione Falletto (CN)
Tel. +39 0173 62814
www.cavallotto.com
info@cavallotto.com

The Cavallotto estate in Castiglione Falletto has been turning out some of the purest expressions of Nebbiolo since 1948, when brothers Olivio and Gildo Cavallotto began bottling their own Barolos from their spectacular Bricco Boschis vineyards. And when Olivio's children Laura, Giuseppe, and Alfio began working at the estate toward the close of the last century—the fifth generation to run the firm—they decided to continue making classic Barolos rather than the dense, highly extracted, and oak-driven wines so in vogue at the time.

FIGURE 9. Giuseppe, Laura, and Alfio Cavallotto. This fantastic family-run winery is located on the stunning Bricco Boschis hill on the crest leading to Castiglione Falletto. It's one of the best sites in the denomination, from which the Cavallottos make classically crafted, age-worthy Barolos that are consistently excellent. Photograph by Paolo Tenti.

Scaling the crest of the Castiglione Falletto hill, one cannot help but notice Cavallotto's Bricco Boschis estate with its impeccable hillside vineyards of old vines that surround the family's sprawling country house and cellars. It is an unusual sight in the Langhe, where, as in Burgundy, the famed vineyard areas are only rarely adjacent to producers' homes and cellars. It was this spectacular setting that initially drew me to the estate while I was touring the Langhe in 2000. Eager to try the wines from these sun-drenched and perfectly maintained vines, on a whim my husband and I made our way unannounced up the tree-lined drive—all the more beckoning for its lack of the usual imposing gate. We were warmly welcomed by what can only be described as a close and joyous family, who treated us to their complex and well-structured wines that were worlds apart from the many fruit-forward, bombastic Barolos that were pouring out of the area at the time.

"We want to make Barolo that tastes and ages like Barolo, a great but unique wine that can't be made anywhere else," Giuseppe said in 2000, adding that the firm tannins and vibrant acidity of their Barolos were crucial for lengthy cellaring. This was a gutsy stance at the time, and more than a decade later, the Cavallottos remain adamant about making balanced Barolos that express the power and purity of Nebbiolo in all its rose petal, tar, and wild cherry glory, and to do so in the most natural manner possible in both the vineyards and the cellars.

Even though the hyped concept of all-natural viticulture has become the wine world's latest marketing tool, the Cavallottos are true pioneers in organic vineyard management. In 1975, Gildo and his older brother Olivio, with the collaboration of Professor Lorenzo Corino, director of Asti's Experimental Institute of Agriculture, were the first in the growing zone to plant grass between rows in their vineyards. The grass creates competition with the vines and "naturally reduces the vine's grape production, generating fewer but better grapes," according to Gildo, whom I interviewed on several occasions before he passed away in 2013. Cuttings are then left on the ground to help stop erosion, and the resulting humus retains water, keeping the soil cool during drought. A year later, the estate introduced predatory insects that allowed it to cease using insecticides altogether. These organic alternatives to the chemical herbicides and insecticides that growers the world over were happily spraying in their vineyards did more than raise eyebrows in Barolo nearly four decades ago. "In 1975 and 1976, my uncle and father were viewed as eccentrics if not downright crazy. But they quickly reached their goal of improving our vines and grapes and hence the quality of our wines by eliminating these harmful chemical substances. Since then, organic agricultural methods have been a way of life for us," explains Alfio, adding that even though they are certified organic, they don't include this information on the label.

In the cellar, Giuseppe and Alfio, both trained enologists, are decidedly noninterventionist, using only wild yeasts for alcoholic fermentation. "We're convinced that because we carefully cultivate our vines with full respect for nature that the indigenous yeasts present on our grapes are the best. Obviously, wild yeasts are only an option for grower-producers who scrupulously follow every phase of the cultivation process and who never buy grapes on the market," says Giuseppe. I admit I was a bit surprised when I first learned that the firm employs rotary fermenters, but, as Alfio points out, they use them very slowly and carefully. "Rotary fermenters, when modified to slowly turn only a couple of times a day in the beginning and after a few days just once a day, gently extract color, aromas, and fine tannins. I think they work better than the pump-over method for Nebbiolo. Nebbiolo skins are slippery and stick together during fermentation, creating solid blocks that make it difficult to fully extract all the best elements of Nebbiolo," says Alfio.

Besides having ideal vineyards, the family's long experience has been key to their success and theirs was the first private winery in their area and one of the first in the entire Barolo growing zone to vinify and bottle their wines commercially. Before World War II, the family sold its grapes to Bonardi, once a famous Barolo firm in Alba. "But between 1944 and 1945, the Langhe's roads and bridges were destroyed and we couldn't get the grapes to Alba. So rather than lose all the grapes, we made the wine ourselves and aged it in our cellars. In the years after the war, our cellars were full of wine but the brokers and buyers didn't want it because there was no demand. So we sold it all directly, in demijohns to local restaurants and trattorie," says Olivio. Fortified by this experience, in 1948, after their father's premature death, eighteen-year-old Olivio and seventeen-year-old Gildo began producing, bottling, and labeling their wines and selling them to what had become a loyal clientele, decades before other local growers became producers.

Then as now, the Cavallottos vinified only their own grapes from their magnificent Bricco Boschis hill, which I have always been surprised was not included in Renato Ratti's now legendary map of Barolo's crus. "Ratti's map is undeniably important, but even he acknowledged that the map was founded on the then prevalent tradition in Barolo of grape buying. There were very few private wineries that made and sold wine, and Ratti's map was based on interviews with a multitude of grape growers who sold their fruit. When Ratti compiled info for the map, all the subzones and crus he included at the time had more than one owner. As a result, many of Barolo's top vineyards are missing from the map, not because they weren't worthy, but because these vineyard areas were owned by a single family and Ratti wanted a general consensus from numerous growers. Besides our Bricco Boschis cru, Falletto, now owned by Bruno Giacosa, and Giacomo Conterno's Francia, are all absent from Ratti's map," points out Alfio.

The Cavallottos are the sole owners of the Bricco Boschis hill, and already in the 1960s, they identified the most important single vineyards on the hill, Vigna San Giuseppe, Vigne Colle Sudovest, and Punta Marcello. "This estate originally belonged to Marchesa Giulia Falletti, as did most of the vineyards and farms," explains Laura Cavallotto, who is in charge of the administrative side of the firm. "When she died childless, the marchesa left this property to Giuseppe Boschis, who used to manage her numerous farms. Of all the land he inherited, Boschis chose to live here," explains Laura who adds that the vineyard area was already marked on a military map dating from 1879. "In 1928, our great-grandfather and grandfather, who were grape farmers here in Castiglione Falletto, bought the property from the Boschis family."

Bricco Boschis, with its varied southern exposures and complex combination of clay and calcareous soil, is unquestionably one of the area's top crus. Many of Cavallotto's vines are also very old, with an average age of fifty, and naturally produce fewer bunches and grapes. According to Alfio, the long roots reach underground minerals, all of which lend better aromas and more complexity to the wines, as well as survive severe drought much better than younger vines, as was proven in the scorching 2003 vintage. The Cavallottos also make an outstanding Riserva from their vineyard in the small Vignolo cru.

Production

Total surface area: 23 ha (54.8 acres)
Barolo: 14.25 ha (35.2 acres), 45,000 bottles

Barolo Bricco Boschis. This is made entirely from estate vineyards located on the Bricco Boschis hill that enjoy south, southwest, and southeast exposures and were planted in 1971. After eighteen to thirty-three days of fermentation and maceration, this ages for three to five years in large Slavonian casks. This is always a beautifully balanced wine and a quintessential expression of Barolo's celebrated complexity and finesse. The 2008 is already a classic, with hallmark rose and earthy aromas, including a whiff of leather. Succulent red berry flavors with impeccable balance and depth. Still young and needs time. Best 2015 to 2028. The 2009 is also outstanding—no small feat given the heat of the vintage. It offers intense rose and berry aromas alongside a creamy palate that delivers cherry, spice, and balsamic notes. Drink after 2019. The compelling 2010 is a textbook Barolo, displaying intense sensations of leather, herbs, black cherry, and spice alongside impressive structure and finesse. Vibrant with great depth, this will age for decades.

Barolo Riserva Bricco Boschis "Vigna San Giuseppe." Made solely with the best grapes from the oldest plants in the firm's San Giuesppe vineyard with vines planted in 1971. This vineyard, located 335 meters (1,099 feet) above sea level, enjoys full southwest exposures. After fermentation and maceration lasting between twenty-two and thirty-eight days, the wine ages for four to five years in large Slavonian casks. The 2006 is a stunning wine with earthy notes of porcini mushroom, truffle, and ripe cherry with rose and leather notes. With its rich fruit, and bracing but fine tannins, this combines elegance and power with an age-worthy structure. It still needs to time to fully develop complexity. Best 2016 to 2046. Compelling. The 2007 offers a fragrance of wild cherry, leather, and truffle. The palate delivers rich black cherry and spice layered with balsamic herbs and mineral notes along with lovely complexity and balance. It's already delicious, but for more complexity drink it after 2019. The 2010 barrel sample I tried in March of 2014 blew me away. It boasts a gorgeous fragrance of rose, balsamic herbs, and even a whiff of leather. This is already stunning, demonstrating both power and grace with red berry and black cherry balanced by a backbone of youthful, bracing tannins alongside nervous acidity. Once it's released (in 2015 or 2016), it will age well for decades.

Barolo Riserva Vignolo. This small cru is named after its former owner, Ferdinando Vignolo-Lutati, who published the landmark work on delimiting the Barolo zone in 1929. The family's tiny parcel is located at 310 meters (1,017 feet) above sea level, and plants are almost fifty years old. Vinified and aged exactly as the Riserva San Giuseppe, Vignolo is more floral and has more finesse than power. The 2006 is still young and tightly woven and needs time to unwind and open. The 2005 is absolutely stunning with rose, leather, and truffle aromas along with creamy wild cherry flavors and a hint of orange peel on the palate. Lovely minerality and elegant tannins. Drink 2014 to 2025. The 2007—another scorching, difficult vintage—is stunning, proving that even in difficult vintages, a quality-driven estate can make fantastic wines. It's vibrant and fresh, with floral aromas and rich cherry, mint, and cinnamon flavors of wonderful depth. I tried the 2010 from the barrel in 2014, and even at this youthful stage, it promises to be a classic Barolo. Slotted for release in 2015 or 2016, the nose was still a bit closed, but it's already demonstrating remarkable energy and an age-worthy structure that will allow it to evolve and develop complexity for decades.

In 2009 the Cavallottos graciously opened up a number of their older Barolos to demonstrate, in their words, how their wines hold up. The bottles were opened at the moment, and the tasting and interview lasted several hours, allowing ample time for the wines to unfold in the glass. The tasting proved beyond a doubt that Cavallotto's wines have a nearly marathon aging capacity during which time they evolve splendidly.

1958 Barolo. A great year for Barolo. Deep brick color, with a hint of orange at the rim. Dried rose petals, toffee, prune aromas. On the palate, hints of maple syrup and a nice length with a tea and tobacco finish. Very much alive, though delicate and somewhat past its prime, but with surprisingly firm acidity holding it altogether. Drink.

1961 Barolo. Another excellent vintage for the area. Solid garnet hue with brick rim. Layered and complex with smoky nose of leather, earth, and mineral. Rich palate of stewed plum and tea with an almost port-like sweetness. Firm acidity and velvety smooth tannins still have a good grip. Has aged majestically and still going strong. Drink.

1967 Barolo Bricco Boschis. Considered a very good year. Smoky aromas punctuated with meat juice extract, herbs, and spice. Spicy flavors and good acidity, but tannins have completely disappeared, leaving a somewhat abrupt finish. Past its prime.

1971 Barolo Riserva Bricco Boschis "Vigna San Giuseppe." An exceptional year. Deep, compact garnet color. Wonderfully youthful with classic aromas of rose petal and a hint of tar and leather. Complex with lovely, creamy cherry-strawberry flavors balanced with vibrant acidity and still firm tannins. Great length that closes on a note of tea and dried fig. An impressive Barolo that still has staying power. Drink.

1974 Barolo Riserva Bricco Boschis "Vigna San Giuseppe." A very good harvest. Garnet with some orange on the edge. Somewhat closed nose but a much better palate of spice and cherries marinated in spirits. Lacks the vibrancy of its predecessors, though still a very valid effort. Past its prime.

1978 Barolo Riserva Bricco Boschis "Vigna Colle Sudovest." A great vintage, as this wine aptly demonstrates. Deep, scintillating garnet. Intense fragrance of cherry and rose with a hint of leather. Mouthfuls of succulent wild cherry and licorice with fantastic length. Impeccably balanced, this is a complex wine of great depth and will continue to age well for decades. Best of tasting and a hallmark Barolo. Drink through 2028.

1985 Barolo Riserva Bricco Boschis "Vigna San Giuseppe." Exceptional year. Dark and deep color. Smoky nose lifted by fresh strawberry aromas with the same fresh strawberry carrying over onto the palate. Burgundy-like with lovely mineral character. At end of tasting, continued to open up and reveal more depth. Gorgeous. Will maintain for another decade or more.

1990 Barolo Riserva Bricco Boschis "Vigna San Giuseppe." Deep color with some brick on the rim. A bit more rustic in nature with lots of earth, leather, and underbrush on the nose. Delicate berry and fruit on the palate, with hint of licorice, but the length is cut short with a somewhat bitter close. Drink.

1997 Barolo Riserva Bricco Boschis "Vigna San Giuseppe." Considered an excellent year. Deep color and at first somewhat inexpressive nose that opened up to reveal classic floral aromas and tar. Ripe fruit palate is very fresh for this notoriously forward vintage and has teeth-coating tannins typical of classic Barolos. Drink through 2022.

1999 Barolo Riserva Bricco Boschis "Vigna San Giuseppe." An exceptional year. Deep and dark, great fresh bouquet with heady floral aromas and a hint of leather and earth. Delicious, succulent cherry-berry flavors punctuated with mineral and Vigna San Giuseppe's hallmark licorice notes. Delicious, and at ten, still a mere baby just developing its complexity. Will evolve into a stunner. Best through 2029.

2001 Barolo Riserva Bricco Boschis "Vigna San Giuseppe." Another superb vintage. Deep solid color. Intense nose of ripe cherry, rose, and spice with mouthwatering wild cherry flavors. Powerfully structured with vibrant acidity and a tannic backbone, this will age for decades to come. A magnificent wine.

Paolo Scavino

Via Alba-Barolo 157
12060 Castiglione Falletto (CN)
Tel. +39 0173 62850
www.paoloscavino.com
info@paoloscavino.com

Founded in 1921, the Paolo Scavino winery makes superlative Barolos from some of the greatest crus in the entire denomination, including the Fiasco cru in Castiglione Falletto, Rocche dell'Annuziata in La Morra, and Monvigliero in Verduno. The firm also makes an excellent Barolo Cannubi from the historic Cannubi vineyard site.

Today the estate is run by Enrico Scavino and his daughters Enrica and Elisa. The winery has been on the cutting edge of Barolo innovations for decades, and reached a milestone in 1978, when Enrico convinced his father Paolo to let him vinify the grapes from their Bric del Fiasc vineyard separately. "Every year we noticed that these were always the best grapes," Enrico told me in 2012. Enrico was also the first in the Langhe to use rotary fermenters, which he introduced in 1993, just before Elio Altare. Scavino's goal was to extract more color, primary aromas, and more fruit from his wines without the harsh tannins. In fact, extracting higher-quality tannins that are friendlier than the massively astringent Nebbiolo tannins of yore is a driving obsession for Scavino. To this end, his first-generation rotary fermenters were specially modified to turn slowly and infrequently, for gentle extraction. Since 2007, he has also been using a patented fermenter, which delivers an even gentler extraction.

Open on top, Scavino's latest steel fermenters are squat and vertical as opposed to his older, horizontally inclined rotary fermenters, and are specially designed with nets that keep the cap and solids constantly submerged. This in turn keeps the grape skins soft and intact, allowing the Scavinos to delicately extract Nebbiolo's noble tannins, color, and other key characteristics, without having to break up the cap, meaning there is less mechanical intervention. And while they do perform pump overs with these new fermenters, these are simply to release CO_2, which is essential to carrying out a complete fermentation. As Enrico's daughter Elisa told me, "We begin fermentation with the skins but after 10–12 days in the new fermenters, 8 days in the old ones, we separate the must from skins and the alcoholic fermentation of the must continues, taking about 20–30 days in total." Fermentation takes place only with indigenous yeasts, and malolactic fermentation occurs in barriques.

Enrico started experimenting with barriques in the late 1980s and early 1990s but decided right away that all new barriques overwhelmed Nebbiolo and suffocated the terroir he was trying so hard to express. He decided that a mix of wood is best, and ages his Barolos for the first year in barriques, with only about 15–20 percent new and the rest used for five and six years, and the second year in large casks made of both French and Austrian oak. "We never want to overwhelm our wines with new wood sensations," says Enrico, and they have succeeded. He uses the barriques mostly to fix the color and stabilize the wines, then racks into 50-hectoliter casks to slow down the maturation process. I must admit, however, that I was very pleased to see six new Austrian casks that had just been delivered when I visited the spacious winery in June of 2012. Enrico's daughter Elisa is experimenting with aging the firm's Barolos solely in these large casks and skipping the barriques entirely, although it will be a few vintages before she makes up her mind.

Enrico Scavino believes in tending his old vines with care and is also a strong believer in thinning the clusters. Selection in the vineyard and after the harvest is crucial for the Scavinos, and the just-picked grapes are selected on a sorting table. The wines are not fined or filtered.

Production

Total surface area: 22 ha (54 acres)
Barolo: N/A, 50,000 bottles

Barolo. This is a blend of Nebbiolo from eighteen different crus from throughout the denomination. The 2008 is a lovely luminous garnet color and has a lovely fragrance of rose and spice with a hint of toasted notes, all of which carry over to the palate. Very elegant and very approachable. Drink 2014 to 2022.

Barolo Carobric. Eighty percent of this Barolo comes from the celebrated Rocche di Castiglione cru in Castiglione Falletto, where vines are situated at 350 meters (1,148 feet) above sea level and have southeast exposures. The soil is predominantly Arenarie di Diano d'Alba, or alternating layers of sandstone and sandy, clay marls. The rest of the grapes come from Cannubi and Bric del Fiasc. The 2008 had a gorgeous bouquet of spice, rose, and balsamic notes with lovely sour cherry and spice flavors and mesmerizing depth. Drink 2015 to 2028.

Barolo Bricco Ambrogio. Located in Roddi, this is one of the Langhe's little-known crus. Realizing it had great potential, Enrico Scavino acquired a parcel in 2001, and just a year later this was his only cru not destroyed by hail during the notorious 2002 vintage. Bricco Ambrogio is the most charming of the Scavino Barolos, with intense perfumes. The 2008 has lovely floral and mineral sensations and mouthwatering raspberry flavors alongside supple tannins. Drink through 2023.

Barolo Monvigliero. From the Grand Cru of the village of Verduno, known for its soils of limestone mixed with veins of chalk. This and the southeast exposure and altitude of 310 meters (1,017 feet) create wines of extreme elegance. The 2010 is exquisite, with an intense perfume of wisteria, rose, red berries, and spice. Delicious cherry, cinnamon, clove, and mineral flavors. Velvety tannins make it tempting now, but hold for complexity. Drink through 2020 to 2040.

Barolo Cannubi. From the historic Cannubi vineyard in Barolo that the Scavinos have leased since 1985 and maintain as if it were their own. Vineyard altitude is 290 meters (951.4 feet) above sea level, and the soil is Sant'Agata Fossili marls mixed with some calcareous marls as well. The advanced age of the vines, planted in 1946, generates intense flavors and complexity. The 2008 is a benchmark Barolo, with intense floral notes and a whiff of leather. Ripe berry and citrus flavors, but it needs time to open up. Best 2016 to 2028. The 2009 is intensely perfumed with rose petal, violet, sage, and eucalyptus and boasts a juicy cherry palate energized with mineral. It's one of the best-balanced Barolos from the vintage.

Barolo Bric Fiasc. This is the darling of the House of Scavino, and the wine that made them famous when they first vinified it separately in 1978. The vineyard—with an average altitude of 260 meters (853 feet) above sea level—has the most complex soil of the firm's crus, and is a mix of whitish-gray limestone and yellowish sandstone. Although much of the vineyard has been replanted in the last few years, the oldest vines hail from 1938, and produce very few grapes. One of my rare 100-point wines, the 2010 is drop-dead gorgeous. Displaying power, grace, and complexity, it delivers sublime Nebbiolo sensations, including rose, underbrush, red cherry, leather, licorice, spice, and balsamic notes. Impeccably balanced. Drink 2018 to 2038.

Barolo Riserva Rocche dell'Annunziata. From the famed cru in La Morra, where vines reach 385 meters (1,263 feet) above sea level and benefit from south and southeast exposures. Vines were planted in 1950 and in 1991, and the subsoils contain sandstone and sand interspersed with calcareous marls. The 2006 has floral, leather, and balsamic aromas accompanied by a gripping palate of rich black cherry, herbs, and spice. It has both power and grace, and is well balanced with firm tannins and vibrant acidity. Drink 2016 to 2036.

Brovia

Via Alba-Barolo 145
12060 Castiglione Falletto (CN)
Tel. +39 0173 62852
www.brovia.net
info@brovia.net

Brovia is making quintessential and classically crafted Barolos of complexity, depth, and elegance from some of the top vineyard sites in all of Barolo, including Rocche and Villero, both in Castiglione Falletto.

FIGURE 10. Alex Sanchez of Brovia. Growers since 1863, the Brovias make quintessential Barolos from top vineyards, such as Rocche and Villero in Castiglione Falletto. Photograph by Paolo Tenti.

Founded in 1863 by Giacinto Brovia, the family firm has a long history of grape growing and winemaking. Giacinto passed the winery down to his son Antonio, whose premature death in 1932, coupled with the Second World War and its aftermath, stopped the family's activity for over twenty years. In 1953, Antonio's children—Giacinto, a trained enologist, Raffaella, a trained agronomist, and Marina—took over and began making quality wines. At the end of the eighties, Giacinto's daughters Elena, now the firm's enologist, and Cristina, the firm's agronomist, began working alongside their father and are now responsible for the daily running of the firm along with Elena's Spanish husband, Alex Sanchez, who joined the firm in 2001.

Over the years, the Brovias have acquired prime vineyards, mostly in Castiglione Falletto, where they own parcels in Rocche, Villero, and Garblet Sue (also known as Altenasso), as well as Ca' Mia from the Brea cru in Serralunga. Although their vineyards aren't certified organic, the family has shunned chemicals for years and keeps yields low. In the cellars Brovia keeps it very simple, fermenting with native yeasts in glass-lined concrete tanks at controlled temperatures followed by maceration for a total of twenty to twenty-five days. The firm then ages their Barolos in 30/40-hectoliter casks of Slavonian and French oak. Wines are not filtered.

Production

Total surface area: 16 ha (39.5 acres)

Barolo: 10 ha (24.7 acres), 32,500 bottles

Barolo Brovia. Blend of the youngest vines in the four estate vineyards in Castiglione Falletto and Serralunga. This is always a beautifully balanced and focused Barolo, with cherry and rose sensations accompanied by firm tannins and vibrant acidity.

Barolo Garblet Sue. Part of the Altenasso geographic mention, Brovia's vineyard borders on Fiasco. Vines face south and southwest, and are situated at about 250 meters (820 feet) above sea level in soils comprised of calcareous clays and marls. This is an earthy and age-worthy Barolo that deftly embodies restrained power, personality, and complexity.

Barolo Villero. From one of Castiglione Falletto's premier vineyard areas that has south and west exposures and where altitude reaches 340 meters (1,115 feet) above sea level. The compact calcareous clay and fifty-two-year-old vines all generate structure and depth. This Barolo displays impressive power, complexity, and finesse with hallmark sensations of rose petal, dark cherry, leather, and spice, with a long licorice finish.

Barolo Rocche. Thanks to sandier soils, a high altitude of 350 meters (1,148 feet), and southeast exposures, this is the most elegant of all Brovia's Barolos, with enticing floral perfume and whiffs of mint and balsamic notes that carry over to the palate with delicious cherry flavors with mesmerizing depth. The 2009 is well balanced with firm but fine tannins.

Barolo Ca' Mia. Made from Brovia's holdings in Serralunga, this is a well-structured and intense Barolo thanks to calcareous soils and a high altitude of 350 meters (1,148 feet). The 2009 shows lush fruit and forest floor along with Serralunga's hallmark spicy, earthy, and licorice notes. While it's already enjoyable, it will have more complexity after 2019. Because of the forward nature of the vintage, this won't be as long-lived as bottlings from more classic years but should drink well through 2024 at least.

Gigi Rosso

Strada Alba-Barolo 34
12060 Castiglione Falletto (CN)

Tel. +39 0173 262369
www.gigirosso.com
info@gigirosso.com

Gigi Rosso is another Langhe institution, and along with Bruno Giacosa and Beppe Colla, knows the area's top crus better than anyone today. According to the excellent book *The Mystique of Barolo* (Gigi's son Maurizio wrote the text), Gigi attended Alba's Enological School from 1947 to 1952, and was surprised to discover that the other students there were far more interested in winemaking than in grape growing. Rosso, who grew up in his grandfather's vineyards, greatly appreciated the new agricultural methods he learned as well as the winemaking methods.

After graduation, he worked for several large Barolo houses, including Fontanafredda, where his duties included buying grapes. He soon met Langhe connoisseur Arturo Bersano, who—years ahead of his time—was advocating vineyard classification and the crucial role of individual parcels. He and Rosso engaged in several projects aimed at understanding the potential for Barolo, and were among the first to separately vinify individual crus and to carry out crop thinning to discard excess bunches in generous years, as well as picking only when grapes had reached optimum ripeness as opposed to when it was convenient for the grower. Bersano even advocated organic fertilizers and minimizing chemicals in the vineyards—unheard-of concepts in 1960 Barolo.

Gigi Rosso was also Renato Ratti's confidant. As Ratti's son Pietro told me, his father, while still working in Brazil but already planning to come back to Piedmont, engaged his friend Rosso to buy grapes for him and to make Barolo, which he did at another friend's cellars—those of Bruno Giacosa. With the stocks of this wine aging in the cellars, Ratti was able to start selling wine as soon as he established his winery in La Morra upon his return to Piedmont.

Knowing all the best vineyard areas, Gigi had his eye on one of the greatest crus in Barolo, Arione. Located in Serralunga and bordering on Giacomo Conterno's Cascina Francia, Arione is the last cru on the southern border of Serralunga. The ideal growing conditions include Serralunga's coveted limestone and clay soils, which lend structure; perfect southern exposures, which encourage ideal ripening; and high altitudes averaging 400 meters (1,312 feet) above sea level. The high altitude cools off the grapes in the evening and creates marked day and night temperature changes that in turn encourage the development of complex aromas. Gigi bought the property in the early

1960s, and for many years sold the grapes to his friend Bruno Giacosa, who made Barolo Arione until 1978.

In 1979 Gigi decided to start making his own wine and founded Cantina Gigi Rosso in Castiglione Falletto, where all the grapes for the firm's properties are vinified and the wines aged. His sons Claudio and Maurizio, and Maurizio's American wife, Mia, have joined him in the firm and have taken over the daily running of the winery. The family adheres to the principles of sustainable agriculture, and has abolished chemical treatments in the vineyards, using sulfur and copper instead and only organic fertilizer. In the cellars, they take a noninterventionist approach. Fermentation occurs with wild yeasts and takes place in temperature-controlled stainless steel tanks, after which the wines are racked into glass-lined cement tanks for decantation for a couple of weeks before aging in large Slavonian casks—three years for Barolo and five for the Barolo Riserva.

Production

Total surface area: 25 ha (62 acres)
Barolo: 4.5 ha (11 acres), 23,000 bottles

Barolo Arione. This is a textbook Barolo from Serralunga, showing both structure and elegance and an ample and refined bouquet. The 2007 has classic leather, truffle, and dried rose petal aromas with the vineyard's own trademark of mint and aromatic herbs. Rich fruit and spice on the palate. Vibrant and fresh—no small task for this hot vintage—with firm but ripe tannins. Best 2015 to 2027. The 2009 offers classic aromas of black cherry, leather, truffle, and rose petal that carry over to the palate truffle, mint, and the vineyard's hallmark licorice. A gorgeous Barolo.

Barolo Arione Riserva dell'Ulivo. In the best vintages, Gigi Rosso also makes a Riserva from the Ulivo vineyard, a parcel in the heart of their Arione cru, so named after a century-old olive tree—the only one that has survived the cold Piedmont winters. The warm microclimate in this part of the vineyard helps perfectly ripen grapes and yields a wine of great complexity and longevity. The 2006 is young but already stunning, with delicious, dense fruit balanced by herbs and mineral notes. It already shows impressive depth and complexity and is impeccably balanced. Drink 2016 to 2036.

Barolo Arione Riserva 1989. Tasted in 2012, this is gorgeous, with an enticing fragrance of spice, mint, balsamic notes, truffle, and leather. Succulent, creamy wild cherry and zabaglione flavors are accented with cedar notes alongside silky tannins and still fresh acidity. This is wonderful now but will continue to evolve and maintain for at least another decade or more. Gripping intensity.

Giuseppe Mascarello

Via Borgonuovo Basso 108
12060 Monchiero (CN)
Tel. +39 0173 792126
www.mascarello1881.com
mauromascarello@mascarello1881.com

Although this historic estate, founded in 1881, has its cellars just outside Barolo's delimited growing area, the family firm is closely associated with Castiglione Falletto, where it owns prime property. The name Giuseppe Mascarello is practically synonymous with that of Monprivato, indisputably one of the very best crus not just in Castiglione Falletto, but in all of Barolo. I still have clear memories of trudging through this vineyard for the first time with Mauro Mascarello in 2008 after days of rain had turned the vineyard's trademark white, calcareous soils into a thick gray paste. In his tweed blazer, rolled-up trousers, and high rubber boots, and with his infectious enthusiasm, he cut the figure of an eccentric college English professor, oblivious to the fact that we were sinking ankle deep into the thick silt.

Mauro's family, who in the mid-1800s were tenant farmers working for Marchesa Giulia Colbert Falletti, acquired a large chunk of Monprivato in 1904, and over the years gradually acquired nearly the entire cru. Mascarello now owns 93 percent of the entire surface area, and they are the only ones to use the Monprivato name on their labels. As Mauro points out, the vineyard area was already referred to in land registries in 1666, and Ratti gave it his equivalent of Grand Cru status on his vineyard classification map. During the run-up to the official delimitation of Barolo's vineyard areas, other growers descended on the outskirts of Monprivato like flies, and Mauro won a hard-fought battle with officials in Rome. Thanks to his tenacity and almost ferocious attachment to Monprivato, Mauro successfully blocked the proposed expansion of his famed cru, which would have allowed unsuitable areas to use the hallowed Monprivato name. Part of the reason for his successful petition was that his family has used the name Monprivato on their labels for

FIGURE 11. Mauro Mascarello in Monprivato. Mauro Mascarello is at the helm of the Giuseppe Mascarello winery, which was founded in 1881. The firm is synonymous with the celebrated Monprivato vineyard site, from which it makes one of the denomination's cult bottlings as well as a Riserva in outstanding years. Photograph by Paolo Tenti.

more than four decades. "These grapes in this vineyard were always the best, so in 1970, I decided for the first time to vinify them apart," says Mauro.

Since then, Mauro has made his iconic Barolo Monprivato, while in excellent years he also makes a Riserva, Ca' d'Morissio, from a particular selection of Monprivato. Ca' d'Morissio is planted with the estate's own genetic material, which hails from very old vines of Michet that were already in this part of the vineyard when Mauro's grandfather Maurizio bought his first large parcel of Monprivato in 1904. In 1921, Maurizio (or Morissio in the Langhe dialect) carried out a massal selection of the best Michet vines located in the Ca' d'Morissio section, and in 1922, he replanted the parcel with these clones. His son Giuseppe carried out another massal selection in 1959, and replanted Ca' d'Morissio and a few other parcels of Monprivato with this estate clone of Michet in 1963. The rest of Monprivato is cultivated with Lampia clones that according to Mascarello were planted in the early 1960s, although they also replanted a few sections in 1996. Besides the advanced age of most plants, and the unique clones in Ca' d'Morissio, Monprivato boasts ideal growing conditions, which include southwest exposures, an average altitude of 280 meters (919 feet) above sea level, and perhaps more importantly, according to the Mascarellos, Serravallian soils composed of clay and silty marls that contain active limestone.

Mascarello also makes a fine Barolo Villero from vineyards acquired in 1985 and a S. Stefano from estate vineyards in the Perno district of Monforte d'Alba. Average plant age for all the firm's Barolo vines is fifty-five years old, with one portion of Monprivato reaching seventy-eight years old. While the advanced age of the vines naturally regulates production, Mauro and his son Giuseppe also lower yields to 60/65 quintals per hectare, and then harvest only the best grapes. The firm also works with famed consultant enologist Donato Lanati, who shares Mauro's approach to crafting classic Barolos. Mauro and Giuseppe use custom-designed steel vats as well as glass-lined cement tanks for fermentation, which they start by inoculating with a strain of selected Barolo yeasts, BRL 97, created by the University of Turin. Fermentation and maceration in a typical year last about twenty-five days. Afterward, the firm ages its Barolos in large Slavonian casks.

Production

Total surface area: 17 ha (42 acres)
Barolo: 8 ha (19.7 acres), 31,000 bottles

Barolo Monprivato. Made from the eponymous vineyard, this is the firm's flagship bottling and a truly iconic Barolo, thanks to its extreme elegance and great depth of flavors. This is one of Barolo's prime sites because of its southwest exposures and ideal altitudes, which average 280 meters (919 feet) above sea level. The advanced age of the plants, averaging fifty-five years old, further generates complexity and intense aromas. Together with the help of celebrated consultant enologist Donato Lanati, Mauro designed stainless steel vats for fermenting Monprivato grapes. These are outfitted with internal pumps that automatically pump must over the floating cap to gently extract color, aromas, and tannins. Although these vats are also thermo controlled, Mauro says he almost never needs to insert this function but lets the temperatures adjust naturally, and only cools down the fermenting juice in particularly hot vintages. If the year is generous and the four vats are not sufficient, Mauro also ferments Monprivato in cement tanks, with fermentation and maceration lasting about twenty-five days in both types of tanks. The 2008 has the wine's hallmark light but luminous color, as well as an enticing fragrance of rose petal, sage, and spice. Very elegant, with creamy strawberry and spice palate and smooth tannins. Surprisingly approachable in 2013, but don't let this fool you—these wines evolve for decades. Best 2015 to 2023. The 2010, tried as a barrel sample in April 2014, is gorgeous. It already showed impeccable balance and supple tannins that supported the bright cherry, strawberry fruit.

Barolo Riserva Monprivato Ca' d'Morissio. Made in the best years from a small parcel in Monprivato that is entirely planted with a very old estate clone of the Michet subvariety of Nebbiolo. Not only is Michet far less common than Lampia, the dominant Nebbiolo subvariety, but it is far less productive; however, as Mauro points out, their clone is the fruit of massal selection on plants that have had "well over one hundred years to adapt to this specific vineyard." Every year, Mauro vinifies and ages Ca' d'Morissio apart, and in the best vintages it undergoes a further one to two years aging in 28- to 30-hectoliter Slavonian casks. In years where the firm doesn't feel the vintage is up to its rigid standards and it doesn't make Riserva, Ca' d'Morissio is blended in with Monprivato. The 2004 is simply exceptional, with intense floral and spicy aromas and succulent berry, mineral, and spice palate. It combines elegance and structure and has mesmerizing depth, concentration, and complexity. Drink 2014 to 2034.

Barolo Villero. This is another hallowed cru in Castiglione Falletto. Like Monprivato, it also has southwest exposures and altitude averages 280–300 meters (919–984 feet) above sea level. One difference, however, is soil: while Monprivato has calcareous, silty soil, Villero has calcareous clay interspersed with veins of sand. Mauro planted much of Villero with his estate clone of Michet, and vines average twenty-six years old. Villero is fermented entirely in concrete tanks and aged in large casks. The 2008 is all about finesse and purity. It is almost ethereal, with delicate rose and spice notes, fine cherry, strawberry, and mineral palate with polished tannins and fresh acidity. Lovely. Drink 2014 to 2023. The 2010, tried in 2014 before it was released, offered lovely floral aromas and is structured but extremely elegant with fine tannins.

Barolo S. Stefano. This is the firm's only wine not made from its holdings in Castiglione Falletto, but rather from its vineyard in Monforte d'Alba. S. Stefano, the famed vineyard area in the Perno district of Monforte d'Alba, has long been famous, and Fantini designated S. Stefano as a Prime Location in his nineteenth-century monograph, while Ratti's map indicates the vineyard has "special characteristics." Mascarello's vineyards boast west and southwest exposures and average 300 meters (984 feet) above sea level. While this may be the firm's least well-known bottling, it is a beautiful Barolo. The

2008 is a classic vintage for S. Stefano, and I was blown away by its combination of restraint and ripe fruit, power and complexity. Classic tar, rose, and leather sensations, creamy cherry and mineral with fabulous depth and length. Drink 2018 to 2038. The 2010, tried as a barrel sample in 2014, offers less perfume but has rich fruit, spice, and an impressive structure thanks to its tannic backbone. This will be one to lay down for years.

Other Wineries of Note

Giovanni Sordo
Roccheviberti
Vietti
Roagna (see under Barbaresco)

EIGHT

Serralunga d'Alba

THE ENTIRE MEDIEVAL VILLAGE of Serralunga d'Alba, commonly referred to simply as Serralunga, is located in the Barolo denomination, and accounts for 16.49 percent of total Barolo production. Dominated by its imposing fourteenth-century castle soaring vertically, high above the vineyards, Serralunga turns out the most complex and age-worthy Barolos from its thirty-nine crus, a number of which are among the most coveted sites in all of Barolo. Serralunga's lightly colored, almost white soil hails from the Serravallian (locally still often referred to as Helvetian) age of the Miocene epoch. This smooth and uniform calcareous marl, which is void of pebbles and rocks, takes on the consistency of fresh cement when wet but becomes flaky, even dusty, when dry, and consists of numerous, compact layers of limestone, marl, and sandy marl. Although it is rich in calcium carbonate, it is poor overall in other nutrients, and while nearby villages share similar soil, Serralunga's vineyards are said to contain the highest levels of calcium carbonate. The village's most prized vineyards are among the highest in the production zone, and many parcels boast full southern exposures. This fortuitous combination of high vineyard altitudes and southern exposures prolongs Nebbiolo's growing season, yielding some of the most austere and powerfully structured Barolos of great complexity that in top vintages can evolve and maintain for decades.

Even though Serralunga is perennially associated with muscular Barolos, and indeed many Barolos from the commune can boast tannic structures of heroic proportions that need time to open up and fully develop, wines hailing from the highest altitudes, from Falletto, for example, possess an enviable combination of power and finesse. Today many Serralunga producers are crafting wines that can be approachable six or seven years after the harvest

MAP 4. Serralunga d'Alba.

but that still stand the test of time beautifully. To reach this fine balance, producers need to tame the monumental tannins generated in Serralunga vineyards by employing practices such as green harvesting, planting grass between the rows, scrupulous canopy management, and turning the earth to keep the soil fresh, all of which help grapes reach ideal ripening and generate rounder tannins. Improved cellar methods are also crucial, such as reducing postfermentation maceration times as compared to the marathon maceration periods of yore, so as to extract less but more refined tannins. While a number of the village's top single-vineyard bottlings still require years to come around, most producers also make a straight Serralunga Barolo assembled from what are usually the youngest vines in various crus. Even though these Serralunga Barolos are enjoyable in their youth, some also have great depth and will keep for years.

Local growers and winemakers have long understood the exceptional quality of Nebbiolo planted in Serralunga d'Alba. King Vittorio Emanuele even chose to create his own Barolo estate in Serralunga in 1858, and up until the 1970s, when Alba's fledging Barolo houses made the wine exclusively by assembling Nebbiolo from different villages to create natural balance, Serralunga's grapes were in the highest demand and fetched the best prices because they gave these blended Barolos their tannic backbone and structure. By the mid-twentieth century, the village's celebrated vineyards were the favorite of the local *négociants,* whose job was to secure grapes for the larger houses, and perhaps the most famous grape buyer in the history of Barolo, Bruno Giacosa, bought his first vineyard in Serralunga on the magnificent hill of Falletto after purchasing grapes from this same vineyard for years. Of all Barolos, the mere mention of single-vineyard bottlings from Serralunga d'Alba's hallowed crus, including Vigna Rionda, Lazzarito, and Cascina Francia, can cause Barolo lovers to go weak in the knees.

However, since many of Serralunga's most famed vineyards have full southern exposures, the climbing summertime temperatures and lower precipitation levels of the last two decades are pushing alcohol levels to the extreme, and it is becoming more common to see Barolos from Serralunga sporting 15 percent alcohol on the label, which most likely means 15.5 percent, since regulations allow a half point of flexibility. As global warming pushes up summertime temperatures, many producers with vineyards boasting southeast exposures, once considered not quite as desirable as full southern and southwestern exposures, are finding that the former are bestowing a measure of welcome freshness to the wines in hotter years. Producers are at a crossroads over whether to decrease or stop green harvesting altogether in an effort to combat soaring alcohol levels, and these days most producers in Serralunga are careful not to trim leaf canopies too early, which could result in the sun burning the grapes, and they are less likely to let the grapes overripen on the vines. But as producers are quick to point out, as long as the wine has enough fruit richness and is balanced with fresh acidity and firm but with refined tannins, most Serralunga Barolos can support these higher alcohol levels. At least for now. As summertime temperatures soar and water levels in the same period are plummeting, many of Serralunga's producers have a renewed appreciation for their older vines, whose roots can reach far beneath the surface to the water and nutrients below, and it is not uncommon to find vines forty years and older in this hallowed part of Barolodom.

Fontanafredda

Via Alba 15
12050 Serralunga d'Alba (CN)
Tel. +39 0173 626100
www.fontanafredda.it
info@fontanafredda.it

Founded by King Vittorio Emanuele II in 1858, Fontanafredda, a magnificent estate surrounded by quiet woods, is one of Barolo's genuinely storied properties. With its iconic buildings painted in terracotta and pale yellow stripes, Fontanafredda remains an important benchmark for the denomination, and the firm's roller-coaster ride of highs and lows is practically a metaphor for Barolo's own fluctuating history. Fontanafredda is also an enormous operation, and is the largest contiguous estate in the denomination. Besides owning prime vineyards in Serralunga and around Barolo, as well as in other areas, the winery also sources grapes from hundreds of growers. Throughout its long history the firm has consistently made good, and at times even very good, if not always inspiring, Barolos. Quality is on the rise, however, and is especially noticeable in the three single-vineyard bottlings, and even if Fontanafredda Barolos have yet to reach their full potential, they are beginning to match the grandeur of the estate's splendid setting.

As this winery played a crucial role in the history of Barolo, I have already written about it in chapter 3, but I feel some of this info warrants repeating in this profile as well. King Vittorio Emanuele's father, Carlo Alberto, was an avid Barolo enthusiast and was already producing the wine in his own right at the royal estates in Verduno and Pollenzo when he passed both his kingdom and his passion for the noble nectar down to his son in 1849, after the former gave in to political pressure and abdicated the throne. After years of stopping at Fontanafredda in Serralunga on his frequent hunting trips to change horses at the estate's stables, Vittorio Emanuele decided the property would be an ideal place to cultivate Nebbiolo for Barolo, as well as provide the perfect residence and future business venture for the two illegitimate children he had with his mistress, Rosa Vercellana, known as "La Béla Rosin." In 1864 the king began planting new vineyards at Fontanafredda, which he had already put in the name of the couple's two natural children, Maria Vittoria and Emanuele Alberto.

According to the estate's chronicles, a document in the Turin State Archives records the first reference to a wine hailing from the property: a "Barbera Fontanafredda 1867." The same document also mentions a "Nebiolo [sic] Barolo 1868" and a "Barolo 1865," and it is assumed the latter two refer to wines made from grapes grown in the vineyards at Fontanafredda and Barolo.

Royal accounts show the first specific mention of a Barolo vineyard acquired by the king in 1866, and this seems the origin of brand Tenimenti di Barolo e Fontanafredda. The royal accounts also attest to the presence of stables, vineyards, and cellars in 1870, as well as the planting of more vine-yards and the construction of new buildings and cellars. By all indications, Vittorio Emanuele was gearing up wine production at Fontanafredda, including his prized Barolo, which he made for his own consumption and which supplied all the residences and estates of his royal family. After Vittorio Emanuele died in 1878, Fontanafredda was no longer funded by the king's private estate. The king's natural son Emanuele di Mirafiore, an expert win-emaker, created the E. Mirafiore winery with the goal of producing and sell-ing wine, with particular focus on Barolo.

This business venture changed the fortunes of Barolo by allowing connoisseurs—and not just members of the royal family and European elites—access to the wine by bringing it to the open market. Price lists on display at Fontanafredda show Mirafiore was already selling Barolos from the 1891 and 1892 vintages in both barrels and cases of twelve bottles. Emanuele Mirafiore, who had traveled extensively around Europe's famed wine regions to better understand winemaking, was also way ahead of his time with regard to pro-moting his wines. In 1887 he became the first producer to open up his estate cellars to the public, and entered his Barolo in major national and international wine competitions, winning gold medals in 1888 at the Brussels Fair and in 1892 in Berlin, just to cite a few wine events from that period.

Unfortunately a series of tragic events starting at the close of the nineteenth century eventually forced the decline of the Fontanafredda estate and the E. Mirafiore firm, which would last for several decades, and halted the escalating fortunes of Barolo just as the firm had begun exporting it throughout the world. In 1894, at the age of only forty-three, Emanuele Alberto di Mirafiore passed away, apparently from liver disease, and just two years later his eldest son, Vittorio, died from complications suffered after falling from his horse. The Fontanafredda property and the E. Mirafiore Company passed to Emanuele's second son, Gastone. By all accounts, Gastone brought the estate to the height of its glory at the beginning of the twentieth century before its astounding reversal of fortune.

The young Mirafiore acquired the most modern winemaking equipment available, including a pioneering mechanical press in 1913, and he introduced new fermentation and aging methods. He also hired Fontanafredda's first estate manager, Sebastiano Mollo, and by the time Italy entered the First World War in 1915, Fontanafredda employed two hundred men whose wives and children also lived with them on the estate. Mirafiore treated Fontanafredda's farmhands and other workers exceptionally well—a rarity in this period when large landowners in Italy adhered to the sharecropping system known as the *mezzadria*, a remnant of feudalism, to drastically cut down on expenses. Mirafiore's grandfather, King Vittorio Emanuele, had already begun paying the estate's farmhands in gold coins and food staples, and his son Emanuele not only employed more farmers and laborers but became the founding president of a mutual aid society in 1893 for all of Fontanafredda's workers. Gastone took things to a whole new level by opening up a school at Fontanafredda for the farmers' and workers' children, building a church for their weddings and christenings as well as a communal oven for bread baking, and adding new lodgings for the estate's swelling population. He even paid dues on behalf of all of Fontanafredda's employees into a state pension plan—completely unheard-of at the time. World War I hit the Langhe hills hard. Fontanafredda's workers were called to arms, leaving their wives and children, as well as Austrian prisoners of war, to tend the harvests and winemaking, but clearly without the same results as before. The Great War coincided with several other developments, including Gastone's move into politics—his true passion—which kept him away from the estate for extended periods. Outbreaks of some of the most devastating grape vine diseases in history, including phylloxera, the pest that nearly wiped out vineyards across Europe, thwarted production, as did other isolated incidents, such as devastating hail in 1917. To complicate matters further, in 1915, Gastone struck a deal with sparkling wine giant Gancia that gave the latter worldwide distribution of E. Mirafiore's products. In 1919, already elected as a member of Parliament, Gastone entered a partnership with a lawyer from Liguria, and together they bought vineyards and cellars from Opera Pia Barolo, but Gastone was excluded from management. Gastone began unloading his shares, and in 1927 a group of businessmen bought all the remaining shares, and Gastone Mirafiore no longer had anything to do with Fontanafredda or the firm that bore his surname. Ownership changed hands several times in just a few years, and new managers fired most of the workers who had helped make Fontanafredda the pride and joy of Serralunga as the new owners began relying instead on the sharecropping system. In 1930, unable to recover from the crash of the world's economies in 1929 and without a stable direction, Fontanafredda went into bankruptcy.

In 1932, the Siena-based Monte dei Paschi, one of Italy's most powerful banks and already a creditor of Fontanafredda, took control of the ailing estate and began the long process of returning it to its former glory. Fontanafredda survived the hardships of World War II and the economic hardships of postwar Italy and flourished again during Italy's economic boom of the 1960s and 1970s, when Monte dei Paschi made substantial investments in the firm, including building new cellars and a large bottling plant. The firm also focused again on Barolo, which it began aging for longer than required, and in 1964 it began vinifying some of the top Barolo crus separately. Besides their own vineyards, the firm hired the Langhe's top grape mediators, such as Bruno Giacosa, to source high-quality grapes.

Yet by the 1980s, Fontanafredda once again went into decline. A number of grape growers turned to winemaking and became boutique producers, crafting a new breed of softer Barolos. Production and quality at Fontanafredda on the other hand became stagnant. By the 1990s, in Italy the brand became associated with supermarket wines. Realizing that bank managers could not run farms, in 1996 Monte dei Paschi hired Giovanni Minetti, a specialist in agronomy and viticulture who was an adviser to Piedmont's Department of Agriculture. Minetti created a team of specialists to revamp vineyards and winemaking, and to overhaul the firm's outdated image as a quantity rather than quality wine producer. Once again Fontanafredda toiled back from the edge of ruin.

In 2006, Monte dei Paschi made a corporate decision to pull out of all "nonstrategic" ventures, and sold Fontanafredda to a group of investors headed by Oscar Farinetti and Luca Baffigo Filangieri, with the latter becoming the sole owners in 2009. Farinetti, an entrepreneur and founder of the Eataly chain of Italian supermarkets and restaurants, is trying to restyle Fontanafredda's dour image into that of a more dynamic firm. The current owners are also transforming Fontanafredda into a "bio-natural reserve." The long-term goals are to reduce the firm's carbon footprint, and to produce better grapes and wine that will eventually be free of added sulfites and selected yeasts. To these ends Fontanafredda claims to have banned chemical herbicides and fertilizers on its estate and reduced treatments against insects. In 2009 the company was the first in Piedmont to be officially recognized for sustainable viticulture, a project started by managing director Minetti (who retired in 2013) some years before. However, a number of growers and producers in the area, who have been committed to sustainable viticulture for years without public recognition, feel this public acknowledgement was attributable to the firm's impressive political connections, as well as its committment. The firm has also hired a full-time agronomist to follow suppliers' vineyards to ensure that they adhere to these rigid standards.

Even though the large firm makes a dizzying number of wines, including more than a dozen sparkling wines and over twenty red wines (not including Barolo), and not all of those particularly exciting, Fontanafredda remains best known for its Barolos, especially its three single-vineyard bottlings—La Rosa, Lazzarito, and La Villa. In 2010, Gancia sold back the Mirafiore brand to Fontanafredda, and to honor the return of the historic name after nearly eighty years, Fontanafredda is now producing a line of traditionally crafted Barolo, Nebbiolo, Barbera, and Dolcetto under the Mirafiore name.

Production

Total surface area: 97 ha of vineyards (239.6 acres)
Barolo: 38.26 ha (94.5 acres), plus purchases grapes; 439,000 bottles
Barbaresco: purchases grapes, 50,000 bottles

Barolo. Fontanafredda's Barolo is made from a blend of Nebbiolo from different Barolo villages, and the firm purchases about 40 percent of the grapes for this bottling. Aged for two years in large casks, both Slavonian and

French, this is a straightforward bottling and is made in large quantities by Barolo standards, averaging 250,000 bottles annually.

Barolo Serralunga.   Made from exclusively Serralunga grapes, this wine is vinified and aged the same way as the straight Barolo but possesses more structure and depth. The 2008, tasted in 2012, is a solid Barolo boasting classic Nebbiolo sensations of wild cherry, earth truffle, and hints of leather along with dense cherry and spice. Still very tannic and tightly wound, it needs time but should gain complexity when it fully develops. Best 2016 to 2028. The 2009 offers dark berry and black cherry flavors with layers of mint, licorice, and spice with big but silky tannins balanced by just enough fresh acidity.

Barolo Riserva.   Made only in exceptional vintages from a blend of the best lots of just fermented wine hailing from estate vineyards. As of 2012, the last Riserva was made in 2005. Aged for three years in medium-sized and large casks from 20 to 140 hectoliters followed by another year aging in concrete, this is also aged for a final year in bottle before release.

Barolo Vigna La Rosa.   Of all the firm's Barolos, Barolo Vigna La Rosa is Fontanafredda's calling card. While some say the vineyard was named in honor of the La Béla Rosin, others claim the name derives from wild roses that bloom along the walls of the farmhouse crowning the hill. Owned entirely by Fontanafredda and situated on the estate between 250 and 300 meters (820 and 984 feet) above sea level, La Rosa is lower than most of Serralunga's vineyards, which means it is usually harvested seven to ten days earlier than many other crus in the area. Its well-draining soil is also sandier than other Serralunga vineyards, which have predominantly calcareous marl that yields more tannic and muscular wines. La Rosa on the other hand produces structured Barolos tempered by elegance, and boasts intense floral aromas that are uncommon in Serralunga Barolos. Aged for one year in barrique, 50 percent of which are new, Vigna La Rosa then goes one year into 20- and 30-hectoliter Allier casks for another year. While the 2008 has wonderful potential, I must confess that when I tried this in 2012, I found the oak-driven aromas and flavors of toast and espresso too invasive for my tastes.

In May 2012, during my visit at the estate, Giovanni Minetti opened some of the estate's most precious bottles of older vintages from Fontanafredda's library of Grandi Annate Storiche, including the following years of Barolo Vigna La Rosa:

—————*2007.* This is an impressive effort for what was a very hot vintage. Shows hallmark floral aromas, but the palate is very round, ripe, and evolved. Tannins are somewhat bitter, as is typical of this vintage, since the intense heat shut down the plants before tannins could reach optimum ripeness. This is not a vintage destined for lengthy aging and should be consumed in its youth.

—————*2006.* The polar opposite of the 2007 vintage, this still needs a lot of time to open and develop complexity. Lovely rose and violet fragrance with just a hint of truffle. Hallmark cherry, spice, and mineral palate with great depth balanced by still racy acidity and refined but youthful tannins. Very elegant and should age well for decades. Best 2018 to 2026.

—————*2005.* Surprisingly youthful with underbrush, truffle, and floral aromas. Classic Nebbiolo flavors with a hint of licorice. Very fresh but still closed, with impressive length. Possesses La Rosa's trademark elegance and should develop more depth in a few years. Best to drink at the ten- to fifteen-year mark.

—————*2004.* Toasted wood and espresso are evident on both the nose and the palate along with wild cherry, spice, and even a hint of tobacco. Fresh and still evolving, and needs time to develop its full potential.

—————*2001.* Classic Barolo perfume of tar and dried rose petal with a whiff of saddle leather. Wild cherry, spice, and earthy flavors show great depth. Very refined with impressive length and still youthful. Should drink well for another decade and more. A stunning wine and my favorite of the tasting. Best through 2021.

—————*2000.* Some sawdust and espresso aromas along with very ripe berry flavors. True to the vintage, this is not very complex and does not boast an age-worthy structure. Drink now.

—————*1999.* Intense rose bouquet. Complex and richly yet gracefully structured, this Barolo shows great breeding and depth. Impeccable balance with impressive length, it should drink well throughout the next decade.

—————*1998.* Intense cherry, raspberry, and spice with very elegant tannins. Young and fresh, and drinking beautifully. While this has reached its peak evolution, it should maintain until 2018 at least.

—————*1997.* After 2000, this is one of the most overrated vintages in Italian wine history, and this Barolo is no exception. All underbrush and bitter tobacco leaf sensations. Very evolved palate, with most of the fruit already dried up, leaving green tannins and alcohol. Drink.

————*1996.* Earthy, floral fragrance with rose, truffle, and leather. This is still very youthful and somewhat closed, but thanks to vibrant acidity and bracing tannins, it promises to evolve into a classic Barolo of heroic structure. Best after 2016 and should age well for a decade or more after this.

Barolo Riserva. 1982. Surprisingly intense floral scents of dried rose petals, truffle, and leather with mint and sage undertones. Nebbiolo sweetness on the palate, with carob, dried cherry, and Alpine herbs. Silky and remarkably fresh, this is a very good example of what was one of the greatest vintages in Barolo and Barbaresco. Should drink well for another decade.

Barolo. 1974. Hallmark tar and rose aromas of a well-aged Barolo. Dried cherry, tobacco, and tea on the palate, which is remarkably fresh. Delicate, silky, and beautifully balanced. While this has reached its peak, it should maintain for another five to ten years.

————*1967.* Complex bouquet of sweet pipe tobacco, truffle, and leather, with Nebbiolo sweetness, carob, and tea flavors. Impressive length. This won't improve but should maintain for a few more years.

————*1961.* All tobacco, tar, and mineral with little fruit or tannins left. Has started its inevitable decline.

Germano Ettore

Loc. Cerretta 1
12050 Serralunga d'Alba (CN)
Tel. +39 0173 613528
www.germanoettore.com
germanoettore@germanoettore.com

High on the Serralunga ridge and right in the middle of the Prapò vineyards, the genial and *molto simpatico* Sergio Germano is making polished Barolos of great character from some of Serralunga's best crus: Cerretta, Prapò, and Lazzarito.

The Germano family has owned land on the Cerretta hill since 1856, and Sergio's great-grandfather and grandfather were established growers who mostly sold grapes, but like most farmers back then, they also vinified a small

FIGURE 12. Sergio Germano in the Cerretta vineyard. Located smack in the middle of the Prapò cru, the Germano Ettore firm is run by Sergio Germano and makes fabulous offerings from Prapò, Lazzarito, and Cerretta. It also recently acquired a plot in Vigna Rionda that it replanted in 2011. Photograph by Paolo Tenti.

amount of wine for family and friends. Sergio's father, Ettore, carried on the business and also became highly skilled at grafting the local grape varieties on American rootstocks, a much sought-after art in the mid-twentieth-century Langhe. In the 1950s, Ettore began carrying out massal selections in his vineyards, and replanted the estate with the firm's own genetic material at a far-sighted density of four thousand plants per hectare to maximize grape quality.

In 1985, Sergio, fresh out of enological school, joined his father in the winery and convinced Ettore to start vinifying even more grapes. In 1987, the firm released its first Barolo, and by 1993 the winery no longer sold any grapes and was producing its own wine. Over the years the family has acquired vineyards in other prime sites in Serralunga, namely, Prapò, Lazzarito, more parcels of Cerretta, and most recently a plot of Vigna Rionda, which they replanted in 2011.

Sergio, who runs the winery with his wife, Elena, feels that Barolo is often misunderstood by consumers, and has clear ideas about how a quintessential Barolo should be. As he explained during one of my visits to the winery, "Many people assume that Barolo is supposed to be this huge, powerful wine, but Barolo should be elegant and complex, as well as structured. When

Barolo is instead excessively rich and concentrated, it loses its drinkability as well as its true character." To this end Sergio favors long, and at times very long, fermentation and maceration times of up to thirty to thirty-five days for his single-vineyard Barolos to impart complexity without overextracting bitter tannins that can result from shorter but more tumultuous fermentation and maceration periods. He also believes that while a small amount of grape thinning and green harvesting is necessary to improve grape quality, it is crucial not to thin out too much to avoid overconcentration.

Sergio makes four excellent Barolos: one from a blend of Nebbiolo from his three vineyard areas, and three separate bottlings of his three Serralunga crus currently in production, with a Barolo Vigna Rionda slated for the future once these vines mature. It is impossible to label Sergio Germano a traditionalist or a progressive; above all he is a down-to-earth and serious winemaker using the tools he believes exalt the particular characteristics of each of his individual Barolos. And it works—these are stunning wines from a producer who surprisingly remains under the radar, but I doubt for long.

Besides other classic Langhe offerings, Sergio, a sparkling wine enthusiast, also makes a delightful *metodo classico* sparkler from Pinot Nero and Chardonnay planted in vineyards he acquired in Cigliè, in Piedmont's Alta Langa area, and a fantastic *metodo classico* made from early-picked Serralunga Nebbiolo.

Production

Total surface area: 15.5 ha (38.3 acres)

Barolo: 7 ha (17.2 acres), 32,000 bottles

Barolo Serralunga. The firm's straight Barolo is a blend of the younger Barolo vines in the three crus, all in Serralunga, which gives Sergio the right to add the village name to the label. After a twenty-day fermentation and maceration, the wine ages in used (some even ten years old) 700-liter barrels for two years. Tasted in 2012, the 2008 had a heady bouquet of earth, leather, herbs, and sage with delicious sour cherry and spice. With bracing but fine tannins and nervous acidity, this youngster needs time to come together. Best 2016 to 2020.

Barolo Prapò. This is a classic Barolo with firm but fine tannins and expressive bouquets. Prapò's southeast exposure helps keep vines fresh, as does the average altitude of 340 meters (1,115 feet), where day and night temperature changes create complexity and depth. The advanced age of the plants, averaging between forty and forty-five years old, generates intense flavors, while calcareous soils, not as heavy as in other Serralunga vineyards, impart fine tannins. Sergio keeps winemaking traditional for Prapò, saying the wine's refined tannins do not need more contact with the increased oxygen levels offered by smaller barrels, and therefore he ages the wine for two years in botti. The 2008 has floral notes of rose and dense cherry, raspberry flavors coupled with spice, mint, and mineral. Fantastic length. Still tightly wound, but will be glorious when it comes around. Best 2016 through 2028. The 2009 offers a classic cherry, leather, and balsamic fragrance. The creamy palate shows delicious cherry, cinnamon, spice, and a hint of vanilla alongside firm, ripe tannins.

Barolo Cerretta. The Cerretta hill boasts Serralunga's archetypical, highly calcareous, lightly colored—almost white—soil, which produces the most powerfully structured, tannic, and age-worthy Barolos in the denomination. The Germano family's 4 hectares (9.8 acres) are among Cerretta's prime real estate thanks to their southern and southeastern exposures and their location in the upper reaches of the cru at 380 meters (1,246.7 feet). Thirty-four-year-old vines impart rich flavors, adding another dimension to this full-bodied wine. After about thirty to thirty-five days of fermentation and maceration, but just before the process is completed, Sergio racks the Cerretta juice into 225-, 500-, and 700-liter French barrels of various ages (only 20 percent new) where it ages for at least two years. According to Sergio, the oxygen-to-wood ratio in the smaller barrels helps soften the tough tannins faster than large botti would, while the seasoned wood minimizes oak sensations. And it works: the 2008 is a quintessential Serralunga d'Alba with dense raspberry, cherry, new leather, and licorice sensations. Well balanced but young with massive tannins and nervous acidity. A classic Barolo for the ages. Best 2018 to 2038.

Barolo Riserva Lazzarito. Made from the firm's oldest vines planted back in 1931 and located in a prime section of Lazzarito, this hallmark Barolo combines elegance with sheer tannic power. As Sergio explains it, besides a southeastern exposure and an average altitude of 320 meters (1,049.8 feet), Lazzarito's complexity is a result of the octogenarian vines, which naturally keep yields very low, while the cru's calcareous soil, lightly layered with a low percentage of iron-rich sandstone, imparts both structure and refined tannins and energizing minerality. Making this only as a Riserva, Sergio carries out a lengthy fermentation and maceration of up to forty days, followed by two and a half years aging in 20-hectoliter botti succeeded by another two years of bottle aging. The 2006, tasted in 2012, is both heroic and gorgeous, with rose, tar, and leather aromas accompanied by sweet cherry, spice, orange peel, and licorice. Very complex, with fabulous length. Already enjoyable, but far from its prime. Best 2016 to 2036.

Guido Porro

Via Alba 1
12050 Serralunga d'Alba (CN)
Tel. +39 0173 613306
www.guidoporro.com
guidoporro@alice.it

On the Serralunga crest, almost directly below the castle, Guido Porro's small winery, passed down from father to son for four generations, sits on top of the Lazzarito hillside. At this little-known jewel of a property, Guido, who has run the family firm since 1996 and is assisted by his father, Giovanni, makes some of Serralunga's most soulful Barolos. With their rich fruit, intense earthy notes and rugged structures, these Barolos are not for the faint of heart, but have all the hallmark rose, violet, truffle, and leather sensations of Nebbiolo coupled with depth and complexity.

Guido Porro's family began vinifying its estate grapes in the 1950s and like many wineries at the time, sold the wine in bulk. It wasn't until the 1980s that the firm began selling bottled Barolo and not until 1996 that Guido began vinifying and bottling their two historic Barolo vineyards, Lazzairasco and Santa Caterina, separately. Both vineyards are located in the Lazzarito cru, which was already mentioned in land registries back in 1610, and much of the hill at one time belonged to Opera Pia Barolo, a sure testament to the historical significance of this celebrated cru. Both vineyards have Serralunga's typical limestone and calcareous clay soils while sun exposures, vine altitudes, and plant age create subtle differences. Lazzairasco is somewhat lower, averaging 350 meters (1,148 feet) above sea level, and boasts full southern and southwestern exposures, while Santa Caterina's vines climb up an average of 400 meters and have exclusively southwestern exposures. Both vineyards have decades under their belt, with plants averaging fifty years old in Lazzairasco and thirty-five in Santa Caterina. Besides these two vineyards, both monopolies that have been in the family for decades, in 2008 Guido acquired a small parcel in the Gianetto cru, just on the other side of the road from the winery, and in 2011 he inherited 1.4 hectares of Barolo vineyards, part of which are in the illustrious Vigna Rionda, which he replanted in 2012.

Guido is a serious noninterventionist, and keeps things as natural as possible in both the vineyards and the cellars, where he uses for the most part ultratraditional methods. He uses sustainable farming methods, forgoes herbicides and fungicides, and keeps his Nebbiolo yields to 65–70 quintals per hectare, well below the minimum of 80 allowed under the production code. He eschews selected yeasts, allowing fermentation with wild yeasts to happen spontaneously, and ferments in concrete tanks follwed by maceration for a minimum of between fifteen and twenty days. As one would expect from such a stalwart traditionalist, the wines are then aged in 25-hectoliter Slavonian botti for three years and are unfiltered.

Production

Total surface area: 11 ha (27.1 acres)

Barolo: 4.5 ha (11.11 acres), 15,500 bottles as of 2012 but from 2015, another
    6,000 bottles when the Gianetto vineyard goes into production

Barolo Santa Caterina. Both the 2007 and the 2008 initially had rustic aromas when first opened, but these burned off after just a few minutes in the glass to reveal intense earthy, truffle sensations and rich ripe fruit, all beautifully balanced. Both vintages were surprisingly approachable, but also have the tannic structure and fresh acidity to age well. With time these should develop more depth and complexity. This is one of those enticing wines that is so alive, in great part thanks to Guido's hands-off approach, that it changes continuously in the glass.

Barolo Lazzairasco. This is a hallmark Serralunga Barolo, with a classic fragrance of rose, violet, truffle, and leather and concentrated flavors. Thanks to very old vines and full southern exposure that pushes ripening to the limits, the 2008 boasts sumptuous, creamy cherry and spice flavors along with powerful but ripe tannins that make it easy to approach while it also shows great aging potential. Fantastic length. Best 2015 to 2025.

Massolino-Vigna Rionda

Piazza Cappellano 8
12050 Serralunga d'Alba (CN)

Tel. +39 0173 613138
www.massolino.it
massolino@massolino.it

The Massolino family name is synonymous with Vigna Rionda, one of Barolo's most illustrious and coveted crus and part of the name of the family's winery. Founded in 1896 by Giovanni Massolino, the first cellars were built by Giovanni's son Giuseppe, who became not only one of the founding fathers of the Barolo and Barbaresco Consorzio in 1934, but who, together with his sister Angela, began buying prime vineyards. This expansion continued with Giuseppe's children, who acquired parcels of Serralunga's greatest crus—Margheria, Parafada, and Vigna Rionda—between the end of the 1940s and the late 1950s. Up until the end of the Second World War, the family sold the wine in bulk, but in 1947 they began selling their first bottled Barolo.

Brothers Franco and Roberto Massolino, trained enologists, began working at the firm in the 1990s and now run the estate, which is headquartered in their recently renovated cellars in Serralunga's historic town center. Although Franco and Roberto have always respected traditional Barolo, they also have experimented with what purists would consider controversial vinification and aging techniques, including rotary fermenters to extract more color and tannins for their Barbera and Dolcetto, while they use barriques for their top Barbera and, from 1990 until 2006, also for their Barolo Parafada.

Franco Massolino points out that when he started in 1990, almost every winery had at least one Barolo aged in barriques, and he decided to add Parafada to this core of what were once considered "modern Barolos." "But in 2006, we decided to bring all of our Barolos back into the classic style, including Parafada. We also decided it was time to make wines that we like, and not what the market supposedly wants," declares Massolino today. Franco insists that all improvements in their Barolo production over the years come from intense focus on vineyard management. The family keeps plant density to an average of five thousand plants per hectare, and Barolo vines are between twenty-eight and fifty-eight years old. For all their Barolo crus, plants hail from massal selection of the best vines in that particular vineyard, and this is still the system used today to replace individual vines that have died.

The Massolinos allow grass to grow between the vines. According to Franco, this isn't only to help improve balance; it's also a measure against

FIGURE 13. Franco Massolino. Franco and his brother Roberto run the Massolino-Vigna Rionda winery. The firm owns prime vineyard land throughout Serralunga, including in the coveted Vigna Rionda site, where its flagship Barolo hails from forty-five-year-old vines. Photograph by Paolo Tenti.

erosion, one of the biggest threats to the steep vineyards. The firm periodically turns the soil directly beneath the plants, which not only helps keep the soil fresh, but, again according to Franco, improves grape quality by encouraging plants to develop thicker grape skins and more pulp. While Massolino performs a green harvest, they leave the leaf canopy intact to avoid grapes getting burned, which is crucial now as temperatures throughout the Langhe are on the rise and summers are drier. And what does Franco think of the rising alcohol levels in the wines, apparently a result of global warming combined with quality-improving measures such as grape thinning? "As long as the wine is balanced and has sufficient acidity for freshness, higher alcohol is acceptable in Barolo," he says.

To highlight the characteristics of each cru, all of Massolino's single-vineyard Barolos are fermented in glass-lined concrete tanks under temperature control, and are aged in large Slavonian botti. Nowadays the firm makes four Barolos, and a Riserva, all of which are exemplary expressions of their respective terroirs.

Production

Total surface area: 23 ha (56.83 acres)

Barolo: 15 ha (37 acres), 61,000 total bottles (35,000 bottles Barolo, 16,000 cru bottlings, 10,000 bottles of Riserva)

Barolo. Massolino's straight Barolo is a blend of Nebbiolo from different vineyards all located in Serralunga. Vineyards range in altitude from 320 to 360 meters (1,049 to 1181 feet) above sea level, and the plants are between ten and forty-five years old. The Massolinos carry out temperature-controlled fermentation and maceration for about fifteen days and then age the wine for thirty months in large casks, most of them Slavonian, although the firm still ages a percentage of its Barolo in three French casks it purchased some time ago as an experiment, preferring in the end to stay with Slavonian wood. This is a lovely, unpretentious, and very drinkable Barolo that quells the myth that Barolo is a "difficult" wine. The 2008 is very elegant, with lovely rose and violet aromas alongside bright berry fruit accompanined by silky, fine tannins. Best after 2015 and will age well for another decade at least. According to Franco, the firm's younger vineyards that currently produce Langhe Nebbiolo will soon be mature enough to produce Barolo, which will allow them to increase production to about 45,000–50,000 bottles in the near future.

Barolo Margheria. Massolino's Margheria vineyards boast a good percentage of sand, giving this wine a unique combination of the village's hallmark structure tempered by elegance and punctuated by intense floral and spice aromas. The 2008, tasted in 2012, is a classic, with rose perfume, wild cherry flavors, and wonderful balance. Although this was already drinking well, it will also age well for another decade and more.

Barolo Parafada. Local growers have long considered the small Parafada cru, which borders the celebrated Gabutti vineyard area, as one of the best plots in Serralunga. Parafada's soil is the classic, lightly colored calcareous marl of Serralunga. The 1.2 hectares (2.9 acres) owned by Massolino is situated between 300 and 330 meters (984 and 1,082 feet) above sea level and boasts a full southern exposure. On top of these near-perfect conditions, the advanced age of Massolino's vines, averaging fifty-eight years old, generates great depth and concentration. And yet, until recently, all of the potential and character of this wine was compromised by dominant oak sensations, which smothered its greatness in my opinion. From 2006, Massolino no longer ages this in new barriques but only in 40-hectoliter Slavonian casks. The 2010 is one of the best Barolos from this magnificent vintage. Vibrant with juicy black cherry, spice, and licorice flavors, it displays breeding, power, grace, and balance. Drink 2020 to 2050.

Barolo Parussi.   In 2006, the Massolinos acquired a vineyard in the Parussi cru of Castiglione Falletto, the only vineyards they own outside of Serralunga. Even though Castiglione Falletto is known for its more elegant as opposed to powerful Barolos, Massolino's Parussi seems as if it too hailed from Serralunga thanks to its bracing tannins and energetic structure. The 2008, with its creamy cherry flavors and teeth-coating tannins, will be best after 2018 and should age well for years. The 2009 delivers concentrated cherry, white pepper, mint, and menthol. It has a delicious creamy texture and big, brooding tannins. While this will evolve nicely for the next few years, it also shows the forward nature of the vintage and will be best at the ten-year mark.

Barolo Riserva Vigna Rionda.   This is Massolino's calling card, and was first bottled separately in 1982. Starting with the 1995 vintage, the firm has made Vigna Rionda as a Riserva, and ages it for six years before release, with a minimum aging period of three and a half years in 50-hectoliter Slavonian casks. Vigna Rionda is perhaps the quintessential expression of Nebbiolo from Serralunga thanks to its heroic structure combined with uncanny depth and complexity that evolves for years. Massolino's 2.5 hectares (6 acres) of Vigna Rionda Nebbiolo, situated between 280 and 340 meters (919 and 1,115 feet) above sea level, are in one of the prime locations of this celebrated cru.

According to Franco, one of the secrets to Vigna Rionda's quality grapes is that the famed hillside is protected from cold winds and frost by the hill just in front of it, which forms a unique microclimate in Vigna Rionda. "Nebbiolo grown in Vigna Rionda bud earlier thanks to the warmer temperatures here, and the vines have a longer growing season than they do in our other vineyards," explains Massolino. While the cru possesses the lightly colored, nearly white, calcareous soil typical of Serralunga, it also contains darker soils composed of oxidized iron elements. Made from forty-five-year old vines, Massolino's 2006 Riserva is a hallmark Serralunga Barolo. With its rich fruit and licorice notes balanced by austere tannins and vibrant acidity, this is a connoisseur's Barolo, reaching a whole new level of complexity compared to the firm's other bottlings. In 2012, the 2006 still needed time to tame tannins and develop complexity. Best 2016 to 2036.

Vigna Rionda 1989.   Tried in May 2013, this is an incredibly youthful, gorgeous wine from a classic vintage. It had the quintessential sensations of aged Nebbiolo—tar, rose, and leather—alongside fig, carob, dried cherry, and pipe tobacco notes. It was incredibly complex and still remarkably fresh, with years ahead of it.

Barolo Riserva 1978.   I tried this stunning wine in 2013, and it did the famed vintage proud. It showed intense rose petal, tar, and leather aromas and still had a core of dry cherry flavors with carob notes. Very young at heart, with gripping tannins, fresh acidity, and layers of complexity, this is a textbook bottling showing remarkable depth and pedigree.

Cappellano

Via Alba 13
12050 Serralunga d'Alba (CN)
Tel. +39 0173 613103
www.cappellano1870.it
info@cappellano1870.it

Cappellano, the tiny winery in Serralunga that is turning out some of the finest wines in the denomination, is one of the oldest Barolo firms and was founded in 1870 by wealthy notary and landowner Filippo Cappellano. Cappellano, who had a passion for both the land and wine, amassed some 60 hectares (148 acres) of vineyards. However, unlike most firms founded at the end of the nineteenth and the beginning of the twentieth century that were exclusively dedicated to either grape growing or winemaking, Cappellano did both. Filippo was also light years ahead of his time: back when other wineries were selling wine in bulk or in demijohns, he was already bottling his wine. Upon Filippo's passing in 1886, his oldest son, Giovanni, took over and by 1889 was already winning medals for his wines at international competitions, including a bronze medal that same year at the Exposition Universelle in Paris. Giovanni also established two hotels, one in Alba and one in Serralunga, for the many visitors coming to the area from Liguria, and even ran a horse-and-carriage service to take them from Alba to Serralunga. At some point during this period Cappellano also transferred his cellars from Alba to the center of Serralunga.

   However, in 1912 Giovanni died prematurely from a tropical fever he contracted in Tunisia, where he had been searching for phylloxera-resistant vines. His brother Giuseppe, a trained pharmacist, had already invented Barolo Chinato, an elixir that boasted curative properties and was made by steeping a blend of exotic spices in a base of Barolo. The wine is still Cappellano's trademark, and while I'm not sure about its curative properties, I can vouch that it pairs beautifully with chocolate. The recipe by the way remains a secret, and has been passed down through five generations of the family, with each new generation following the custom of copying it over in his own handwriting from his father's version and storing the prized instructions under lock and key.

Giuseppe Cappellano added to the firm's holdings and acquired vineyards in the best sites, becoming one of the area's largest grape growers. He was evidently quite good at making wine as well, and the large Gancia Company, which owned the Mirafiore brand at the time, entrusted Cappellano with its winemaking. To keep up with demand, Cappellano also purchased grapes, and according to records still in the family firm's possession, he was the biggest buyer of the area's grapes until his death in 1955. Since his only daughter had died years before of the Spanish flu (Cappellano, who owned a large amount of property in Serralunga, dedicated the main piazza to her, and it is still called Piazza Maria Cappellano today), the firm passed to Giuseppe's extended family of nieces and nephews. Cappellano's holdings became fragmented and were eventually dispersed as family members sold off their inherited property.

The end of the 1960s saw the rebirth of Cappellano when Giuseppe's nephew and eventually his grandnephew Teobaldo Cappellano returned to Serralunga from Eritrea in Africa. Teobaldo's father had moved the family to Eritrea and had eventually founded a plantation with vineyards and produced wine, although he went back and forth for several years once he inherited what was left of the Serralunga firm. Teobaldo and his wife soon joined him in Piedmont, having left Eritrea shortly before the country plunged into civil war, and Teobaldo went about reestablishing the Cappellano brand. However, since there were no more cellars and no more vineyards, he started from zero. In the beginning, Teobaldo purchased grapes and vinified in different cellars—even using the ancient cellars of the Serralunga castle for one of his earliest harvests—until he was able to buy his own cellars and house at the foot of the hill that climbs up to the historic center of Serralunga.

Teobaldo had learned to make Barolo from his father during the many trips they had made to Serralunga, and Teobaldo's disarming personality, philosopher's outlook, and relentless conviction in traditionally crafted

Barolo soon allowed him access to the best growers in Serralunga. In the 1980s he bought prime vineyards in the Gabutti cru, one of the most prestigious and coveted hillsides in the entire Barolo denomination. He bought 2 hectares (4.94 acres) in two contingent blocks in two separate transactions years apart from a grower named Otin Fiorin. Even though other estates offered far more than Cappellano, once they realized the prized property was for sale, Fiorin kept his promise and respected his agreement with Teobaldo. For his part, Teobaldo named his Barolo "Otin Fiorin."

Situated just below the village of Serralunga and boasting full southern exposures, Gabutti's vertiginous slopes offer protection from strong winds and create a unique microclimate where Nebbiolo excels. The white, calcareous marl gives Gabutti Barolos their imposing tannic structure, while the median altitude of Cappellano's vines of 300 to 350 meters (984 to 1,148 feet) imparts vibrant acidity. In 1989, Teobaldo began a risky experiment that he had been studying and researching for years. In the middle of his seventy-year-old Gabutti vines, he planted ungrafted Nebbiolo, chosen from massal selection from his other vines. "I was sick of hearing the old-timers tell me, 'Barolo before phylloxera was much better than the Barolo made today on grafted American rootstocks,'" he told me in an interview back in 2003. And if phylloxera should eventually attack the ungrafted vines? "At least I could say I had fun trying," he responded with a laugh, and knowing Teobaldo's nonconformist nature, he meant it.

Several visits to Cappellano's vineyards demonstrated the physical differences between the vines: the ungrafted plants are sparser, with fewer grape bunches, when compared to the lush vegetation of the grafted vines. "Veteran growers used to tell me they always felt the real reason behind grafting on American rootstocks was to increase production, since the ungrafted vines were less vigorous and produced fewer grapes," explained Cappellano. And looking at the differences between the two vineyards, they may not have been completely wrong.

Teobaldo, one of the founders of Viniveri, a united group of wine producers who proudly describe themselves as "anarchical naturalists," deplored overoaked and overextracted wines, and respectfully asked that wine writers never demean or belittle his wines with numerical scores or other classifications.

After Teobaldo passed away unexpectedly in 2009, his son Augusto, who had joined his father in 2003 after graduating university with an engineering degree, took over the firm. To his merit, Augusto is every bit as passionate, nonconforming, and determined as his father was. Young Cappellano is maintaining Teobaldo's traditional style while adding his own mark, beginning with an exhaustive and much-needed renovation of the cellars. Augusto also commissioned a thorough soil analysis of his Gabutti vineyards. While the chemical composition is unsurprisingly calcareous marl, the analysis revealed that the specific composition, or granular material, is 11–16 percent sand, 61–65 percent silt, and 22 percent clay. "Langhe's previous generations of growers knew what they were doing when they created Gabutti's borders. At the extreme limit of the confines, this composition changes dramatically to 27 percent sand, 49.6 percent silt, and 23.1 percent clay," declares Augusto.

Like his father, Augusto forgoes chemicals in the vineyard, shunning herbicides and fungicides, and any treatments he uses are certified organic methods. In the cellars, Cappellano remains a die-hard traditionalist, avoiding selected yeasts and allowing fermentation with ambient yeasts to occur spontaneously in wooden vats with no temperature control, followed by three and a half to four years of aging in traditional Slavonian botti ranging from 16 to 50 hectoliters. The wines, unsurprisingly, are unfiltered.

Production

Total surface area: 5 ha (12.35 acres)
Barolo: 2 ha (4.9 acres), ca. 7,500 bottles

Barolo Otin Fiorin Piè Rupestris. Made from seventy-year-old vines grafted onto one of the first American rootstocks that successfully kept phylloxera at bay, this classically crafted Barolo undergoes lengthy fermentation and maceration times that vary with every vintage, followed by three and a half to four years aging in Slavonian oak, and is usually released a year later than most other producers' Barolos. These are quintessential Serralunga Barolos. The 2006, tasted in 2012, shows textbook Nebbiolo aroma of rose and truffle with ripe sour cherry and mineral flavors. Best 2014 to 2031.

Barolo Otin Fiorin Piè Franco. Made exactly like the firm's other Barolo, this wine hails from ungrafted vines planted in 1989 from a massal selection of Cappellano's best Gabutti vines. This isn't just one of my favorite Barolos; it is one of my favorite wines. The ungrafted vines, which naturally produce fewer grapes than their grafted counterparts, also produce a more austere Barolo with downright heroic structures as well as a more persistent bouquet.

The 2006 is compelling, offering a complex bouquet of dried rose petals, clove, new leather, and orange peel along with cherry, truffle, and mineral flavors of great depth and fantastic length. This was still very youthful and aggressively tannic in 2012, and appears to have marathon aging potential. Best 2016 to 2036 at least.

Villadoria

Località Cappallotto 5
12050 Serralunga d'Alba (CN)
Tel. +39 0173 626211
www.villadoria.it
paola.lanzavecchia@villadoria.it

Founded in 1959 by Daniele Lanzavecchia's father, Pietro, this large, handsome winery is located at the foot of the Serralunga hill. Surrounded by parkland and vineyards, in particular the Cappellotto cru, the estate also offers a unique view of the tower of Castiglione Falletto on the opposite hillside. In 2004, Daniele's outgoing daughter Paola, a trained enologist, joined her father in running the company, and she is adamant in her perennial quest to raise the bar on quality.

Villadoria owns vineyards throughout Serralunga, including in crus Lazzarito, Cappallotto, and Meriame. Even though altitudes and plant ages vary somewhat, the median altitude of all its Barolo holdings is 300 meters (984 feet), while plant age averages out to twenty years old, although vines in some crus are far older, even up to fifty years old. The firm makes several solid Barolos, but not all are made every year, depending on the quality produced by individual vineyards in any given vintage. The Lanzavecchias use for the most part traditional methods for Barolo and Barbaresco with the exception of their Barolo Lazzarito, which is aged in new barriques. They also make a good Barbaresco with grapes they outsource from trusted growers in San Rocco Seno d'Elvio, with whom they've been working with for thirty years.

Production

Total surface area: 23 ha (56.8 acres)
Barolo: 12 ha (29.65 acres), 85,000 bottles
Barbaresco: purchases grapes, 20,000 bottles

Barbaresco. This is a lovely, straightforward Barbaresco of the classic style. Aged for one year in traditional botti, it demonstrates bright Nebbiolo aromas of rose, earth, and spice, with wild cherry and mineral flavors. The 2008 was still closed in 2012, but should open up nicely and develop complexity. Best 2014 to 2018.

Barbaresco Riserva. Aged for three years in Slavonian casks ranging from 30 to 50 hectoliters, this wine boasts quintessential Nebbiolo aromas and flavors and the elegance of Barbaresco, with more complexity than the straight Barbaresco. Made only in top years. The 2006 Riserva, tasted in 2012, was showing beautifully with leather, licorice, and cherry notes, along with lovely balance and depth. Best through 2021.

Barolo. Hailing from their various Serralunga vineyards, this undergoes twenty-five days of fermentation/maceration followed by two and a half years aging in large traditional casks. Despite its traditional aging, the 2007, tasted in 2011, showed evident oak-driven sensations of chocolate and espresso, perhaps due to new botti. On the other hand, the 2008, tasted in 2012, although still closed and tannic, offered the violet and underbrush aromas, sour cherry and spice sensations, of a traditionally crafted Barolo. It should soften and develop complexity over the next few years. Best 2016 to 2028.

Barolo Riserva. Aged for four years in 30- and 50-hectoliter Slavonian casks followed by a year in bottle, this wine is made exclusively in the best years. The 2000 Riserva, tasted in 2012, and the latest Riserva at the time of writing this book, showed evident oak, again perhaps because the casks were new. The next Riserva will be the 2004.

Barolo Sorì Paradiso. This is my favorite Villadoria wine and is produced only in what Daniele and Paola feel are outstanding vintages for the vineyard. Made from the best grapes from twenty-five- to fifty-year-old vines in the Sorì Paradiso vineyard in the Cappallotto cru surrounding the winery, the wine is aged for between two and three years in 30-hectoliter Slavonian botti. Sorì Paradiso is quintessential Barolo: it has raspberry, leather, and mineral perfumes alongside gorgeous ripe fruit and spice flavors. This shows Serralunga power and age-worthy structure with layers of complexity and fine balance. The 2005, tasted in 2012, showed superb depth, impeccable balance, and great length. Will go for decades, best through 2025 at least. The next Sorì Paradiso slotted for release will be the 2008.

Barolo Lazzarito.   From the eponymous cru, this is aged two years in barriques of varying ages. While it should be the estate's flagship bottling, I found that coffee, espresso, and chocolate sensations overwhelmed the Nebbiolo.

Anselma Giacomo

Piazza Maria Cappellano 2
12050 Serralunga d'Alba (CN)
Tel. +39 0173 613170
www.anselmagiacomo.it
info@anselmagiacomo.it

This small winery, which turns out soulful, earthy Barolos, is another one of Serralunga's storied Barolo firms and was a favorite of Italian wine maestro Luigi Veronelli. In the early 1900s, Felice Anselma, whose father, Giacomo, ran a small osteria just below Serralunga's castle, began making the Langhe's classic red wines, scouring the vineyards in order to source grapes from the best vineyards in Serralunga. Felice eventually acquired parcels in top sites, including in the heart of Vigna Rionda and Collaretto, releasing his first bottled Barolo in 1930. In the 1920s, Felice and his wife opened one of the Langhe's first restaurants combined with a small hotel, Albergo Ristorante Italia. Still run by the family today, the clientele has always been the key market for Anselma's wines.

The firm has passed down through the generations, and today Felice's grandson Franco Anselma and his wife, Maria, run the winery, restaurant, hotel, and wineshop—all located in the historic center of Serralunga. For several years now Anselma's wines have been certified as "biotipico," meaning the firm has eliminated using harsh chemicals in the vineyards, including industrial fertilizers, and applies only biomineral treatments to the leaves to nourish the plants. In the cellars Franco is a die-hard noninterventionist, and his Barolos, from some of the best crus in Serralunga, are among the last of the earthy, heroic Barolos of yesteryear, and are chock-full of personality and soul. Franco ferments in concrete tanks, allowing spontaneous fermentation to occur with wild yeasts only. He then ages in large Slavonian botti for a minimum of three years, and does not filter or fine the wines. Although these days there is a huge return to traditionally crafted Barolos, things have not always been easy for Anselma.

"In the 1990s and up until the mid-2000s, during the heyday of barriques and oaky, concentrated wines, it was very difficult to sell our Barolos, and I begged my husband to buy barriques. He refused, saying he had to make a wine that he would drink, not what the market wants. Then, in 2007, we went to a wine show in Denmark with thirty-five other producers, and our Barolo won the competition. Now there are a lot of people who love and want our wines, so my husband was right," says Maria, who can usually be found in the firm's wineshop in Serralunga's main square. Like other storied producers that have witnessed recent changes in the denomination, Franco and Maria feel that in the past decade and a half a number of growers have planted Nebbiolo for Barolo in places the site-sensitive grape should never be cultivated. "Before, when someone wanted to plant Nebbiolo for Barolo, the chamber of commerce would send a technician out with a compass, to guarantee that the vineyard had southern exposures. Now no one checks. And in other instances, woods that have sustained the hillsides for centuries have been pulled out for vines, resulting in frequent landslides," stated Franco during my visit to the winery in 2012, proving he is as passionate about defending Barolo's historic vineyards as he is about defending classically crafted Barolos.

Production

Total surface area: owns 3 ha (7.41 acres), leases 2 ha (4.9 acres)
Barolo: 4 ha (9.8 acres), 20,000 bottles

Vigna Rionda Riserva. This is the firm's flagship wine, made from their 0.7-hectare (1.7-acre) parcel situated at 400 meters (1,312 feet) above sea level. With its calcareous clay soil, southern and southwestern exposures, this is a prime site, and yields earthy, age-worthy Barolos with ripe fruit and refreshing acidity. Franco ages this for five years in traditional botti and releases the wine as a Riserva. The 2006, tried in 2012, opened with classic truffle, leather, rose, and tar aromas. The palate delivered a great depth of flavors, including juicy black cherry, spice, and balsamic herbs. This will develop more complexity over the next few years and will age well for decades. Best 2016 to 2036. The 2005 Riserva offers intense underbrush and floral aromas along with leather and eucalyptus sensations. The vibrant acidity and firm tannins are supported by ripe berry, mint, and licorice notes. Drink 2015 to 2025. The

2003, also tried in 2012, has lovely depth and surprising freshness for this scorching vintage.

Barolo Collaretto. Running practically parallel to Vigna Rionda, this vineyard is also situated at 400 meters (1,312 feet) above sea level and enjoys south-southwest exposure, with perhaps more southwestern exposures. The 2007, tried in 2012, was big and ripe, with almost funky aromas of turned soil, meat juices, leather, and truffle. The palate was delicious, with dense, dark berry, licorice, and spice. Already very drinkable. Anslema also makes an outstanding Langhe Nebbiolo from its Collaretto holdings.

See also the following:

Giacomo Conterno (under Monforte d'Alba)
Bruno Giacosa (under Barbaresco, Neive)
Gigi Rosso (under Castiglione Falletto)
Bruna Grimaldi (under Grinzane Cavour)
Pio Cesare (under Alba)

Other Serralunga Wineries of Interest

Zunino

NINE

La Morra and Cherasco

WHILE LA MORRA IS A CORE Barolo village, Cherasco is the tiniest player in terms of Barolo production, and is included in this chapter for the sole purpose of the maps, since it borders La Morra.

La Morra has the largest surface area dedicated to Barolo vineyards, 479 hectares (1,198 acres), which account for 24.9 percent of the denomination's total production. Located above the village of Barolo, La Morra also has the greatest difference in altitude among its vineyards, which range from 200 to 500 meters (656 to 1,640 feet) above sea level. While a few of Monforte's vineyards also reach 500 meters, and a sliver of Monforte's Bussia goes as low as 220 meters (721 feet), this gap in altitude is very common in La Morra.

The village, whose summit offers the ultimate views of the surrounding mountains and the Langhe hills below, produces some of the most graceful Barolos in the growing zone, which are celebrated for their enticing bouquets. Unsurprisingly, the village has long played a key role in the age-old custom of blending Nebbiolo for quintessential Barolos, lending intense floral aromas to the mix. In a 2011 interview, Pio Boffa of famed Barolo house Pio Cesare told me when his grandfather and father were assembling their iconic Barolos, they always relied on "La Morra for elegance and fragrance."

While altitude and microclimate certainly play a role in La Morra's finesse, many producers insist that soil is perhaps the deciding factor. The Tortonian soil in La Morra consists mainly of Sant'Agata Fossili marls. Besides these bluish-gray marls, La Morra's soil has the highest amount of clay and the least amount of sand, sandstone, and calcium carbonate according to the study conducted by Soster for the Piedmont Region, which is backed up by the region's data banks of analysis on farming land. The higher clay content

FIGURE 14. Vineyards after a snowfall in La Morra. This is the view of La Morra after the January 24, 2013, blizzard. Photograph by Paolo Tenti.

means that soils in La Morra tend to be more humid and are able to create water reserves, especially when compared to the better draining soils in Serralunga, for example. Generally speaking, thanks to these water reserves in the soil that keep vines fresh, La Morra tends to perform better than other parts of the growing area in those years when rainfall is scarce in the summer and autumn, and while this was the case, for example, in 2007, it was not the case in 2009, because of uneven ripening that many producers apparently tried to mask with new oak. In very wet vintages on the other hand, much of La Morra can suffer as the ground absorbs and retains too much water, making it difficult for Nebbiolo to reach ideal ripening and increasing the risk of fungal diseases. According to several local producers, La Morra's soil also boasts more magnesium than other areas, as well as a high amount of potassium, which lends more refined perfume, ranging from floral notes of wild rose and violet to balsamic notes of mint and eucalyptus.

However, La Morra Barolos generally do not possess Barolo's archetypical tannic structures, although winemaking preferences obviously play a crucial role as well in the final wine style. Barolos from La Morra tend to be more

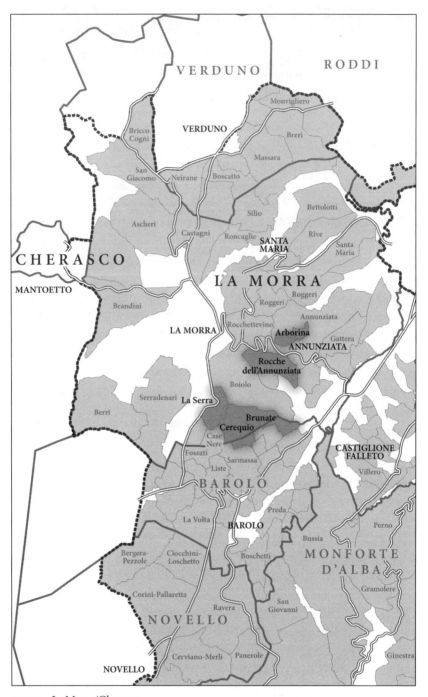

MAP 5. La Morra/Cherasco.

approachable earlier than Barolos from other areas, though they continue to evolve and improve with modest aging and can maintain well for another fifteen to twenty years after the harvest year depending on the vintage.

Back when inky dark, overly concentrated, and brawny wines were the only ones garnering top scores from those critics who didn't—and many still don't—appreciate Nebbiolo's uniqueness and finesse, producers in La Morra were at a disadvantage. Perhaps this is why so many wineries here have turned to more invasive winemaking techniques that extract more color and tannins, such as extreme grape thinning, short, tumultuous fermentation in rotary fermenters, or fermenting in all new barriques, as well as aging in barriques, in attempts to beef up structure and add complexity. The result has often been overly extracted wines with overwhelming wood sensations that can easily strangle Nebbiolo. Although these days some producers here, like many producers across Italy, have stepped back toward more Nebbiolo-friendly methods and have become proficient at using barriques, too many from this village still abuse their wines with new wood in my opinion.

However, a number of producers who are using less new wood and more used barriques, as well as some of the more traditionally minded producers using large casks, are turning out stunning Barolos that combine structure and complexity with La Morra's trademark elegance and perfume. Masters of barriques in La Morra include Elio Altare and Mauro Veglio. "I no longer carry out malolactic fermentation in barriques but in steel because malo in barriques leaves dominant wood sensations," says Veglio, who now uses less new wood, and only slightly toasted, for aging.

If after tasting the 2008s I detected a distinct step back from new wood and felt that quality across the board in La Morra had never been higher or more uniform, I was sorely disappointed by the majority of 2009s from La Morra when I tried them at Nebbiolo Prima, the annual five-day press tasting, in 2013. This was a difficult year across the denomination, but Barolo aged in new oak suffered the most, and overall, La Morra, which had a stellar showing at Nebbiolo Prima in 2012 with the 2008s, showed the worst at the 2013 event. Not only was Nebbiolo overwhelmed by espresso, vanilla, and toast, but the barriques also imparted astringent wood tannins that only compounded the bitterness of green tannins that resulted from uneven grape ripening, and I don't foresee these wines getting any better with age. The best 2009s from the village were generally aged in large casks or used barriques, and a number of these were in fact very good despite the challenges of the vintage.

Like their counterparts in other villages, the best producers in La Morra are focusing on better farming methods to improve quality, such as careful canopy management, eschewing harsh chemicals, and adopting a less extreme green harvest. La Morra boasts a number of celebrated vineyard areas, most of them in the eastern part of the township with many bordering Barolo. Top sites include Cerequio, Brunate, and La Serra, which are all clustered together and close to Barolo, and the crus near the Annuziata zone, in particular Rocche dell'Annuziata, and Gattera, situated on the eastern side of La Morra facing Castiglione Falletto.

Oddero

Poderi e Cantine Oddero
Fraz. S. Maria 28
12064 La Morra (CN)
Tel +39 0173 50618
www.oddero.it
info@oddero.it

With viticultural roots stretching back to the eighteenth century and its first bottled wines from the 1878 vintage, Oddero is one of the oldest established Barolo houses, and Giacomo Oddero, the fifth generation to run the firm, is Barolo's senior statesman. When I first visited this lovely estate in 1994, Giacomo was still running the L-shaped winery with his brother Luigi, but in 2005 the two brothers divided their holdings, and a year later Luigi founded his own Luigi Oddero estate. Giacomo, a spry eighty-eight year old at the time of the writing of this book, stayed on at the family's historic head-quarters in the Santa Maria hamlet of La Morra, long considered one of the best areas of the township. Today Giacomo's daughters Mariacristina, who holds a degree in agriculture from the University of Turin with a specializa-tion in viticulture and enology, and Mariavittoria, a doctor, and her daughter Isabella, have taken on many of the daily responsibilities, although Giacomo remains a driving force.

Giacomo has been a Barolo ambassador for decades, and he has also done much to help the area, most notably through his crusade to construct the first aqueduct in the Langhe. Over the years, he has been the mayor of La Morra, president of the Chamber of Commerce for fifteen years, and as a long-time councilman on the province's Board of Agriculture, he signed in the DOC and DOCG laws regulating the Langhe's wine production. And the whole while, he continued to improve production at his own estate. For years, this was one of the übertraditional wineries, and I have wonderful memories of Oddero's 1988 and 1989 Barolos, which we thoroughly enjoyed in the early years of the New Millennium while they were in the prime of their wild cherry, tar, rose, and leather glory.

Oddero has holdings in prime areas throughout Barolo and Barbaresco, including Brunate in La Morra, Vigna Rionda in Serralunga, Villero in Castiglione Falletto, and Gallina in Neive as well as others. In 2011, the firm began the arduous process of converting some of their vineyards—spread out in numerous parcels all over Barolo as well as in Barbaresco—to organic farming, which will eventually be certified. In the cellars, the firm is no longer ultratraditional and for its single-vineyard Barolos, carries out malolactic fermentation in barriques of varying ages that can, however, occasionally impart evident albeit not invasive wood sensations (the straight Barolo on the other hand undergoes malolactic fermentation in steel). Aging takes place in large casks between 15 and 30 hectoliters made of Austrian oak and French oak, although according to Mariacristina they are relying more on Austrian oak these days. Oddero still has some Slavonian casks, which it uses for the straight Barolo and Nebbiolo Langhe, but these are being phased out.

Production

Total surface area: 35 ha (86.5 acres)
Barolo: 17 ha (42 acres), 50,000 bottles
Barbaresco: 2 ha (5 acres), 6,500 bottles

Barbaresco Gallina.   Oddero leases a parcel of the famed Gallina cru in Neive (they have a long-term thirty-five-year contract) from the Diocese of Alba and maintains the vineyard as if it were its own. The 2010 opens with toasted aromas along with rose sensations. The palate is delicious, loaded with juicy cherry and raspberry punctuated by white pepper and cinnamon notes. This is very elegant, with firm but fine tannins and plenty of length.

Barolo.   A blend of Nebbiolo from Oddero's holdings in La Morra and Castiglione Falletto, this is a straightforward Barolo with hallmark aromas and bracing but fine tannins, and while usually approachable while young, it also ages well for a decade or so depending on the vintage. The intense 2010 boasts a beautiful rose and violet fragrance with whiffs of leather, spice, and balsamic notes. The vibrant palate delivers red cherry, mint, and menthol alongside supple tannins. Drink 2018 to 2035.

Barolo Bussia Vigna Mondoca. Made from thirty-five-year-old plants, this is quite structured and complex. The 2007 has an intense bouquet of rose, leather, and truffle, with rich fruit, spice, and licorice flavors accompanied by some toasted notes and drying tannins. Drink through 2027. The 2004, tasted in 2013, is stunning, with concentrated floral and balsamic notes accompanied by marinated cherry flavors and rich licorice notes. Drink through 2024.

Vigna Rionda. Made from a prime parcel in the famed vineyard, Oddero has long aged this for five years (four in wood) before release, and while it is for all intents and purposes a Riserva, the firm never designated it as such on labels. However, starting with the 2006 vintage, in top vintages, Oddero will age its Vigna Rionda for ten years before release and will label it as a Riserva.

Renato Ratti

Frazione Annunziata 7
12064 La Morra (CN)
Tel. +39 0173 50185
www.renatoratti.com
info@renatoratti.com

Located in a contemporary winery just below the fourteenth-century Abbey of L'Annunziata, and surrounded by a breathtaking amphitheater of vineyards in an area historically known as Marcenasco, this firm is turning out more internationally styled interpretations of Barolo that, in varying degrees, still retain their Nebbiolo pedigree.

Renato Ratti, who founded the winery in 1965, was a pioneer in the modern age of Barolo. Unlike most of the Langhe's producers, Ratti, whose father was a veterinarian and his grandfather a doctor, was free from all ties to winemaking traditions that were normally passed down through the generations. Because of the difficult postwar conditions that made it impossible to send Renato to university to study medicine, his family sent him to Alba's enological school. After graduation, Ratti was hired by the industrial Vermouth producer Cinzano, who in 1955 sent him to Brazil, where he oversaw production for ten years. His experience abroad gave him a forward-thinking outlook, which would shape his views on Barolo and Barolo production when he returned to Piedmont in 1965. That same year, he bought his first small vineyard in the Marcenasco subzone, from which he created Barolo Marcenasco.

Ratti was convinced that the secret to great Barolo depended on the vineyard, and after years of talking with veteran Barolo growers and producers, and thanks to his own experience sourcing grapes and acquiring vineyards, in the mid-1970s, he compiled his first map of the Barolo crus. On this first version of his now famous map, Ratti indicated the historical subzones in Barolo as well as select areas with "particular characteristics"; and in 1976 he created a similar map of Barbaresco's vineyard sites. In 1985, he updated his Barolo map by adding the first category classification of the best vineyard areas. These maps were milestones for the denominations, especially for Barolo, where it is still referred to today, as are his Barolo vintage charts.

Ratti also experimented with updated cellar techniques with the goal of making fruitier, less tannic Barolos, and to this end cut alcoholic fermentation and maceration down from its customary one to two months to ten to fourteen days. He advocated the pump-over method to keep the fermenting wine and skins in contact, as opposed to the traditional and lengthy submerged-cap method that Ratti felt extracted an excess of tannins, "especially from the skins,"[1] from prolonged contact between the fermenting wine and solids. Ratti also put his wines through malolactic fermentation, a practice few producers were using in the area at the time. Moreover, he supported decreasing barrel aging—which up until the late 1970s lasted anywhere from four to eight years—down to two years, and favored longer bottle aging instead.

Renato's son Pietro, who is currently the president of the Consorzio, as was his father before him, took over the winery in 1988 when he was only twenty, after Renato's premature passing. Pietro, a trained enologist, had the huge task of not only continuing the family business, but of having to buy vineyards, because so many growers who had supplied his father were becoming wine producers themselves. Pietro also built brand new cellars, completed in 2006, where he introduced his own innovations, such as rotary fermenters and barriques, although he also uses 25-hectoliter casks as well. In the last few vintages, according to Pietro, he uses less new wood for aging.

Production

Total surface area: 35 ha (86.5 acres)

Barolo: 16.5 ha (41 acres), 57,000 bottles

Barolo Marcenasco. This is Ratti's most important Barolo in terms of volume, and it's my favorite of the firm's three selections, combining rich fruit and Nebbiolo *tipicità*. Made from different southeast- and southwest-facing parcels located around the Abbey of L'Annunziata that range in altitude from 240 to 290 meters (787 to 951 feet) above sea level, and grown in La Morra's typical Tortonian soils, this is a lovely expression of La Morra's perfume and finesse. The 2008, aged 70 percent in Slavonian cask and 30 percent in barriques of varying ages, has enticing aromas of violet, rose, spice, and balsamic notes. The palate offers tart cherry, spice, and present but ripe tannins and nervous acidity. Best 2014 to 2023.

Barolo La Conca. Made from the eponymous cru that lies just below the Annunziata Abbey, this bowl-shaped vineyard traps in the heat, creating a hot microclimate, which in turn yields a tannic, structured Barolo. This undergoes malolactic fermentation in wood and is aged in barriques and botti. The 2008 is darkly colored with intense balsamic notes and licorice, as well as espresso and very evident oak, all of which carry over onto the palate. Drink 2016 to 2028.

Barolo Le Rocche. Le Rocche dell'Annunziata is one of La Morra's most important vineyards, and Renato Ratti classified it as a first category subzone. Although it is lauded for its intense perfume and refinement, I personally find that elegance and bouquet are often overwhelmed by oak in Ratti's bottling of this famed cru. Le Rocche 2008, which like Conca undergoes malolactic fermentation in wood and ages for one year in barriques and one year in cask, is darkly pigmented and very extracted with dense, almost overripe black fruit sensations—strange, given the more austere nature of the vintage. Wood is subtle on the nose, but more evident on the palate. Drink 2016 to 2023.

Elio Altare

Frazione Annunziata 51
12064 La Morra (CN)
Tel. +39 0173 50835
www.elioaltare.com
elioaltare@elioaltare.com

Elio Altare, an intense and passionate winemaker with remarkable charisma and energy, is undoubtedly one of the most controversial figures in

FIGURE 15. Elio Altare. Elio Altare's approach to winemaking and vineyard management was influenced by his many trips to Burgundy. Altare played a major role in the revolution in Barolo and Barbaresco that encouraged many growers to become producers of quality Barolo and Barbaresco. Photograph by Paolo Tenti.

Barolodom. Loved by advocates of the so-called modernist style—a term Altare himself ridicules—he is also criticized by many Barolo purists. My take: while Altare's Barolos are not typical, they can be gorgeous, and while sleek and polished, they still manage to maintain their Nebbioloness. They are not the fruity oak bombs some die-hard Barolo fans have made them out to be; nor are they quintessential expressions of Barolo and Nebbiolo. They are, like their creator, highly original, fascinating, and deserving of their cult status.

"Whatever you do—don't call me a *modernist*," the usually affable Elio says emphatically when I bring up the subject of the different Barolo styles during a January 2013 interview. Nothing apparently makes Altare more upset than defining him as a modernist—a now passé definition for winemakers producing more internationally styled wines. Except of course lauding tradition, which really gets Altare going. "Don't talk to me about tradition either! *This* is tradition," exclaims Elio as he shows me a picture of himself as a ten-year-old wearing a straw hat and guiding a large ox through the vineyards. "I worked the fields and vineyards with an ox-drawn plough until I was twenty, in 1970. And until the early 1970s, many people here were so poor, during the winter months they spent their days in the barn with the farm animals to stay warm. That's tradition, along with old, rotting casks," says Altare more calmly.

Tradition in Langhe in the late 1960s and early 1970s also meant that the father was the ruler supreme and what he said went. Period. The change and rebellion that began in the United States and exploded in Italy in 1968 reached rural Langhe, and Elio, born in 1950, began to question everything while in his late teens, much to his father's chagrin. By the mid-1970s, their relationship was more than tense, according to Elio. Like most of their contemporaries, Elio's family grew grapes and other crops, and while they also made and even bottled a small amount of wine, the bulk of their income derived from selling grapes to the large Barolo houses. Elio wanted to improve not just the quality of the wine, but also the grower's life.

Altare recalls the status quo that severely penalized the local growers, and recounts standing in the main square in Alba with hundreds of other growers just before the harvest, all of them jostling to sell their grapes still ripening on the vine: "It was 1975, and we had the most beautiful grapes that year. But the buyers purposely waited another two weeks to the point where the grapes were rotting on the vines, forcing us to sell at a loss. And of course, we weren't paid until a year later." In 1976, Elio and a group of other young growers took a trip to Burgundy, which proved a life-altering experience. "It was another world in terms of vineyard management and wine production," says Elio today. He returned and began thinning out the bunches and short pruning the vines in order to lower yields, and tried to implement changes in winemaking. Father and son clashed for years until things reached a brutal climax in 1983, when Elio took extreme measures to change both farming and winemaking methods.

"After the war, sellers of chemical herbicides and industrial fertilizer descended like flies in rural Italy and convinced small farmers that these products saved time and money and would create even healthier plants," according to Elio. His father, like most of his peers, eagerly began using the new wave of products. But according to Elio, by the mid-1970s, the leaves on their vines and other crops were turning yellow and many were dying while weeds, grass, and insects had disappeared. After trying out several remedies suggested by "experts" that did nothing to resolve the problem, Elio had the soil analyzed by the University of Turin, which determined that the land had been rendered completely sterile from harsh chemicals. A professor there suggested that Elio ban all chemicals in the vineyards and fields, and start revitalizing the soil with manure. Convincing his father wasn't so easy.

Then, in 1979, Elio, who by now was leasing the vineyards and cellars from his father, suffered severe intoxication from the pesticides his father sprayed on the fruit trees, which resulted in a lengthy hospital stay. For the next few years he battled with his father over their use. "By 1983 I couldn't take it anymore. I bought a chainsaw and cut down our eight hundred fruit trees. And I didn't stop there. I went into the cellars and cut up my father's crumbling casks to make room for brand-new barriques," recounts Elio with a note of sadness. He was promptly disinherited, and when his father died in 1985, Elio took out a large mortgage to buy back the farm from his sisters.

Elio then began his long journey of experimenting and discovery, all recorded in a notebook that he has kept every year, documenting his successes as well as what didn't work. And judging by the number of empty bottles of Burgundy's most famous Grands Crus displayed throughout the winery, he also spent vast sums trying the wines he wanted to emulate. "I never cared for the terms 'modern' or 'traditional.' There are only two kinds of wine: good and bad. I want to make good wine, and to do that in Barolo, controlling tannins is crucial," says Altare, adding that one shouldn't have to wait fifteen or twenty years before a wine is approachable. Yet with his trademark frankness, Altare also admits that one of the greatest wines he has ever had, tasted blind during a dinner a few years ago, was a 1971 Bartolo Mascarello.

In La Morra, Elio owns vineyards in the Arborina cru surrounding the winery, and for protection from hail, these are fitted out with special nets that he can open when the weather appears ominous. Elio also has a vineyard in Cerretta in Serralunga, and his first release was from the 2005 vintage. In the vineyards, Elio has avoided all chemical treatments and chemical fertilizers since 1983, using sulfur and copper treatments and cow manure instead. He also hoes the weeds and grass just beneath the vines exclusively by hand, which he says helps the plants live longer. In the cellars, Elio was among the first wave of Langhe growers to break with traditional methods, starting by introducing shorter maceration times and aging in barriques since 1984. Since 1993 he has used rotary fermenters for the first three to four days of maceration and fermentation to extract noble tannins and push the seeds to the bottom, where they are collected and removed regularly to avoid harsh tannins. The still-fermenting juice is then racked into barriques, 20 to 30 percent new while the rest are up to eight years old. Barolos finish their fermentation in barriques, and are also aged in barriques for two years. Altare, joined in the firm by his wife, Lucia, and daughter Silvia, does not filter or fine his wines, and uses well below the minimum amounts of sulfur dioxide just before bottling to stabilize the wine.

Production

Total surface area: 12 ha (30 acres)

Barolo: 5.5 ha (13.5 acres), owned and leased; 25,000–30,000 bottles

NB: From 1995 to 2009 Altare made Barolo Brunate from a leased vineyard but after the lease expired no longer produces this. He has recently acquired vineyards in Cannubi, to be released in the near but as of yet undetermined future. He also makes a straight Barolo with Nebbiolo from Serralunga d'Alba, La Morra, Castiglione Falletto, and Barolo.

Barolo Arborina.   This is Elio's standard-bearer, made from vineyards surrounding his house and winery, much of it planted by his grandfather, Giovanni, in 1948. Vine age ranges from twenty-five to sixty-five years old, and vines, located between 220 and 280 meters (721 and 918 feet) above sea level, benefit from southern and southeastern exposures and are planted in La Morra's typical marl and clay soils. The 2008 is extremely polished, with dark fruit and floral sensations along with hints of coffee and espresso from the barriques. Very elegant with nervous acidity but soft tannins. Best 2018 to 2023. In 2013 I tried Altare's Arborina 1990, which had lovely floral and spice aromas but even after a few hours in the glass, showed bracing acidity but not much fruit while tannins were almost nonexistent. The next day however, the wine had developed more fruit sensations, but was still off its peak.

Barolo Cerretta "Vigna Bricco."   Since 2005, Altare has leased 1 hectare (2.471 acres) of vineyards in Serralunga's Cerretta cru, 0.38 hectares of which he purchased in 2011. The ten-year-old plants average 350 meters (1,148 feet) above sea level and are planted in the village's classic calcareous soil. Elio himself admits that at first he was very surprised at the stark differences between his Serralunga and La Morra Barolos, and tends to age the Cerretta longer in bottle before release in order to tame the more evident tannins. The 2006, which I tried in 2013, is an outstanding effort, and is perhaps the most elegant Barolo I've ever had from Serralunga. Rose, truffle, and meat juice aromas are classic Barolo as are the cherry, menthol, and licorice flavors. The tannins—big but smooth and supple—are signature Altare. Beautiful balance and great length. Best 2016 to 2036. Gorgeous wine.

Mauro Veglio

Frazione Annunziata-Cascina Nuova 50
12064 La Morra (CN)
Tel. +39 0173 509212
www.mauroveglio.com
mauroveglio@mauroveglio.com

Mauro Veglio lives right next door to Elio Altare, and the two even share a courtyard of what generations ago was the single Cascina Nuova property. "I've been hugely influenced by Elio," says Mauro today. Veglio makes it clear that besides being a friend and neighbor, Elio was, especially in Veglio's formative years, his mentor.

Veglio, whose father bought the small property in 1979, recalls that until the 1980s their vineyards were interspersed with grain and fruit trees in the *coltura promiscua* cultivation that used to sustain farmers. He also clearly remembers working the land with his father using an ox-drawn plough the first few years. Like most farmers, the Veglios sold off most of their grapes while making a small amount of wine for family consumption and to sell in bulk. The farming life was so harsh that when he came of age, Veglio had no desire to take over the family farm. Then, in 1992, Altare convinced the younger Veglio to join him in what Veglio now refers to as "a great adventure." Thanks to Altare, Veglio participated in the massive changes occurring in Barolo at the time that gave poor growers a shot at earning a decent living—an unthinkable concept less than a decade before. Under Elio's guidance, Veglio, who is helped by his wife, Daniela, started green harvesting and bunch thinning, carried out shorter maceration times, invested in new barriques, and later hired the services of consulting enologist Beppe Caviola. Like Elio, Veglio avoids all chemicals treatments in the vineyards and uses only organic fertilizer.

With bank financing, Mauro soon built a new cellar, invested in rotary fermenters, and as he puts it, watched the Barolo prices jump up 15 percent every year throughout the 1990s. "Every year the prices went up, fueled by demand, and producers kept expanding. Only Altare warned not to continuously increase production, advocating instead to keep production low and prices high," says Veglio. "It was a bubble that eventually exploded," he noted, adding that as production went up, most producers could no longer justify their high prices. The bubble finally burst after 2008's global economic downturn, when cellars were full across the Langhe, until things began to turn around again in 2012.

Veglio freely admits that many Barolo producers swinging away from tradition swung too far, and agrees that in the late 1990s and part of the first decade of the new century there were excesses: a lot of overoaked and overconcentrated Barolos. For his part, Veglio has pulled back. He parted ways with Caviola and now ferments using only wild yeasts. Maceration and the first part of fermentation take place for eight days in rotary fermenters before Veglio racks the wine into vertical, stainless steel tanks to finish fermentation. Up until 2010, he carried out malolactic fermentation in barriques, but now does this in steel to minimize wood sensations. He also uses less new barriques and, perhaps most importantly, now uses only lightly toasted wood for aging.

Production

Total surface area: 13 ha (32 acres)
Barolo: 7 ha (17 acres), 30,000 bottles

Barolo Arborina.   Made from the vineyards surrounding the winery, located at 270 meters (886 feet) above sea level, where clay keeps the vines fresher, especially important in hot, dry years. Southern and southeastern exposures help ripening, and thirty-five-year-old plants generate intense flavors. The 2008 has a lovely rose and violet bouquet with earthy notes accented with nutmeg. The elegant, approachable palate shows rich flavors of juicy cherry and spice. Best 2014 to 2023.

Barolo Gattera.   Located in La Morra, the Veglios have long owned vineyards in Gattera, which, thanks to its slightly lower altitudes of 250 meters (820 feet) above sea level and southern and southwestern exposures, has a warm microclimate that helps grapes reach ideal ripening. The 2008 is a bigger wine than Arborina, due in part to the sixty-year-old plants, which generate more concentrated flavors and structure. It's loaded with dense cherry, truffle, and licorice flavors, combining structure and finesse. With energizing minerality and great length, this is the most classic Barolo of Veglio's impressive lineup. Drink 2015 to 2028. Compelling.

Barolo Rocche dell'Annunziata. Made from vines situated at 300 meters (984 feet) above sea level with southern and southeastern exposures and more calcareous soils. The 2008 is full-bodied and round, with rose, mint, and dark fruit sensations but also some drying wood sensations on the finish. Best 2015 to 2028. The 2009 on the other hand, despite the challenging vintage, offers a gorgeous floral fragrance of rose and violet alongside succulent black cherry and spice flavors. It shows the forward nature of the vintage and is already drinking well. Best through 2019.

Barolo Castelletto. This vineyard belongs to to the family of Veglio's wife, and is located in Monforte d'Alba. Vines are located at 350 meters (1,148 feet) above sea level in calcareous soil and have southern and southeastern exposures. Replanted in 1994, vines are still relatively young for Barolo. The 2008 has very enticing and earthy aromas with balsamic notes. Dense black cherry fruit and spice, as well as notes of espresso and oak, are supported by a tannic backbone. Best 2016 to 2033.

Aurelio Settimo

Frazione Annunziata 30
12064 La Morra (CN)
Tel. +39 0173 50803
www.aureliosettimo.com
aureliosettimo@aureliosettimo.com

Located right in front of the beautiful and open Le Rocche dell'Annunziata cru, where the Settimo family owns prime vineyards, this small winery, originally founded in 1943, is turning out classic Barolos of elegance, restraint, and Nebbiolo purity. Tiziana Settimo, who worked alongside her father, Aurelio, for years, has been in charge since 2007 when she inherited the estate, and she is a proud and self-proclaimed traditionalist.

This firm is yet another one of the Langhe's little-known gems, and having prime vineyards in Le Rocche dell'Annunziata is key to the finesse and complexity of its earthy, floral Barolos. On my visit to the estate in 2011, I found Tiziana working in her vineyards surrounding the winery. She pointed out Le Rocche dell'Annunziata's unique panorama—"From here, you can see all eleven communes in the Barolo denomination"—a truly stunning view of all the Barolo hills that I have never before seen from a single vantage point. All of the firm's vineyards are around the winery in the Annunziata area of

La Morra, and most are in Le Rocche. For years the firm has adhered to the regulations of Lotta Guidata e Integrata, or Integrated Vineyard Management, which aims to regulate and reduce chemical treatments in the vineyards and encourages more natural alternatives, and also involves being followed by viticultural specialists appointed by the region.

In the cellars, Tiziana follows the classic school, and although she is updating her equipment, she chooses only technology that does not interfere with the authenticity of her wines. Up until 2008, the firm fermented in resin-lined cement vats for fifteen to twenty days, but starting with the 2009 vintage, she ferments for ten to twelve days in temperature-controlled steel tanks. After the alcoholic fermentation, Tiziana transfers the just fermented wine to the concrete vats where it undergoes malolactic fermentation and stabilizes for one year, two for the Riserva, before long aging in 25- and 35-hectoliter French casks.

Production

Total surface area: 6.64 ha (16.40 acres)

Barolo: 5.67 (14 acres), 32,000 bottles

Barolo. This is a blend of the firm's holdings around Annunziata that have southeastern exposure and are situated between 270 and 300 meters (886 and 984 feet) above sea level. This always has a cherry, mineral, and earthy character and ripe but fine tannins. The 2008 has succulent black cherry and energizing mineral. Very fresh and young with bracing tannins, it will age beautifully. Best 2014 to 2028. The 2009 reflects the forward nature of the vintage, with ripe berry and leather aromas along with juicy cherry, sage, and mint flavors. Best through 2019. In 2011, Tiziana opened up a Barolo 1980, which was a mesmerizing wine with the hallmark Nebbiolo sensations that develop in aged Barolos. Intense leather, tar, dried rose petal, and truffle aromas with zabaglione, truffle, licorice, and spice flavors. Layers of complexity and impressive freshness with great length. This evolved continuously in the glass. A memorable experience. Ready but will maintain a decade or more.

Barolo Rocche dell'Annunziata. Made entirely with the fruit from this celebrated cru known for its fragrant Barolos. The section where Aurelio Settimo has its vineyards is one of the best, shielded by adverse weather and winds by the hills of San Martino and Cerequio-Brunate. With their vineyards' ideal southern and southwestern exposures, the sun hits the vines first thing in the morning and stays until late in the afternoon, allowing grapes to reach perfect ripening. The altitude of 270 meters (886 feet) above sea level is optimal, while the plant age, between eighteen and forty-six years old, generates concentrated flavors, and the calcareous clay soil yields structure. The 2008 has a hallmark Nebbiolo fragrance of intense rose and violet accompanied by earthy notes. The palate delivers bright red fruit and spice with energizing mineral notes alongside bracing but fine tannins and nervous acidity. Needs time. 2016 to 2033. The 2009 opens with overripe berry, truffle, and forest floor aromas accompanied by a ripe but delicious palate of juicy cherry and spice. Drink soon. Best through 2019.

Barolo Le Rocche dell'Annunziata Riserva. In outstanding vintages, the firm also makes a Barolo Riserva from Le Rocche that shows more complexity and depth and has a more age-worthy structure. This undergoes six years aging before release: two in cement, three in wood, and one in bottle. The 2004 has a gorgeous bouquet of leather, truffle, and rose and mouthwatering berry and spice flavors. Complex with mesmerizing and gripping tannins, this is all about the fine balance between power and finesse.

Marcarini

Piazza Martiri 2
12064 La Morra (CN)
Tel. +39 0173 50222
www.marcarini.it
marcarini@marcarini.it

Marcarini makes classic Barolos that beautifully convey La Morra's quintessential perfumes and polish. Although five generations have owned vineyards, the firm was founded by the Marcarini family in 1959, and today Luisa Marcarini Marchetti and her husband, Manuel, are in charge. The family's cellars are housed in an eighteenth-century building situated in a square just below the summit of the hilltop town of La Morra, with lovely views of the Barolo valley below.

Once again, the combination of prime vineyards and nonintrusive cellar techniques are the secret to these refined but structured Barolos. Marcarini owns some of the best vineyards in Brunate (spanning both La Morra and Barolo) and La Serra, and although they share similar calcareous clay soils with high percentages of magnesium and have identical southern and southwestern exposures, each cru has its own distinct microclimate that yields remarkably different Barolos. Brunate, where there are more hours of sunlight, hotter temperatures, and more humidity, creates more structured Barolos with earthy aromas of underbrush and truffle that develop into tar as they age. La Serra on the other hand has a fresher microclimate thanks to higher altitudes and constant breezes that in turn produce more elegant and floral Barolos. Like most top producers, the estate limits the use of harsh chemicals in the vineyards.

In the cellar, the firm is very traditional. Fermentation lasts fifteen days followed by thirty-two days of maceration with the skins with the cap submerged. The firm then ages the wines for two years in 25- to 40-hectoliter botti that average forty years old.

Production

Total surface area: 25 ha (62 acres)

Barolo: 7 ha (17 acres), 40,000 bottles

Barolo Brunate.   Situated both in La Morra and partly in Barolo, this vineyard is located 300 meters (984 feet) above sea level, and shows a more structured side to these villages. The 2008 shows dark fruit, truffle, tobacco leaf, and hints of leather with balsamic notes. Drink after 2018. The 1998, opened in 2014, had an intense perfume of rose petal, tar, exotic spice, and white pepper. The remarkably fresh palate delivered dried cherry layered with fig, carob, and balsamic herbs balanced with velvety tannins and still lively acidity. Like most 1998s, this was a late bloomer but well worth the wait.

Barolo La Serra.   Located at 380 meters (1,247 feet) above sea level, this is a quintessential expression of La Morra, with enticing floral aromas and captivating finesse. The 2008 is beautiful, with intense rose and iris aromas, bright red fruit, and elegant tannins. This needs some time to tame nervous acidity and unwind but will be a classic. Drink after 2018. The 2009 shows more balsamic aromas along with succulent black cherry, spice, mint, and Alpine herbs. Drink soon through 2019.

Michele Chiarlo

S.S. Nizza Canelli 99
14042 Calamandrana (AT)
Tel. +39 0141 769030

www.chiarlo.it
info@chiarlo.it

Even though Michele Chiarlo's vinification and aging cellars are outside of the Barolo denomination, I've inserted the firm here because the family's lovingly restored Barolo vineyards and impressive estate are in the Cerequio area of La Morra. I visited Cerequio with Michele's son Stefano during a snowstorm that quickly became a blizzard in January 2013 (in fact we barely made it back up the very steep hill to the main road after my visit and tasting) and was stunned by the sheer beauty of the hillside vineyards and ancient hamlet.

Although best known for its Barbera d'Asti, the family firm, founded in 1956, has made Barolo since 1958 and Barbaresco since 1971. Until the early 1980s, Chiarlo made the latter two wines exclusively with grapes sourced from top growers in Serralunga's Vigna Rionda and other prime vineyard areas. "But by the early 1980s, we knew we had to buy vineyards to have control over grape quality," says Stefano. "We simply couldn't get the growers to green harvest or thin out the grape bunches to lower yields and raise quality. We even offered to pay for the discarded bunches, but they simply wouldn't do it," says Stefano. His father began scouting for just the right vineyards, and in 1983 leased prime vineyards in the long-abandoned Cerequio hamlet and cru in La Morra. According to Stefano, locals were so outraged that first year when they saw Chiarlo grape thinning and "wasting perfectly good grapes" that they sent the parish priest to reprimand Michele and to try to talk him out of such sacrilege.

Incredibly, Cerequio, one of the vineyards Lorenzo Fantini designated as a Prime Location at the end of the nineteenth century, and classified by Renato Ratti as a first category area in 1985, had been entirely abandoned in the 1950s. Chiarlo has now restored both the hamlet and its vineyards to their former glory, and some years ago even Angelo Gaja invested in vineyards in the cru. The Chiarlos have also opened up a luxury hotel surrounded by their Barolo vines. In 1990 the Chiarlos purchased another abandoned vineyard, this time in the heart of Cannubi, which had been deemed too steep to work according to Stefano. The family solved the problem by constructing earthen terraces, the first in Barolo. They also lease vineyards in Barbaresco.

Chiarlo—like most top producers—uses no chemical herbicides or pesticides in their estate vineyards. They also plant grass between every other row to help with erosion and absorb rain, and every few years they also plant peas and legumes that are eventually uprooted to act as a natural fertilizer. Manure is put down every five years or so and only if necessary.

In the cellars, Stefano, who is a trained enologist and agronomist, ferments in steel for his straight Barolos and Barbarescos, and in large wooden vats of French oak for his single-vineyard bottlings. Aging takes place in large 55-hectoliter French casks for the straight bottlings and in 700-liter tonneaux, 50 percent new and 50 percent used once before for the single-vineyard selections.

Production

Totals surface area: 60 estate ha, 50 ha leased (148 acres + 125.5 acres)

Barolo: 13 ha (32 acres), 90,000 bottles

Barbaresco: 5.5 ha (13.6 acres), 25,000 bottles

Barolo Tortoniano.   Made from grapes hailing from vineyards located in Tortonian soil in La Morra and Barolo, with half of the grapes coming from the firm's Cerequio holdings. Average altitudes are 350 meters (1,148 feet) above sea level, and plants average twenty-five years old. The 2009 is very earthy with porcini mushroom and truffle notes. Ripe fruit reined in by nice acidity and firm but ripe tannins. A lovely Barolo. Best 2015 to 2024.

Barolo Cerequio.   Made entirely with the best grapes from the estate's vineyards in Cerequio, where vines are located at 350 meters (1,148 feet) above sea level and enjoy southern and southwestern exposures. According to Stefano, Cerequio's soil is particularly rich in magnesium, which gives the wine its marked balsamic notes. The 2007 shows very ripe cherry, sage, and eucalyptus along with rose petal and toasted notes. I would love to see this wine aged in large casks someday to cut down on the toasted notes that I feel muffle Nebbiolo, but overall this is a very nice wine.

Barolo Cannubi.   Located in the heart of one of Barolo's most celebrated crus, where thirty-year-old vines are situated at 280 meters (919 feet) above sea level. In the Chiarlo's part of historic Cannubi, Tortonian meets Helvetian, as the locals say, and the soil is a mix of calcareous marls and iron-rich sand. The 2007 is elegant and structured, with floral aromas, ripe fruit, and licorice flavors accompanied by notes of toasted coffee beans that I would prefer to have only in my coffee. Drink through 2022. The 2009 shows poise and balance, no small feat given the vintage. It opens with violet, rose, and truffle aromas alongside creamy sour cherry and spice flavors. A stunning Barolo. Drink through 2019.

Barbaresco Reyna. Made from the firm's leased vineyards in Barbaresco and Treiso ranging between 250 and 320 meters (820 and 1,050 feet) in altitude. The 2010 is a classic Barbaresco from a classic vintage, with violet and rose aromas and creamy cherry and mineral flavors. All elegance and finesse. Best 2018 to 2025.

Barbaresco Asili. Made from twenty-two-year-old vines located 250 meters (820 feet) above sea level in one of Barbaresco's most hallowed crus. The 2009 shows very ripe fruit and the heat of the vintage in the hot midpalate. Once again, the toasted notes of oak and espresso restrain the bright cherry and mineral of Nebbiolo. Drink 2014 to 2019. Would love to see this aged in large casks.

Other La Morra Firms of Note

Cordero Montezemolo
Cascina Ballarin
Ciabot Berton
Vigneti Luigi Oddero

Cherasco

While Cherasco has played a role in the history of Piedmont—becoming the seat of the Royal Court of Savoy in 1630 when the plague engulfed Turin, in terms of Barolo production, it is the least significant of the denomination's eleven communes. Only a sliver of this township is devoted to Barolo production, a total of 2 hectares (less than 5 acres) to be exact, accounting for a mere 0.13 percent of total output. Cherasco's only delimited subzone, Mantoetto, is owned entirely by producer Umberto Fracassi.

TEN

Monforte d'Alba

MONFORTE D'ALBA IS ANOTHER ONE of the denomination's core villages, and makes a wide range of Barolo styles, from structured with gripping tannins to perfumed and complex. A number of the denomination's most acclaimed wineries are located in this large municipality, including Giacomo Conterno, whose iconic Barolo Monfortino—which since the early 1970s actually hails from Vigna Francia in Serralunga—is named for the producer's hometown. Other renowned producers in Monforte d'Alba include Aldo Conterno, Elio Grasso, Rocche dei Manzoni, as well as cult favorites Giacomo Fenocchio and Attilio Ghisolfi, to name but a few. Not only do winemaking styles vary notably among the town's producers—swinging from dense and fruity with very evident oak to austere, complex, and age-worthy—but this municipality's growing areas boast a wide variety of exposures, soils, and microclimates, making it impossible to define a typical expression of Nebbiolo from this commune.

Monforte d'Alba, commonly referred to simply as Monforte, reportedly takes its name from the Latin *mons fortis,* a reference to the medieval castle that once stood on top of the town's high hill and was surrounded by fortified walls. According to historians, in 1028 the archbishop of Milan razed the castle as retaliation for the area's reported heresy and to punish the local feudal lords. Today, the municipality's large territory accounts for 20.36 percent of total Barolo output, and after La Morra, Monforte is the second largest commune in terms of volume. Monforte's Serravallian soil is composed predominantly of sandstone and clay, and although many people compare its soils to those found in Serralunga d'Alba, according to Dr. Stefano Dolzan, head of the Piedmont Region's Agricultural Department, in terms of soils, Monforte is actually more similar to Castiglione Falletto. "In the commune

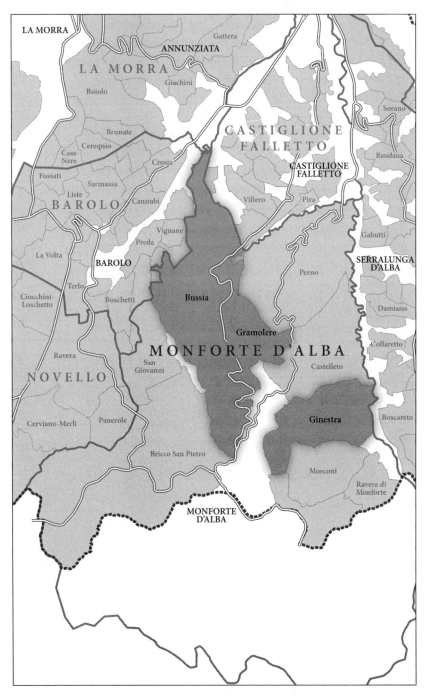

LA MORRA

ANNUNZIATA

Gattera

LA MORRA

Giachini

Boiolo

Sorano

Brunate

CASTIGLIONE
FALLETTO

Cerequio

Case
Nere

Crosia

Baudana

Fossati

Sarmassa

CASTIGLIONE
FALLETTO

Liste

BAROLO

Cannubi

Villero

Pira

Vignane

Gabutti

Preda

La Volta

BAROLO

SERRALUNGA
D'ALBA

Terlo

Perno

Ciocchini-
Loschetto

Boschetti

Bussia

Damiano

Gramolere

MONFORTE D'ALBA

Collaretto

Ravera

San
Giovanni

Castelletto

NOVELLO

Ginestra

Boscareto

Cerviano-Merli

Panerole

Bricco San Pietro

Mosconi

Ravera di
Monforte

MONFORTE
D'ALBA

MAP 6. Monforte d'Alba.

of Monforte d'Alba, soils can be classified as Castiglione di Falletto units and La Morra units. Castiglione di Falletto units originate from Arenarie [sandstone] di Diano d'Alba and are characterized by a higher presence of sand when compared to other areas," explains Dolzan. The region's soil map of the entire Barolo growing zone, which demonstrates the results of the study headed by Dr. Moreno Soster, shows that Monforte has a large section of Castiglione Falletto units (mostly around the Pian Polvere area), La Morra units dispersed throughout, and in the area considered the classic part of Bussia (before the latter was recently expanded), Barolo units—composed of calcareous marls interspersed with layers of sandstone in the subsoils.

Monforte d'Alba has a number of prime vineyard areas, and those with the best growing conditions have been noted for decades including historical names such as Pianpolvere, Pugnane, Dardi, Bussia, Munie, and S. Stefano di Perno. However, it has to be noted that the commune has been rightly criticized for its poor effort to officially map out the town's vineyard boundaries, and it did not protect many of Monforte's historical growing zones. In what can only be described as the commune's botched—if not downright butchered —attempt at delimiting its famed crus, the whole purpose of which was ostensibly to stop the progressive expansion of the most lauded vineyard areas, Monforte did just the opposite. Rather than delineate the numerous smaller vineyard areas, the town instead consolidated most of them into far fewer, but massively expanded areas, with what is now an enormous Bussia area being the prime example of Monforte's widely questioned attempt at delimiting its Barolo crus.

Critics of Monforte's geographic mentions lament that by merging many of the smaller vineyards into the now-oversized official areas, namely, Bussia and Perno, Monforte has erased historical names such as Pianpolvere, Pugnane, Munie, and S. Stefano from the official map of Barolo. Yet producers in the heart of Bussia say they are the real victims, now that their specific growing area has been so blown out of proportion. Estates located in Bussia's classic area (widely considered to be a stretch of vineyards situated between what used to be called Bussia Soprana and Bussia Sottana) tell me that during the numerous and contentious town meetings held over creating official vineyard perimeters, they don't recall any producers fighting to delimit their small vineyard areas or arguing to be excluded from the legendary Bussia area.

On the contrary, according to Bussia's historic growers and producers—who decline to go on record since this remains an almost explosive issue—all the producers involved wanted their vineyards to be part of Bussia because of the latter's undeniable name recognition among Barolo lovers. And since the main road in this part of Monforte d'Alba is called Località Bussia, town officials sanctioned Bussia's amplification to accommodate everyone with a Bussia address, even if Bussia's road extended way beyond the classic viticultural area. Bussia isn't the only expanded area authorized by Monforte d'Alba; Perno is another area and has swallowed up legendary names such as S. Stefano.

Despite the town's oversimplified and homogenized geographic mentions, Monforte d'Alba's producers do have options that allow them to use the names of more specific vineyard areas that have been wiped from the official Barolo map. One of these is establishing trademarks, although these names had to have been registered before 2009. To this end, some producers wisely trademarked their specific vineyard names, such as Poderi Aldo Conterno's Bussia Colonello and Romirasco. And all producers in Barolo and Barbaresco can elect to make a vineyard-specific wine from within a larger geographic mention. To do so the vineyard has to be part of a recognized register that lists all the smaller vineyard names. On top of the official geographic mention, producers then add the name of their recognized vineyard on the label after the term *Vigna*, like Fontanafredda's Barolo Vigna La Rosa, for example. But there is a catch: for vineyard-specific Barolos the denomination's regulations require that producers further reduce yields by 10 percent, making this a more costly option, and one that for the moment most producers are not taking advantage of.

Giacomo Conterno

Loc. Ornati
12065 Monforte d'Alba (CN)
Tel. +39 0173 78221
www.conterno.it

The stately wrought-iron gate at the entrance to Giacomo Conterno's modern winery in Monforte d'Alba already suggests the grandeur of the estate's celebrated wines aging inside, including Barolo Cascina Francia and the family's crown jewel, Monfortino. Monfortino is not simply one of the best Barolos, whose name alone can make die-hard Barolo fans weak in the knees; it is one of the finest wines in the world. Although it is named after the family's hometown, for the past four decades the grapes that go into Monfortino actually come from the Francia vineyard in Serralunga.

FIGURE 16. Roberto Conterno of Giacomo Conterno. Roberto Conterno now runs the firm behind one of the most celebrated bottlings from the Langhe, if not all of Italy: Barolo Riserva "Monfortino." The wine actually hails from a selection of the best grapes in the family's Francia vineyard in Serralunga. Photograph by Paolo Tenti.

The Conternos have been making wine in the Barolo area since the early 1900s, and like nearly all Barolo firms back then the family bought grapes from local growers, made wine, and sold it in bulk. Then, in the 1920s, young Giacomo Conterno helped usher Barolo into the modern age by creating and bottling a Barolo Riserva destined for lengthy aging. Giacomo took over the family business at about this same time, and at his now eponymously named winery continued making his Barolo Riserva, which he renamed Monfortino in honor of his home village of Monforte d'Alba. Between the late 1950s and early 1960s, Giacomo passed the reins to his two sons, Giovanni and Aldo, who had worked alongside their father for years. The brothers went their separate ways in 1969, with Giovanni keeping the family's Giacomo Conterno business and name.

Giovanni continued his father's custom of purchasing only top-quality grapes and crafting heroic Barolos using staunchly traditional methods. These practices included leaving the just fermented wine in contact with the skins for an extended maceration period to extract color, complexity, and above all the tannic backbone that helps give Monfortino its age-worthy structure. Like his father, Giovanni aged his Barolos for several years in large, old casks.

By the early 1970s, Giovanni realized high-quality grapes were destined to become scarce as a number of growers began producing their own wines rather than sell grapes, so he began scouting for just the right vineyard that would guarantee his wine's quality. He set his sites on Serralunga—the village famed for its long-lived and structured Barolos—and in 1974 purchased Cascina Francia. Thanks to this vineyard's southwest exposures and high altitudes of between 370 and 420 meters (1,214 and 1,378 feet) above sea level and its calcareous soils layered with sandstone, it proved ideal for producing age-worthy Barolos of stunning depth and uncommon complexity.

When Giovanni passed away in 2004, his son Roberto, working full-time at the winery since 1988, took charge and has remained faithful to his father's philosophy of producing traditional Barolos that often need thirty years or more to reach full maturity. Roberto, whom I've interviewed several times over the years, is always very guarded in his responses and gives the strong impression he'd much rather be in the cellars or in the vineyards, attending to the business of winemaking instead of being interviewed. Yet like his Barolos, which are initially closed, with time, Roberto opens up.

Unlike many scions of Italian winemaking families who decide to break with the customs of their fathers, Roberto, now in his mid-forties, has remained faithful to his father and grandfather's winemaking philosophy. He continues to employ long maceration times for Barolo and the Riserva, followed by years of aging in large casks—far longer than the mandatory aging requirements stipulated by production codes.

Roberto, however, has made his own impact on the Conterno legacy. "Basically I make wine the same way my father did," explains Roberto, adding that the changes he has made over the years haven't modified the fundamental character of the firm's wines. Such changes include abandoning stainless steel and fermenting in conical wooden vats, which Roberto feels better maintain the steady, high temperatures required for the long maceration process (fermenting in wood is also known to help maintain color thanks to micro-oxygenation). About fifteen years ago Roberto also introduced large, neutral Austrian casks for aging, which he uses alongside traditional Slavonian casks.

But as Roberto is quick to point out, when you have outstanding raw material and generations of winemaking experience at your back, things like fermenting vessels are mere details. "People often lose sight of what's really important. My grandfather and father made extraordinary wines, first fermenting in wood, then cement, then stainless steel, and now I'm fermenting in wood. Give me great grapes and I'll make great wine, even if I only had to ferment in a plastic container," Roberto told me during an interview in 2012. It goes without saying that Roberto has always shunned any radical changes, refusing to use barriques or rotary fermenters, which would drastically change his wines.

Like his father, Roberto makes Barolo Cascina Francia, which he ages for about four years, and in exceptional vintages, he makes Barolo Riserva Monfortino, which is aged on average for seven years. Roberto is quick to point out that aging times can vary somewhat depending on the vintage. Grapes for both wines hail from the Cascina Francia vineyard, but the Monfortino comes from a selection of the best grapes. Both wines boast Cascina Francias's hallmark licorice notes as well as quintessential Barolo sensations of cherry, earth, mineral, and hints of leather. Conterno also makes an outstanding, mouthwatering Barbera from Barbera vines planted in Cascina Francia.

In 2008, Roberto acquired a vineyard on the celebrated Cerretta hill in Serralunga. Conterno's first Cerretta Barolo will be from the 2010 vintage, and even though there is no official debut date, it is already one of the most highly anticipated new Italian releases ever.

Production

Total surface area: N/A
Barolo: N/A

Barolo Cascina Francia. Cascina Francia is everything a Barolo should be: restrained power, depth, and finesse. The 2008 was still very young when I tried it in late 2012, with vibrant cherry sensations, slate, licorice, and mineral notes balanced with fine but bracing tannins. A classic Barolo that needs time to develop complexity. Best 2016 to 2038.

Barolo Riserva Monfortino. Monfortino is in a league of its own, with dazzling complexity and intensity accompanied by an astonishing depth of flavors, all impeccably balanced in an age-worthy structure. The 2005, tasted in late 2012, has a quintessential Barolo fragrance of dark cherry, leather, truffle, and licorice, all of which carry over to the palate along with mint and menthol notes. Stunning depth of flavors, but still young with ripe, teeth-coating tannins. Best 2020 to 2040.

Poderi Aldo Conterno

Località Bussia 48
12065 Monforte d'Alba (CN)
Tel. +39 0173 78150
www.poderialdoconterno.com
info@poderialdoconterno.it

Aldo Conterno, who passed away in 2012 and was the brother of the above-mentioned Giovanni Conterno, was a pioneer of modern-day Barolo and one of the denomination's most revered protagonists for over five decades. He played a crucial role in Barolo's rebirth as a world-class wine and helped transform Barolo from a harshly tannic wine needing decades to soften into one of Italy's most sought-after bottlings. In the process, he inspired an entire generation of Piedmont winemakers.

Conterno descended from generations of Barolo producers. His father was the renowned Barolista Giacomo Conterno, one of the denomination's twentieth-century trailblazers, who started bottling the family's Barolo Riserva in 1920, heralding the birth of Monfortino, arguably Barolo's most iconic wine. In 1961 Giacomo handed the family winery over to his sons Giovanni and Aldo, but in 1969 the two brothers decided to separate. Besides philosophical differences with his sibling over Barolo production, Aldo had long nurtured a dream to have his own winery. That same year Aldo created his own estate, Poderi Aldo Conterno, located in the magnificent Bussia hills in Monforte d'Alba. To ensure a consistent supply of high-quality grapes, he also began acquiring top vineyards at a time when most Barolo producers were still purchasing their grapes from a large network of local growers.

One of the secrets of Conterno's success, besides owning prime vineyards, was his open-mindedness and outgoing nature—qualities few other Barolo producers from his generation possessed and traits that blossomed when Aldo moved from the Langhe hills to California in the 1950s to help his uncle establish a winery in Napa Valley. During his time in America, Aldo opted to complete his mandatory Italian military service in the U.S. Army and served during the Korean War. By the time he got out, his uncle had abandoned the winery venture, and Aldo eventually returned to Piedmont. Despite the crippling economic hardships in rural Italy during this period, Conterno's five years abroad left him with a spirit for innovation along with a desire to experiment with methods that would help revamp Barolo and attract wine lovers from around the world.

FIGURE 17. Giacomo Conterno of Poderi Aldo Conterno. Founded by Aldo Conterno, whose father established the Giacomo Conterno winery, this winery possesses some of the most coveted crus in all of Barolo from the best sections of Bussia. Its Riserva Gran Bussia is one of the most sought-after Barolos. Photograph by Paolo Tenti.

Once on his own, Aldo balanced tradition with new techniques in an effort to make friendlier Barolos that still maintained the wine's essential character and personality. By the 1970s, in his quest to minimize Barolo's massive tannins and preserve primary fruit sensations, Conterno had already reduced the marathon fermentation and maceration times that were once customary for Barolo, and he also abandoned the submerged-cap method in favor of pumping over—radical decisions for the times. His willingness to try new techniques while also respecting fundamental traditions—including his dedication to aging Barolo in large Slavonian casks, insisting that the vanilla and spice sensations imparted by new barriques had no place in Barolo— defied the simplistic categories of "traditionalist" and "modernist." From his stately winery crowning the Bussia hills, Aldo Conterno made his celebrated single-vineyard Barolos—Romirasco, Cicala and Colonello—and in outstanding vintages Granbussia Riserva, an assembly of the best grapes in all three vineyards and one of Piedmont's cult Barolos.

These days Aldo's grown sons, Franco, Stefano, and the ever affable Giacomo, run the winery after years of working alongside their father, and they have no intention of making any radical changes. Nor should they: these are polished versions of classic Barolos that beautifully express Nebbiolo purity and the varied terroirs of their vineyards. According to Giacomo, who tends the vineyards, since 1995 the firm has stopped using any industrial fertilizers or systemic chemical products against insects or diseases. Over the years the estate has replanted its Nebbiolo from the offspring of estate vines selected by careful massal selection. The firm selects only the very best of their grapes for their celebrated bottlings, and despite having enough fruit to produce about 200,000 bottles on average they bottle less than half this amount, about 80,000 bottles total. Fermentation is carried out exclusively with wild yeasts, and the wines are not filtered or fined.

Production

Total surface area: 25 ha (61.7 acres)
Barolo: 12 ha (29.6 acres), 35,000 bottles

Barolo/Barolo Bussia.   From 2004 to 2008, Aldo Conterno produced a straight Barolo blended from its various Bussia vineyards and from its holdings in the Barolo township. After a mudslide destroyed its vineyards in Barolo, however, starting with the 2009 vintage, the firm has made Barolo Bussia, a blend of the various estate-owned vineyards in Bussia from plants averaging fifty years old. Soils are calcareous marls layered with sandy deposits, and average altitude is 380 meters (1,247 feet) above sea level. The 2008 offers a lovely fragrance of dark fruit and spice with dense black fruit and white pepper flavors lifted by vibrant acidity. Long licorice finish. Classic and approachable but will also age gracefully. Drink 2016 to 2028.

Aldo Conterno's cru bottlings all hail from vineyards that average 400 meters (1,312 feet) above sea level and enjoy southern and southwestern exposures. Plant age for these bottlings averages fifty-five years old, and all are fermented in steel and aged in 25-hectoliter Slavonian casks for twenty-nine months.

Barolo Bussia Colonello.   Made from a vineyard that according to local legend was named after a colonel in Napoleon's army who bought the hillside in 1797 because he loved wines produced from its grapes. Soils in this celebrated parcel are sandy with magnesium. This is the most elegant and floral of the firm's single-vineyard bottlings. The 2008—clocking in at an undetectable

15 percent alcohol—offered floral aromas, lush dark fruit, and balsamic notes of leather and eucalyptus. Elegant with great structure and bracing but fine tannins. Best 2016 to 2038.

Barolo Bussia Cicala.   Made from the eponymous vineyard where the calcareous soil also contains a higher than usual amount of iron, this is a spicy and structured Barolo with rich fruit. The 2008 was still a bit closed in 2012, but is a powerful Barolo with spice, leather, earth, and truffle sensations that seamlessly support the 15 percent alcohol. Fantastic length. Best 2018 to 2040.

Barolo Romirasco.   This has always been one of the most coveted crus in Barolodom, and Aldo had long leased the vineyard before the family that owned it finally sold it to him in 1982. Romirasco combines the different soils found in Colonello and Cicala, producing a powerful Barolo of great depth. The superb 2010 delivers underbrush, leather, violet, black cherry, sage, spice, and menthol sensations. Still young, tightly-knit, and vibrant with brooding tannins. Give this time to fully develop. Drink 2020 to 2040.

Barolo Riserva Gran Bussia.   In exceptional years, Aldo Conterno makes a Riserva by blending the best grapes from all three of its Bussia vineyards in varying proportions: 70 percent from Romirasco, 15 percent from Cicala, and 15 percent from Colonello. Until 2005, the grapes from each vineyard were vinified separately, and fermentation and total skin maceration lasted about five weeks. But starting with 2005, the firm has reverted to the grand tradition of blended Barolos. To this end, the grapes are now vinified all together for Gran Bussia: fermentation takes place in wooden vats with no temperature control, and total maceration time lasts an average of sixty days. This is undoubtedly one of the truly great Barolos, and the 2005, tasted in 2012, expresses all the beauty, complexity, and depth of the classic Barolo: rose, leather, spice, and mineral with layers of depth and complexity. A gripping, gorgeous wine. Best 2015 to 2030.

Elio Grasso

Località Ginestra 40
12065 Monforte d'Alba (CN)
Tel. +39 0173 78491
www.eliograsso.it
info@eliograsso.it

FIGURE 18. Elio Grasso. Elio Grasso's richly textured Barolos, from prime vineyards like Ginestra and Gavarini, helped elevate Monforte to its current prestige. From the family's stunning winery, one has magnificent views of Serralunga and the distant Alps. Photograph by Paolo Tenti.

At their stunning winery with its breathtaking views of Serralunga's castle and the distant Alps, Elio and Marina Grasso and their son Gianluca make gorgeous, polished and richly textured Barolos that have helped elevate Monforte d'Alba to its current prestige. The family is the sole owner of one of the best vineyards in the township, Gavarini, and also owns prime vineyards in Ginestra. The vineyards' ideal growing conditions include perfect southern exposures and an average altitude of 330 meters (1,083 feet) above sea level. According to Marina, the thick woods crowning the hillside—a rarity in the Langhe, where trees and woods have been ripped up to make way for more lucrative vineyards—also play a key role in producing quality Barolo: "The woods not only provide a healthy ecosystem, but they protect our vineyards from violent storms and hail that sometimes hit this area."

The Grasso family knows something about these hailstorms, and while the woods generally offer great protection, in the past the estate has been devastated by hail, as Elio's grandfather described in detail in 1885. Scrawled on the inside of a cabinet door that Marina and Elio preserve to show visitors just how difficult life once was in the Langhe, Gioanni [sic] Grasso wrote in

Italian, "1885, 13 April: the hail fell for 47 minutes and has stripped every single plant and vine of leaves. There will be no harvests this year."

Elio himself remembers how tough times were when he was growing up in postwar Italy, with only a single fireplace for heat in the large house and no running water. His father, a grape grower, struggled to give his children a better life, and when Elio was sent to a boarding high school in Turin, his father told him to study hard and added: "Don't come back here. Don't be a grape grower." Elio went on to university and had a successful career in banking. Yet he and his wife, Marina, a native of Turin, came to the farm in Monforte on weekends and in the summer, and in 1978 Elio could no longer resist the countryside and vineyards. "I am first and foremost a farmer—a *contadino*," Elio says today. "And even though society made my father and grandfather ashamed to be growers, I'm proud to be the son of *contadini* and to be one myself."

And well he should be: over the years Elio has restructured the estate and built a state-of-the-art winery. He and son Gianluca tend the manicured vineyards and make the wines with the guidance of consultant enologist Piero Ballario. The approach in the cellars is a mix of cutting-edge technology and tradition that yields dazzling Barolos of breeding and class. The firm ferments all Barolos in temperature-controlled steel tanks with skin contact lasting another twenty-five to thirty days postfermentation. The single-vineyard Barolos are aged in 25-hectoliter Slavonian casks for thirty months, while the Riserva is aged for forty months in new 228-liter barriques. The wines are not filtered or fined.

Production

Total surface area: 30 ha (74 acres)
Barolo: 10 ha (25 acres), 33,000 bottles

Barolo Gavarini Chiniera. Located between 320 and 360 meters (1,050 and 1,181 feet) above sea level, Chiniera has calcareous and slightly sandy soil, yielding an exquisite, floral Barolo of remarkable finesse. The 2008 offers lovely rose, cherry, and spice aromas that carry over to the palate. Still youthful but extremely elegant and fresh with firm but fine tannins. Great depth and wonderful length. Drink 2017 to 2033.

Barolo Ginestra Casa Matè. Ginestra's vineyards are situated between 300 and 350 meters (984 and 1,148 feet) above sea level, and the calcareous soil has more clay than Gavarini, producing wines with more structure and tannic backbone. The 2010 is a classic Barolo that beautifully expresses this outstanding vintage. Vibrant and structured, it boasts crushed black cherry, leather, tar, spice, herbs, and balsamic notes alongside gripping energy. It's still young, so hold for more complexity. Drink 2020 to 2040.

Barolo Riserva Runcot.　In outstanding vintages Elio Grasso also produces a Riserva from the Runcot vineyard in the larger Gavarini cru. This is aged between forty and forty-three months in 228-liter French barriques and seamlessly combines power and grace. The 2006 Riserva opens up to reveal classic Nebbiolo fragrance of truffle, leather, rose petal, and tar. Ripe but restrained fruit accompanied by a whisper of oak that in no way interferes with the beauty of Nebbiolo. Big, ripe tannins and a long finish. Compelling and complex. Drink 2016 to 2036.

Franco Conterno

Loc. Bussia 62
12065 Monforte d'Alba (CN)
Tel. +39 0173 78627
www.francoconterno.it
infor@francoconterno.it

Franco Conterno's quintessential Barolos are one of Piedmont's best-kept secrets, but I doubt for very long. The winery makes solid, serious Barolos that lovers of classic Nebbiolo would love to get their hands on.

Once again, the main factor behind these solid Barolos is superior vineyards. The sprawling Franco Conterno winery and farm, the latter known locally as Sciulun, is immersed in an amphitheater in the Munie cru, which borders what used to be the hallowed Bussia Sottana district. Many would argue, including the Conternos, that Munie, long known for its elegant and perfumed Barolos, has always been a part of the classic Bussia area. Regardless of its history, Munie—the word in the local dialect for "monks," as monks used to run what is now the Bofani estate owned by Batasiolo—is now officially part of Bussia. The Conterno's winery itself marks the very edge of the Monforte d'Alba municipality and lies on the border with Castiglione Falletto, and a portion of the surrounding vineyards, including part of the firm's Pugnane holdings—defined as a first category vineyard area by Lorenzo Fantini—are actually in Castiglione Falletto. This area is the nucleus of the family's estate, and according to Daniele Conterno, Franco's son, benefits from a unique microclimate: high hills protect from cold and storms, perfect exposure keeps vines warm and bathed in sunlight, while frequent breezes keep humidity and fungus diseases at bay. All these conditions conspire to encourage ideal ripening. The family also has Barolo vineyards in Novello.

The family relies on integrated vineyard management practices and since 2000 hasn't used chemical herbicides, turning and working the soil instead. In 2008, they began planting beans and clover between the rows, and rely on leaf thinning to ensure bunches receive adequate ventilation to discourage fungus, and they also perform a green harvest to control yields. In the cellars, Franco Conterno and his sons Andrea and Daniele use a mix of technology. All the Barolos are fermented with wild yeasts in rotary fermenters, while the Riservas are fermented in open wooden vats. Barolo ages predominantly in Slavonian casks (Barolo Petrin is also aged in a small percentage of French casks) ranging in size from 15 to 48 hectoliters.

Production

Total surface area: 15 ha (37 acres)

Barolo: 6.8 ha (17 acres), 37,000 bottles

Barolo Bussia Pugnane. With its southwest exposures and calcareous, sandy soil, this is elegant, approachable, and classic. The 2008 has an earthy nose with leather and balsamic notes accompanied by rose and spice. Gorgeous creamy raspberry and spice flavors balanced by fine tannins and bright acidity. Lovely *tipicità*. Very tannic and tight with a long finish. Best 2014 to 2028.

Barolo Bussia Munie. Made from the Munie vineyard where vines range between 280 and 320 meters (919 and 1,050 feet) above sea level. The predominantly calcareous clay soil and advanced plant age of forty-five years generates concentrated flavors and structure. The 2008 delivers rose, leather, flint, and spice aromas with succulent but restrained cherry and spice flavors. Dusty tannins and fresh acidity. A textbook Barolo but still young. Best 2016 to 2033.

Barolo Riserva "Sette7anni" 2004. Made only in outstanding vintages from Nebbiolo from Bussia Munie, Pugnane e Panerole, this is aged for seven years in traditional botti. The 2004, tasted in 2012, is a gripping, stunning old school Barolo that is also polished enough to appeal even to uninitiated palates. It has an intense perfume of leather, rose, violet, truffle, and clove alongside a palate of succulent sour cherry, raspberry, and balsamic herbs with great depth and velvety tannins. A little-known gem just waiting to be discovered by the world's Barolophiles, this will continue to develop complexity for years. Drink through 2034.

Giacomo Fenocchio

Loc. Bussia 72
12065 Monforte d'Alba (CN)
Tel. +39 0173 78675
www.giacomofenocchio.com
info@giacomofenocchio.com

My visit in 2012 to this cult winery offered a real insight into how hard the Langhe's small winemakers work: while he was showing me the cellars, current owner Claudio Fenocchio received several calls from his field hands in the vineyards asking for advice, his cellar master wanted him to taste the Arneis before sending the sample off to the Consorzio for the DOCG tasting panel, and halfway through our tour and interview, two large trucks arrived simultaneously and without warning to pick up deliveries for his importers in northern Europe. Claudio even had to load the trucks himself, since loading the trucks "is not part of the drivers' job descriptions." I was exhausted just watching him and shocked when he said this was actually "an easy day." And lest I forget, he also had to tend to all the usual winemaking practices in the cellars.

Despite wearing many hats, Claudio, who was born in the heart of what the locals still refer to as the Bussia Sottana district (in other words, part of the true Bussia) is a master at crafting classic Barolos that beautifully express their pedigree. Not only does he have prime vineyards in the heart of classic Bussia, in Villero, and on the Cannubi hillside, but his noninterventionist approach in the cellars ensures that their individual terroirs shine through.

From the terrace of his house and cellars on top of the hill overlooking his Bussia Sottana vineyards, Claudio demonstrates how small the entire Barolo growing zone really is: two hills over to the left of his Bussia vineyards is Cannubi, while on the right, on the next hill over, is Villero. "The altitudes for all are pretty much the same—300 meters [984 feet] above sea level for Bussia and Villero and 280 meters [919 feet] for our vineyards in Cannubi.

FIGURE 19. Claudio Fenocchio of Giacomo Fenocchio. The Giacomo
Fenocchio winery is located in the heart of what used to be called Bussia
Sottana—part of the classic Bussia zone. From these vineyards as well
as holdings in Villero and on the Cannubi hillside, the firm makes delicious Barolos boasting complexity and Nebbiolo purity. Photograph
by Paolo Tenti.

While Bussia and Villero both have Serravallian soil rich in limestone and
iron, for some reason Bussia Barolo always demonstrates more minerality.
Cannubi on the other hand has Tortonian marls with more sand," says
Claudio.

In the cellars, Claudio keeps winemaking simple and traditional: fermentation occurs spontaneously with wild yeasts in steel tanks for Barolo, and in
wooden vats for the Riserva. He then ages his wines in 35- and 70-hectoliter
Slavonian casks.

Production

Total surface area: 15 ha (37 acres)

Barolo: 7 ha (17 acres), 39,000 bottles

Barolo Bussia.   Made in the classic Bussia area with southern and south-western exposures from thirty-year-old vines. The 2006 is gorgeous, with intense cherry, spice, and licorice notes. Great depth. Still very young and needs time to develop complexity. Drink 2016 to 2036. The 2008 delivers structure and grace, with sour cherry, white pepper, cinnamon, spice, and mineral sensations. Great length, depth, and beautifully balanced. Drink 2015 to 2033. The 2009 is forward and delicious, and is already developing some complexity. Drink through 2019. The 2010, which Claudio compares to the wonderful 2001 vintage, delivers floral, incense, bright red berry, graphite, mineral, and licorice sensations alongside bracing tannins and lively acidity. It has a classic structure for lengthy aging and should develop layers of complexity over time. Drink 2020 to 2035.

Barolo Villero.   Thirty-year-old vines and southwest exposures generate concentrated flavors. The 2006 boasts enticing floral and truffle bouquet, succulent fruit flavors. Very elegant and young, with a long licorice close. Drink through 2031. The 2008 has a sweet nose of rose and strawberry jam that carries over to the palate with sour cherry and spice. Fresh, and still very tannic, but this should open up beautifully. Drink 2016 to 2028. The 2009 has remarkable energy and balance for the vintage, with layers of intense cherry, raspberry, and spice. Already approachable. Drink now through 2024. The 2010 is a hallmark Barolo with black cherry, white pepper, mineral, and balsamic sensations alongside youthful, brooding tannins that need time to tame. Drink 2020 to 2035.

Cannubi.   Made from forty-year-old vines kept fresh with southeast exposures in the Cannubi Boschis part of the hillside. The 2008 is exquisite with an intensely floral and balsamic fragrance, wild cherry, spice, and mineral flavors of stunning purity and balance. Hallmark Barolo. Drink 2016 to 2033. Even in difficult vintages this winery produces outstanding Barolos: the 2009 Cannubi has aromas of roses and irises along with berries and Alpine herbs. The palate offers a core of rich black cherry, white pepper, and clove, along with firm but elegant tannins. Drink 2015 to 2024. The 2010 is gorgeous, with elegant floral aromas and vibrant red berry fruit accented with spice and mineral alongside bright acidity and firm but fine tannins. It has structure, finesse, and impeccable balance. Drink 2020 to 2035.

Barolo Bussia 90di.   To extract all the complexity and perfume from Bussia, starting with the 2008 vintage, Claudio makes a Barolo Bussia selection that slowly ferments in contact with the skins followed by extended maceration for a total of ninety days in steel. Afterward, the wine rests for another six months in steel vats before aging in Slavonian casks for "as many years as it takes." The 2008, released in 2013, is a gorgeous, fascinating wine. It boasts layers of berry, spice, truffle, leather, and balsamic sensations along with depth you can get lost in. The 2010 barrel sample, tasted in 2012, already shows mesmerizing depth and complexity and will be a wine for the ages. Tasted again from the barrel in 2014, this has developed an even greater depth of flavors, including concentrated red berry fruit, licorice, and mineral. It already has wonderful balance and breeding.

1978 Barolo. Tasted in 2013, this superb Barolo, made by Claudio's father from one of the greatest vintages in the Langhe, was shockingly youthful. In fact, the 1978s, notoriously closed, are just now beginning to open up, but these are wines to will down to the kids, maybe even the grandkids. This showed black cherry, carob, zabaglione, and licorice with hints of leather and tar. Still fresh acidity and surprisingly strong-willed tannins. One of my most memorable Barolos, for sure.

Attilio Ghisolfi

Loc. Bussia 27
12065 Monforte d'Alba (CN)
Tel. +39 0173 78345
www.ghisolfi.com
ghisolfi@ghisolfi.com

Yet another of Monforte d'Alba's little-known treasures that flies under the radar of the media, Attilio Ghilsolfi's winery produces outstanding Barolos of finesse and depth.

Gianmarco Ghisolfi, a trained agronomist and enologist, took over the winery in 1988 and that same year began bottling the firm's Barolos, which had been produced already for three generations but until then had always been sold in bulk. All of the firm's vineyards are in Monforte, in the Visette district. Visette, now officially incorporated into Bussia, has long been known for its quality grapes, and according to Gianmarco, documents from the twelfth century refer to the cultivation of Nebbiolo in Visette, which again according to Ghisolfi, is a derivative of *vis*—a term in the local dialect for *vite,* or "grapevine." Regardless of its ancient history, Visette, running parallel to the ridge of Pianpolvere, has ideal growing conditions that include southern and southwestern exposures and near-perfect altitudes of 350 meters (1,148 feet) above sea level that allow for day and night temperature changes that prolong the growing season and create complex aromas.

Ghisolfi is a firm believer in massal selection after having mixed results with purchasing commercial Nebbiolo plants from various grapevine nurseries. "I had perfect results with one nursery, but then bought the same clones from another nursery and many of the plants were sick and failed," says Gianmarco, adding that he feels that the dreaded *flavascenza dorata,* or grapevine yellows, was spread by infected plants sold by some nurseries. He is also not a fan of some of the newer clones. "The need for grape thinning was born in the 1990s, when vineyards were planted with vines purchased from the nurseries, which in my opinion were very vigorous clones," says Ghisolfi. In his oldest Visette vineyard, called Fantini, Gianmarco has carried out a massal selection of his best plants and replaces vines that have died with the offspring of these mother vines from his own genetic stock. He has also done this to a small extent in Visette. As can be imagined, Ghisolfi reveres his older vines, and plant age for his Barolo Bricco Visette and the Riserva ranges from twenty to sixty-four years old. To keep vines healthy, the firm uses only organic fertilizer and rather than herbicides, mechanically turns the soil instead. To combat fungus diseases, Ghisolfi treats vines with the traditional copper and sulfur mix.

Gianmarco mixes things up in the cellars, using various types of vats for fermenting as well as different-sized barrels for aging. He uses only wild yeasts for fermentation, and also ferments about 40 percent of his Barolo production in rotary fermenters. "Rotary fermenters permit me to take away the seeds right away and extract finer, softer tannins," says Gianmarco. He also uses short, wide steel vats that keep the cap softer and less compact, facilitating pump-overs and complete fermentation. Aging takes place in 15- to 50-hectoliter Slavonian casks for Barolo Bussia, in the same botti as well as a small portion of used barriques for Bricco Visette, and in tonneaux and casks for Riserva Fantini.

Production

Total surface area: 6.5 ha (16 acres)
Barolo: 3.5 ha (9 acres), 20,900 bottles

Barolo Bussia. This is made with the firm's youngest vines—between five and fifteen years old—situated in the Visette microzone. The Barolo Bussia is aged for three years exclusively in large 25-, 30-, and 50-hectoliter casks. The 2008 offers smoky, earthy aromas of flint and underbrush with a hint of rose alongside a lovely cherry palate with a hint of mineral. Very refined and approachable. Drink through 2023.

Barolo Bricco Visette. Plant age ranges from twenty to forty-five years old, generating great depth and structure. This is aged for two and a half years in wood; 80 percent in large 25- and 30-hectoliter casks, 20 percent in used barriques averaging five to six-years old. The 2006 is exquisite with an intense floral-leather perfume and a classic palate of cherry and pipe tobacco with notable mineral notes. Archetypical Barolo of structure and complexity. Drink through 2031. The 2008 was still a bit closed in 2012, but showed classic Nebbiolo sensations of creamy wild cherry, spice, and mineral accompanied by firm but ripe tannins and racy acidity. Drink 2016 to 2028.

Barolo Riserva Fantini. In outstanding years, Ghisolfi makes a Barolo Riserva from the estate's oldest vines that average between fifty and sixty-five years old and are located in the Fantini vineyard in the larger Visette area. According to Gianmarco, these old vines are actually the highly rare Rosé, which until recently was thought to be a clone or subvariety of Nebbiolo, although researchers now say it is a distinct grape variety that is, however, a close relative of Nebbiolo. The Fantini vineyard also has sandier soil than the rest of Visette, giving more elegance to its imposing structure. The firm ages its Riserva for one and a half years in tonneaux and three and a half years in 25-hectoliter casks. The 2006 is magnificent, with Barolo's classic rose, tar, and leather aromas and cherry, spice, and mineral flavors. Shows extraordinary depth and length. Still young and needs time to develop complexity but will age beautifully. Drink 2016 to 2036.

Principiano Ferdinando

Via Alba 47
12065 Monforte d'Alba (CN)
Tel. +39 0173 787158
www.ferdinandoprincipiano.it
info@ferdinandoprincipiano.it

Ferdinando Principiano is one of Italy's practicing advocates of the natural wine movement, although he admits his real priority is making good wine.

FIGURE 20. Ferdinando Principiano. Ferdinando Principiano is one of the early advocates of Italy's natural wine movement, although he says his only goal is to make good wine in the most natural way possible. And he has succeeded admirably. Photograph by Paolo Tenti.

"But if I can make good wine with more natural methods, all the better," says Principiano. He'd also like to see more research into *vini naturali,* and admits that many people these days are jumping into the marketing side of the natural wine movement, although he himself goes to extremes to limit as much as possible all chemicals and harmful products from his vineyards and cellars. To this end, he is trying to buy the woods near his vineyards in Serralunga so that they can continue to provide an invaluable ecosystem of predator insects and birds. The woods also act as life-giving lungs that keep the air clean and fresh.

Principiano uses no herbicides, but cuts and leaves the grass between the rows; he has even reduced tractor use, which he says can damage the ground. Like most natural wine supporters, Ferdinando has abolished chemical fertilizers and fungicides but at the same time tries to avoid the customary copper and sulfur solution against mold and fungus, which he feels is overused in the vineyards. "Copper is a heavy metal that can build up on the grapes, and this in turn can end up in our systems, while sulfur, which kills off natural yeasts, can also be harmful," declares Ferdinando.

To reduce and even eliminate copper sulfate treatments—which most producers say they prefer to chemical fungicides and which are allowed under organic farming regulations—Ferdinando is experimenting with treatments made from aloe, algae, and propolis, which he says is keeping his fifty-year-old plants in his Boscareto vineyard healthy. Because he drastically limits all treatments, Ferdinando is forced to keep yields remarkably low, about 30 to 40 quintals per hectare in Boscareto.

In the cellars, Ferdinando maintains his noninterventionist approach: fermentation is carried out with wild yeasts only and without temperature control, and he adds no sulfites during the winemaking process. He is also a fan of whole-cluster fermentation—but only under the right circumstances. Without de-stemming, Principiano crushes grapes from his forty-year-old vines in the Boscareto vineyard in Serralunga d'Alba, and then ferments with no selected yeasts. "You can ferment with whole clusters only when vineyards are treated naturally and have perfect growing conditions—including ideal exposure—because these vineyards can yield healthy, ripe grapes and bunches," says Principiano. "When stems are perfectly ripened, they add noble tannins to the wine, and also acidity. These are both natural wine preservatives, and help me make a wine that will age well over many years." His three Barolos are then aged in Slavonian casks. The results are impressive wines that are lightly colored and luminous, with layers of depth and personality. They are some of the most fascinating Barolos out there.

Production

Total surface area: 18 ha (44.5 acres)

Barolo: 7 ha (17 acres), 30,000 bottles

Barolo Serralunga.   Made from the younger vines in the Boscareto vineyard in Serralunga that are on average twenty years old, Ferdinando ages this for two years in 20- to 40-hectoliter Slavonian botti. The 2007 offers floral, truffle, and cherry sensations with hints of orange peel, and shows surprising freshness for the hot vintage. Layers of flavors and bracing tannins. Best 2014 to 2022.

Barolo Boscareto.   Located just below Conterno's lauded Cascina Francia, this is a prime vineyard site in Serralunga, just opposite Monforte d'Alba's Ravera and Ginestra crus. Boscareto is made from the vineyard's fifty-year-old vines situated at 350 meters (1,148 feet) above sea level. Sun exposure is ideal, south and southwest, and the soils are the village's typical calcareous marls. This is the firm's nod to the Barolos of yore: grapes are crushed by foot and maceration—with the perfectly ripened stems—takes place in wooden vats for up to sixty days with temperature control. The wine is then aged for four years in 25-hectoliter Slavonian casks. The 2006 is gorgeous, with extraordinary intensity and purity of flavors. Incredibly elegant expression of Serralunga, and a complex wine that will age for decades but is already enjoyable. Drink through 2031.

Barolo Ravera. Located in Monforte d'Alba, this very steep slope faces south and southeast and has combination soils of calcareous marls and clay layered with veins of sand. These are Ferdinando's oldest vines, planted in 1934, which generate concentrated flavors and remarkable depth. The 2008 possesses an intense bouquet of rose, leather, and smoke with a succulent wild cherry and spice palate. Structured but refined, this is an archetypical Barolo of class and breeding. Drink 2016 to 2038.

Other Wineries of Note

Gianfranco Alessandria
Rocche dei Manzoni
Domenico Clerico

See also Poderi Colla and Giuseppe Mascarello.

ELEVEN

Verduno, Grinzane Cavour, Roddi, and Diano d'Alba

OF THESE FOUR VILLAGES, grouped together to facilitate a single map of the northern and northeastern quadrants of the growing zone, Verduno is the clear star, although it too is not as well known as the core Barolo villages. Modern-day Barolo production has taken a back seat in these villages, although like Verduno, Grinzane Cavour's history is closely linked to the mid-nineteenth-century creation of Barolo. With the exception of Verduno, these townships possess fewer great and good vineyards when compared to the more celebrated Barolo communes, and their overall impact on volume is minimal; altogether these four areas produce just a little over 10 percent of the entire Barolo output. Verduno's output is by far the largest of the four communes, accounting for 4.97 percent of the denomination's total production. Verduno, on the northern edge of the Barolo growing zone, also makes more single-vineyard bottlings than the other three towns combined, thanks to its superb vineyard areas.

VERDUNO

I've long been a huge fan of the elegant, floral, and spicy Barolos of Verduno, and lately even more so, since the area appears to have suffered less in the recent bout of exceedingly hot and dry vintages: the 2007s and 2009s from Verduno generally possess freshness and a vibrant energy lacking in many other bottlings from the same vintages hailing from other villages. And even though Verduno Barolos tend to be approachable sooner than many other Barolos, they also have essential structures for lengthy aging, as was beautifully demonstrated by a magnificent 1982 Castello di Verduno La Massara, tried in December of 2011.

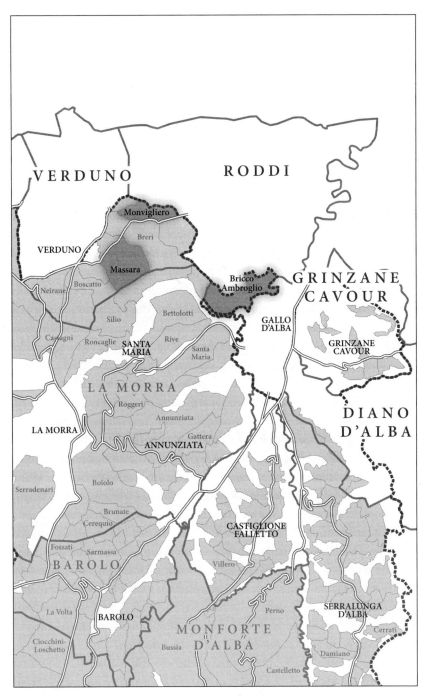

MAP 7. Verduno/Grinzane Cavour/Roddi/Diano d'Alba.

Yet most of Verduno's estates fly under the radar, and the village remains little known by all but the most passionate Barolophiles. One reason for this obscurity is the town's comparatively small output, which makes these Barolos harder to find. Another is that many of Verduno's small growers have always sold their grapes to bigger houses, including the Terre del Barolo cooperative cellars, resulting in few Barolos mentioning Verduno or its crus on their labels (although Terre del Barolo does produce a Barolo Monvigliero). While this has changed somewhat over the last decade as growers in the village have started making their own Barolos, even today only a small number of estates in Verduno make and bottle Barolos made entirely from Verduno grapes. And finally, seeing that Verduno doesn't produce the most-structured Barolos, the area has long been underappreciated—even disregarded—by many wine critics who prefer a more bombastic style.

But as more fine-wine lovers now look for wines of finesse and complexity as opposed to concentration and sheer power, the village is recovering some of the prestige it held in the nineteenth and early twentieth centuries, when it was a cradle of nascent Barolo production. In 1838 King Carlo Alberto, of the Royal House of Savoy, purchased the Castle of Verduno—more a grand mansion or manor house than a fortified castle—that had been rebuilt in the mid-1700s. The king—a huge fan of Barolo according to contemporary chronicles—hired General Paolo Francesco Staglieno to run the estate and above all the winery. Staglieno, the author of a very successful manual on winemaking, *Istruzione intorno al miglior modo di fare e conservare i vini in Piemonte*, published in 1835, is perhaps Italy's first consulting enologist, and even though he has often been overlooked by historians in favor of Oudart, these days many experts and Barolo makers alike now consider him to be the true Father of Barolo.

Another Barolo pioneer, Giovan Battista Burlotto, who eventually bought Castello di Verduno from the House of Savoy in 1909, helped cement Verduno's fundamental role in the initial rise of Barolo's fortunes when he bought a property—complete with a private chapel—in Verduno in the latter part of the nineteenth century. There he created a cellar and began vinifying Nebbiolo from Verduno's most famed vineyard, Monvigliero, as well as from the Cannubi hillside in Barolo. Unlike other wine producers of the day, Burlotto sold at least some of his wines in bottles rather than in barrels and demijohns only, and these early bottlings soon became a favorite with the royal court.

In 1929 Ferdinando Vignolo Lutati, in his treatise on Barolo, wrote that Verduno's soil was complex, formed partly in the Tortonian age and partly in the Messinian age, and this is confirmed by today's researchers. According to

Stefano Dolzan, head of Piedmont's Agrochemical Laboratory, Verduno is composed of Barolo Units, Serralunga Units, and Verduno Units. While the Barolo Units have calcareous clays and marls, and the Serralunga Units contain lightly colored calcareous soils and sandstone, the Verduno Units are unique in Barolo. "The Verduno Units differ from the others in terms of lithology. They are from the Messinian Gessoso-Solfifera Formation and have chalky deposits," says Dolzan. Yet according to Fabio Alessandria of leading Verduno estate Comm. G. B. Burlotto, "In all the deep plowing and earth turning we've done in our Verduno vineyards—namely, Monvigliero, Breri, Neirane, and Rocche Olmo—we've never seen any chalk. Some chalk fragments can be seen on the borders of a few vineyards, those facing Roero. But the zone richest in chalk is the Castagni hamlet, on the border with Verduno but situated in La Morra's territory."

While even educated opinions differ on the township's soil composition, most producers say it is Verduno's soil that imparts the spicy character to the village's Barolos, although once again there is no scientific evidence to support this claim. Yet the theory is backed up by the village's exclusive production of Pelaverga, made from the rare native grape of the same name that performs well only in Verduno. Very light and fruity, and joyfully drinkable young, Pelaverga is also intensely spicy.

The lookout point aptly known as Belvedere in the center of the sleepy village offers dazzling views of the township's wide-open and luminous vineyards, which mark the northern edge of the denomination, and it instantly becomes clear why Verduno, wedged between La Morra and Roddi, is known as the Sentinel of the Langhe. Of all Verduno's vineyards, the 11-hectare (27-acre) Monvigliero is the village's Grand Cru, and offers ideal growing conditions on par with the very best vineyard areas in all of Barolo. Monviglierio's best parcels are situated between 280 and 300 meters (919 and 984 feet) above sea level and have silty, calcareous clay and full southern exposures.

According to Professor Vicenzo Gerbi, who teaches enology at the University of Turin and who participated in the region's Barolo study published in 2000, "Monvigliero is the only cru in the denomination that faces fully south." While global warming has made many begin to doubt that perfect southern exposures and their now-soaring summertime temperatures are indeed the best, the Tanaro River just below Monvigliero generates cooling evening breezes that refresh the grapes and create the cru's signature aromatic intensity and complexity.

Other great vineyards in Verduno include Breri, Pisapola, and Massara.

Comm. G. B. Burlotto

Via Vittorio Emanuele 28
12060 Verduno (CN)
Tel. +39 0172 470122burlotto@burlotto.com
www.burlotto.com

Fabio Alessandria is the fifth generation to run this historic family winery that was founded in the mid-1800s by his maternal great-great-grandfather, Giovan Battista Burlotto, who was known as Commendatore, a title of distinction awarded by the king to civilians who showed particular merit in business. In the case of Giovan Battista Burlotto, his particular merit may very well have been his fundamental contribution to the early days of Barolo production.

In 1850, a young and self-made Giovan Battista Burlotto founded his winery in a sprawling country residence, complete with its own private chapel, which still houses the firm today. Unlike other nineteenth-century Barolo makers who purchased all their grapes from a number of small growers, by the late 1800s Burlotto had bought vineyards in Monvigliero and on the Cannubi hillside. And according to the estate's invoices and labels, he was already selling his Barolo in bottles, unheard-of at this time, when Barolo was sold in barrels or demijohns. By all accounts, Burlotto was also fanatical about the latest techniques in enology, and between 1886 and the first two decades of the twentieth century, he won thirty-two medals for his Barolo at international wine fairs.

Among the admirers of Burlotto's Barolo were members of the royal family, and the winery still sports its proudest achievements, "Supplier to the Savoy Royal Household" and "The Only Supplier to the Duke of Abruzzi's Arctic Expedition to the North Pole 1899," on its labels. Giovan Battista, who eventually bought the Castello di Verduno from King Carlo Alberto, passed his firm and holdings down through the generations, and besides making Barolo, the family also helped revive the nearly extinct Pelaverga vine and wine in the 1970s.

Today Fabio, a trained enologist, runs the firm along with his mother Marina Burlotto and his father Giuseppe, an agronomist. Together they make cult Barolos from estate grapes from their various holdings in Verduno and from a small parcel in Barolo. Fabio keeps things ultrasimple in the vineyards and the cellars, normally using wild yeasts but in the rare instances when alcohol levels start to climb too high, he uses BRL97, a strain of specific

FIGURE 21. Fabio Alessandria of Burlotto. Fabio Alessandro is the fifth generation to run this historic winery, which was founded by his great-great-grandfather Giovan Battista Burlotto in the mid-1800s. The firm's flagship Barolo, Monvigliero, shows breathtaking elegance. Photograph by Paolo Tenti.

Barolo yeasts created by the University of Turin. Fermentation is carried out in conical wooden vats, and Fabio uses temperature control only when necessary, with the exception of Monvigliero. The latter is the firm's übertraditional wine made by soft-pressing whole clusters by foot, no temperature control ever, and marathon maceration times. All the Barolos are then aged in large, 35-hectoliter casks of both Slavonian and French oak.

Production

Total surface area: 15 ha (37 acres)

Barolo: 6 ha (14.8 acres), 24,000–28,000 bottles

Barolo.   Made from their holdings in Verduno, this is aged for two to two and a half years in large casks. Very enjoyable and approachable Barolo with the village's spicy sensations. The 2007 shows vinous, raspberry notes along with white pepper and cinnamon, firm tannins. Best 2014 to 2017.

Barolo Acclivi.   Made from a selection from Burlotto's top Verduno vineyards (Monvigliero, Rocche dell'Olmo, and Neirane), this is one of the best expressions of the village. The 2008 has a classic Nebbiolo nose of rose, wild cherry, and truffle with the barest hint of leather. Lovely Nebbiolo palate of sour cherry. Aggressive tannins need time to tame, but should evolve beautifully. Best 2016 to 2033. The 2009 boasts a gorgeous floral fragrance accented with balsamic herbs, while the palate is rich but elegant, with sweet black cherry fruit layered with spice. It's silky smooth and already approachable but will gain more complexity over the next few years. Drink 2015 through 2024.

Barolo Cannubi. Made from the family's small parcel in Valletta on the Cannubi hill, this is always very elegant but also boasts a solidly tannic backbone. The 2008 has layers of rose, truffle, and leather accompanied by hallmark varietal flavors of wild cherry, mineral, and spice. Still tight and tannic in 2012 but should develop well. Best 2015 to 2028. The 2009 has an expressive perfume of rose, underbrush, porcini mushroom, and cinnamon. The palate shows bright red cherry, white pepper, mint, and balsamic notes, with uplifting mineral tones. Drink through 2024.

Barolo Monvigliero. This is the firm's calling card and is all about finesse, structure, and fragrance. Made from vines ranging between twenty and sixty years old from the best parcels, this is a Barolo-lovers Barolo and perhaps the most stunning expression of this famed cru. Fabio crushes whole bunches of his best Monvigliero grapes by foot directly in wooden vats. He then ferments with wild yeasts, followed by lengthy maceration—generally two months—with the cap submerged to slowly extract perfume, complexity, and noble tannins.

The 2010 is fantastic, offering layers of scent including crushed violets, exotic incense, smoky mineral, Alpine herbs, pine forest, and leather. The smooth, supple palate delivers dark cherry, thyme, and sage along with vibrant acidity. Drink 2018 to 2038.

Castello di Verduno

Via Umberto I 9
12060 Verduno (CN)
Tel. +39 0172 470284
www.castellodiverduno.com
cantina@castellodiverduno.com

Castello di Verduno is another premier Verduno estate as well as a key Barbaresco producer, turning out exquisite wines of fascinating complexity and depth. Owned by another branch of the aforementioned Burlotto family, the current generation also descends directly from the trailblazing Commendatore Giovan Battista Burlotto. This side inherited the prestigious castle and accompanying vineyards, which were abandoned from the 1930s until 1950 when Giovanni Battista (his grandfather's namesake) returned from Eritrea. He immediately set to work restoring the castle and the vineyards of the stunning property crowning the hilltop village, and in 1953 he turned part of the residence into a hotel and restaurant. Today his three daughters, Gabriella, Elisa, and Liliana, and their children run the estate along with Gabriella's husband, Franco Bianco, a fourth-generation Barbaresco producer who incorporated his family's business and prestigious holdings, including Rabajà and Faset, into the Castello di Verduno firm.

Like their cousins, this Burlotto family also has prime Barolo vineyards in Verduno, including Monvigliero and Massara. Franco Bianco carefully tends all the vineyards using the least invasive methods possible, and to free up his time so that he could dedicate himself fully to vineyard management, he personally trained the firm's in-house enologist Mario Andrion, who took over winemaking some years ago. Castello di Verduno's Barolos and Barbarescos are made with traditional methods, including fermenting with wild yeasts, lengthy, submerged cap maceration, and aging in large Slavonian casks. The wines are not filtered or fined. The firm also believes in extended bottle aging before releasing its Barbarescos and Barolos.

According to Franco Bianco, who good-naturedly points out that at home and at work he is surrounded by women (his wife and their grown daughters, his two sisters-in-law and their daughters), "All of Castello di Verduno's wines are made and aged at my family's Barbaresco winery. Then we bottle and store the wines in the Castello's historic cellars." He quickly adds, "This was my decision—the only one I've ever been allowed to make," before happily walking off to tend his vineyards.

Production

Total surface area: 9.35 ha (23.1 acres)

Barolo: 2.3 ha (5.68 acres), 7,700 bottles

Barbaresco: 2.8 ha (6.9 acres), 14,900 bottles

Barolo Massara. This is Castello di Verduno's signature wine, and it is always an impressive effort. Made entirely with grapes from the Massara vineyard, where vines have east and southeast exposures and average altitudes of 265 meters (869.5 feet) above sea level and calcareous clay soil. Vinified entirely in wooden vats, this undergoes a total thrity-five-day maceration followed by thirty-two months aging in Slavonian casks and another thirty-seven months bottle aging. The 2008 shows lovely red fruit and spice aromas and a creamy cherry and spicy palate with white pepper, cinnamon, and tea-berry notes. Firm but fine tannins and great length and balance. Still young with an age-worthy structure and impressive depth. Drink 2015 to 2028. In 2011, I tried the Massara 1982, which was exquisite: fresh with leather, rose, and spice fragrance and layers of cherry, tobacco, and fig flavors. Remarkable depth and complexity and still going strong.

Barolo Riserva Monvigliero. The firm makes just two thousand bottles of their single-vineyard Riserva Monvigliero, produced only in the best years. Perfect southern exposure and an altitude of 280 meters (919 feet) above sea level encourage ideal grape ripening, while the roots of the forty-year-old plants go down deep to reach water and nutrients below, helping ward off heat stress in hot years. The 2006, vinified in steel with the cap submerged, was aged for forty-four months in botti followed by eighteen months of bottle aging. The 2006 shows intense rose petal fragrance with hints of leather and truffle and a touch of espresso. Succulent berry palate, with the cru's hallmark spicy tones. Still very young with gripping tannins. Needs time to develop complexity but should blossom into a beauty. Drink 2016 to 2036.

Barbaresco Rabajà. From one of the most famed crus in the denomination, this is the firm's calling card for Barbaresco. Made from forty-year-old vines situated at 300 meters (1,050 feet) above sea level in the village's classic Sant'Agata dei Fossili marls, this is vinified in wooden vats with the tried-and-true submerged-cap method, and then aged for twenty months in large Slavonian casks. The elegant and structured 2010 has a vibrant character with quintessential floral and underbrush aromas. The savory palate offers layers of juicy cherry, mint, cinnamon, and orange peel. Drink 2018 to 2038.

The firm also makes a wonderful single-vineyard Faset Barbaresco and a Barbaresco blended from Faset and Rabajà. In outstanding vintages it also makes a complex and age-worthy Rabajà Riserva.

Fratelli Alessandria

Via Beato Valfrè 59
12060 Verduno (CN)

Tel. +39 0172 470113
www.fratellialessandria.it
info@fratellialessandria.it

The owners of the Fratelli Alessandria firm are also relatives of the proprietors of Comm. G. B. Burlotto: the Alessandrias are cousins of Fabio and his father, Giuseppe Alessandria. Located in an imposing and just-restored eighteenth-century palazzo, Fratelli Alessandria is yet another historic Verduno house that not only makes sublime Barolos, but has Barolo roots stretching back to the first half of the nineteenth century. In 1843 the winery, then owned by the Dabbene family, received two gold medals in an agrarian competition organized by King Carlo Alberto in October in Alba that same year. The first medal was for "the improvement in wine making through the method... being used in the royal winery as well by the oenologist Staglieno," and for the successful shipments of their wines overseas." The second gold medal was for a tie for "the best method to arrange a winery," which Count Camillo Benso Cavour also received for his winery. The firm has been in the Alessandria family since 1870 after marriage united them with the Dabbene family.

Today Giovan Battista Alessandria, his wife, Flavia, his brother Alessandro, and his son Vittore run the firm. In the small, vaulted cellars of the winery, built in the mid-1700s, the firm turns out polished Barolos from such coveted sites as Monvigliero, San Lorenzo, Pisapola, Rocche dell'Olmo in Verduno, and Gramolere in Monforte d'Alba. Things are kept very straightforward in the cellars, with temperature-controlled fermentation with wild yeasts (though they don't rule out resorting to BRL 97 if they have to for extremely difficult vintages) in steel. Aging for the straight Barolo takes place only in 30- to 40-hectoliter casks made of both French and Slavonian oak, while the single-vineyard Barolos age the first six to ten months in tonneaux, ranging from 15 percent new to ten years old. After tonneaux, the crus pass into 25-hectoliter French and Slavonian casks for twenty-two to twenty-four months.

Barolo. This blended Barolo is made from the firm's Riva Rocca, Pisapola, Rocche dell'Olmo, Campasso, and Boschetto vineyards in Verduno and Gramolere in Monforte. Vineyard altitude ranges from 300 to 450 meters (984 to 1,476 feet) above sea level, with various exposures. Vibrant and enjoyable, this also ages well. The 2007 delivers great varietal character: floral and underbrush aromas with wild cherry and spice flavors. Great freshness for the vintage and big but ripe tannins. Drink through 2019.

Barolo Monvigliero.   Fratelli Alessandria's parcel of Verduno's most lauded hill is one of the highest at 300 meters (984 feet), where the firm's thirty-five-year-old vines enjoy southern and southwestern exposures and significant day and night temperature changes. The 2008 is a stunning wine with an enticing bouquet of wild cherry, rose, and spice that carry over to the palate along with succulent cherry-berry flavors, spice, and cinnamon. In 2012, this was still tannic and tight, but with remarkable depth and impeccable balance. An archetypical Verduno Barolo of power and finesse. Best 2015 to 2028. The gorgeous 2010 weaves together classic Nebbiolo sensations of black cherry, spice, leather, and uplifting mineral notes. It's a textbook expression of the vintage, with polished tannins and bright acidity. Drink 2020 to 2040.

Barolo Gramolere.   Made from the eponymous cru in Monforte, where forty-five-year-old vines are situated 400 meters (1,312 feet) above sea level, and the soil is a mix of limestone with veins of sand. This is a very earthy but savory Barolo with an age-worthy structure. The 2008 shows hallmark berry and underbrush notes with a long spice finish. Still young and tightly wound, but already shows fantastic depth. Great length. Drink 2016 to 2028.

Other Wineries

Bel Colle
See also Paolo Scavino.

GRINZANE CAVOUR

This village is perhaps best known for the Grinzane Cavour castle. Although the structure was originally built in the eleventh century, most of the current building was constructed in the sixteenth century. By the early 1800s the property belonged to Count Camillo Benso of Cavour's family. From 1832 to 1849, the grand fortress was the residence of the count, who was the first prime minister of a unified Italy and one of the architects behind the unification of the country. His revolutionary agricultural reforms not only improved farming and winemaking but also bettered the squalid conditions of the *contadini,* or peasant farmers. Cavour was also a pioneer in Barolo production, and to this end he hired General Paolo Francesco Staglieno as a consultant winemaker to improve Barolo making. The count also briefly worked with Oudart, who, as a merchant at the time, bought grapes and vinified them at the castle in return for cash and wine.

These days, the village accounts for 3.15 percent of overall Barolo production, counting 51 hectares (127 acres) of vineyards registered to Barolo, and at last count, four Barolo producers resident in the village itself. According to *Atlante delle vigne di Langa*, the benchmark guide to the area's vineyards published by Slow Food Editore in 2000, Castello is "the only vineyard of significance" in the township, but by 2009, with the authorization of the "official geographic mentions," Grinzane's area was divided into eight microzones. Many of the vineyards in Grinzane are quite young, having only recently been planted, and it remains to be seen if they will produce Barolos of complexity. For the moment, wines from these vineyards demonstrate varietal Nebbiolo *tipicità,* albeit of the youthful, easygoing kind. Some producers are opting for heavy-handed cellar practices, including overextracting during fermentation (with brief and violent fermentations in rotary fermenters, for example) or aging entirely in new barriques, perhaps hoping to give the wines a semblance of structure and complexity that most don't normally possess at this point in time.

However, since many vineyards are still young, it can't be ruled out that these newly planted vines could one day naturally yield more interesting wines with less intrusive measures as opposed to being forced in the cellars.

Bruna Grimaldi

Via Parea 7
12060 Grinzane Cavour (CN)
Tel. +39 0173 262094
www.grimaldibruna.it
vini@grimaldibruna.it

While Bruna Grimaldi's cellars are in Grinzane Cavour, the firm has long been associated with Serralunga, where it owns 2 hectares (5 acres) in Badarina, one of the highest vineyard areas in this township. Once considered too high for optimum Nebbiolo ripening, Badarina used to be dominated by Dolcetto vines, but as Barolo demand increased while Dolcetto began its decline in popularity, the situation is reversed. Global warming, however, has taken care of the ripening problems, and apparently Nebbiolo has no problem reaching ideal maturation, while it is able to maintain freshness in the hottest vintages.

Bruna and her husband, Franco Fiorino, now run the family firm that Bruna's father handed over to them in 1998. While they are both trained enologists, according to Bruna the pair learned a lot from her father and grandfather, who founded the original family firm in 1954. Although in the recent past they relied on 500- and 700-liter tonneaux for aging—both new and seasoned for up to nine years—since 2011 they also use some larger casks, 16 and 20 hectoliters.

Production

Total surface area: 11 ha (27 acres)
Barolo: 5.3 ha (13 acres), 28,000 bottles

Barolo Camilla.   This is made from young vines in the south-facing Camilla vineyard in the larger Raviole cru in Grinzano, where altitude ranges between 270 and 300 meters (886 and 984 feet) above sea level. The 2008 is very expressive for the vintage, with a pretty floral fragrance and just a whiff of leather. The palate opens with classic Nebbiolo cherry and underbrush followed by hints of vanilla and espresso that subdue the pure varietal character.

Barolo Bricco Ambrogio.   The firm started making Barolo Bricco Ambrogio, the village of Roddi's only geographic mention, in 2007. Vine altitude lies between 280 and 300 meters (919 and 984 feet) above sea level, and plants range between twelve and fifty years old. This is a delicate, soft expression of Barolo and very drinkable. The 2008 has lovely violet and rose petal aromas and bright, strawberry Nebbiolo sweetness on the palate. Approachable early but will maintain a decade or more.

Barolo Badarina.   Badarina is the firm's signature wine and hails from Serralunga. The Grimaldi's parcel, located between 380 and 420 meters (1,247 and 1,378 feet) above sea level, has southern and southeastern exposures, while plant age is a healthy and hearty twenty-eight years old. The 2007 boasts a beautiful Nebbiolo fragrance with just a hint of oak along with ripe berry and mineral flavors and bracing tannins. Drink through 2022. The 2008 opens with underbrush, porcini mushroom, truffle, and leather aromas, while the palate delivers succulent black cherry flavors, balsamic notes, and well-integrated oak. The rich flavors, big tannins, and structure easily support the 15 percent alcohol. Drink after 2018 for more complexity.

RODDI

Roddi has a mere 23 hectares (57 acres) of registered Barolo vines and accounts for 1.29 percent of total Barolo output.

The medieval hamlet on the northeastern edge of the denomination is best known for its solid and austere castle that dates back to the eleventh century with towers added in the twelfth and fifteenth centuries. In terms of Barolo production, however, until recently Roddi elicited very little excitement: about the best thing Slow Food's *Wine Atlas of the Langhe* could say about Roddi, besides mention of its castle, was that the village "is also famous for handball, and it is no coincidence that it was home to one of the greatest players of all time." However, Roddi's fortune as a forgotten Barolo outpost began to change when top-ranking producer Enrico Scavino acquired land there in the zone known as Bricco Ambrogio.

Today Bricco Ambrogio is the sole geographic mention in Roddi, and yields lovely Barolos with intense floral aromatics, ripe, round fruit, and finesse. These are not the most complex Barolos, but they are among the most vibrant and enjoyable.

See Paolo Scavino and Bruna Grimaldi.

DIANO D'ALBA

In the prestigious world of Barolo production, Diano d'Alba is one of the minor protagonists, with just 14 hectares (35 acres) turning out 0.88 percent of Barolo's overall output. It ranks tenth in terms of volume, just above Cherasco, the tiniest Barolo contributing village of all.

Noted above all for its Dolcetto production, the sliver of the township devoted to Barolo vineyards lies between Grinzane Cavour and Serralunga, just on the other side of Serralunga's crest. Although there are three geographic mentions—Sorano, La Vigna, and Gallaretto—the most notable is Sorano. Most of Sorano is situated in Serralunga's territory, and in his late nineteenth-century monograph, Lorenzo Fantini classified this cru—under Serralunga—as being one of the best in the denomination. However, Fantini made no mention of the village of Diano d'Alba in his publication, making it doubtful whether Fantini considered this side of hill to be of the same quality as the side in Serralunga, or perhaps he simply disregarded Diano d'Alba. The latter might indeed be the case, since the original boundaries for Barolo production—authorized in 1927 with the founding of the first Barolo and Barbaresco *consorzio,* which was created to protect the authenticity of these wines—did not include any part of Diano d'Alba. The Vigna vineyard area is located on the lower part of Sorano.

Regarding Gallaretto, Alessandro Masnaghetti's comments accompanying his 2011 vineyard map that included the township sum this area up by saying it is just on the other side of the Serralunga hill, where it is "cool and less suited to Nebbiolo; it is thus no accident that up until now these grapes have never been vinified on their own."

PART THREE

Profiles of Key Barbaresco Producers by Village

TWELVE

Barbaresco

FROM DOMIZIO CAVAZZA TO SUBZONES

PLEASE SEE CHAPTER 4 for more details on the history of Barolo, which had an impact on the start of winemaking in Barbaresco, and chapter 5 for a description of the Barolo Wars, which had a profound effect on both denominations.

Barbaresco, long seen as Barolo's junior partner—albeit it in a very successful venture—has always lived in the shadow of its more famous neighbor. Although die-hard fans of Italian wine may passionately debate which of the two wines they prefer and the reasons why, many more Italian wine lovers, even those familiar enough with Barolo to know it as the King of Wines, the Wine of Kings, know on the other hand relatively little about Barbaresco, other than perhaps the name of Angelo Gaja. One reason why Barbaresco remains less famous than its neighbor is simply volume: there is two-thirds less Barbaresco produced than there is Barolo. Another reason is the still too common yet wholly undeserved perception that Barbaresco is not quite up to par with Barolo.

Those who dismiss Barbaresco as simply Barolo's kid brother are not only making a serious mistake, they are also missing out on one of the world's most mesmerizing and compelling wines. Not only is Barbaresco both elegant and complex, it comes with the added benefit that, at least for now anyway, it also costs significantly less than Barolo (with some notable exceptions—namely, Angelo Gaja and Bruno Giacosa, whose wines carry notoriously hefty price tags). While American wine lovers have a healthy respect for Barbaresco, and the United States is its number one export market, annually absorbing more than 20 percent of the denomination's entire output according to the Consorzio's estimates, other key markets have yet to discover the wine. A classic example is the United Kingdom, which imports 14 percent of

Barolo's annual production but only between 2 and 3 percent of Barbaresco's output. However, when connoisseurs do discover Barbaresco, they usually become lifelong fans, and some even join in on the debate: Barolo or Barbaresco?

Comparisons between the two wines are unavoidable, since both Barolo and Barbaresco are made from 100 percent Nebbiolo, and their respective growing areas are only separated by Alba; with Barolo spreading out to the south and west of the city, and Barbaresco radiating to the east and north. The small Barbaresco denomination counts for just 684 hectares (1,690 acres) and covers the three villages of Barbaresco, Neive, and Treiso as well as a sliver of San Rocco Seno d'Elvio, the latter two areas having been incorporated into the commune of Barbaresco until 1957. Given the number and size of Barbaresco's communes, this growing area is more uniform when compared to Barolo. Barolo's much larger and generally higher growing area includes eleven communes and dedicates 1,984 hectares (4,903 acres) of Nebbiolo to Barolo, and as was discussed in the Barolo chapters, while growing conditions in some communes are very similar, there are also significant variations between certain villages, such as between La Morra and Serralunga.

Barbaresco's significantly smaller annual production of roughly 4.6 million bottles, as opposed to Barolo's 13.9 million,[1] is one of the major reasons why Barbaresco remains less well known. While the vast majority of producers in both denominations are third- or fourth-generation farmers who inherited their vineyards and wineries (unlike the situation in Tuscany, where waves of wealthy outsiders flocked in over the last few decades to invest in winemaking), Barbaresco is dominated by small growers-turned-winemakers whose tiny productions may be hard to find abroad. Barolo on the other hand has always boasted a number of large firms with substantial volumes whose wines have long been readily available internationally, and this is still the case even if many growers who once supplied grapes to these large houses have become boutique Barolo producers in their own right over the last twenty years.

Regarding the actual wines, both have a luminous garnet color that turns to brick with aging. Both generally waver between 14 and 14.5 percent alcohol, although wines containing 15 percent alcohol, while still rare, are no longer unheard-of in Barolo and Barbaresco as a result of global warming. Unsurprisingly, since they are made from Nebbiolo and thanks to the proximity of their respective growing areas, wines from both denominations have similar fragrances and flavors, great depth, and tend to be more complex as opposed to being simply powerful, despite Barolo's undeserved reputation as a colossal wine rippling with muscle. While the similarities between Barolo and Barbaresco are many, there are also fundamental differences in the history of the denominations, and their growing areas, as well as differences between the wines themselves that set them apart from each other.

While Barolo as we know it today was created sometime in the mid-1800s by a handful of pioneering estates owned by Italian nobles (including the Marchesi Falletti; Camillo Benso, the Count of Cavour, who later became Italy's first prime minister; and Vittorio Emanuele, the first king of Italy, and then his son, Count Mirafiore at Fontanafredda), Barbaresco has a specific and widely accepted birthdate of 1894 with the founding of the first Cantina Sociale di Barbaresco. It is generally assumed that before this, most Nebbiolo grapes from Barbaresco ended up in Barolo, and there is little information about a wine specifically called Barbaresco before 1894. However, by that time Barbaresco was already well known for the quality of its Nebbiolo, both the grape and the wine, as is aptly demonstrated in several documents, and it appears that some growers were already vinifying their grapes at the end of the eighteenth century. According to a document now housed in Barbaresco's parish church, in 1799, after Austrian forces beat the French at the battle of Genola, the commander, General De Melas, ordered "the commune of Barbaresco to deliver a *carrà* [a 600-liter barrel] of excellent Nebbiolo." to the camp in Bra.[2] The oldest bottle of Barbaresco in existence today is a "Barbaresco 1870," still preserved at Cascina Drago,[3] although to be fair while the bottle looks ancient and is most likely authentic, it has merely a generic, hand-scrawled label with no mention of the producer and only confirms that bottled Barbaresco before the end of the nineteenth century was a rarity.

Another significant mention of Barbaresco (the wine) appears in Lorenzo Fantini's *Monografia*, which he began writing in 1879 and published in 1895. Fantini gives a very precise description of Barbaresco in a chapter entitled "Luxury Red Wines." According to Fantini, "Next to Barolo . . . is Barbaresco, also made with Nebbiolo. It has the same alcohol potential as Barolo, but a bouquet that is quite different, that some would say is more refined."[4] Fantini goes on to say that the quality of the wine had improved over the last few years and that now "Barbaresco rivals Barolo."[5] Unfortunately, it is impossible to pin down exactly when this statement was written as the manuscript spans almost two decades, but it appears that Fantini's observations of the recently improved Barbaresco coincide with the wine's official debut. Besides these few mentions, there is no other known documentation of a wine called Barbaresco. As stated previously, although growers sold the bulk of their Nebbiolo to Barolo producers, those who made wine called it simply Nebbiolo, or sometimes Nebbiolo di Barbaresco. Domizio Cavazza changed all this.

Credited as the Father of Barbaresco, Cavazza was among the first to believe in the great potential of Barbaresco and to consider it on a par with Barolo, and not merely as a source of high-quality grapes that helped give a touch of elegance and ripe fruit to soften the austere Barolos of the late nineteenth century. By all accounts, Cavazza was a wunderkind: born in Modena, he graduated with honors from the University of Milan in agronomy. He continued his studies abroad, mainly in France, first at Versailles, then Montpellier. During this tumultuous period for European viticulture, Cavazza witnessed firsthand in the vineyards of France the ravages of several diseases imported from the United States, mainly downy mildew and phylloxera. The young agronomist was on the cutting edge of studying and developing treatments for these diseases, which threatened to obliterate Europe's *Vitis vinifera* vines and wine production. In 1881, when Cavazza was only twenty-six, Italy's Ministry of Agriculture called on him to be the founding director of Alba's newly created Royal Enological School.

Although the aristocratic wine producers of Barolo assumed that Cavazza would settle in Alba or in one of the celebrated Barolo villages, he surprised everyone by choosing to settle in Barbaresco instead. According to a 2008 interview with Cavazza's grandson Mario Cavazza by Attilio Ianniello, author of *Produttori del Barbaresco 1958–2008*, Domizio Cavazza developed his passion for Barbaresco shortly after arriving in Alba in 1881. As recounted by Cavazza's grandson, the young director of the Enological School caught a persistent cold soon after he arrived in Piedmont and was treated by Gino Rocca, a doctor from Barbaresco who was working at Alba's hospital. The two became friends, and Rocca frequently invited Cavazza to Barbaresco, where he had him try the local wines: "My grandfather had a lot to laugh about with respect to how the local farmers maintained their vineyards, but regarding the wines, he had no doubts: they were the best wines he had tried from the wine areas around Alba, but he also knew they could be even better."[6] Barolo or Barbaresco? Cavazza chose Barbaresco, and given his experience and position, this was quite a coup for Barbaresco.

In 1886, Cavazza bought his first property in Barbaresco, the Casotto farm, a vineyard area now incorporated into the Ovello cru in the section historically known as Loreto. Cavazza immediately began to cultivate the vineyards with Nebbiolo, using the avant-garde techniques he had learned at the University of Milan as well as in the most renowned universities and vineyards in France, and during his five years in the Barolo and Barbaresco growing zones. He evidently understood the need to unite local producers to improve overall quality, and in 1894, together with a group initially composed of nine growers, he founded a cooperative cellar, the Cantina Sociale di Barbaresco. That same year he also bought the Barbaresco Castle from Oscar Rocca, taking out a large loan from a bank in nearby Cuneo. Cavazza enlarged the castle's cellars and outfitted it with the barrels and equipment needed for serious winemaking. In the autumn of 1894, in this grandiose setting, the united producers made what are considered the first wines to be officially called Barbaresco.

After a propitious beginning, Barbaresco soon fell on hard times when Cavazza died in 1913. His son Luigi, also an agronomist, took over but was called to arms in 1915 when Italy entered World War I. The war was followed by a period of intense poverty throughout rural Italy, and in some areas fields and vineyards lay abandoned during and even after the war because of a shortage of labor resulting from the high mortality of young men who fought in the conflict. To make matters worse, in the Langhe, fresh outbreaks of phylloxera and downy mildew decimated the vineyards, and food shortages abounded as a result of the low productivity of the countryside, sending prices soaring. Not only did demand for quality wine understandably plummet, but starting in 1922, the newly instated Fascist regime encouraged grape growers to grub up their vines and cultivate grain instead, so that the country could avoid importing staple foods, culminating in Mussolini's Battle for Grain campaign in 1925. In the midst of the social and economic turmoil of the mid-1920s, the Cantina Sociale closed.

Even though Barolo suffered as well during these difficult years, it was able to survive thanks to its already established reputation and a patronage that included the House of Savoy, Italian diplomats, and a new class of entrepreneurs that emerged after the war. Barbaresco's fledgling wine scene, however, was throttled as all but a few growers completely abandoned winemaking. It would not be until the late 1950s and early 1960s that Barbaresco would stir to life again thanks to a new generation of dynamic young winemakers, including Angelo Gaja and Bruno Giacosa as well as the Produttori del Barbaresco cooperative cellar, the successor to Cavazza's original Cantina Sociale di Barbaresco.

Founded in 1958 by the local parish priest, Don Fiorino Marengo, as a way to stop the exodus of Barbaresco's young farmers who were abandoning the countryside to find work in the cities, the new cooperative resuscitated Cavazza's vision of uniting local growers to make outstanding Nebbiolo on a par with their more famous neighbor. Their efforts paid off, and not only did Produttori become one of the best and most respected cooperative cellars in Italy, it inspired more landholders in Barbaresco to return to their vineyards and to make quality wine. Barbaresco was included, along with Barolo, Brunello di Montalcino, and Chianti in the first tier of denominations to be regulated under Italy's DOC (Denominazione di Origine Controllata) in 1966 and DOCG (Denominazione di Origine Controllata e Garantita) in 1980.

Although Piedmont's dynamic duo share many traits, and it can be argued that the more delicate Barolos from La Morra have a similar structure to the hearty Barbarescos from Neive, there are clear distinctions between the two wines. Barbaresco is often described as more feminine or refined because it has less tannic force than fuels an archetypical Barolo, and Barbaresco's production code obligingly calls for two years of aging, at least nine months of which must be spent in wood before release, and it must have a minimum alcohol of 12.5 percent. Barolo on the other hand must undergo three years of aging, eighteen months of which must be in wood, to tame more forceful tannins, and have a minimum alcohol content of 13 percent. This does not mean, however, that "light" is an appropriate descriptor for Barbaresco.

Both Barolo and Barbaresco are complex wines with full-bodied, tannic structures that permit long cellaring, though Barbaresco is generally more elegant, less austere, and more approachable earlier. Barbaresco is also more flexible with meals, even pairing with pasta and risotto as well as chicken, while Barolo on the other hand tends to pair better with more demanding dishes. While both wines have age-worthy structures, Barolo needs more time to come around and can age longer, and Barbaresco usually maintains more freshness than Barolo in hot years, as the 2007 and 2009 vintages aptly demonstrate. While many 2007 and 2009 Barolos suffered from noticeably high alcohol and cooked fruit sensations combined with bitter tannins, the latter a result of picking when sugar levels were already very high but before phenolic maturation of the seeds was complete, the 2007 and 2009 Barbarescos are generally better balanced overall and have riper tannins. With the undeniable advent of global warming, this is a clear advantage for Barbaresco, for the time being anyway.

Barbaresco's finesse is a direct consequence of microclimate and soil. Unlike Barolo, which is blocked from the Tanaro River by the ridge of La Morra, the Barbaresco production zone is wide open to the influences of the Tanaro and its valley. While it creates fog in the winter, according to producers, in the summer the river influence gives the Barbaresco growing zone hotter morning temperatures when compared to Barolo. The river also generates evening breezes that keep the vines fresh and healthy. Essentially this means that grapes are picked at least a week earlier in Barbaresco and tend to mature with greater regularity. Soil is another crucial factor that gives Barbaresco its more graceful demeanor. Even if soils for both of Piedmont's flagship wines are predominantly calcareous marls, the main element responsible for the wines' tannic structures, Barbaresco's soil can be divided into two formations: the bluish-gray marls of the Sant'Agata Fossili formation from the Tortonian age, and the lighter-colored marls alternating with beds of sand of the Lequio formation.

While different townships in Barolo share the aforementioned soil formations, there are more macro- and microelements in Barbaresco's soil, and it is therefore more fertile than Barolo's, according to Aldo Vacca, who is not only the director of the Produttori del Barbaresco cooperative cellar, but also the vice-president of the Consorzio. "Barbaresco's soil has more nutrients, such as potassium and phosphorous," says Vacca, who adds that this "soil fertility leads to more plant vigor, which in turn yields a more refined structure and more supple tannins when compared to Barolo." Because of the many similarities between the two wines, it can be difficult to distinguish a Barbaresco from a Barolo in blind tastings, and this is most definitely the case when Barbaresco is forced into being a bigger, more concentrated wine by drastically lowering grape yields and overextracting tannins during fermentation and maceration. Moreover, it is nearly impossible to tell Barbarescos from Barolos if they have both been aged in new barriques, thanks to the standardizing effect of new oak. Thankfully, most producers these days are stepping back from these practices and focusing instead on making more terroir-driven wines, but the Barolo Wars certainly made an impact also in Barbaresco.

As in Barolo, by the late 1980s and early 1990s, there was a marked division among wine producers in Barbaresco between those who used traditional winemaking methods and those who advocated radical change. This led to clear misuse of the new barriques, and lightening-fast fermentations in rotary fermenters that resulted in many overoaked and overextracted wines, until experience eventually taught moderation. However, the Barolo Wars proved crucial to improving Barbaresco across the board: it forced grower-producers—especially those who had been making wine for family consumption or to be sold in bulk to locals—to focus for the first time on cellar hygiene and to turn in their old, rotting casks for new ones. In the process, they raised quality throughout the denomination.

These days most wineries in Barbaresco rely far less on new, toasted French oak than they did just a few years ago. Rather than struggle to please New World palates that readily embrace dominant wood sensations that can mask the wine's natural flavors and aroma profile, the great majority of Barbaresco producers now prefer to allow Barbaresco's trademark sensations of violets, sour cherry, spice, truffles, and licorice to thrive unfettered by invasive wood. Many winemakers and bottlers here now agree with what I have been writing for years, that overoaked wines are not only unpleasant to drink, but there is nothing modern about them—they are in fact outdated expressions of what was a passing trend. Or as a number of producers say when they refer to Barbarescos aged in new barriques, they are "Old School Barbarescos."

While the great wine wars threatened to tear apart the Barbaresco denomination, as in Barolo, today many Barbaresco makers have found common ground when it comes to wood aging. A number have gone back to medium and large casks, normally between 20 and 50 hectoliters, made of Slavonian, French, and even Austrian oak. Others use a combination of new and used barriques and large casks, so that drastically overoaked wines, while still around, are now a minority rather than the status quo of the 1990s and much of the first decade of the new century. It goes without saying, however, that there are still some winemakers who insist on new oak, inevitably telling me that even if they personally don't like the style, "this is what the market wants." Of all the villages, for reasons I don't fully understand, many winemakers across the board in Neive still rely too much on new barriques and produce wines with evident wood and espresso sensations that strangle Nebbiolo.

Yet Barbaresco's real threat came not from barriques versus large casks, but from internal politics. The denomination was shaken up in late 1999 when Angelo Gaja shocked the wine world by declassifying his beloved mono-cru Barbarescos from DOCG status, the most coveted designation in the country, to Langhe Nebbiolo DOC, starting with the 1996 vintage. Rumors abounded that Gaja's unprecedented decision was based on a desire to blend his various Barbarescos with Barbera to add freshness, which is strictly prohibited in the Barbaresco DOCG but which is allowed under the Langhe DOC. At the time Barbaresco came under almost microscopic scrutiny as both Italian and international wine critics bemoaned the demise of Barbaresco's hard-earned reputation, and winemakers in other elite and restrictive denominations watched and waited to see if local winemakers would follow Gaja's initiative.

Fortunately for the Barbaresco denomination, other firms did not imitate Gaja in his risky gamble. "I don't agree with Gaja's decision to withdraw any of his wines from the DOCG. I think it potentially could have damaged the denomination, and if any other producer had tried this, it would have meant suicide," Aldo Vacca told me in 2006. Tino Colla, who founded Poderi Colla along with his niece Federica and famed older brother Beppe Colla, formerly of Prunotto, feels downgrading the area's greatest wines is counterproductive given the instability of the international wine scene. "While I don't want to judge anyone's decisions, I firmly believe that we producers must stay united in order to face the very real threat of large multinational companies from the New World that are buying up and merging small wineries all over Italy. Our future depends on our unique wines but alone our small wineries cannot stand up to large beverage groups or compete against the deluge of New World wines. Our only hope is to strengthen our position by staying together and confronting as a group the trend towards globalization," Colla told me in an interview for this book.

Beppe Colla, who defines his noninterventionist philosophy of winemaking as "classic," since the term "traditional" often connotes antiquated winemaking practices, confirms a large return among producers to more Nebbiolo-friendly practices. "In the past few years we've seen numerous cellars here return to more natural winemaking techniques that better suit Barbaresco, and thankfully fewer producers are now trying to force their wine into resembling something out of Australia."

Barbaresco's producers realized relatively early—by Italian standards—the important role individual vineyards play in making unique wines and the necessity of protecting their growing area. In the 1990s, in a first step toward delimiting the best areas, the denomination began identifying the zone's various crus with the intent of having them officially recognized by the government. However, those not in the best vineyard areas created an uproar, so the government grandfathered in fantasy names and other registered place-names within the growing area, even if the majority of these designations are not associated with any special characteristics or superior quality.

These subzoning efforts came to fruition in 2007 when Italy's minister of agriculture approved what is now a whopping sixty-six designated micro-zones within Barbaresco, defined with the uninspiring name of *menzioni geografiche aggiuntive,* or "additional geographic mentions," since terms such as *subzones* and *cru* seemed to imply superior quality. Italy seems committed to promoting inequality for all, and insisted that the language regarding the zoning remain neutral. Even though the sheer number of authorized mentions undoubtedly creates some consumer confusion, and the ridiculously large number has taken some prestige away from the much smaller number of truly great vineyard areas, they have at the same time played a crucial role in stopping what had become rampant expansion in the best crus. Before their approval, vineyard areas such as Rabajà, for example, got bigger every year, as producers outside of the classic Rabajà area claimed to be inside. Unfortunately, local politics played a predicted role in drawing up the borders, and many producers complain that the fixed borders are too generous. And in the case of Rabajà, the former Rabajà vineyards of one of the most lauded producers in the denomination, Bruno Giacosa, were excluded.

All of the vineyard areas are now legally delimited, and the borders are closed. Barbaresco was the first Italian denomination to reach this crucial milestone, followed in 2010 by Barolo.

THIRTEEN

(Village of) Barbaresco

WHEN THE ROMANS CONQUERED the local population and founded the city of Alba Pompeia in 89 B.C., the territory of Barbaresco was a vast forest. The Stazielli tribes from Liguria took refuge from the troops in the dense woods, and the Romans, who called all those who were not Roman "barbarians," named the area Barbarica Silva, meaning "woods of the barbarians." Over time, Barbarica Silva transformed into the name Barbaresco. According to local history, the "barbarians" were devoted to the god Mars, and their exact place of worship was the hill and valley called Martinengen, which is undoubtedly the Martinenga hill today. Still another testimony to the ancient tribes who took refuge in the hills of Barbaresco is the celebrated cru Asili, which derives from the Latin *asylum,* or "place of refuge." The name Barbaresco appears often in medieval documents, as the town was violently fought over by both Alba and Asti for centuries until it became part of the Duchy of Savoy in 1631 following the Cherasco Peace Treaty.

Barbaresco's monolithic medieval tower, which was once part of a large fortification that was demolished centuries before the construction of the eighteenth-century castle standing in the center today, is all that remains from the town's turbulent past. Today the tower stands guard over 1,690 acres of peaceful vineyards, and Barbaresco, which lends its name to the eponymous wine, is the heart of production. It was the expression of Nebbiolo from the Barbaresco commune, which until 1957 also incorporated the village of Treiso and the hamlet of San Rocco Seno d'Elvio, that inspired Domizio Cavazza to purchase property here and establish Barbaresco's first cooperative cellar, officially creating the wine called Barbaresco. The township accounts for 35 percent of the denomination's total output and boasts the majority of the registered vineyards for its namesake wine, including

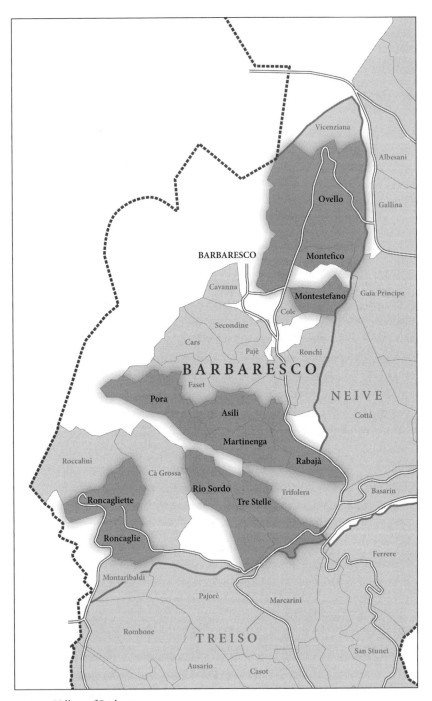

MAP 8. Village of Barbaresco.

many of the best vineyard sites, such as Asili, Rabajà, Roncaglie, Roncagliette, Rio Sordo, and Montestefano. The best vineyards are located between 200 and 350 meters above sea level, and the village's location, perched on a hill just above the Tanaro River, creates a mild microclimate.

The soil in Barbaresco is composed of the compact, bluish marls of Sant'Agata Fossili, and of all the villages in the denomination, Barbaresco has the highest percentages of both silt and calcareous clay. The village produces some of the most complex and age-worthy Barbarescos, combining structure with elegance. The village of Barbaresco is also home to two of the denomination's leading players, Angelo Gaja and the Cantina Sociale dei Produttori del Barbaresco.

Gaja

Via Torino 18
12050 Barbaresco (CN)
Tel. +39 0173 635256
info@gaja.com

Angelo Gaja, one of Italy's most successful not to mention extravagant winemakers, is credited not only with drawing Barbaresco out of obscurity but he also played a fundamental role in triggering the quality revolution that pulled the country's wine scene out of the doldrums. Even though aficionados and pundits automatically associate Gaja with Italy's twentieth-century wine renaissance and sleek single-vineyard bottlings, his wines also boast fantastic aging potential, as I learned firsthand in January 2007 when Angelo and his daughter Gaia opened up four decades of their wines for me at their winery in the heart of the Barbaresco village.

Founded in 1859, the house of Gaja is the oldest winery in the denomination, and Angelo's father had already improved on overall quality and acquired some of Barbaresco's best vineyards before Angelo, the fourth generation, took the reins in 1961 at age twenty-one. Angelo Gaja has always been on the cutting edge, and many of his numerous innovations that initially seemed outrageous were soon copied throughout Italy. One of the pioneers of single-vineyard bottlings, Gaja's seductive *sorì* bottlings first appeared in 1970 from the 1967 vintage, and their debut sent prices soaring. Nearly ten years after experimenting, Gaja released his first barrique-aged Barbaresco in 1978, the same year he planted Cabernet Sauvignon in the sacred heart of

FIGURE 22. Angelo Gaja. One of Italy's most successful and celebrated producers, Angelo Gaja is credited with pulling Barbaresco out of obscurity, in great part through his single-vineyard bottlings. He also played a key role in triggering Italy's Quality Wine Revolution. Photograph by Paolo Tenti.

Nebbiolo country. He was also among the first to advocate short pruning back in the 1960s to lower yields, as well as replanting at higher densities.

Since 1978, the winery has broken from the custom of planting vines in horizontal rows, and replanted in vertical columns (the so-called *ritocchino* system), not only to facilitate tractors but also to allow sun exposure on both sides of the rows in Gaja's south-facing vineyards. However, local growers have not followed suit because the area's severe erosion makes vertically planted rows more susceptible to landslides. The firm has replanted gradually, and the average age of the vines is between thirty and forty years old.

Although Gaja has employed temperature-controlled fermentation since 1982, he had previously tried to control fermentation with more artisanal methods. These included busing in blocks of ice from Alba's slaughterhouse to cool down the must during skyrocketing temperatures in 1971 and pumping the juice through a hose that had been laid between the giant blocks of ice. Although this certainly raised eyebrows at the time, the unconventional tactic worked.

While Gaja's many fans applaud his world-class wines, cynics often claim that his modern winemaking methods have changed the *tipicità* of his

Nebbiolo. Yet these same critics fail to note that Gaja is one of the few top wineries in Italy that does not use selected yeasts for the alcoholic fermentation, although in very difficult years he will add a small amount of nutrients to feed the native yeasts if needed. Gaja's use of barriques has also come under fire from advocates of traditional Nebbiolo. However, while he ages his Barbaresco for the first year in barriques, he also uses giant, perfectly maintained Slavonian casks that are on average one hundred years old for the second year.

Starting with the 1996 vintage, Gaja pulled his single-vineyard Barbarescos (Sorì San Lorenzo, Sorì Tildin, and Costa Russi) out of the Barbaresco DOCG and into the less prestigious Langhe DOC. He also did the same for his single-vineyard Barolo Sperss, although he still makes Barolo DaGromis from La Morra. Gaja's unorthodox declassification sent shock waves rippling throughout the wine world amid speculation that he wanted to blend Nebbiolo from his beloved crus with other grape varieties, a practice strictly prohibited under Barbaresco's production code.

Many quickly bemoaned the demise of Barbaresco now that its leading producer had seemingly abandoned the denomination. "I know what journalists and others in the industry have said and continue to say," acknowledges Gaja. "But my decision was actually to support Barbaresco. My family has always made Barbaresco, but as the single-vineyard bottlings grew in prestige, our flagship wine was suddenly referred to as 'basic' or 'normale' and was considered inferior to the crus, which I never intended. My family has been making wine and striving for excellence for over 150 years, and I don't want anything we make to be considered 'regular.' So now I have one Barbaresco only," Gaja told me in 2007. His former single-vineyard Barbarescos and Barolos are now blended with between 5 percent and 8 percent Barbera.

Gaja has long since moved on, and these days he and his team, which includes his daughters Gaia and Rossana, are focusing more than ever on viticulture and vineyard management. As Gaia Gaja told me in 2012, the firm has abolished chemicals in the vineyards and uses only copper and sulfur to combat fungus, and only when needed. The winery has also been working with the University of Turin since 2003 to choose the best clones from the oldest plants on their estate, which they have now narrowed down and planted in an experimental vineyard. Every year, grapes from this test site are microfermented and aged separately to see how well they perform. Gaja also confirms that thanks to global warming, they have made other changes to adapt to rising temperatures, including planting new vines (to replace those that have died) in October as opposed to April. While April is the customary time for this procedure, the extreme summer heat in recent vintages, namely, in 2012, killed off the young plants that were only a few months old. And even though they have allowed grass to grow between the vines for years as a measure against erosion, they no longer cut the grass but leave it to protect the soil and roots from extreme heat.

According to Gaia, one of the most crucial measures against global warming is managing the leaf canopy. "We used to cut the top leaves, and this forced the plants to produce more sugar. Now we want less leaves below, and a higher leaf wall to ensure that the seeds will reach ideal ripening, while at the same time trying to encourage the plant to produce less sugar," she explains. Starting with the 2009 vintage, the firm is also experimenting with fermenting with the stems (also known as whole bunch fermentation), for some vineyard lots that go into the firm's Barbaresco, "to give more color, add another dimension and more complex aromas," according to Gaia, who stresses that this can be done only if stems are perfectly ripened.

Although the firm still makes its single-vineyard Langhe Nebbiolo DOC bottlings and a Barolo, Da Gromis, I've concentrated on Gaja's standard-bearer, the straight Barbaresco.

Production

Total surface area: 64 ha (158 acres)
Barbaresco: 37 ha (91.4 acres), 50,000 bottles
Barolo: 27 ha (66.7 acres), bottles N/A

Barbaresco.   Made from fourteen separate vineyards and aged for one year in new and used barriques and one year in large Slavonian casks, Gaja Barbaresco is elegant and complex with an age-worthy structure. The 2008 is gorgeous, with classic floral notes and finesse. In 2012, this was just starting to open up and will benefit from more bottle age. Give this time to fully develop. Drink 2014 to 2028. The 2009 showed less fruit and more under-brush and dried tobacco leaf with a hint of spice and toasted oak. While Gaja's Barbarescos are usually approachable upon release, which often belies their age-worthy structures, I found the 2009 fiercely tannic and needing time to soften. This was also the first year that the firm fermented with the stems from five of the fourteen vineyards. Best after 2019. The 2010 is destined to become a classic and is already impressive. It offers an intense perfume of violet, earth, and ripe red fruits punctuated by balsamic notes. The palate delivers rich wild cherry layered with mint, cinnamon, and eucalyptus. Structured but balanced and elegant, this will develop more complexity over time. Drink 2020 to 2035.

The tasting notes that follow are from an informal private tasting held for me by Angelo and Gaia on January 12, 2007. This unique vertical, the results of which I wrote about in *The World of Fine* a few months later (issue 15), allowed me not only to experience changes at the estate, but to experience Italy's quality metamorphosis firsthand. Changes and improvements in planting, vinification, and aging were subtle though apparent throughout, while Gaja's hallmark elegance was evident in every bottling, like a family resemblance.

Barbaresco 1961. This was Angelo's first vintage and a stellar year, but the young winemaker's debut proved problematic, as the extreme heat resulted in an exasperatingly prolonged fermentation. Thankfully, only a tiny amount had been bottled before Gaja realized that the fermentation had been incomplete, and he left the rest in wood for marathon aging before bottling. Still dissatisfied, he initially refused to release the wine but decades later discovered that it had aged majestically and evolved into a quintessential Barbaresco.

A great vintage marked by extreme heat. Garnet with brick edges. Concentrated aromas of tar and dried rose petals with a hint of tea. Still very much alive with surprisingly fresh acidity and ultrasmooth tannins balanced with pronounced cherry flavors for its age. Just heading past its peak.

————*1964.* Another stellar vintage for the Langhe. Luminous but deep garnet with slight oranging on the rim. Dazzling bouquet of violets, rose petals, and a hint of sandalwood. Wild cherry flavors and still firm acidity are balanced by velvety tannins. Incredibly youthful for its age, and complex, this is the only Barbaresco in the lineup to include grapes from the San Lorenzo vineyard acquired that same year, which starting from the 1967 vintage was bottled separately. A gorgeous expression of Nebbiolo and full of personality.

————*1971.* Another very hot year. Spicy nose loaded with ripe, almost stewed fruit, with whiffs of black pepper and tea. Rather firm acidity and evolved tannins. Port-like texture and sweetness. Flavors of cherries preserved in spirits with truffle and thyme notes. Not as youthful as the previous two but still in very good condition.

————*1978.* The first Barbaresco to be aged one year in barriques as well as one year in large casks. According to Gaja, this wine was very closed for the first fifteen years. Dark but luminous garnet color. Leather, tea, and tobacco aromas with a hint of animal and smoke alongside ripe plum and cherry flavors. More power than finesse and still surprisingly youthful.

————*1982.* Outstanding vintage and the first year of temperature-controlled fermentation, which perhaps explains the richer, darker garnet color. Tantalizing nose, with Nebbiolo's hallmarks of violets, ripe berry, truffle, and spice sensations. Impeccably balanced and youthful with fresh cherry flavors, balsamic herbs, and a long tobacco finish.

Barbaresco Sorì San Lorenzo 1982. Darker ruby-garnet color. Complex and stunning bouquet of rich fruit, tea, and spice. Lush berry and mineral flavors accompanied by firm tannins and vibrant acidity. A gripping wine with great depth and structure that will keep going strong for decades.

————*1985.* At first closed, this opened up beautifully in the glass after a few hours to reveal ripe plum berry and licorice on the nose with mouthwatering black cherry on the palate along with well-integrated oak. Opulent with firm acidity and bracing tannins.

————*1988.* Very dark color and more international in style. Initial wood and vegetable-herbaceous aromas give way to spicy black pepper and truffle after some hours in the glass. Oak dominates the lush plum flavors. Not my favorite of the lineup.

Barbaresco Sorì San Lorenzo 1988. Wonderfully spicy nose of white and black pepper, and cinnamon. Very concentrated plum flavors, but elegant, not jammy. Big round structure and long spicy finish with a hint of oak.

————*1989.* Classic Nebbiolo with heady aromas of violet and rose petals, cinnamon, leather, and truffle. Lovely concentration with fresh acidity and a seriously tannic backbone. Long, wild cherry finish and a tobacco close. This is a keeper and will continue to age gracefully for decades. Superb.

————*1990.* Another hallmark Barbaresco with a luminous ruby-red hue and a complex bouquet of dried cherries, violets, licorice, and a hint of truffle that carried over to the palate. Later, graphite emerged as the wine continued to evolve. Elegant structure and impeccably balanced with smooth tannins and fresh acidity. Gorgeous.

————*1996.* Deep dark ruby. At first austere, with a wood-dominated nose that soon dissipated once the wine opened up in the glass after a few hours. Then very ripe fruit and leather came out, and later still notes of flint. Round and full-bodied with rich black cherry flavors and a hint of vanilla accompanied by a long tannic finish. Still youthful and rather aggressive. Needs to be opened several hours before serving.

————*1997.* Hailed as one of the best years of the last century, its hot conditions resulted in rounder, more immediate wines that are the polar opposites of 1996. Dark ruby hue and ripe black fruit on the nose with whiffs of licorice, tobacco, and truffles. Rich berry and truffle flavors with hints of tea and figs. Long finish.

————*1998.* Overshadowed by the 1997 and 1999 vintages, which were hailed for their forwardness, 1998 has never been fully appreciated. Gaja's 1998 is a classic late bloomer and proved to be one of the best of the tasting for the younger set. While at first austere, stunning floral aromas soon developed. Classic berry, licorice, and tobacco palate. Perfectly balanced with vibrant acidity and bracing tannic backbone. Very young, with a long life ahead.

————*1999.* More international in style with initial oak and burnt aromas that soon vanish. Exuberant chocolate and coffee aromas dominate nose. Lavish fruit palate with oak and vanilla notes. Teeth-coating tannins and a long spicy close. Needs time to evolve.

————*2000.* Deep dark ruby color. Lush dark fruit and espresso fragrance with a hint of vanilla and oak. Rich and ripe black cherry and plum flavors are concentrated but not jammy. Bold tannins and a long toasty finish.

————*2001.* Alluring perfume of violet and rose with layers of strawberry and truffle. Bright and succulent black cherry and strawberry flavors with bracing tannins that need time to soften. Incredibly long and elegant finish of spice and mineral.

————*2003.* One of the hottest and driest vintages ever recorded. Fruit-forward aromas of ripe berries and plum with hints of rose. Juicy raspberry flavors and floral sensations with the warmth of alcohol on the palate. Remarkable freshness for the vintage balanced with firm tannins. Long cherry finish has telltale Gaja finesse.

Produttori del Barbaresco

Via Torino 54
12050 Barbaresco –(CN)
Tel. +39 0173 635139
www.produttoridelbarbaresco.com
produttori@produttoridelbarbaresco.com

Produttori del Barbaresco is not only one of the best and most consistent Barbaresco producers, but this *cantina sociale* is also one of the very best cooperative cellars in all of Italy, offering unbeatable quality-price ratios. Today the winery is run under the steady hand of managing director Aldo Vacca, and has fifty-two members who possess 100 hectares (247 acres) of vineyards, many among the most coveted sites in the denomination. The history of the Produttori is intertwined with the history of Barbaresco, and its roots go back to local legend Domizio Cavazza. Cavazza, the first director of the Royal Enological School of Alba, which was founded in 1881, decided shortly after his arrival in Piedmont to settle in Barbaresco. He realized early on the huge potential of the Barbaresco hills for creating great wines that were enjoyable earlier than Barolo but that were also long-lived and complex. In 1894, Cavazza gathered together nine Barbaresco growers and producers and created the original Cantina Sociale, where he encouraged grape growers to make wine in the cellars of his newly acquired Barbaresco castle.

The Cantina Sociale thrived for nearly two decades before a series of events forced it to close, starting with Cavazza's premature death in 1913 followed by World War I and its aftermath of poverty and misery. The cellar's death knell came with the rise of Fascism, which stipulated that farmers focus on only the barest necessities, mainly wheat, cereals, and cattle breeding and forced Barbaresco's cooperative cellar to finally close in 1925. Although Barolo, already a well-established wine with a die-hard following among Italy's elite, survived this difficult period, the first half of the twentieth century signaled the darkest time in Barbaresco's young history.

In 1958, Don Fiorino Marengo, Barbaresco's parish priest, realized that there would soon be no more parish in Barbaresco if local families continued their mass exodus out of the countryside to Turin and Alba to find work in the cities' thriving factories. Don Marengo gathered nineteen grape growers and convinced them it was time to revive the village's cooperative, and together they founded Produttori del Barbaresco.

FIGURE 23. Aldo Vacca of Produttori del Barbaresco. Largely considered one of the best if not the best cooperative cellar in all of Italy, this winery, managed by Aldo Vacca, makes Barbarescos with unbeatable quality-price ratio, especially their single-vineyard Riservas. Photograph by Paolo Tenti.

Today the members own one-sixth of the vineyards in Barbaresco, and have set an impressive quality benchmark. The winery keeps things very traditional in the cellars, with twenty-eight days of fermentation and maceration followed by aging in large casks (22–55 hectoliters) of both French and Slavonian oak. While Produttori makes cru Riservas in outstanding vintages, it also makes a textbook Barbaresco from a blend of various crus, mostly from Ovello and Pora, where its growers own the most land. The straight Barbaresco is aged for two years in botti while the crus, all designated as Riservas (made only in good years), are aged for three years in botti.

Production

Total surface area: 110 ha (271 acres) of Barbaresco owned by members
Barbaresco: 400,000 bottles

Barbaresco. This is consistently a straightforward, archetypical Barbaresco thanks to scrupulous selection, almost unheard-for cooperative cellars, which usually focus on quantity. The 2010 is a classic Barbaresco. It delivers quintessential Nebbiolo sensations of rose, black cherry, red berry, cinnamon-spice, and a hint of leather. It's intense but already accessible with firm, round tannins and just enough fresh acidity. Drink through 2020.

Pora Riserva 2008. Intense perfume of incense and spice. Bright and delicious berry flavors, with a round structure and firm but ripe tannins and racy acidity. Needs time to develop complexity but this should age beautifully. Drink 2015 to 2024.

Ovello Riserva 2008. Lovely, enticing floral fragrance with a hint of leather and balsamic notes. Succulent cherry fruit with spice and mineral notes. Great depth of flavors. The most accessible of the cellar's 2008 single-vineyard bottlings, this too will benefit with more age. Drink 2014 to 2023.

Rio Sordo Riserva 2008. This offers intense underbrush aromas of truffle, pine forest, leather, and balsamic notes. The palate has a core of juicy black cherries layered with cinnamon-spice and shows plenty of depth. Drink this after 2018 to let it develop more complexity.

Muncagota Riserva 2008. Up until 2007, the name of this famed vineyard was actually Moccagatta, but to avoid confusion with a winery bearing that same name, the cru has been officially renamed Muncagota, as it was often referred to in the local dialect. This is the most closed of all the 2008 crus, but it eventually opened up to reveal floral aromas and ripe black cherry accented with spice and mineral notes. This is still young, with bracing tannins and nervous acidity but has all the components and balance to become a spectacular Barbaresco. Drink 2018 to 2028.

Montestefano Riserva 2008.   Spicy with cinnamon, mint, and licorice notes along with ripe cherry-berry flavors. Powerfully structured with firm but fine tannins and vibrant acidity. Needs time. Best 2016 to 2023.

Cascina delle Rose

Via Riosordo 58
12050 Barbaresco (CN)
Tel. +39 0173 638322
www.cascinadellerose.it
cascinadellerose@cascinadellerose.it

This small estate is one of the true gems of Barbaresco and produces some of the most elegant and delicious wines in the entire Langhe. The estate's owner, Giovanna Rizzolio, left the fast-paced world of fashion design in 1985 and transferred full-time to her grandparents' farm in the Rio Sordo area of Barbaresco. There she revived the family's vineyards on the Rio Sordo and Tre Stelle hills and began making her own wine. In 1992 she also converted part of the property into a welcoming bed-and-breakfast, the first in Barbaresco. I'm not sure if Giovanna found the peace and tranquillity she was expecting when she moved to the countryside, but I do believe she has gotten immense satisfaction now that her small production cannot keep up with the growing demand from wine lovers around the world.

Founded by Giovanna's grandmother in 1948, the firm released its first bottled Barbaresco in 1952, decades ahead of most of today's Barbaresco producers, who sold their grapes until the end of the 1980s and in the early 1990s, and she continued releasing miniscule amounts of Barbaresco until the early 1980s. Giovanna released her first Barbaresco "Rio Sordo" in 1985, adding the name of this celebrated cru, which had already been defined as a "Prime Position" by Lorenzo Fantini at the end of the nineteenth century.[1]

Today Giovanna and her husband, Italo Sobrino, along with his sons Davide and Riccardo, run this boutique estate. As with most family firms, everyone wears more than one hat, but Davide is in charge of the vineyards

FIGURE 24. Giovanna Rizzolio and Italo Sobrino of Cascina delle Rose. This boutique estate is one of the real jewels of the Langhe. From their Rio Sordo and Tre Stelle vineyards, Giovanna and Italo make what are among the most elegant and delicious wines in Barbaresco. Photograph by Paolo Tenti.

and also helps his father and Giovanna in the cellars, while Riccardo runs the on-site accommodations. Patrons who stay at the winery tend to return every year and are among the firm's die-hard fans, and if you stay here you'll know why. Giovanna, whose positive energy permeates the estate, and Italo are handcrafting compelling, elegant wines of depth and breeding that also boast age-worthy structures. And because nature and a healthy environment are priorities for Giovanna, she eschews chemicals in the vineyards, relying instead on strict vineyard management and careful grape selection, although she is never radical when it comes to green harvests, searching instead to find the right balance for each plant.

Although the firm replanted some vineyards in 2004, it also has a high percentage of vines that were planted in 1950, which naturally produce fewer but superior grapes. Their holdings in Rio Sordo and Tre Stelle benefit from southern and southwestern exposures, while altitude ranges between 240 and 310 meters (785.4 and 1,017 feet) above sea level—optimum conditions for ripening Nebbiolo. Soil is a complex layer of calcareous marls and blue marls interspersed with veins of well-draining sand and darker soil rich in minerals. The estate's vineyards further benefit from an abundant quantity of underground water that encourages vines to penetrate far beneath the surface where they can find nutrients and minerals. This water reserve also ensures that vines do not suffer from water stress, which is now a major problem throughout the Langhe.

Giovanna and Italo adopt a noninvasive approach in the cellars, shunning selected yeasts and allowing wild yeasts to spontaneously start fermentation. They age their Barbarescos in 10- and 20-hectoliter Slavonian casks and do not filter their wines. Situated in the middle of these Slavonian casks with their classic red borders is a spacious tasting area, complete with red leather chairs—one of the most stylish and welcoming tasting rooms I've been in, and a perfect setting to try these lovely wines.

Production

Total surface area: 5 ha (12.35 acres)

Barbaresco: 1.65 ha (4 acres), 5,500–5,900 bottles

Barbaresco Tre Stelle. Aged between fifteen and twenty months in Slavonian casks, this luminous and vibrant Barbaresco is all about elegance and breeding, and even in hot years like 2007 and 2009, it still boasts fresh acidity thanks to underground water reserves. The 2009 has an exquisite floral bouquet with dark cherry and mineral flavors. Silky, long, and linear. Drink 2014 to 2024. The 2010 is stunning, offering an enticing Nebbiolo perfume of forest floor, Alpine herbs, ripe berry, truffle, and a hint of leather. The palate delivers cherry notes sprinkled with spice, and shows great depth and balance. It's elegant and already shows gripping complexity but will continue to evolve for years. Drink through 2030.

Barbaresco Rio Sordo. Aged for about twenty-two months in Slavonian casks, Rio Sordo has more structure and depth than Tre Stelle. The 2009 boasts ripe cherry-berry and earthy aromas with hints of spice, truffle, and leather. Gripping tannins and fresh acidity. Drink 2014 to 2024. The 2010 is a textbook Barbaresco. It has an alluring and multifaceted bouquet of lilac, violet, and wisteria, along with hints of spice, truffle, and earth. The palate is focused, with intense cherry and spice notes balanced by firm but fine tannins and freshness. It already shows ample complexity and will age beautifully. Drink 2015 to 2035.

Barbaresco Rio Sordo 1999. Tasted in 2012, this 1999, a fantastic vintage, demonstrates the undeniable aging potential of top Barbarescos. Enticing dried rose petals and dried cherries, with leather and white truffle notes, fig and black tea. Long and linear, with great depth balanced by velvety tannins and still vibrant acidity. Drink through 2024.

Langhe Nebbiolo. Cascina delle Rose makes one of my favorite Langhe Nebbiolos. Aged in steel, this is always fresh, vibrant, and delicious, with floral aromas and strawberry, cherry, and spice flavors and silky tannins.

Roagna

Loc. Paglieri 9
12050 Barbaresco (CN)
Tel. +39 0173 635109
www.roagna.com
info@roagna.com

Alfredo and Luca Roagna, the fourth and fifth generations of a family of long-established Barbaresco grape growers and winemakers, are handcrafting fascinating, soulful Barbarescos and Barolos of mesmerizing depth. Roagna's Barbarescos, made from estate grapes grown in the heart of the village's top crus, and their Barolos, from their holdings in Castiglione Falletto (they also used to make Vigna Rionda), are earthy, structured wines with mind-blowing complexity and exceptional character and are the result of ideally ripened Nebbiolo from prime vineyards coupled with a scrupulous disdain for convention and a near-fanatical obsession with nature.

A walk through the Roagna's vineyards with Luca on a cold, rainy day in late November 2012 proved that while many winemakers merely talk up a good tale about natural farming and natural winemaking, the Roagnas are die-hard naturalists who truly live out this unyielding philosophy. The family's Barbaresco vineyards are in the most protected parts of the most desired crus, including Asili, Crichët Pajè, Pajè, and Montefico in Barbaresco, and Pira and Carso in the Barolo village of Castiglione Falletto.

Standing in the pelting autumn rain in the firm's untamed vineyards in the heart of Montefico, I was stunned to find a thick carpet of green grass, wild mint, and wild peas—even the occasional bright purple wildflower—all still thriving despite being so late in the season. "We're considered the savages of Barbaresco because we never cut the grass but instead trample it down. The grass is at the heart of the biodiversity in our vineyards, which is crucial for healthy vines. It also protects from erosion," says Luca, who is intensely passionate about his vineyards and winemaking but who also has a wonderful sense of humor, particularly when it comes to describing his family's unorthodox vineyard and cellar practices.

Roagna turns the earth only "once every four or five years," never uses chemicals of any kind, and never puts down fertilizer of any sort, not even organic. The firm also shuns commercial clones, which Luca feels are too susceptible to disease and suffocate the biodiversity among the vines, which he maintains is crucial to achieving naturally balanced vines and wines. And their underlying philosophy of working around nature rather than forcing nature's hand seems to be succeeding: Roagna's vines average fifty-five to sixty years old, among the oldest I've ever seen in the Langhe, and are still apparently very healthy overall. When individual plants die because of old age, the firm used to plant rootstocks grafted with young plants from the same vineyard, chosen by massal selection, but now Luca is substituting plants by propagating from the plant next to it. In other words, he uses the technique before phylloxera forever changed planting vineyards around the globe: he buries a vine shoot from the closest vine without grafting onto a rootstock. In the firm's Barolo holdings in Castiglione Falletto, where the subsoil contains a high percentage of sand, a natural enemy to phylloxera, Roagna even has some seventy-five-year-old ungrafted vines.

The noninvasive approach extends to the cellars located in the heart of the Pajè cru in Barbaresco. Roagna ferments in conical wooden vats made of both Slavonian and French oak, with no temperature control, and it goes without saying that they never use selected yeasts. Postfermentation maceration recalls the days of yore, and depending on the vintage, the total maceration period, including skin contact during the ten to fifteen days of alcoholic fermentation, can last a whopping seventy to one hundred days. Roagna still favors the time-honored submerged-cap method, known locally as *steccatura,* for complete but gentle extraction of color, fine tannins, and polyphenols. The wine then ages in large Slavonian casks for years: five, six, or more, depending on the wine and the vintage. According to Luca, when it comes to fermentation and aging times, "the only rules here are that there are no rules."

Production

Total surface area: 20 ha (49.4 acres)

Barbaresco: 3 ha (7.4 acres), 10,000–12,000 bottles

Barolo: 5 ha (12.35 acres), 25,000 bottles

Barbaresco Pajè 2007. Very floral, earthy aromas with hints of truffle. Big, ripe berry flavors. Surprisingly fresh for this hot vintage, with teeth-coating but fully ripe tannins. An excellent 2007.

Barbaresco Pajè 2007 "Vecchie Vigne." As the name states, this is made from the oldest plants, between sixty and sixty-five years old, in a cru that boasts ideal southwest exposures. Concentrated perfume of rose, violet, and sandalwood, this is way more intense than the straight Pajè. Rich cherry and mint flavors of great depth balanced by dusty, youthful tannins and racy acidity. Fantastic length. Best 2017 to 2027+.

Barbaresco Asili 2007 "Vecchie Vigne." Intense floral fragrance of wild rose and violet with sweet cherry, berry, and spice flavors. Extremely elegant and supple with intriguing complexity and poise all wrapped up in a solid structure. Impeccably balanced. This may be the best Barbaresco I've tried so far from this vintage. It is also a hallmark Asili, perhaps Barbaresco's equivalent of Chambolle-Musigny Les Charmes. Drink 2015 to 2032.

Barbaresco Montefico 2007 "Vecchie Vigne." More masculine than Asili, with impressive power. This could easily be a Barolo. A compelling wine that will age well for another decade or more.

Barolo La Pira 2007. This intense wine is initially closed but then unfolds in the glass to reveal layers of cherry, leather, and balsamic herbs. This is austere and still quite young and closed. Rich fruit flavors are balanced by nice acidity and powerful but sweet tannins. This needs more time to develop complexity and let tannins tame down. Best after 2017.

Barbaresco 1997. Blended with Nebbiolo from Montefico, Asili, and Pajè, this was a stunning and surprisingly youthful 1997 when tasted in 2012. Still bright cherry flavors with leather, truffle, and tobacco leaf alongside rather fresh acidity and velvety, evolved tannins. Great length and mineral finish. Complex and balanced. Best 2014 to 2022.

Barbaresco Crichët Pajè 1988. Produced only in the greatest vintages, Crichët Pajè is Roagna's calling card. Made from a small parcel of land in the heart of the family's Pajè holdings, this is a monument to Nebbiolo. Tasted in 2012, this twenty-four-year-old boasted dried rose petal, tar, leather, and tobacco sensations. It's powerfully structured, yet more complex than muscular, with fabulous depth. A soulful and gorgeous Barbaresco with aged

Nebbiolo's unparalleled tertiary sensations balanced by astonishingly youthful freshness. Best through 2028.

Albino Rocca

Strada Ronchi 18
12050 Barbaresco (CN)
Tel. +39 0173 635145
www.albinorocca.com
roccaalbino@roccaalbino.com

At the 2012 Nebbiolo Prima annual press tastings held in Alba to showcase the latest vintages, I was surprised that several of my high-scoring wines from these blind tastings were from the Albino Rocca firm. In the past I found these wines delivered more oak than fruit so I was pleasantly surprised and more than intrigued by the polished but pure Nebbiolo sensations and finesse of the estate's recent releases.

As is the typical story of so many Langhe wineries, the Rocca family has been growing Nebbiolo for more than a century in Barbaresco. In 1955, Albino Rocca founded the firm, and he and his father, Giacomo, began bottling their wines from the family's vineyards in Barbaresco. Albino's son Angelo began working at the winery in the mid-1960s, and in 1971 the firm released its first Barbaresco labeled Albino Rocca. The mid-1980s were a pivotal time for the denomination and for Angelo, who had been working at the winery since he was fifteen. "In 1986, we began bottling our entire production, and I also started spending time with Elio Altare and other Barolo producers who were making a softer, fruitier style of Barolo. That same year, a group of us went to France, and we came back determined to improve quality for Barolo and Barbaresco. I started lowering yields and thinning out the grapes with a green harvest, which was quite radical at the time in Barbaresco and in Barolo, and even my own uncle told me I was crazy. In 1986, I also began aging our wines in barriques," Angelo told me during an interview and visit to the winery in May of 2012. Soon after, he started working with consulting enologist Beppe Caviola. Caviola was pivotal in creating more internationally styled Barolos and Barbarescos for many of the Langhe's young winemakers who were taking over family wineries in the 1980s and 1990s but who wanted to break with tradition.

By the late 1980s, Angelo understood the great potential of two of his vineyards, Ronchi and Loreto, and in 1990 he began vinifying and bottling these two crus separately. Angelo was a trailblazer when it came to vineyard management. In the 1970s, Barolo and Barbaresco producers, like winemakers throughout the world, had embraced a new generation of industrial and chemical agricultural products designed to combat weeds and parasites. Yet by the mid-1980s, Angelo realized these products had sterilized the soil, and "had effectively poisoned the environment." In 1992, he converted to Italy's regulated Lotta Guidata method of vineyard management, eschewing harsh chemicals and using only organic fertilizers and only small doses of copper and sulfur to combat fungus.

In the cellars, the firm ferments in rotary fermenters with maceration lasting on average a total of eight days. In 2004, Angelo's innovative spirit shone through once again when he decided that he was fed up with barriques and started using large, neutral casks. After several years of experimenting, he decided on 20-hectoliter casks made of both German and Austrian oak, saying during our interview, "I was never very happy with barriques, and am very pleased that the market now wants more elegant, less evidently oaked wines, which is what I prefer."

Besides wine, Angelo, who according to other winemakers in Barolo and Barbaresco was one of the most generous and outgoing of their colleagues, had a true passion for flying. One of his greatest pleasures was flying above the vineyards and just over the rooftops of the tiny historic center of his home village. His yellow and blue ultralight plane had in fact become a fixture in the skies over Barbaresco and was in the backdrop of many of my recent visits there. Sadly, Angelo, who struck me in the brief time I knew him as one of the nicest and most down-to-earth winemakers in the denomination, died when his plane crashed in October 2012. His three grown daughters, Daniela, Monica, and Paola, and his son-in-law Carlo, all of whom worked at the firm alongside Angelo for years, have taken over the winery.

Production

Total surface area: 23 ha (57 acres)
Barbaresco: 6.5 ha (16.06 acres), 33,000 bottles

Barbaresco. This is made from the Montersino vineyards in San Rocco Seno d'Elvio. Located 310 meters (1,017 feet) above sea level and with full southern exposures, grapes usually reach ideal maturation, while the high altitude cools down the vines during the growing season. Aged for two years in 20-hectoliter casks made with Austrian and German wood, this a succulent and floral Barbaresco that is approachable but can age as well. The 2008 shows vibrant dark cherry, mint, and a hint of anise with juicy berry flavors, spice, and supple tannins.

Barbaresco 2010 Duemiladieci. Elegant with an intensely floral bouquet of rose, violet, and iris, plus whiffs of sage and balsam. The palate offers juicy, wild cherry flavors punctuated with truffle and balsamic notes of Alpine herbs. It's impeccably balanced, with ample length.

Barbaresco Vigna Loreto. From the eponymous vineyard in the Ovello cru, where Rocca's thirty-five-year-old vines are situated 240 meters (787 feet) above sea level and enjoy southeastern exposures and a certain percentage of sand in the subsoil. This is very elegant and perfumed, with mouthwatering fruit. The 2008 is classic, with floral, cherry, and spice fragrance and creamy cherry-berry fruit with a long mineral finish. Radiant with lithe tannins and beautiful balance. Gorgeous.

Barbaresco Ronchi. From Rocca's Ronchi vineyard where vines are between fifty and seventy years old, and where there is more compact soil and calcareous clay, both of which give the wine more structure than Loreto. Since 2004, the Roccas have been reducing barrique aging in favor in large casks, and starting in 2012 they will be eliminating barriques entirely. The 2008 boasts dark, plump cherry, spice, and mineral sensations with subtle toasty notes and a hint of espresso. The 2010 boasts lovely violet and sage aromas sprinkled with coffee and espresso notes. The palate shows creamy red fruit layered with chocolate and spice and firm but refined tannins. This is very elegant but still a bit shy, and so best to drink after 2014.

Barbaresco Vigneto Brich Ronchi Riserva. This is a fantastic, compelling wine. Made only in the best years and from the best grapes from the oldest plants in Ronchi, this is aged for four years in 20-hectoliter Austrian and German casks. The 2006 is loaded with concentrated but vibrant dark cherry fruit, earth, leather, and spice with stunning depth and layers of complexity. A gripping and delicious wine.

Cantina del Pino

Strada Ovello 31
12050 Barbaresco (CN)
Tel. +39 0173 635147

www.cantinadelpino.com
renato@cantinadelpino.com

Renato Vacca's small winery boasts an impressive lineage and has a special place in the history of the village of Barbaresco, for it was once owned by none other than Domizio Cavazza, hailed as the Father of Barbaresco. Cavazza, the founding director of Alba's Royal Enological School from 1881 until his death in 1913, decided not to settle in the more celebrated Barolo zone, as the noble families of Piedmont had expected. Instead, Cavazza settled in Barbaresco, at the time an undervalued area where he saw tremendous potential for Nebbiolo. He acquired the Castle of Barbaresco and other property, including a farmhouse and surrounding land on the Ovello hillside, known as Cascina Ovello. After the birth of his first son, Cavazza planted a Mediterranean pine tree, and the area soon became known to locals as the Cascina del Pino, or Pine Tree Farm. After Cavazza's premature death, his family moved to Turin, and Renato Vacca's great-grandfather purchased the Cavazza's vineyards where the Vacca family has been growing grapes and eventually making Barbaresco ever since.

Renato's father and uncle were founding members of Produttori del Barbaresco, and Renato, a graduate of Alba's Enological School, worked in the cooperative's cellars for five years before taking over the family firm and producing his first estate-bottled Barbaresco in 1997. In the celebrated Ovello cru, Renato's family owns a block of vineyards situated at 300 meters (984 feet) above sea level with southern and southwestern exposures. The advanced age of the plants, nearly seventy years old, generates intense flavors, while the clay and sandy soil give the wines both body and elegance as well as its bright character. Vacca also owns vineyards in the Albesani subzone on the celebrated Santo Stefano hill in the village of Neive. Thanks to full southern exposures and higher clay content, this Barbaresco is darker, spicier, and more powerfully structured than Ovello. Renato also makes a Barbaresco from blending four vineyards. The firm uses no chemical fertilizers, and plant age averages forty years old for Nebbiolo.

Renato keeps things simple in the cellar, and more than a straight traditionalist, he is a noninterventionist, guiding his wine through the vinification and aging processes to produce terroir-driven wines with character. He also believes that Nebbiolo should never be entirely destemmed, but drives home the crucial point that the 10–15 percent stems he allows in the fermentation process "must be perfectly ripe." According to Vacca, these ripe stems

FIGURE 25. Renato Vacca of Cantina del Pino. Renato Vacca now runs the family winery acquired by his great-grandfather, which once belonged to Domizio Cavazza, the Father of Barbaresco. In the celebrated Ovello cru, the firm owns a block of vineyards that average seventy years old and generate concentrated flavors and complexity. Photograph by Paolo Tenti.

impart noble tannins that add an extra element to his wines. Fermentation and maceration last for about thirty days for Barbaresco. In his minimalist cellars, built in 2005 in the heart of Ovello, Vacca ages his Barbarescos for two years in wood, one year in barriques, 30 percent of which are new, and one year in 25-hectoliter Slavonian botti. He then ages Barbaresco for one year in bottle, while his single-vineyard Barbarescos undergo two years of bottle aging. Renato does not filter or fine his wines.

Production

Total surface area: 7 ha (17.29 acres)

Barbaresco: 5.5 ha (13.59 acres), 20,000 bottles

Barbaresco.   Made by blending estate Nebbiolo from Ovello in Barbaresco and Gallina, Albesani, and Starderi in Neive. This is a lovely and approachable wine with good aging potential. The 2009 offers dark cherry, cinnamon, and clove with black pepper. Very fresh and vibrant with firm but round tannins. Best 2014 to 2019.

Barbaresco Ovello.   Made with the best grapes in the Ovello vineyard and aged for four years before release (two in wood, two in bottle), this is full-bodied, with delicious dark cherry, spice, and mineral flavors. The 2009 has ripe, red fruit sensations but is still young and nervous with bracing tannins. Long and linear with a hint of licorice. Best 2014 to 2021.

Barbaresco Albesani.   Made from a selection of the best grapes in the eponymous vineyard, this is made just like the Ovello Barbaresco. Richer, darker, and more structured.

La Spinona

Via Secondine 30
12050 Barbaresco (CN)
Tel. +39 0173 635169
www.laspinonabarbaresco.it
info@laspinonabarbaresco.it

Owned by the Berutti family, this small winery is just a short walk down the hill from the Enoteca Regionale del Barbaresco and overlooks the stunning Faset hill, where the family has their vineyards. Here ninety-two-year-old Pietro Berutti, his son Gualtiero, and grandson Pietro Paolo are crafting archetypical and long-lived Barbarescos that combine elegance and restrained tannic strength that develop layers of complexity with bottle age.

La Spinona takes its name from a particular race of Piedmont hunting dogs that the winery owner, Pietro Berutti, breeds. The original dog that lent its name to the winery was another member of the family for the Beruttis, and accompanied Gualtiero everywhere, to the vineyards and even occasionally to the university when Gualtiero was studying to become a veterinarian. Sadly, the dog, like so many other dogs before and after him living in the Italian countryside, was poisoned by eating a nugget of meat laced with poison that had been purposefully left by hunters. According to the many local winemakers who have also witnessed their pets' demise, a shocking number of hunters apparently have no qualms about causing a slow and painful death to family pets in order to ensure that nothing—especially a barking dog—will interfere with a day's hunting. In the Langhe, this tragedy happens even more often during the truffle season, when jealous truffle hunters deliberately poison their competitors' truffle dogs. To honor their beloved pet, Pietro named his winery La Spinona, and the dog's image adorns the firm's labels.

FIGURE 26. Pietro Berutti of La Spinona. Just a short walk from the center of Barbaresco this winery overlooks the splendid Faset vineyard where the firm has prime holdings. Ninety-two-year-old Pietro, his son, and grandson produce archetypical and age-worthy Barbarescos and Barolos. Photograph by Paolo Tenti.

Nonagenarian Pietro, a Barbaresco native and a decorated soldier-turned-partisan, founded the winery in 1958, and his first Barbaresco hails from the same year. Having camped and fought in the Langhe hills for three years during World War II, he knows the hills intimately, and knew that the high, central part of the Faset vineyard, known as Bricco Faset, was ideal for Nebbiolo. Although the family owns land in other parts of Barbaresco, they bottle only the best from their prime holdings in Faset. Since 1996, the firm has also produces an excellent Barolo from vineyards they acquired in Novello. Pietropaolo, a trained enologist who has recently taken on most of the winemaking responsibilities while his father Gualtiero looks after the vines, is keeping things rather traditional. He avoids commercial yeasts, opting instead for the "pie di cuve" method of allowing a small amount of pre-harvested estate grapes to ferment and then inoculating the tanks with the fermenting wine. Aging takes place in 25-hectoliter casks, of both Slavonian and French oak.

These are textbook Barbarescos and Barolos, with lovely fruit, bracing tannins, vibrant acidity, and energizing minerality. They are consistently well balanced, and with time develop the hallmark nuances of Nebbiolo: dried rose petal, tar, and leather, with layers of complexity. They are also an outstanding value even in U.S. wineshops.

Production

Total surface area: 27 ha (66.7 acres)

Barbaresco: 11 ha (27 acres); much of this is sold in bulk; 4,000 bottles

Barolo: 4 ha (9.8 acres), 5,000 bottles

Barbaresco Faset.   This is a classic Barbaresco that seamlessly combines elegance, great depth of flavors, and a firm tannic backbone brightened by fresh acidity. The 1999 was a breath of fresh air when I first came across the wine in the early years of the New Millennium, when so many wines were overoaked and underwhelming. I've tried the wine every year since then, and find it is very consistent, and thanks to careful selection, this is outstanding in good and even not-so-good vintages. The 2009 had rounder fruit than usual, thanks to the warmer vintage, but still had vibrancy, and should drink well through 2019. The 2008 is more classic and is almost Burgundy-like with strawberry sensations and lovely mineral purity and bracing but fine tannins. Lots of energy and depth. Best 2014 to 2028. In truly outstanding years, generally once every five or six years, the estate also makes a Barbaresco Faset Riserva, which shows more complexity and needs more time to develop.

Barolo Sorì Gepin.   Like the Barbaresco Faset, this Barolo is crafted in the classic style. While it boasts a bracing tannic structure, its layers of bright fruit support both the tannins and fresh acidity, and it too develops wonderful complexity at about the ten-year mark. The 2007 offers juicy, mouthwatering cherry and strawberry fruit with leather, menthol, and spice notes. Surprisingly fresh for the vintage, this has compelling depth of flavors and a long finish. Best 2017 to 2027.

De Forville

Via Torino 44
12050 Barbaresco (CN)
Tel. +39 0173 635140
www.deforville.it
info@deforville.it

FIGURE 27. Paolo and Valter Anfossi of De Forville. Founded in 1860, the De Forville family was one of the trailblazers of Barbaresco, and the family winery is now run by Paolo and Valter Anfossi, the fifth generation. The Anfossis continue to make authentic, terroir-driven Barbarescos from their select estate vineyards such as Loreto. Photograph by Paolo Tenti.

Right in the center of the village of Barbaresco and next to the tower, De Forville, one of the oldest producers in the denomination, turns out textbook Barbarescos from its coveted holdings in Barbaresco. De Forville's prime real estate includes the excellent Loreto vineyard—now part of the proven Ovello cru, where the firm also has other first-rate vineyards—and Cavanna.

The family-run firm is one of the true trailblazers of Barbaresco, and was founded in 1860 by Gioacchino De Forville, born in Alba but of Walloon origins, from the eponymous region in Belgium. De Forville was one of the earliest Barbaresco producers to believe wholeheartedly in Nebbiolo, and he was soon following the teachings of Domizio Cavazza, founder of Alba's Royal Enological School, who would also create the first cooperative cellar in Barbaresco at the close of the 1800s. The firm has always produced Barbaresco, originally sold in bulk to restaurants and retailers, who in turn would bottle the wine for their patrons, but by 1940, De Forville was bottling its own Barbaresco. Today the fifth generation of the family, Paolo and Valter Anfossi, run the winery in a refreshingly down-to-earth style and rightly so: no need for the flash and extravagance relied on by some of Barbaresco's more celebrated producers, here the authenticity and quality of the wines speak for themselves.

Like all the best producers of terroir-driven Barbarescos, the Anfossi have a decidedly hands-off approach in both the vineyards and the winery, and one reason for this is the outstanding quality of their raw material. Their Barbaresco vineyards have predominantly southwestern exposures and are situated on average at 250 meters (820 feet) above sea level, while plant age averages thirty-five years old—the prime for healthy and productive Nebbiolo plants. In the cellar, the brothers eschew selected yeasts, allowing fermentation to occur in temperature-controlled stainless steel tanks. Fermentation and maceration generally last about four weeks depending on the vintage. De Forville's Barbarescos are then aged for eighteen months in large Slavonian casks.

Production

Total surface area: 11 ha (27 acres)

Barbaresco: 3 ha (7.4 acres), 20,000 bottles

Barbaresco. This is De Forville's flagship Barbaresco, made from a blend of Nebbiolo from four separate estate vineyards—all situated in Barbaresco—that give natural balance to the wine. This is a quintessential Barbaresco with hallmark aromas of violet, rose, leather, and truffle. The palate offers delicious but restrained fruit and spice with bright acidity and sweet but firm tannins. The 2009 has an intense bouquet of rose and truffle with delicious cherry flavors and ripe, dusty tannins. Best 2014 to 2019.

Barbaresco "Vigneto Loreto." This is more structured and has more depth than the straight Barbaresco, and is made entirely from the best grapes in the superb Loreto vineyard. The 2009 boasts intense floral and earthy aromas and delicious cherry, truffle, and black tea flavors. Still incredibly youthful with racy acidity and bracing tannins, this needs time to develop complexity and to find itself, but it should blossom into a compelling wine. Best 2017 to 2029.

La Ca' Nova

Via Ovello 4
12050 Barbaresco (CN)
Tel. +39 0173 635123

This estate has quietly been making outstanding, terroir-driven Barbarescos for generations from two of the denomination's top crus, Montestefano and

Montefico. And perhaps the most remarkable aspect is that these polished and compelling wines are made with almost no use of modern technology.

Pietro Rocca, the family's smiling and modest patriarch, is the fourth generation of grape growers. In the early 1970s, he began making and bottling Barbaresco; before that, his family sold grapes to none other than Angelo Gaja and to his father before him. There is no secret as to why these wines are quintessential expressions of Nebbiolo—it all starts in the vineyards with healthy grapes that have reached ideal ripening. Their single-vineyard bottlings come from two of the most coveted sites in Barbaresco. Montestefano produces some of the most structured Barbarescos, and the Roccas own prime parcels situated at 270 meters (886 feet) above sea level with full southern exposures. Montefico, where the Roccas own the Bric Mentine vineyard, has the same altitude, southern and southeastern exposures, and less marly soil. Local legend has it that Montefico was once owned by Domizio Cavazza, the founding father of Barbaresco.

Today Pietro is joined by his sons Marco, an enologist, and Ivan, an agronomist who tends to the vineyards. The firm adopts a strictly hands-off approach in the winery, using only wild yeasts for fermentation, which takes place mostly in steel tanks and in three wooden conical vats, but with no temperature control. Just before fermentation is completed, the firm continues fermentation and maceration with the antique tradition known as *steccatura,* whereby wooden planks keep the cap (a mass composed of the grape skins and seeds) submerged in the tank. This time-consuming method gently extracts more color and polyphenols. For the firm's single-vineyard bottlings, fermentation and maceration generally take twenty-five to thirty days.

After fermentation the firm ages its Barbarescos in 30-hectoliter casks, but rather than Slavonian oak, Pietro prefers Austrian oak: "They are untoasted and neutral, and are the best-quality barrels I have ever seen. In fourteen years, not one has ever leaked a drop." Pietro recounts that eschewing barriques a decade ago was very difficult, especially since his children were pushing him to switch over. "Now they're glad we didn't because these days there is a strong interest in traditionally crafted wines, but it was a battle for a few years," he says. The wines are also unfiltered, and besides being quintessential Barbarescos with finesse and structure, they are also extremely well priced.

Production

Total surface area: 10.8 ha (26.68 acres)

Barbaresco: 10.8 ha (26.68 acres), 18,500 bottles

Barbaresco Montefico "Bric Mentin" 2009. Hallmark Barbaresco with a bright, garnet hue. Lovely floral fragrance punctuated by mushroom and truffle. Silky and bright. Although this is approachable soon after release, will age well for a decade or more. Drink 2013 to 2019.

Barbaresco Montestefano 2009. More intense and structured than Bric Mentin. Intense perfume of black cherry, spice, and hints of leather. Delicious cherry and spice flavors balanced by gripping tannins and racy acidity. This needs time but will develop complexity as its tannins tame. A compelling wine. Drink 2015 to 2029.

Giamello Silvio—La Licenziana

Strada Ovello 14
12050 Barbaresco (CN)
Tel. +39 0173 635157
s.giamello@email.it

The singular rose, cherry, and mineral purity of Nebbiolo shines through these quintessential Barbarescos made by artisanal producer Silvio Giamello, whose firm is known as La Licenziana, an area that traces its roots back to ancient Rome. According to documents analyzed by Silvio, and as reported in a history of Barbaresco written by Domizio Cavazza, it seems the land was once owned by a Roman noble by the name of Lollio Gentiano, who built Villa Gentiano. As the local theory goes, over the millennia the name was transformed to Licenziana, and eventually Vicenziana, now the names of Silvio's estate and Barbaresco, respectively.

Silvio is the fourth generation of growers and winemakers to work the Vicenziana cru. Thanks to the vineyard area's cooler, eastern exposures it greatly benefits from fresher conditions as opposed to many crus with full southern exposures, which are suffering from the climatic changes of the last fifteen years or so that have led to much drier and hotter growing seasons in the Langhe. Silvio adds that there are more hours of daylight in his vineyards than in other areas, which helps grapes reach ideal ripening in this cooler corner of Barbaresco, as does vineyard altitude, which ranges between 180 and 240 meters (590 and 787 feet) above sea level.

Silvio's great-grandfather founded the farm, which, typically for the times, was planted with mixed cultivation, including vines, cereal, fruit trees, and grazing land, which produced everything the family needed in order to survive.

He passed the farm down through the family, with each generation wisely replanting more land to vineyards. His son bottled a small amount of the family's production and sold the rest of the grapes and wine in bulk. By the mid-1960s, his son, Silvio's father, regularly bottled and sold more of the production, increasing amounts each year while he too continued to sell grapes. From 1990 until 1995, because of several family issues, the firm suspended bottling but continued to sell both grapes and wine until Silvio took over in 1995.

Silvio, who is helped by his wife, Marina, now concentrates on making outstanding Barbaresco solely from their estate grapes. His family never used chemical herbicides or fungicides in their vineyards, and these days Silvio plants legumes between every other row, which he then cuts and leaves to break down for natural fertilizer. Today, their healthy plants average forty-five years old and generate just the right amount of controlled vigor in the field and intense flavors in the wine. In his modest cellars beneath his house, Silvio allows spontaneous fermentation with wild yeasts carried out in temperature-controlled steel tanks. He then ages his Barbaresco for between two and three years in traditional Slavonian casks.

Production

Total surface area: 5 ha (12.3 acres)
Barbaresco: 2 ha (4.9 acres), 4,000–5,000 bottles

The following offerings were all tasted in 2012.

Barbaresco Vicenziana 2006. Classic Nebbiolo fragrance of just-picked cherry, rose, tar, and leather with layers of succulent cherry flavors accompanied by spice, menthol, and licorice. Extremely elegant with gripping tannins and vibrant acidity. Will age beautifully. Drink through 2036.

Barbaresco Vicenziana 2001. Hallmark Barbaresco from one of the best of the recent vintages. Enticing bouquet of saddle leather, dried rose petals, tar, and cooking spices that all carry over onto the palate with mineral and black tea notes. Incredibly elegant and drinkable, changing with each sip. A stunning wine with great personality. Drink and enjoy through 2031.

Barbaresco Vicenziana 1998. Gorgeous perfume of violet, rose, and sandalwood, with berry and mineral on the palate. Silky smooth and impeccably balanced with supple tannins and vibrant acidity. Drinking beautifully. Best through 2018.

Giuseppe Cortese

Strada Rabajà 80
12050 Barbaresco (CN)
Tel. +39 0173 635131
www.cortesegiuseppe.it
info@cortesegiuseppe.it

Rabajà is one of the most celebrated crus in the Barbaresco denomination, although many locals say that the officially delimited cru is far bigger than the historic zone where grapes truly excelled. The Giuseppe Cortese winery has 8 hectares (20 acres) in Rabajà, laid out like out an amphitheater on the famed hillside.

The estate was founded in 1971 by Giuseppe Cortese, who began bottling Barbaresco made from estate grapes that same year. Today Giuseppe still follows the vineyards, while his son Pier Carlo, a graduate of Alba's Enological School who joined the firm in the 1990s, is the winemaker, turning out a refined, straightforward Barbaresco and a more complex and age-worthy Riserva, all from Rabajà.

Besides southern and southwestern exposures and an ideal altitude for the vines, Giuseppe, whose father was also a grower, has long believed in short pruning, bunch thinning, and scrupulous grape selection, all of which encourage grapes to reach ideal ripening. Once they are in the cellar, Pier Carlo allows the healthy grapes to spontaneously ferment, without using selected yeasts. He then ages his wines in 17- to 25-hectoliter casks made from both Slavonian and French oak.

Production

Total surface area: 8 ha (19.76 acres)
Barbaresco: 4 ha (9.88 acres), 23,000 bottles

Barbaresco "Rabajà."   Made from thirty-five- to fifty-five-year-old vines situated at 250 meters (820 feet) above sea level and aged for eighteen to twenty-two months in casks. This is a consistently outstanding effort vintage after vintage, showing hallmark Nebbiolo sensations. The 2008 is fantastic, with a bouquet of wild rose, bright cherry, raspberry, spice, and balsamic notes. The palate is vibrant with rich cherry and spice flavors accompanied by bracing but round tannins. Drink 2014 to 2023. The 2010 offers up intensely floral and balsamic fragrances alongside delicious cherry-berry and spice flavors. Its tannins are firm but elegant, and while still tightly wound, this will be drinking beautifully after 2015 and will continue to evolve for another decade at least.

Barbaresco Rabajà Riserva. This is the firm's flagship wine, and it is only made in exceptional vintages. The Riserva, which is aged for forty months in large casks followed by three years fining in bottle, hails from Cortese's best and oldest vines in Rabajà, averaging forty to sixty years old. Plant age and full southern exposure generate complex aromas, rich flavors, and an ageworthy structure. The 2006 is a hallmark Nebbiolo, with intense aromas of rose, leather, and spice. The palate is full and rich, with succulent cherry punctuated by spice and tobacco. Tasted in 2012, this is still very young with youthful but ripe tannins and nervous acidity. Needs time to develop complexity, but should blossom into a classic for the ages. Drink 2014 to 2028.

Olek Bondonio

Via Riccardo Terzolo 14
12050 Barbaresco (CN)
Tel. +39 3387 421620
www.olekbondonio.it
info@olekbondonio.it

Hands down, this is my favorite of Barbaresco's young wineries. Olek Bondonio is making gorgeous, earthy Barbarescos of intensity and balance that I'm sure will soon be discovered by many more critics and wine lovers, although I doubt his tiny production will ever be able to keep up with demand.

Olek, whose mother is Polish and whose father was born in Alba, grew up in Turin, but his family has owned some of the most coveted vineyards in Barbaresco for more than two hundred years. The firm's holdings are in Roncagliette, one of the most celebrated crus in all of Barbaresco, and already described as being a prized vineyard area by Lorenzo Fantini in his nineteenth-century tome *Viticoltura ed enologia.* Roncagliette is also home to some of the most celebrated vines in the denomination: Angelo Gaja's Sorì Tildin and Costa Russi vineyards.

Olek's great-great-grandfather was one of the founding members of Domizio Cavazza's cooperative cellar in 1894, and almost one hundred years earlier, another ancestor was already commercializing wine for the Kingdom of Sardinia. In more recent times, Olek's family made a small amount of wine for their own enjoyment, but mostly they sold the grapes to other local producers. Olek, who spent his adolescence competing in international half-pipe snowboarding competitions, studied enology and agronomy at the University of Turin before taking over the family winery in 2005.

Olek spent his summers at the winery while growing up and credits two local farmhands who looked after the vineyards for his grandfather as inspiring him to become a winemaker. But before taking over the winery, Olek traveled and worked in wineries all over the world, including Medoc, Australia, Oregon, and New Zealand. After his global experience, he decided to stick to Langhe's traditional winemaking methods. Olek's fifty-year-old vines are located 350 meters (1,148 feet) above sea level on the very top of the Roncagliette hill, just above the hallowed vines of Angelo Gaja, from which the latter produces his Sorì Tildin Langhe DOC. Olek's parcel of Roncagliette, separated from Gaja's holdings by a small hazelnut grove, enjoys a unique microclimate thanks to the southern and southwestern exposures and proximity to the Tanaro River. The compact clay soil and vine age generate structure and intense, rich flavors. To keep the vineyards healthy, Olek avoids all harsh chemicals and industrial fertilizers. He also sources grapes from the Starderi cru in Neive for the firm's straight Barbaresco, and even though Olek doesn't own the vineyard, he manages every aspect of it as if it were his, using the same philosophy he applies in Roncagliette.

In the winery's cramped cellars, the enthusiastic winemaker adopts a rigid hands-off approach: he ferments with only native yeasts in concrete tanks where maceration lasts for up to thirty-five days, half the time with the cap submerged. He then ages his wines in 16-hectoliter Slavonian and French casks. Bottling is done by gravity, with no pumps, and Olek does not filter or fine his wines.

Production

Total surface area: 3.5 ha (8.64 acres)

Barbaresco: 1.3 ha (3.21 acres), 4,000 bottles

Barbaresco 2009.   This is a blend of Nebbiolo from the Starderi vineyard and Roncagliette. Intense rose and cherry aromas. Succulent wild cherry, strawberry, and mineral flavors with hints of truffle and spice. Very elegant with great depth and very good length. Drink 2014 to 2019.

Barbaresco Roncagliette 2009.   Made entirely from the best grapes in the eponymous cru, the 2009 is the debut vintage of Olek's single-vineyard bottling and is a stunning effort. Classic Nebbiolo fragrance of rose petal, cherry, leather, and truffle with hints of white pepper. Delicious, creamy wild cherry flavors layered with spice, earthy, and mineral notes and a hint of licorice. Silky and vibrant with lovely depth and balance. Gorgeous. Drink 2015 to 2024. The 2010 is loaded with juicy black cherry and raspberry notes layered with mint, carob, and white pepper. It has big but ripe tannins balanced by lovely acidity and a long finish. This should gain more complexity over the next few years, so drink 2015 to 2025.

Musso

Via D. Cavazza 5
12050 Barbaresco (CN)
Tel. +39 0173 635129
www.mussobarbaresco.com
valtermusso@tiscali.it

This is another established estate making classic Barbarescos that are both charming and structured. Located on the road going into the tiny town center, the winery was founded in 1920 by the grandfather of Valter Musso, who now runs the family firm. Musso's family owns prime vineyards in Rio Sordo and Pora, two of Barbaresco's most lauded crus. Rio Sordo, with its southwestern exposures, has long been celebrated, and Fantini considered it "a Prime Location" in his late nineteenth-century publication. With its southern, western, and southeastern exposures that border Asili, Pora has long been known for producing some of the longest-lived Barbarescos that, while austere in their youth, develop splendid depth and complexity with bottle age. Musso is one of the very few producers with coveted holdings in Pora, which at the end of the nineteenth century reportedly belonged almost entirely to Domizio Cavazza.

Valter, a graduate of Alba's Enological School, is refreshingly down-to-earth, and recounts that his grandfather first began bottling Barbaresco in 1937. Before this, the family made wine that it sold to other producers and restaurants in bulk. Like most serious grower-producers, Musso keeps his vines as healthy as possible and is careful in how he manages his vineyards. Fermentation is carried out in temperature-controlled steel tanks using selected yeasts that have been chosen in Barbaresco and reproduced by researchers, according to Valter. Musso then ages both his Barbarescos for one year in 50-hectoliter Slavonian casks followed by a second year in 25-hectoliter Slavonian casks. The very noticeable differences between the two wines, vinified and aged in the same way, is the individual expression of the two vineyards—the elusive terroir.

Production

Total surface area: 13 ha (32 acres)

Barbaresco: 6 ha (14.8 acres), 19,000 bottles

Barbaresco Bricco Rio Sordo.   Musso's vines, up to forty-two years old, enjoy a southwestern exposure in this famed cru known for its calcareous clay soils. The 2009 has a refined fragrance of wild rose with cherry and ginger notes. The palate is rich yet elegant with ripe cherry and balsamic flavors of great depth. A delicious wine that in 2012 was surprisingly approachable. Best through 2019.

Barbaresco Pora.   Musso's holdings are in the historical center of the Pora hillside, the most coveted position, as vines are more protected from cold and winds not only by the surrounding hills but also from the rows of vines above and below. Pora also boasts southwestern exposure, but it has more marly soil, both of which give these Barbarescos their structure and complexity. The 2009 Pora is more robust and austere than the firm's Bricco Rio Sordo. Very structured, with spicy, earthy, and truffle notes and bracing tannins. This could be a Barolo in terms of structure and tannic strength. Best 2017 to 2024.

Socré

Via Riccardo Terzolo 7
12050 Barbaresco (CN)
Tel. +39 0115 211154
www.socre.it
info@socre.it

This is one of Barbaresco's up-and-coming estates and is getting better every year. Owner Marco Piacentino, an architect, was born in Turin but spent weekends and summers at his family's home in Barbaresco. Piacentino has no time for the poetry that too often surrounds wine and winemaking, and he fully understands the sacrifice and hard work involved: "My mother didn't just leave Barbaresco; she fled from what was then a life of hardship and backbreaking work."

Since 1871, Piacentino's family has owned prime land in the Roncaglie cru, near Gaja's Sorì Tildin and just above Poderi Colla's vineyards. The family always made a little wine for its own consumption but sold off the bulk of their grapes to private producers. In 2000, Piacentino decided to vinify and bottle a portion of his production, and every year since then he has invested more in winemaking equipment and sold fewer grapes to other producers. By 2012 the firm was no longer selling any of its grapes. Piacentino works with enological consultant Guido Busatto, with whom he seems to have a solid relationship, even if they do not always see eye to eye. Busatto initially pushed for excruciatingly low yields for the firm's single-vineyard selection Roncaglie, as well as wooden fermenting vats. "I've slowly managed to convince Busatto that the yields were too low for Roncaglie, and since 2007, I've cut back on grape thinning," explains Piacentino. He also stresses that while he never used all new barriques, he now uses only 30 percent new wood, and starting with the 2011 vintage, he is also experimenting with aging his wines in 20-hectoliter French casks for one year after one year in barriques. But he maintains that barriques are essential to stabilize the more delicate color generated by Roncaglie grapes.

I actually prefer the firm's straight Barbaresco, and while the Roncaglie shows lovely depth, I can't wait to see the results once Roncaglie sees less barrique and more large casks, which should minimize the oak nuances and wood tannins. In late 2012, Piacentino was just completing expansion of his cellar, located right above his vineyards. With more space including an underground aging cellar, this winery is going to continue improving what are already very good wines.

Production

Total surface area: 5.5 ha (13.6 acres)
Barbaresco: 3 ha (7.4 acres), 14,500 bottles

Barbaresco 2009. Classic floral nose with spice and bright cherry flavors with just a veil of oak. Clarity of fruit and energizing mineral make this very approachable yet it will benefit with a few more years of bottle age. Drink 2015 to 2024.

Barbaresco Roncaglie 2009.   Made from the best and oldest grapes, this is more intense and concentrated than the straight Barbaresco. Ripe, candied fruit flavors with hints of espresso and toasted notes, and a touch of licorice alongside aggressive tannins. Drink 2016 to 2029.

Other Wineries of Note

Marchesi di Gresy—Martinenga

FOURTEEN

─────────

Neive

NEIVE OWES ITS NAME TO the noble Roman family Gens Naevia, or the Naevii, who once owned what is now the town of Neive and much of its surroundings during the rule of the Roman Empire. Neive, which became a municipality in the twelfth century, is divided into the walled medieval town on the top of the hill, known as Neive Alta, with charming cobblestoned streets and old stone buildings, and the urbanized sprawl constructed during the 1960s and 1970s below. In terms of total surface area, it is the largest township in the Barbaresco denomination. In 2000 the commune accounted for a little more than 28 percent of total Barbaresco production, and this number has grown to 37 percent today, demonstrating the growing appreciation of the wine. And even though Moscato, and not Nebbiolo, is still the most planted grape in this large township, Neive has surpassed the village of Barbaresco in terms of Barbaresco production.

For many Barolophiles, some of Neive's vineyards produce Barbarescos that are similar to Barolos, or to put it in the language of the local producers, the village can produce Barbaresco *che Baroleggia*: in other words, a number of Barbarescos hailing from Neive vineyards often possess firm, tannic structures and noted longevity, which are more reminiscent of Barolo than a quintessential Barbaresco. One of the reasons for Neive's brawny Barbarescos is soil. The part of Neive that lies adjacent to Barbaresco has very compact soil composed predominantly of bluish, calcareous marls that yield structured wines. When combined with just the right altitude and microclimate, these areas of Neive, such as the Albesani cru, famous for its celebrated Santo Stefano vineyard, and Gallina, can produce complex, age-worthy, and even austere Barbarescos that need time to develop. In the eastern part of Neive on the other hand, to the south of the town center, the soil has more sand and

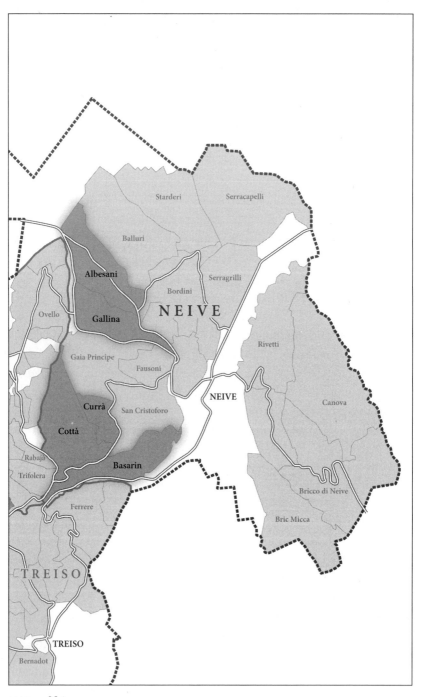

MAP 9. Neive.

is less compact. These areas of Neive produce less-structured but refined wines that are more approachable sooner.

Neive is also the home to famed producer Bruno Giacosa, the "Genius of Neive," whose complex and extremely elegant Barbarescos and Barolos are sought after by wine lovers the world over.

Bruno Giacosa

Via XX Settembre 52
12057 Neive (CN)
Tel. +39 0173 67027
www.brunogiacosa.it
brunogiacosa@brunogiacosa.it

Bruno Giacosa has been one of Piedmont's leading lights for more than five decades, and he has not only made some of the greatest Barolos and Barbarescos, but was a trailblazer in understanding the vital role of the best vineyards. It is undisputed, even among the highly individualistic growers and winemakers in the Langhe, that no one knows the Barolo and Barbaresco vineyards better than Bruno Giacosa, who spent much of his career as a *négociant*, sourcing grapes for other large producers and later buying the very best grapes to vinify under his own label. Thanks to Giacosa, many of today's most recognized vineyards in the Langhe are now celebrated worldwide, including Santo Stefano in Neive and Vigna Rionda in Serralunga (Giacosa stopped making the latter bottling in the early 1990s). And while it's true that great wine starts in the vineyard, Giacosa's stunning bottlings also prove beyond a shadow of doubt the equally vital role of an experienced and scrupulous winemaker, and one who knows enough to intervene as little as possible during the winemaking process.

Bruno was born in 1929, the same year his grandfather Carlo died and his father, Mario, took over the family's firm. Carlo had been making and bottling wine since the end of the nineteenth century, but in 1929, as a result of the global economic crises that drastically reduced demand, Mario stopped selling bottled wine. Instead, he concentrated on buying and reselling grapes directly, and vinifying a portion of the fruit that he sold in bulk to other producers. Bruno began his illustrious career at the tender age of fifteen, when he began working full-time for his father's grape-buying and winemaking firm in 1944. He spent his days walking in the Langhe hills in what are

FIGURE 28. Bruno Giacosa. Bruno Giacosa has been one of the Langhe's luminaries for over five decades. Not only does he make some of the greatest bottlings in both denominations, but he was among the first to understand the vital role of top vineyard sites and was a pioneer in bottling single-vineyard Barbarescos and Barolos. Photograph by Paolo Tenti.

the most coveted vineyards in Italy in search of the best grapes—namely, Nebbiolo, but also Barbera and Dolcetto. Young Giacosa soon became known for what many have described as his golden palate, but which the man himself says is actually his keen olfactory perception. As Giacosa told me during an interview in 2011, "Smelling the just pressed grapes, the must, the fermented and aging wine, is even more important than tasting them."

After years of buying grapes and helping his father vinify the wine they sold in bulk, Bruno was keen to make and bottle quality wines. To this end, in 1960 he created the Bruno Giacosa firm, with his first Bruno Giacosa Barbaresco "Riserva Speciale" hailing from the 1961 vintage, and the firm's first Barolo "Riserva Speciale" from the celebrated 1964 vintage. While he still bought grapes for other large houses, he also purchased the very best grapes for his own label, and he paid for quality not quantity, going directly to the growers and bypassing whenever possible Alba's squalid grape market. He went on to create Barolos and Barbarescos of extraordinary complexity from the most renowned vineyards while also discovering lesser-known vineyards that he would make famous through his elegant and impeccably balanced wines. In the mid-1960s,

Giacosa was among the very first producers, along with Gaja and Beppe Colla, to make single-vineyard bottlings of Barolo and Barbaresco, starting with his 1964 Barbaresco Santo Stefano Riserva Speciale (made with grapes hailing from a small parcel of Nebbiolo vines in the now-celebrated vineyard that was acquired by the Stupino family that same year) followed by the 1967 Asili Riserva Speciale and the 1967 Barolo Vigna Rionda di Serralunga.

Today Bruno's acclaimed bottlings read like a wish list for wine connoisseurs, and include some of the most hallowed names in Piedmont, including Barolo Falletto, Barolo Le Rocche del Falletto, Barbaresco Asili, and Barbaresco Santo Stefano, while his Riserva bottlings, distinguished with red labels and made only in the best years, are among the most sought-after wines in the world. Bruno even makes exceptional sparkling wines, crafted in the classic tradition and made from Pinot Noir grapes from Oltrepò Pavese, not to mention his Arneis, Barbera, and Dolcetto.

By the 1970s, it became harder to source quality grapes, not only because many growers were becoming producers and stopped selling grapes, but also because, as Bruno pointed out during one of our many interviews between 2004 and 2011, by that time many small farmers were using chemical herbicides, pesticides, and fertilizers. "These products lowered the quality of the grapes. They made the skins on Nebbiolo too thin, making everything from harvesting to fermentation more difficult," according to Giacosa. By this time, Bruno had already decided he wanted full control over the production chain and knew just which vineyards he wanted to own. After years of saving and waiting for just the right properties to become available, in 1982 Giacosa purchased the magnificent Falletto farm and vineyards in Serralunga, with its perfect south-southwest exposures, and in 1996 he acquired Barbaresco vineyards in the best part of Asili and in Rabajà. Giacosa continues to make wines from sourced grapes as well, and has divided the company accordingly: wines labeled Casa Vinicola Bruno Giacosa are made from purchased grapes, while those labeled Azienda Agricola Falletto di Bruno Giacosa are made exclusively with estate grapes.

Giacosa has the utmost respect for the Langhe's great vineyards and uses the least amount of products and treatments possible on his vines. He also keeps yields low to naturally increase concentration. In the cellar, Bruno, an enlightened traditionalist, is decidedly hands-off, preferring to let perfect grapes express themselves with as little intervention as possible. His cellar methods include avoiding selected yeasts in most years, but when in very difficult vintages the firm resorts to selected yeasts for their Barolos and Barbarescos, Giacosa uses only Langhe Nebbiolo yeasts created by the

University of Turin. Bruno prefers to age in large casks, between 55 and 110 hectoliters, made of untoasted French oak. The resulting wines express Nebbiolo's hallmark floral aromas, concentrated wild cherry and mineral flavors combined with the mesmerizing depth, power, and grace that has made the Langhe, and Bruno Giacosa, famous.

Bruno, a man of few words and a rare but stunning smile, whom I am lucky enough to have interviewed and tasted with on numerous occasions at the winery despite his reputation for avoiding journalists, suffered a devastating stroke in 2006. After a year of convalescing, Bruno slowly made his way back to the cellars—albeit on a very limited basis—participating in the most important steps in the winemaking process and tasting regularly. Yet two years after Bruno's stroke, Dante Scaglione, the cellar master who had worked alongside Bruno since 1992, folded under the pressures of being almost solely in charge of one of the most celebrated wineries in Italy. A gifted winemaker who had been groomed by a master, Dante admitted during an interview in 2011 that he had not been prepared to take charge and make crucial decisions on his own. Bruno and his daughter Bruna, who has been head of marketing and sales at the winery for over twenty years, were forced to let Dante go in 2008. In his place, they hired Giorgio Lavagna, who had been a winemaker at Batasiolo. While Lavagna had the driving ambition needed to take control, he could not fulfill the unimaginably difficult role of successor to Bruno Giacosa, and though the firm's wines made under Lavagna were good, they were not up to Giacosa's notoriously high standards.

In 2011, the Giacosas asked Dante to come back. Thankfully, for fans of Bruno Giacosa, Dante, who is now a thriving consultant-enologist for other wineries in the Langhe, graciously accepted and is now consulting winemaker for Bruno Giacosa. He is also helping groom Francesco Versio, the young in-house enologist hired by the Giacosas to oversee daily running of the cellars. Even though Dante still works with other wineries, he makes no secret that Bruno Giacosa is a priority and that he will be there as much as they need him, especially in the most crucial phases of the winemaking process.

Bruno has admitted several times over the years that he regrets never putting aside any bottles, not even in great years, to create a vintage library, choosing instead to sell every bottle. Giacosa is one of the only truly prestigious Italian firms with decades of history that has never been able to hold a vertical to demonstrate the aging potential and evolution of its wines. *Che peccato!*

A note on Bruno Giacosa's recent production changes.

Bruno created an uproar in 2009 when he announced that he would not bottle any Barolo or Barbaresco from the 2006 vintage. While Bruno maintains the vintage was not up to par, most local producers strongly disagree, saying that 2006 is a classic, outstanding vintage. I agree with the latter camp, that 2006 is an excellent vintage. I assume that Bruno's decision was far more personal, seeing that 2006 was obviously a difficult year for him and for his winery because of his stroke, and it was a vintage he couldn't follow at all. In 2013, the winery revealed that they will not make any 2010 Barolos or Barbarescos, again creating surprise among the estate's fans and local producers. The year 2010 has proven to be a classic vintage in the Langhe and has yielded superb Barbarescos and Barolos with age-worthy structures. Once again, this seems to be a decision based on the estate's own production situation rather than a vintage issue.

Starting from the 2007 vintage, the firm no longer makes a Barbaresco Rabajà because their vines were excluded from the eponymous vineyard's official delimitation, thereby prohibiting them from using this geographic mention. So where do these grapes end up now? The official word from the winery is that their Rabajà vineyard "has been reclassified as Asili and a small portion of the grapes go into their white label Barbaresco Asili." However, because Barbaresco made from the vineyard previously known as Rabajà has a more robust and riper character than the more refined and graceful Asili, none of Rabajà's grapes ever go into the Asili Riserva according to Bruna. And rather than end up in the straight Barbaresco, again according to Bruna, the rest of the juice from the Rabajà grapes is now sold in bulk. In January of 2013, Bruna told me that 2011 will be Giacosa's last vintage of Barbaresco Albesani Vigna Santo Stefano. According to Bruna, this was because the owner of the vineyard, Italo Stupino, not only replanted the vineyard, meaning the grapes are very young, but her firm "no longer has any control or input in the management of the vineyard." This surprising decision to renounce Santo Stefano, (which got a lot of interest and generated more feedback than I expected when I tweeted about it after I spoke with Bruna), seems to signal a shift in the firm's direction. In my opinion, now that Bruno can no longer walk the vineyards and personally choose the grapes or make any suggestions regarding vineyard management, and since there seems to be no one at the winery stepping up to this task, I think the winery will focus more on wines made from their estate grapes and less on wines made with sourced fruit. Finally, the firm also owns vineyards in La Morra, where they have planted Nebbiolo, but so far has only made one single-vineyard bottling, Vigna Croera 2004, from the property.

Production

Total surface area: 22 ha (54.3 acres)

Barolo: 10 ha (24.7 acres) in Serralunga, 51,000 total bottles

Barbaresco: 4 ha (9.8 acres), 54,000 total bottles (This bottle figure includes 14,500 bottles of Santo Stefano from purchased grapes.)

Barbaresco Asili.   Asili is the greatest confirmation of the firm's Barbarescos. Bruno has told me on several occasions, even when the firm was still actively producing single-vineyard bottlings of Rabajà and was still satisfied with how things were going over at the Santo Stefano vineyard, that Asili is the Barbaresco vineyard closest to his heart. "Even out of a line up of dozens of Barbarescos, I can always pick out Asili, thanks to its intense floral perfume and its extraordinary elegance," says Bruno. According to Bruno, Asili's soil has more fine silt and sand, which contribute to the cru's finesse. The 2008 is stunning, with intense perfume of rose, violet, cedar, and sandalwood. Extremely elegant with delicious raspberry and mineral flavors and smooth, polished tannins. Drink through 2028.

Barbaresco Asili Riserva.   In outstanding vintages the firm also makes an Asili Riserva that it ages for two years in large French casks, as opposed to fifteen to eighteen months for the straight Asili. Since 2007 Giacosa now adds a small portion of grapes from their former Rabajà vineyard into the straight Asili to lend more structure, but it does not add these grapes to Asili Riserva. The 2007 boasts the cru's hallmark rose, violet, and ripe cherry aromas with ripe cherry and earthy cedar flavors. Wonderful depth, reminiscent of a fine Burgundy with an energizing and seducing lift from mineral notes coupled with supple tannins. Fabulous length. Drink through 2022.

Barbaresco Rabajà.   I for one am very disappointed that the firm isn't still bottling this great vineyard—change the name, who cares? It's the fruit that counts. If Bruno Giacosa chose to buy this vineyard and vinify these grapes, there was good reason, as he proved over and over again. In 2013, we opened up our last bottle of the Rabajà Riserva 2001, and I wish we had more. This is a hallmark Barbaresco, with an intense fragrance of ripe raspberry, cedar, leather, and spice. The palate delivers concentrated wild cherry, mineral, truffle, and balsamic herbs alongside fresh acidity and silky smooth tannins. Impeccable balance and great length.

Barbaresco Santo Stefano.   And while I'm at it, I'll add this to my wish list of Wines I Wish Bruno Giacosa Still Made. With ripe fruit and hearty structure, Giacosa's Santo Stefanos showed the tannic backbone usually reserved for Barolo. In 2014, I opened up the 2000, and must admit, however, that I was underwhelmed, but this could be the forward nature of the vintage. It doesn't have much intensity and is already rather evolved, with dried cherry, fig, spice, and carob alongside fleeting tannins.

Barolo Falletto.   Giacosa started sourcing grapes from Falletto in 1967, and when the former owners decided to sell in 1982, Giacosa swooped in and bought the property before anyone even knew it was for sale. Located in the venerable village of Serralunga, perhaps the most prestigious of all the Barolo villages, Falletto has ideal southwest exposure that allows the grapes to mature slowly but fully, while its calcareous soil adds complexity and structure. The 2007 has an exquisite bouquet of rose petals, iris, and leather alongside succulent wild cherry and mineral flavors. It's well balanced with surprising freshness for the vintage and firm but refined tannins. Drink 2014 to 2022. In outstanding years, Giacosa also makes a Barolo Falletto Riserva. In 2014, I opened a magnum of the 2000. It had a classic fragrance of leather, truffle, and berry that carried over the palate alongside creamy cherry, licorice, Mediterrenean herbs, and mineral notes. It's extremely elegant, even subtle, and while it will maintain for years, this is already in its ideal drinking window.

Barolo Le Rocche del Falletto.   Along with Giacomo Conterno's Monfortino, this is one of Barolo's most iconic bottlings. Le Rocche is a small parcel of the Falletto vineyard, with the highest altitude and oldest vines. Before Le Rocche's debut vintage in 1997, Le Rocche went into Giacosa's Barolo Falletto Riservas. Le Rocche undergoes longer maceration with the skins when compared to Falletto, while both are aged for eighteen to twenty-two months in large French casks. While Le Rocche can be austere and tight in its youth, with age it develops layers of gripping complexity and the bright, red fruit sensations develop quintessential Nebbiolo sweetness. These also have the structure to age for decades. The 2009 is more delicately structured and forward than usual but still bears Giacosa's hallmark finesse and complexity. It has mesmerizing perfumes of rose, violet, cherry, strawberry, and hints of cedar. The palate shows lively cherry, mineral, and spice notes and has a smooth, silky texture. Drink now or hold for more complexity. In great vintages Giacosa also makes a Riserva version that is aged for three years in large French casks and boasts even more complexity.

Castello di Neive

Via Castelborgo 1
12052 Neive (CN)
Tel. +39 0173 67171
www.castellodineive.it
info@castellodineive.it

The imposing Castello Neive rises up behind a high, stone wall in the historic center of Neive. Standing on the foundations of a much older fortress, the current castle was built in the mid-1700s by Manfredo Bongioanni, the Count of Castelborgo, who made sure to include spacious cellars that were specifically designed for winemaking. The cellars are still used by the current owners, the Stupino family, who purchased the property in 1964.

Today, Italo Stupino manages the winery, which he owns together with his siblings. Natives of Neive for four generations, the family already owned vineyards in prime areas of the township, including Gallina and Basarin, but the purchase of Castello di Neive included what has become one of the most illustrious vineyards in Langhe—Vigna Santo Stefano. According to Italo, when his father was negotiating the purchase of the castle and parcels of land, he had the choice of a parcel in Gallina, already under vine, or the hill of Santo Stefano, which in the early 1960s was largely uncultivated, with the exception of a small amount of Nebbiolo vines. The rest was overgrown with blackberry bushes and pockmarked with deep gullies caused by rainstorms. Aware of the great potential of the vineyard, Giacomo Stupino chose Santo Stefano, and, with the help of expert grafters who worked directly in the vineyards, he planted new vines and restored the ones that were already there.

Santo Stefano, located in the Albesani cru, owes its success to a number of factors, including perfect south-southwest exposures, an ideal altitude of 280 meters (918 feet) above sea level, remarkably steep slopes, and calcareous clay and marls. Its vicinity to the Tanaro River is also important, as the river mitigates the negative effect of dry vintages like 2003 and 2007, according to Claudio Roggero, the firm's in-house enologist and general manager. Still another major factor in Santo Stefano's success, says Italo Stupino, is the selection of Nebbiolo clones, most of which were planted in the mid-1960s: "We started a collaboration with the University of Torino, and Anna Schneider, one of their most famous researchers, discovered that about 30 percent of our Nebbiolo is of the Rosé variety. This gives Santo Stefano its innate elegance that counterbalances the wine's tannic structure." Stupino seems unfazed that Schneider and her colleagues have since determined that Rosé is not a variety of Nebbiolo, but is instead a distinct variety. However, he and other growers who already have the grape in their designated vineyards are still allowed to use it in Barbaresco and Barolo—for now anyway.

From the outset, Castello di Neive, which first bottled Santo Stefano under its own label in 1967, sold grapes to Bruno Giacosa, who went on to make this cru one of the most famous in the entire denomination. Over the years the Stupino family has gradually increased their own bottlings from their holdings while selling off fewer grapes and bulk wine. By 2012, the firm was bottling its entire production, and moved the vinification cellars to a newly constructed building nearby. Stupino now uses the vaulted cellars beneath the castle exclusively for aging.

The firm avoids using harsh chemicals as well as excess amounts of copper and sulfur in the vineyards and is a member of VignEtico, a united group of local producers, researchers, and agronomists working to improve vineyard management while keeping a low environmental impact. In the cellars, Castello di Neive ferments in temperature-controlled stainless steel, and ages in barrels of different sizes. Although it used more barriques and tonneaux in the past, the firm now uses mostly large casks, between 32 and 37 hectoliters, made of untoasted French oak, while a small part ages in tonneaux and barriques. And the wines have improved immensely in just the last five or six vintages.

Production

Total surface area: 54 ha (133.4 acres)
Barbaresco: 11 ha (27 acres), 20,000–30,000 bottles

Barbaresco. A blend from the firm's various vineyards throughout Neive with plant age averaging thirty years old. The 2009 shows ripe berry, bright acidity, and textured but ripe tannins. Best 2014 to 2019.

Barbaresco Gallina. First bottled as a single-vineyard Barbaresco in 2008, this is a very elegant expression of this famed vineyard made from the firm's two separate holdings in Gallina that were planted thirty years ago with estate clones. Both areas have southwest-facing slopes, and are situated on average 280 meters (918 feet) above sea level. The 2009 is a glowing garnet color with an intensely floral bouquet and a strawberry-mineral palate. Drink 2014 to 2019.

Barbaresco Santo Stefano. If you haven't tried this one in awhile, you may surprised by its Nebbiolo purity and elegance, which are much more in evidence now that Stupino is aging this wine for eighteen months almost exclusively in 32- to 37-hectoliter casks made of untoasted French oak. As mentioned above, this vineyard area incorporates optimum growing conditions for Nebbiolo, and the grape excels here. The 2009 possesses a luminous garnet hue, and an enticing, multifaceted fragrance of cherry, rose, earth, truffle, and a hint of orange peel. Creamy strawberry, wild cherry, and spice palate with energizing minerality, gripping but fine tannins, and impeccable balance. Focused and compelling. Best 2015 to 2022.

Barbaresco Santo Stefano Riserva. Made only in outstanding vintages and from the best grapes, this undergoes two years of aging mostly in large casks. The 1999 Riserva, tried in 2013, is a throwback to a different time: dark and concentrated with lingering oak sensations of espresso and vanilla and wood tannins from tonneaux and barriques in which it was partly aged.

Piero Busso

Via Albesani 8
12052 Neive (CN)
Tel. +39 0173 67156
www.bussopiero.com
bussopiero@bussopiero.com

Founded in 1953, the Piero Busso winery is a textbook example of Barbaresco's small, family-run estates that make exceptional wines of authenticity and character. According to Piero, who is joined in the winery by his wife, Lucia, daughter Emanuela, and son Pierguido, "The key words in our family are 'grape variety,' 'vineyard,' 'harvest,' and 'wine.'" "We don't follow any trends in winemaking, but only look for the best ways to express the grape variety in each individual vineyard, taking into account the specific conditions of each harvest."

The Bussos, whose small winery is located in the celebrated Albesani vineyard area, a stone's throw from Santo Stefano and just opposite the outstanding Gallina cru, make wine exclusively from their own vineyards. Following Piero's scrupulous standards, not only are vinification and aging tailored to suit the specific characteristics of each vineyard area, but each vineyard has distinct parcels, and each parcel has its very own vinification tank. Since the small firm has vineyards in four distinct areas, this dedication to separate vinification of numerous parcels within each vineyard is more than impressive; it is almost obsessive. The family's holdings include some of the top sites in Neive, including the Borgese vineyard in the Albesani cru, vineyards in the heart of Gallina, and a parcel in Mondino, which is now incorporated in the larger Balluri cru. The family also has vineyards in the hamlet of Treiso, from which they make San Stunet.

In the cellars, Busso mixes up traditional and nontraditional methods. To maintain the integrity of each vineyard's special characteristics, he ferments only with wild yeasts in temperature-controlled steel tanks. Until the 2010 harvest, Busso also employed some barriques, most notably for Barbaresco Gallina, which was aged entirely in barriques. Now the firm's four Barbarescos, all designated with geographic mentions or individual vineyard names, are aged almost entirely in 20-hectoliter Slavonian casks. In 2015, the firm will release its first ever Riserva, from the 2010 vintage, which hails from seventy-year-old vines in the Albesani cru that were vinified and aged in conical wooden vats made with Slavonian oak, with no sulfites added.

Production

Total surface area: 10 ha (24.7 acres)

Barbaresco: 5.5 ha (13.5 acres), 17,500 bottles

Barbaresco Borgese. Located in the Albesani cru and right next to Santo Stefano, this is Busso's hallmark Barbaresco. Thanks to vineyard altitude of 320 meters (1,049 feet) above sea level, southern and western exposures, and compact calcareous clay soil, Borgese boasts impressive tannic structure, while the advanced age of the vines, up to eighty years old, generates a fabulous depth of flavors. The 2008 offers beguiling and elegant aromas of violets alongside juicy berry, spice, and mint flavors balanced by firm tannins. Lovely mineral finish and beguiling complexity. Drink 2016 to 2028.

Barbaresco Mondino. Located in the Balluri cru, which has similar growing conditions to those in the Borgese vineyard, Mondino is fleshier, with more fruit than Borgese and rounder tannins, demonstrating the mysterious role of terroir. The 2008 is very floral and packed with succulent red fruit and supple tannins. This is already approachable but will age for a decade or more. Drink 2014 to 2018.

Barbaresco Gallina. I have always found this wine dominated by espresso, toast, and vanilla sensations that strangled the Nebbiolo, which seemed clawing to get out. Starting in 2010, Busso stopped aging this wine in barriques and is now using Slavonian botti. Given the superb growing conditions in Gallina and the concentrated grapes hailing from the sixty-year-old vines, I'm expecting a wonderful wine.

Barbaresco San Stunet. This is the only Busso vineyard not in Neive, but located instead in the village of Treiso, where the rockier soils and higher vineyard altitudes of around 400 meters (1,312 feet) yield very graceful, lithe Barbarescos. While this wine is aged mostly in Slavonian oak casks, about 30 percent is also aged in barriques, ostensibly to add complexity. The 2008 is loaded with cherry and spice, punctuated by espresso and coffee notes. Drink 2014 to 2022.

F.lli Cigliuti

Via Serraboella 17
12057 Neive (CN)
Tel. +39 0173 677185
www.cigliuti.it
info@cigliuti.it

Surrounded by vineyards, the Cigliuti farm is located along the crest of the hill in Neive's Serraboella cru, and just across the street from the vineyard area known as Bricco di Neive. The property, spanning both vineyard areas, has been in the Cigliuti family for four generations, and Renato, who began working at the farm as a youngster, took over the farm in 1964. That same year he started bottling the firm's wines, focusing only on estate grapes. Before this, his father and uncle used to vinify grapes and sell bulk wine to private customers who would come to stock up at the winery.

Today Renato, joined by his wife, Dina, and two grown daughters, Claudia and Silvia, makes two outstanding Barbarescos. Both of them are single-vineyard bottlings, from Serraboella and Bricco di Neive. The bulk of the family's holdings are in Serraboella, at an average altitude of 350 meters (1,148 feet) above sea level, where constant breezes help keep fungus diseases under control. The predominantly calcareous soil and older vines, averaging thirty-five years old, produce a rich, tannic, and full-bodied Barbaresco of impressive longevity. According to daughter Claudia, Renato was one of the first to believe in the great potential for Nebbiolo in Serraboella, and until he began planting Nebbiolo for Barbaresco, the now lauded hill had been planted mostly with Dolcetto and Moscato.

Cigliuti's other holdings are just across the narrow street from the winery in Bricco di Neive. The firm's parcel, Vie Erte, has the same altitude as Serraboella and a similar history: for years the altitude was deemed too extreme for Nebbiolo, so producers planted other varieties. Cigliuti once again paved the way for Nebbiolo. One fundamental difference between the two crus is soil: while Serraboella is mostly calcareous, Vie Erte's calcareous soil is layered with a significant percentage of sand, producing more elegant Barbarescos.

Production

Total surface area: 7.5 ha (18.5 acres)
Barbaresco: 4.5 ha (11.11 acres), 11,500 bottles

Barbaresco Serraboella. From the eponymous cru, which the Cigliutis helped make famous, this is a big Barbaresco, with classic Nebbiolo aromas and flavors and great depth. The Cigliutis age 60 percent of this Barbaresco in 20- and 25-hectoliter Slavonian botti, and 40 percent in tonneaux and barriques, both new and used several times over. The 2008 boasted heady floral and earthy aromas and big, ripe red fruit flavors and bracing tannins. This is an intense, structured wine that needs time to develop. Best 2014 to 2028. In 2013, I tried the Serraboella 2001, and was blown away by its youthful, succulent cherry fruit, energy, spice, and balsamic notes. Incredibly alive and complex. Drink through 2031. A serious Barbaresco.

Barbaresco Vie Erte. From the family's vineyard in Bricco di Neive, this is aged entirely in Slavonian casks, and is more elegant and approachable sooner than Serraboella. The 2008 showed surprisingly ripe fruit, and the vineyard's trademark spice and eucalyptus sensations. Very fresh and almost ready in 2012, with fine tannins. Opened up beautifully in the glass. Best 2015 to 2020.

Ugo Lequio

Via del Molino 10
12075 Neive (CN)

Tel. +39 0173 677224
www.ugolequio.it
info@ugolequio.it

In all the Barbaresco tastings—both open and blind—that I've done over the last decade for the many articles I've written on Barbaresco and for this book, I have consistently given Ugo Lequio high and very high scores. Although he is surprisingly under the radar, for Barbaresco cognoscenti, Ugo Lequio is synonymous with Gallina, one of the historically great crus in Neive.

Ugo, who came from generations of farmers, founded his own winery in 1981. He then set out on the momentous task of convincing the owners of the best vineyards to sell their grapes to him rather than to some of the more famous producers, say, Bruno Giacosa, for instance. And Ugo, who had lived opposite Gallina for years, wanted to make wines from grapes grown on Gallina's sun-soaked slopes, and specifically, with grapes grown in the most renowned part of Gallina, Cascina Nuova. Originally part of the properties owned by the Conti Riccardi Candiani nobles, and now owned by the Marcarino family, this is perhaps the ultimate spot on Gallina's famed hillside. Although the Marcarinos began selling Ugo their Barbera grapes in 1981, it took some years before they would sell him their coveted Nebbiolo grapes, which they had been selling to Giacosa for years. "At first, I had to go and buy the Nebbiolo grapes from this grower only under the cover at night," laughs Ugo today.

The Cascina Nuova's Gallina vineyards boast some of the best growing conditions in the cru, with perfect southern exposures, altitudes of 270 meters (885.7 feet) above sea level, and clay soils interspersed with sandstone, yielding Barbarescos of elegance and marked depth. Ugo believes in rigorous grape selection and vinifies only the very best grapes at his modest but functional cellars in the newer section of Neive, just down the street from Bruno Giacosa. Lequio ages his Barbarescos in 25-hectoliter Slavonian casks for between twenty and thirty months, well above the mandatory minimum of nine months. These are textbook Barbarescos from Neive with complexity, structure, and depth.

Barbaresco Gallina. This is Ugo Lequio's calling card, and one of the best expressions of the Gallina cru and of Neive, boasting ripe but restrained fruit, remarkable depth, and an impressive structure along with beautiful floral notes. The 2008 offers intense aromas of violet, leather, meat juices, and spice with layers of intense cherry and mint and eucalyptus flavors. Bracing but refined tannins and a graceful structure. Gorgeous. Best 2016 to 2028.

The 2009 boasts hallmark floral, cherry, and truffle sensations along with succulent red fruit and mineral flavors. Needs time to develop complexity. Nice freshness for what was a warm vintage. Best 2015 to 2019.

Barbaresco Gallina Riserva. In outstanding vintages, Ugo also makes a Riserva, aged for thirty months in Slavonian botti followed by another fifteen months in tonneaux that have been used several times before. This has more structure and complexity, and will age longer. Ugo's 2007 Riserva, a difficult vintage marred by intense heat, is an impressive effort. Leather, eucalyptus aromas with hint of mint and delicious cherry, raspberry fruit balanced with firm but refined tannins. Will develop well over the next few years. Drink 2015 to 2022.

Cantina del Glicine

Via Giulio Cesare 1
12052 Neive (CN)
Tel. +39 0173 67215
www.cantinadelglicine.it
info@cantinadelglicine.it

Founded in 1980 by Adriana Marzi and enologist Roberto Bruno, this boutique winery, located in the center of Neive's Old Town, is turning out stunning Barbarescos from two of Neive's smallest crus, Currà and Marcorino. The seventeenth-century winery itself is also an architectural jewel.

Named after the centuries-old wisteria plant (*glicine* in Italian) that climbs across the garden and courtyard, the winery's vaulted cellars, built between 1582 and 1602, with brick walls and stone floors, are among the most suggestive I've seen anywhere. Snaking 8 meters (26 feet) below ground, the cellars were obviously designed for winemaking, and their original blueprints are conserved in Turin's Accademia di Belle Arti. After more than four centuries, these subterranean tunnels still offer ideal conditions for aging the firm's wines, thanks to their consistently cool temperatures and high humidity—in both summer and winter—that eliminate the need for climate control of any kind.

Roberto Bruno, who is both the winemaker and the agronomist, has almost single-handedly brought the previously unsung Marcorino and Currà vineyard areas to their current respected status for Nebbiolo. Both vineyard areas share similar altitudes of approximately 300 meters (984 feet) above sea level, and soils in both are clay and calcareous marls. However, in the sunniest part of Marcorino, where the firm has its vineyards, vines benefit from the southeast exposures and fresher temperatures, creating elegantly structured Barbaresco with fine tannins. Vineyards in Currà on the other hand are more protected and enjoy southwest exposures. This warmer microclimate produces more robust and complex Barbarescos.

In the cellars, Roberto Bruno has long experimented with both traditional botti and barriques of various ages. When I first interviewed Roberto in 2006, he aged both of his Barbarescos partly in botti and partly in barriques, saying, "Most wine drinkers outside of Italy are accustomed to wines made with barriques and need their sweetening effect that also helps Nebbiolo to be enjoyed earlier." Although he always had a steady hand with barriques, he has now stepped back even further, and uses more botti grandi. When he does use barriques, most have been around the block, or the cellars, for several years.

Production

Total surface area: 6 ha (14.8 acres)
Barbaresco: 2 ha (4.9 acres), 12,500 bottles

Barbaresco Marcorino. Aged for one year in large Slavonian casks and one year in barriques that have been used for several years, this is the more elegant of the firm's two Barbarescos. The 2008 shows raspberry, herbs, and eucalyptus notes with hints of truffle and oak. Nice acidity and firm tannins. Best 2014 to 2023.

Barbaresco Currà. Aged for two years entirely in large Slavonian casks, this is definitely the more classic and intriguing of the firm's two Barbarescos. The 2008 boasts succulent red fruit, spice, and an impressive tannic backbone. Great depth and with time, this should develop fascinating complexity. Best 2016 to 2028.

Sottimano

Loc. Cottà 21
12052 Neive (CN)
Tel. +39 0173 635186
www.sottimano.it
info@sottimano.it

This estate has undergone a radical and very welcome change in all aspects of its winemaking philosophy, starting in the vineyard, which has culminated with the extraordinary 2010 vintage. Sottimano is now turning out terroir-driven Barbarescos that are both exquisite and complex.

Andrea Sottimano is about as passionate a winemaker as you are ever going to meet anywhere, but I have to admit that in the past I had found his wines to be too reliant on new oak and too opulent for my tastes; they were flashy, fleshy, and anonymous. So I was happily surprised—shocked even—when I tried his 2009 and later 2010 Barbarescos in early 2013 at a tasting of wines from Piedmont and Burgundy, and found them to possess the character, authenticity, and sense of place that they had lacked before, and I said as much to Andrea. "I've drastically cut down on new wood, but I've also made other fundamental changes in the vineyard, starting with eliminating all chemicals. No more herbicides, no more chemical fungicides or insecticides," he told me.

As Andrea explained, eliminating all chemicals in the vineyards then allowed him to eliminate selected yeasts. His wines now ferment spontaneously with wild yeasts for about twenty-two days. After which, the fermented wine is racked into used Burgundy 228-liter barrels (*pièces*), with only 15 percent new wood. According to Andrea the barrels are not only lightly toasted, but toasted through to the middle, not just on the surface. The wine then undergoes a very long malolactic fermentation starting in the following spring, when the cellar naturally heats up, and malo then finishes between the summer and fall. Afterward, the wine is racked into different barrels of the same size, all used, for twenty-four to thirty months aging.

Sottimano, a trained enologist, is a disciple of the classic Burgundian school and a believer in the greatness of Nebbiolo, as is confirmed by his new direction. The changes didn't occur overnight, but little by little, starting in 2004, Andrea has made changes and innovations that have led to these fascinating Barbarescos, which have the finesse of the finest Burgundies and the complexity and structure of Langa's best Nebbiolo bottlings.

Production

Total surface area: 18 ha (44 acres)
Barbaresco: 9 ha (22 acres), 26,800 bottles

Barbaresco Fausoni. Made from Sottimano's Fausoni holdings in Neive, where thirty-five-year-old vines, located at 220 meters (722 feet) above sea level, enjoy southern and western exposures. The 2010 delivers violet, rose, spice, leather, and balsamic aromas with tart cherry, pipe tobacco, and underbrush flavors. Vibrant with lovely balance, firm and fine tannins, and a long anisette finish. Layered and multifaceted. Drink 2015 to 2024.

Barbaresco Cottà. Made from fifty- to sixty-year-old vines situated at 280 meters (919 feet) above sea level, this is a well-structured Barbaresco that used to be all about flashy opulence but has now found the right element of finesse. The 2010 shows classic Nebbiolo aromas of rose, cassis, and hints of menthol. Creamy cherry fruit, orange peel, licorice, and mineral flavors. A Barbaresco of dazzling energy and density. Drink 2016 to 2029.

Barbaresco Currà. Also from Neive, where forty-five-year-old vines enjoy full southern exposures. The 2010 is a very bright, floral wine boasting layers of dark cherry, mint, and spice. Still very young with aggressive but fine tannins, this needs more time. Best 2016 to 2028.

Barbaresco Pajorè. This is Sottimano's only vineyard holding in Treiso, and the famed cru does not disappoint under Andrea's guidance. Situated at 320 meters (1,050 feet) above sea level, old vines between fifty and sixty years old generate lovely depth and an extra dimension. The 2010 is loaded with black cherry and spice with sage and leather notes. Very elegant and refined with impeccable balance. Drink 2015 to 2025.

Luigi Voghera

Fraz. Tetti 6
12057 Neive (CN)
Tel. +39 0173 677144
www.vogheraluigi.com
info@vogheraluigi.com

Voghera makes archetypical Neive Barbaresco with a Barolo-like structure, intense Nebbiolo purity, and the radiant minerality and approachability of Barbaresco. Founded in 1974 by Luigi Voghera, the winery is located in the Tetti hamlet of Neive, down a narrow and only partly paved country road, and so far removed from the main routes that it seems to be part of another era altogether. Yet the Voghera family have continuously updated their winery with all the modern equipment necessary to produce outstanding wines, and outside, at the back of the winery, is an exposed earth wall where Luigi's son Livio takes visitors to see what really makes the wines from this area special: the terroir. I visited the estate with a group of researchers and geologists from the University of Turin in October 2012, who together with a small group of producers, including Voghera, have formed a union called Nuove Realtà, whose goal is to promote the Langhe's terroir-driven wines. We had a fascinating lesson at "the wall," where the geologists, soil scientists, and paleontologists pointed out the various layers of marls, clay, and sandstone that took millions of years to form.

Most of the firm's vineyards are near the winery, where predominantly calcareous clays lend tannic structure and the forty-year-old vines generate concentrated flavors and depth. Voghera also owns a single hectare in the Basarin cru, where the calcareous soils are interspersed with veins of sand that lend elegance and complexity. In outstanding years, the estate bottles Basarin separately. Livio has only recently inherited the winery, and is turning out Barbarescos of the classic school, aged in large casks of untoasted French oak, eighteen months for the straight Barbaresco and twenty-four months for Basarin.

Production

Total surface area: 23 ha (56.8 acres)
Barbaresco: 8 ha (19.7 acres)

Barbaresco. A blend of Nebbiolo from different estate vineyards in Neive that average 200 meters (656 feet) above sea level, grown in Neive's typical soils, which are composed of calcareous marls, clay, and some sand. After temperature-controlled fermentation in steel, the wine ages for eighteen months in large French casks. The 2008 has a complex and enticing bouquet of violet, cherry, spice, truffle, and licorice. With bright but dense red fruit flavors of spice, mineral, and licorice. Radiant with big, ripe tannins. Already enjoyable in 2013 but will continue to develop. Drink 2014 to 2028.

Wineries to Watch

Punset
Mainerdo

FIFTEEN

Treiso and San Rocco Seno d'Elvio

TREISO, WHICH BROKE AWAY from the municipality of Barbaresco in 1957, is not as well known as Barbaresco and Neive, but the village makes what are generally among the most elegant Barbarescos in the whole denomination.

Treiso prides itself on its rich history and its direct connection to ancient Rome. The village is the acknowledged birthplace of Publio Elvio Pertinace, or Publius Helvius Pertinax in Latin, who was emperor in 193 A.D. Pertinace, also known simply as Pertinax, was born into humble circumstances in Treiso in 126 A.D., and after an illustrious career in the army became emperor. He had one of the shortest reigns of a Roman emperor, ruling for a mere three months before he was assassinated during what later became known in history as the Year of Five Emperors. The part of the village where he was born is still known as Pertinace, and even the local cooperative cellar, established there in the 1970s, adopted the emperor's name.

In terms of Barbaresco production, Treiso accounts for 23 percent of total Barbaresco output. Even though several of Treiso's vineyards were already noted at the end of the nineteenth century as being cultivated with Nebbiolo, and Fantini even considered a few as being first-rate for Barbaresco, growers here took a different direction once the town became independent. According to local producers, from the early 1960s until the mid-1980s, when Barbaresco was not yet a very popular wine, farms in Treiso concentrated more on Dolcetto, Barbera, and Moscato. As Barbaresco grew in popularity, growers increasingly converted their vines to Nebbiolo for Barbaresco production, and as with the rest of the Langhe, most of these growers also became producers. Today Treiso has earned well-deserved respect for its polished and compelling Barbarescos. Or perhaps I should say, the area has finally

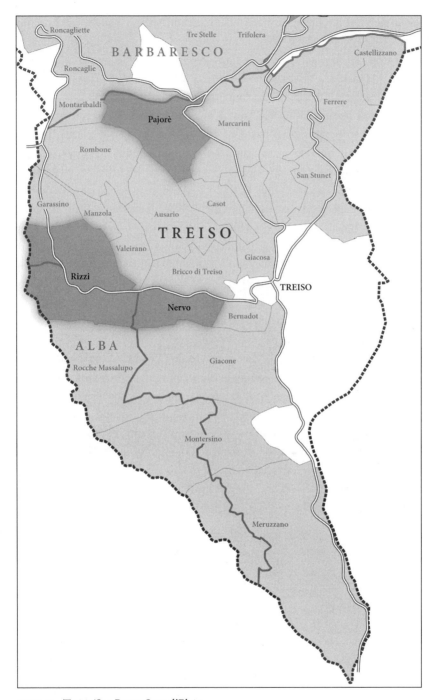

MAP 10. Treiso/San Rocco Seno d'Elvio.

reclaimed the respect it formerly held back in the late 1800s when Lorenzo Fantini designated three vineyard areas around what is now the independent township of Treiso as "Prime positions" for Barbaresco: Casotto (now called Casot), Manzola, and Valeirano.

However, not all of Fantini's contemporaries agreed with his assessment of Treiso, most notably Domizio Cavazza, the Father of Barbaresco, who in 1907 wrote more critically of the "parish of Treiso." According to Cavazza, Treiso's soil, which he defined as "clayey and cold" was "not suitable for Nebbiolo," and he pointed out that the area was "in fact cultivated with Dolcetto, Barbera, Freisa, and other rustic vines but above all there are fields and woods."[1] Cavazza also specified that the best vineyards for Barbaresco were "between 155m and 300m above sea level," which excluded much of Treiso, which has the highest vineyards in the denomination. Nebbiolo's difficulty in reaching ideal ripening in some of Treiso's higher altitudes is therefore another reason why Treiso's growers have traditionally focused less on the Langhe's most noble grape and more on other varieties, although to be sure there are lower vineyards where Nebbiolo has always performed well or had the potential to.

However, since temperatures have undeniably risen since the end of the twentieth century, Treiso's higher vineyards are proving to be an advantage now that Nebbiolo is fully ripening in these elevated reaches while still maintaining freshness. Despite Cavazza's description, growers say Treiso generally has more sand content than either Barbaresco or Neive, and thanks to this soil composition, along with vineyard altitude, Barbarescos from select areas in Treiso are among the most perfumed and graceful in the denomination. While usually approachable early, most will also age well for at least a decade, and others longer. Besides the aforementioned vineyard areas, other crus of note include Nervo, Bernadot, and Pajorè.

Rizzi

Via Rizzi 15
12050 Treiso (CN)
Tel. +39 0173 638161
www.cantinarizzi.it
cantinarizzi@cantinarizzi.it

Rizzi is one of the rising stars of the entire Barbaresco denomination, and father-and-son team Ernesto and Enrico Dellapiana are turning out classic

FIGURE 29. Enrico Dellapiana of Rizzi. Rizzi is one of the Langhe's rising stars. Owned by the Dellapiana family and run by father-and-son team Ernesto and Enrico, the firm turns out quintessential Barbarescos that show the pedigree of top vineyard sites, including Nervo, Pajorè, and Rizzi. Photograph by Paolo Tenti.

Barbarescos of breeding that are both subtle and sublime. As the name suggests, the estate, which has been in the Dellapiana family since the late 1800s, is in the Rizzi cru, perched on the crest of the hill, where the firm's vineyards surround the family home and winery before dropping vertiginously down the steep hill just across the narrow road in front.

In 1973, Ernesto, long a devotee of the Langhe and its wines, decided to leave the city and a booming business in the paper industry to revive the family's country estate, and he founded his winery in 1974. He not only restored the family's Rizzi vineyards, but he soon began acquiring vineyards in other great areas, including Nervo and Pajorè. He also started bottling a portion of the firm's wines, and with the 1974 vintage, produced his first Barbaresco. Ernesto's great love has always been the vineyards, and today he is the firm's agronomist while his son Enrico, who graduated from university with a double degree in enology/viticulture and history, takes care of winemaking. Ernesto's wife and daughter Jole take care of the administrative side and run the winery's bed-and-breakfast.

Despite being polar opposites personality-wise, Enrico and Ernesto work well together. Both are steadfast traditionalists, who refuse to use any methods that could compromise Nebbiolo's natural fragrance and flavor profiles. And to demonstrate the distinct characteristics of the firm's four vineyard areas, Enrico ferments and ages all his Barbarescos in exactly the same manner. "The differences in our Barbarescos are exclusively terroir-driven," says Enrico. Enrico is also an outspoken critic of certain aspects of Barbaresco's geographic mentions—namely, that some are too general and all-encompassing: "Mapping out individual vineyard areas was an important step, but there's a lot of room for improvement regarding the actual borders. Many of the delimited zones currently include large tracts not suitable for Nebbiolo, including areas with full northern exposures and valley floors. This is unacceptable. Some towns were more careful in this respect than others. For example, Castiglione Falletto and Serralunga were able to map out only those areas suitable for Nebbiolo while excluding unsuitable parcels. Other townships, however, like Monforte d'Alba, Treiso, and Neive, have instead 'delimited' large areas that include streams, woods, and valley floors."

Rizzi makes all its wines from estate grapes, and bottles only its top wines, selling the rest to other producers in bulk. Cellar methods are straightforward and nonintrusive and include temperature-controlled fermentation in steel followed by maceration, lasting for a total of twenty to twenty-five days. Enrico then ages his wines in 30- and 50-hectoliter Slavonian casks for twelve to eighteen months followed by another year of aging in either concrete or steel tanks before bottling.

Production

Total surface area: 35 ha (86.5 acres)
Barbaresco: 15 ha (37 acres), 23,000 bottles

Barbaresco Rizzi. This hails from grapes that originate entirely within the estate's large Rizzi cru, where there are variations, both marked and subtle, in soil makeup, exposure, and altitude. Given these differences, including varying plant ages and altitudes that range from 220 to 310 meters above sea level, this Barbaresco is the firm's classic wine, made by blending Nebbiolo grown in what are similar but not uniform conditions. Barbaresco Rizzi is fragrant with a tannic backbone tempered by Treiso's hallmark finesse. The 2008 is a benchmark Barbaresco, with red fruit, violet, and aromatic herbs on the nose that carry over to the palate alongside vibrant acidity and sweet tannins. Lovely balance. Best 2014 to 2023. The 2009 shows darker, riper fruit and a warmer palate with hallmark sage and mint. Already enjoyable but will age for a decade at least. Best through 2019.

Barbaresco Nervo (Fondetta). From the Fondetta vineyard in the larger cru area, this is the most elegant of all the firm's Barbarescos, and a quintessential expression of this celebrated vineyard. Average altitude between 310 and 370 meters above sea level and sandier soil generate complexity and finesse, while well-draining soil helps plants reach ideal ripening, as do the steep slopes, which allow more sun to hit the vines. The 2008 is gorgeous, with a hallmark fragrance of violet, rose petal, forest notes, and spice accompanied by strawberry, cherry, cinnamon, and licorice flavors. Radiant and alive with outstanding purity of fruit and mineral balanced with silky tannins. Drink 2014 to 2030. NB: From 2004 to 2009 this was labeled as Nervo Fondetta, but will be labeled as Nervo starting with the 2010 vintage.

Barbaresco Pajorè. This is another outstanding cru located in Treiso, on the border with Barbaresco. The altitude, 230 to 300 meters (755 to 984 feet) above sea level, is considered perfect for Barbaresco, as is the full southern exposure, especially in wet or humid vintages, while the poor, calcareous marls are also considered ideal for Nebbiolo to produce wines with structure. The advanced age of Rizzi's vines, which were planted between 1960 and 1965, also generates great depth and complexity. The 2008 shows floral, red fruit, and spice aromas punctuated by whiffs of earth and leather. Succulent strawberry and raspberry flavors with spice, licorice, and mineral notes all balanced with firm but fine tannins and fresh acidity. A gripping wine that will develop complexity over the next few years. Best through 2023. The 2010 is gorgeous, showing both structure and finesse along with balsamic notes, spice, and vibrant berry. It will gain in complexity with more bottle age. Drink 2015 to 2030.

Barbaresco Riserva "Boito." Made in the best vintages, this Riserva hails from the best grapes in the Boito vineyard found in the highest part of the Rizzi cru. Altitudes ranging between 240 and 310 meters (787 and 1,017 feet) above sea level are perfect for ripening, as are the southern and southwestern exposures. The white, calcareous marls and clay allow the roots to penetrate deep underground to the water and nutrients below. Postfermentation maceration continues about a week longer for this wine, while wood aging can last up to twenty months. This is an intoxicating mix of power and restraint with an age-worthy structure. NB: From 2000 to 2007 Barbaresco Boito was not made as a vineyard selection. From the 2008 vintage on, the firm has made this wine as a Riserva.

Pertinace

Località Pertinace 2
12050 Treiso (CN)
Tel. +39 0173 442238
www.pertinace.com
pertinace@pertinace.it

Also known as Cantina Vignaioli Elvio Pertinace, this small-scale cooperative cellar makes quintessential Barbarescos of great *tipicità* and authenticity— remarkable for a cooperative. The firm's quality-price ratio is perhaps one of the best in all of Italy.

Located in the hamlet of Pertinace, between Treiso and Barbaresco, where the Roman emperor Elvio Pertinace was born in 126 A.D., the winery was founded in 1973 by Mario Barbero. Barbero united thirteen small growers in Treiso who shared the same goal: to create quality wines from native grapes, mainly Nebbiolo but also Dolcetto, and to form a business that could launch a new brand in what was a growing but difficult market to break into for small growers. Over the years, the winery has invested in new equipment and renovations, and now counts fifteen members that produce wines from about 80 hectares (198 acres) dedicated to native grapes. Recently, the co-op has outgrown its medium-sized cellars, and according to Cesare Barbero, the founder's son and Pertinace's managing director and enologist, they are looking for new headquarters. The extra space will allow them to accept more members and increase production.

Barbero insists that the most important factor at Pertinace is grape quality: "Here the price of the grapes is based on quality, using a range from 1 to 6. And the difference in price between the top of the range and the bottom is double, encouraging growers to bring us only top quality fruit." In the cellars, Barbero keeps things conventional, fermenting in temperature-controlled steel tanks, although some of these are outfitted with an internal ball to gently break the cap and extract more color and noble tannins. Despite having experimented with tonneaux in the past, Barbero now ages the co-op's four Barbarescos for eighteen months in traditional botti ranging in size from 30 to 105 hectoliters that allow the specific characteristics of the individual vineyards and of Nebbiolo to shine through unfettered.

Production

Total surface area: 80 ha (197.6 acres), owned by 15 members
Barbaresco: 30 ha (74 acres), 100,000 bottles

Barbaresco. This is the firm's blended Barbaresco, and the most important in terms of volume. The grapes hail from various vineyards, most of which are located in Treiso and, thanks to the higher altitudes, Pertinace's straight Barbaresco is very approachable and elegant, with bright fruit, spice notes, and fine tannins. The 2008 offers berry, tobacco leaf, and spice aromas with bright cherry, strawberry, and truffle on the palate. Vibrant with graceful tannins. Drink through 2018.

Barbaresco Castellizano. Also in Treiso, with southeast exposures. While this is not one of Treiso's more recognized crus, it is usually a consistent effort with delicious dark fruit, mineral, and supple tannins. The 2008 offers ripe, round fruit and supple tannins. Drink through 2018.

Barbaresco Marcarini. More concentrated, with riper fruit and more depth. The 2008 shows lovely floral notes of violet with spice and a hint of orange peel. Dark fruit flavors accompanied by brooding but ripe tannins. Somewhat austere. Needs time to open up. Drink 2016 to 2028.

Barbaresco Nervo. Thanks to the full southern exposures and near-perfect altitude, Nervo is the epitome of Treiso Barbaresco, embodying both structure and finesse. Pertinace's 2008 has an ample bouquet of violet, earth, truffle, and orange peel with a hint of leather. Remarkably bright cherry and spice flavors with balsamic notes. Still nervous and tightly wound. Drink through 2015 to 2028.

Ada Nada

Loc. Rombone
Via Ausario 12
12050 Treiso (CN)
Tel. +39 0173 638127

www.adanada.it
info@adanada.it

Founded in 1919 by Carlo Nada, this family winery has been handed down through the generations of Nada men named either Carlo or Giovanni or a combination of the two, although now the firm and its future seem to be entirely in the hands of the family's women. Today Anna Lisa Nada runs the estate with her husband, Elvio, who has overseen the vineyards since 2001 and who took over the winemaking in 2012 after a decade of working alongside his father-in-law, Gian Carlo Nada, who was a trained enologist. Anna Lisa and Elvio are the proud parents of three young girls who are growing up at the estate, while Anna Lisa's sister Sara and her two daughters share an active role in the winery.

The surname Nada is as common in Treiso as Jones is in any U.S. suburb, and all are related. Ada Nada, however, sits on the original property created up by Anna Lisa's great-grandfather and company founder, Carlo Nada. To differentiate the name of their estate, Anna Lisa's father added the name of his wife, Ada, to the winery. Over the years, the original property was parceled off through inheritance among generations of siblings, although Anna Lisa's family has bought back some of the original property, while her husband, Elvio, also owns vineyards inherited through his family. The result is that Ada Nada owns vineyards in prime locations, including Valeirano, one of the vineyard areas Lorenzo Fantini designated as "Prime Position" in his celebrated nineteenth-century monograph. Ada Nada's other vineyard areas include Rombone, where they have their winery. Elvio is careful with his vines, some of them verging on fifty years old. He does not use chemical herbicides or other harsh chemical treatments, and puts down manure for fertilizer only where needed and only every two to three years. "The plants must suffer a little; otherwise they produce too many grapes," explains Elvio.

This noninterventionist approach continues in the cellar, where the firm allows spontaneous fermentation with wild yeasts. Elvio, like his father-in-law before him, ages Barbaresco predominantly in 30-hectoliter Slavonian casks, although they also use some used barriques for Valeirano.

Production

Total surface area: 9 ha (22 acres)
Barbaresco: 3 ha (7.4 acres), 18,500 bottles

Barbaresco Valeirano. With its southwest exposures and ideal altitudes of 200 to 350 meters (656 to 1,148 feet) above sea level, this vineyard area has long been noted for near-perfect conditions for Nebbiolo. Aged mostly in large Slavonian casks and partly in used barriques, the 2006, tried in 2012, is somewhat austere but classic, with rose, truffle, and leather aromas with a hint of menthol. Cherry, spice, and herbs on the palate with energizing mineral. Still young and aggressive, with an age-worthy structure. Drink 2014 to 2026. The 2008 is also a bit closed but shows Nebbiolo sensations combined with a vibrant, tannic structure that needs time to develop. Best 2016 to 2028.

Barbaresco "Cichin." From the eponymous vineyard in the Rombone cru, where the family's manicured vines hug the steep hill around the Ada Nada winery and country hotel. The Nadas were among the first to plant Nebbiolo here and have the best parcels. Aged in Slavonian casks, this is always approachable with present but fine tannins and ripe, succulent fruit. The 2008 is very earthy with ripe red fruit, spice, and underbrush aromas with a hint of orange peel all carry over to the palate. Big but sweet tannins and fresh acidity. Thoroughly enjoyable. Drink through 2018.

Barbaresco "Elisa." From a small single vineyard in the Valeirano cru that Anna Lisa's father, Gian Carlo, renamed "Elisa" in honor of Anna Lisa and Elvio's first daughter, this wine is made from a selection of the best and oldest grapes in the parcel, with some rows planted in 1947. Aged entirely in casks, this is the firm's flagship wine, combining structure, depth, and complexity. In 2005 they made this as a Riserva that offers intense aromas of underbrush, truffle, and leather along with succulent cherry and spice flavors. Fresh acidity and big but round tannins. Drink through 2020.

Nada Giuseppe

Azienda Agricola Nada Giuseppe
Via Giacosa 12/a
12050 Treiso (CN)
Tel. +39 0173 638110
www.nadagiuseppe.it
enrico@nadagiuseppe.it

Giuseppe Nada, a cousin of the Nada family who own Ada Nada, founded his winery in 1964. That same year he started bottling the wine he made from the vineyards inherited by his side of the family, but before that, Giuseppe's father and grandfather had sold grapes and wine in bulk. To have more space for a larger cellar and equipment, in 1968 Giuseppe moved his family from their old farmhouse in Casot, one of Treiso's most famous crus, to the current location in the Marcarini cru, where Giuseppe also owns vineyards and built his winery and home. Today the winery is a family affair run by Giuseppe, his wife, Nella, and their grown children Barbara and Enrico, who represent the fifth generation in the business originally founded by Carlo Nada in 1919.

The firm's calling card is Casot, widely recognized as one of the best and most historic crus in Treiso, which goes as far back as Lorenzo Fantini, who pointed it out in his monograph. Casot benefits from a singular microclimate created by southwest exposures, what are some of Treiso's lowest altitudes—290 to 330 meters (951 to 1,083 feet) above sea level—and protection from cold winds provided by the hill directly in front of it. Seeing that Nebbiolo has long excelled in these conditions, it is no coincidence this is one of the few vineyard areas in the town where the noble grape has been traditionally cultivated.

Like many of the Langhe's young winemakers, Enrico, who has been in charge of winemaking since 2008, takes a middle route in the cellars, especially when it comes to aging. For his Barbarescos, he uses a mix of wood and barrel sizes for aging: barriques, only 10 percent new, and seasoned 500-liter tonneaux and 10-hectoliter casks for the first year, all made of French oak, and 30- and 40-hectoliter Slavonian casks for the second year. The final result is complexity without dominant wood sensations.

Production

Total surface area: 7 ha (17.29 acres)
Barbaresco: 3 ha (7.4 acres), 12,000 bottles

Barbaresco Casot.   Made from vines ranging between fifteen and eighty years old, many planted by Enrico's grandfather, this is a structured and age-worthy Barbaresco. In top years, the firm also makes a Riserva from a selection of the oldest vines. In 2012, the family opened up a number of vintages, proving the impressive aging potential of their flagship wine.

The 2009 shows berry, animal, and earth aromas, with mouthwatering fruit and firm but ripe tannins. It still needs time to develop, so drink 2016 to 2024. The 2008 is earthy with leather, spice, truffle, and restrained wild cherry flavors and intense mineral purity. Structured but elegant, this is a lovely wine. Best through 2028. The 2007 shows sumptuous red fruit and balsamic notes of great depth and intensity alongside whiffs of leather. Ready now; drink through 2017. The 2007 Riserva is gorgeous, with an enticing depth of flavors. It's a textbook Barbaresco that belies the heat of the difficult 2007 vintage. Drink through 2027. The 2006 delivers hallmark Nebbiolo pedigree with great fruit, leather, truffle, and an earthy bouquet. Dense red fruit flavors with spice and menthol. Best 2018 to 2036. Stunning. The 2005 Casot Riserva is gorgeous, with intense, earthy perfume of leather, truffle, spice, with dense red fruit. Still closed, needs time to fully develop. Impressive structure for the vintage.

Starting with the 2011 vintage, the firm also makes a Barbaresco from the Marcarini cru.

Pier

Via Giacosa 22
12050 Treiso (CN)
Tel. +39 0173 638178
www.piervini.it
info@piervinit.it

I tasted Pier's Barbaresco Rio Sordo at the 2012 Nebbiolo Prima press tastings, and among the sixty-five wines tried that day, it jumped out at me for its Nebbiolo intensity and mineral purity. And no wonder: not only do they have ideal vineyards, but the firm recently started working with consulting enologist Dante Scaglione of Bruno Giacosa fame. This estate is one of my most exciting discoveries uncovered while researching this book.

Founded in Treiso in the early 1900s by Pietro Grasso, this lovely winery, on the family's restored farm, sits on a high hill just over the town line, between Barbaresco and Treiso, overlooking the Marcarini vineyards on one side and Rio Sordo and Tre Stelle on the other. Today the winery is in the capable hands of the founder's son Giuseppe, who still manages the vineyards, and grandson Pier Paolo, who has taken on the winemaking and many of the everyday responsibilities. The firm owns prime vineyards in Treiso, including Pajorè, while the bulk of its holdings are in the celebrated Rio Sordo in Barbaresco and Currà in Neive, with average plant age a healthy and

FIGURE 30. Giuseppe and Pier Paolo Grasso of Pier. From their lovingly restored farmhouse and winery perched on a high hill between Barbaresco and Treiso, the Grassos make stunning Barbarescos of intensity, finesse, and Nebbiolo purity from their holdings in Rio Sordo, Pajorè, and Currà. Photograph by Paolo Tenti.

mature thirty-five years old. Most vineyards have ideal southwest exposures, are situated between 220 and 250 meters (721.7 and 820 feet) above sea level, and soil in all the vineyards is predominantly calcareous clay, all of which are ideal conditions for producing structured and long-lived Barbarescos that are also approachable in their youth.

The firm's wines come from estate grapes, and Giuseppe and Pier sell much of their overall production in bulk; selecting and bottling only the best wine for their own label. In the cellars, Pier is a converted traditionalist, allowing spontaneous fermentation with wild yeasts followed by lengthy maceration, with the entire process lasting between twenty-five and thirty days. After experimenting with barriques from 2000 to 2009, the firm now ages its Barbarescos exclusively in botti for eighteen months, with each 50-hectoliter cask made of alternating French and Slavonian slats of untoasted oak. Pier's Barbarescos possess classic Nebbiolo fragrances and rich flavors balanced by a weightless complexity that only a few producers can achieve. The firm also makes one of the best Dolcettos I ever have ever tasted. "This is the real Dolcetto, elegant and drinkable with spice and mineral notes and around 12.5 percent alcohol," explains Pier, who adds that the Marcarini vineyard directly below their house, planted in 1985 when Dolcetto was in high demand, would be perfect for Nebbiolo for Barbaresco.

Production

Total surface area: 44 ha (108.7 acres)

Barbaresco: 10 ha (24.7 acres), 30,000 bottles

Barbaresco Rio Villa. This is a blend from all the firm's vineyards, and shows layers of fruit, bracing tannins, and great balance. The 2009 has ripe cherry and spice aromas with hints of cedar and menthol, all of which carry over to the palate. Outstanding length. In very good years, they also produce a Riserva version.

Barbaresco Rio Sordo. A hallmark Barbaresco of structure, finesse, and breeding. The 2009 is a textbook example of classic Barbaresco, with an intense bouquet of violet, spice, and truffle with rich layers of cherry, raspberry, orange peel, cinnamon, and clove. Still very young and tannic, with a long licorice finish. Drink 2015 to 2024.

Barbaresco Rio Sordo Riserva. In the best years Pier also makes a more complex and structured Riserva from the best Rio Sordo grapes. Tried in 2012, the 1999 Riserva was still magnificent, boasting a fragrance of dried rose petal and leather alongside a shockingly youthful palate of dense wild cherry, earth, sage, and rosemary accompanied by licorice and compelling mineral notes. Gorgeous. Drink through 2029.

SAN ROCCO SENO D'ELVIO

When talking about Barbaresco, it is easy to overlook this sliver of the denomination that accounts for a mere 6 percent of total Barbaresco production. The hamlet used to be part of Treiso, but when the latter broke from Barbaresco, San Rocco Seno d'Elvio opted to go under the jurisdiction of Alba. Because of very steep slopes and cooler temperatures, growers here have traditionally preferred to plant other grapes, mainly Moscato and Dolcetto, although Nebbiolo for Barbaresco plantings have increased from 22 hectares (54.3 acres) in 2000 to 38 hectares (94 acres) in 2012. Of the four delimited crus in San Rocco Seno d'Elvio three are shared with Treiso and only one,

Rocche Massalupo, of which there is little or no mention before the official geographic mentions came into play, is entirely in the hamlet.

Adriano Marco Vittorio

Fraz. San Rocco Seno d'Elvio 13A
Alba (CN)
Tel. +39 0173 362294
www.adrianovini.it
info@adrianovini.it

The Italian custom of listing last names first causes a good amount of confusion over the name of this winery, but brothers Marco and Vittorio, whose surname is Adriano, are used to it. "People assume that Adriano is another brother," laughs Vittorio.

This charming family firm has its roots in the early years of the twentieth century when Giuseppe Adriano, a sharecropper, first began cultivating grapes. He and his son Aldo eventually bought a small farm and planted their own vineyards, and years later, the family built their winery. Marco, who follows the vineyards, and Vittorio, who is the winemaker, are the third generation of growers, and in 1994 they began vinifying and bottling their production. After discovering their wines in the early 2000s, I made my way to their winery in 2005, and learned from Vittorio only years later, in 2013, that I had been the first journalist to ever visit their estate.

The firm's Barbaresco Sanadaive, local dialect for Seno d'Elvio, hails from southwest-facing vineyards in San Rocco Seno d'Elvio. According to Vittorio this exposure can leave cooled morning grapes scorched by the impact of the burning sun, but thanks to Marco and Vittorio's scrupulous canopy management, they can prolong the growing season, which in turn helps Nebbiolo reach optimum maturity and ripe tannins. The firm also makes an outstanding single-vineyard Barbaresco Basarin from the eponymous cru located in Neive, where the calcareous marls and veins of sand tend to yield linear but structured wines with remarkable elegance. According to older producers, despite the southern exposures, Basarin, which has extremely steep slopes, is often subject to cool northeast winds that used to impede ripening for Nebbiolo. Now however, these same winds seem to lend freshness to Basarin's Barbarescos in the Brave New World of the Langhe, where soaring summertime temperatures and frequent drought during the crucial growing season are reshaping the vineyard hierarchy. In the cellars, Vittorio has a straightforward approach and a light hand, fermenting in temperature-controlled stainless steel followed by skin maceration, with the whole process lasting about fifteen days for the Barbaresco crus, and up to twenty-five for the Riserva. Afterward, he ages the Barbarescos for at least one year in traditional 35- to 50-hectoliter botti, two years for the Riservas.

Production

Total surface area: 40 ha (99 acres)
Barbaresco: 7.5 ha (18.5 acres), 53,000 bottles

Barbaresco Sanadaive.   This is made from a blend of the firm's various holdings in San Rocco Seno d'Elvio where average altitudes reach 300 meters (984 feet). The 2009 shows the slightly lighter hue typical of San Rocco Seno d'Elvio's southwest-facing slopes, and has an enticing floral and spice bouquet. Gorgeous, ripe cherry fruit and mineral sensations with firm but fine tannins and spice. Long and linear. Drink through 2019. The 2010 delivers classic aromas of red rose, leather, and berry alongside hallmark cherry, raspberry, and spice flavors layered with balsamic notes. Great length and impeccable balance. Give this time to fully develop.

Barbaresco Basarin.   Made from grapes in Neive's Basarin cru. The 2008 shows a very pretty fragrance of wild rose, violet, and spice with ripe and radiant berry, sage, and mint flavors. Best 2014 to 2019. The 2009 offers succulent, round cherry-berry sensations with earth, spice, balsamic, and licorice notes. The tannic structure is balanced by freshness and delicious fruit. Best 2014 to 2019, but this will maintain for even longer. The 2010 offers pure Nebbiolo sensations—violet, rose, and vibrant cherry with layers of white pepper, cinnamon, balsamic notes, and mineral. It's structured but also elegant and well balanced.

Barbaresco Basarin Riserva.   More intense and more structured than the straight Basarin and will benefit from more bottle age. The 2006 has enticing aromas of rose petal, leather, truffle, and balsamic notes. Intense wild cherry, licorice, and menthol flavors balanced by vibrant acidity and firm tannins. Drink through 2026.

Poderi Colla

San Rocco Seno d'Elvio 82
12051 Alba (CN)
Tel. +39 0173 290148
www.podericolla.it
info@podericolla.it

Founded by Tino Colla and his niece Federica in 1994, Poderi Colla owns prime holdings in both Barolo and Barbaresco. The firm also counts on the collaboration of Beppe Colla, Tino's much older brother, and Federica's father, a living institution in the Langhe. Tino's son Pietro has also recently joined the firm.

Wine has been in the family DNA for generations, and the family has long had vineyards on the nearby Moscato hill where initially they grew and sold grapes, and later made and sold wine. Then, in 1909, Beppe and Tino's father, Pietro, was hired at the tender of age of fifteen by Gancia, for more than a century one of the largest sparkling wine houses in Italy. Pietro spent twelve hours a day for more than six decades rotating tens of thousands of bottles in Gancia's damp cellars, and he learned the delicate art of fermenting in the bottle in the classic Champenois method from other Gancia cellar hands who had been sent to France. Pietro was one of the last Italian sparkling wine specialists to have the title of Champagnista, which was used to distinguish his craft. At the same time, Pietro continued to oversee and expand the family's Moscato vineyards, and eventually began making and selling his own wine. Even though his position at Gancia was a well-paying job for the time, the physical sacrifice was immense, but Pietro was undeterred. The solid income allowed him to ensure that all of his children received an education, and Pietro encouraged them to establish their own businesses after completing their studies.

Born in 1930, Beppe, Pietro's oldest son, graduated from Alba's Scuola Enologica and at nineteen was hired as winemaker by the large Bonardi Barolo house. Although defunct since the 1970s, this was once a prestigious Barolo producer, and his time there provided invaluable experience for young Beppe. Not only did he learn to vinify large quantities of grapes and still make quality wine, but he was also sent to scout out the best grapes, allowing him the opportunity to discover the Langhe's most suitable vineyards.

In 1956, Beppe Colla purchased Prunotto, another well-respected Barolo/ Barbaresco firm located in Alba. Under his ownership and guidance, Prunotto made outstanding wines, in great part due to Beppe's firsthand knowledge of the top vineyard sites in both Barolo and Barbaresco. Beppe was ahead of his

time when it came to highlighting the importance of the Langhe's single vineyards, and in 1961 he was the first to vinify separately and bottle single-vineyard
selections of Langhe's classic wines, including a single-vineyard Barolo Cru
Bussia and a Barbaresco Cru Montestefano. He was met with widespread criticism and resistance. "At the time Barolo and Barbaresco were blended from
different sites, so this was considered a sacrilege. I was just a few years too early,"
Beppe told me during one of our interviews. By 1967, both Bruno Giacosa and
Angelo Gaja would also be producing single-vineyard bottlings, but Colla
paved the rough road. He was also among the first to buy a temperature-
controlled steel fermenting tank in 1980, which, fearing an uproar among other
producers, he had to hide behind the large oak casks so no one could see it.

By the mid-1980s, after his business partner passed away, Prunotto ran into
financial problems and Beppe was forced to sell. Through a rather convoluted
chain of events, including defaults and mergers between the original buyers,
Prunotto ended up being acquired by Tuscan scion Piero Antinori in 1990,
with the agreement that Beppe would stay on until 1994. After this, Beppe
began working with his brother Tino and daughter Federica, who are joined
today by Tino's son Pietro, who is taking on many of the winemaking duties.

Thanks to Beppe's firsthand knowledge of the Langhe hills and his connections with vineyard owners, Poderi Colla was able to acquire prime vineyards
in the Bussia cru in Monforte d'Alba for the firm's Barolo, and in Roncaglie in
Barbaresco. The firm is headquartered at Cascina del Drago, an old but charming farm where they make outstanding Nebbiolo d'Alba and other local clas-
sics. They also make a wonderful sparkling wine in the classic method, from
Pinot Nero and Nebbiolo—an Extra Brut named in honor of *nonno* Pietro.

Like most top producers, the Collas avoid harsh chemicals in the vineyards and use treatments and fertilizers (organic) only as needed. In the cellars, the Collas adhere to the Langhe's classic school, making wine using tried
but true methods that include fermentation in glass-lined concrete tanks,
aging in large Slavonian casks, and no filtering. The result is terroir-driven
wines that are elegant expressions of Nebbiolo, but also possess their own
strong personalities that set them apart from the crowd.

Production

Total surface area: 26 ha (64.2 acres)

Barbaresco: 5.45 ha (13.5 acres), 15,000–20,000 bottles

Barolo: 5.9 ha (14.5 acres), 20,000–30,000 bottles

Barbaresco Roncaglie. With its optimum southern and southwestern exposures, calcareous clay soils, and ideal altitude averaging 260 meters (853 feet) above sea level, grape merchants, including Beppe Colla, had long sought out fruit from Roncaglie. However, it was Colla who first bottled a single-vineyard Roncaglie in 1994, demonstrating to all the true potential of the vineyard. This is an archetypical Barbaresco. The 2009 has intense aromas of strawberry jelly and orange peel accompanied by hints of spice and rosemary with delicious strawberry flavors layered with white pepper and mineral. Very elegant, very drinkable with great depth of flavors. Long, lean, and fresh with firm tannins. Drink 2014 to 2019.

Barolo Dardi Le Rose Bussia. Since the early 1960s, Beppe Colla has made wonderful Barolos from the Dardi area in Monforte d'Alba, long known for its excellent Nebbiolo, and when the opportunity arose in 1990, he bought the Dardi Le Rose farm and vineyards. Although Slow Food's *Atlante delle vigne di Langa,* published in 2000, considered Dardi a superior cru, they listed it as a distinct and separate site, but Poderi Colla has always added the mention Bussia, and since 2010, its Dardi Le Rose vineyards have been officially incorporated into the Bussia site. The high vineyard altitude of 330 meters (1082 feet) above sea level, southern and southwestern exposures, and calcareous clays all offer Nebbiolo ideal growing conditions, while forty-year-old vines add to the richness and complexity of Dardi Le Rose Bussia. The 2010 is a textbook Barolo with classic Nebbiolo sensations of ripe cherry and spice with leather, orange peel, and truffle, all of which carry over onto the palate. Great depth and fantastic but bracing tannins need time. Best 2020 to 2040.

SIXTEEN

Wineries in Alba and outside of Barolo/Barbaresco Villages

HISTORICALLY, IN THE NINETEENTH CENTURY and for much of the twentieth century, almost all the Barolo-producing firms were located in Alba. Until the latter half of the 1900s, these large houses did not possess their own vineyards but instead bought grapes from the network of the Langhe's numerous small growers, transported the grapes to the wineries in Alba, and made Barolo. This all began to change in the late 1970s and more so in the 1980s as the Langhe's grape growers began making Barolo themselves, forcing many of Alba's Barolo wineries to close, while others decided to buy their own vineyards. Today only one major winery remains in Alba, Pio Cesare, while others have moved outside the city's limits, including Prunotto and Ceretto.

The city of Bra, 50 kilometers (31 miles) south of Turin and 50 kilometers northeast of Cuneo, is actually not in the Langhe but in the neighboring Roero area; however, it too played a crucial role in Barolo's history thanks to Pollenzo. In 1835, Pollenzo, a hamlet of Bra, became the seat of King Carlo Alberto's royal farming estate, the Agenzia di Pollenzo, where the king began to seriously produce Barolo. Unsurprisingly, given the success of the king's Barolo production, Bra attracted other entrepreneurs to establish Barolo wineries in the town, and according to an article written by present-day Barolo historian Lorenzo Tablino, "In the 1800s Bra was the center of Barolo production."[1] Tablino went on to write that there were at least six large Barolo-making firms in Bra, including Fissore. According to Matteo Ascheri, another producer from the town, Fissore won a Gold Medal for its Barolo at Vienna's World Fair in 1873. Of all the former Barolo wineries in Bra, only Ascheri remains. "The other Bra Barolo firms were quite large and were already exporting. They really suffered after the global economic crash in

1929, and most closed in the years just after this, while a few others hung on for a couple of decades. Our winery was smaller and didn't suffer to the same extent," explains Ascheri.

Pio Cesare

Via C. Balbo 6
12051 Alba
Tel. +39 0173 440386
www.piocesare.it
piocesare@piocesare.it

Founded in 1881, the Pio Cesare winery is one of the oldest and most-respected Barolo- and Barbaresco-making firms. The winery itself is one of the most fascinating I've ever seen, with a labyrinth of two-thousand-year-old fortified walls that snake their way 12 meters (39 feet) beneath the bustling city of Alba, giving a rare insight into the Alba Pompeia of ancient Rome.

Don't expect to find someone actually named Pio Cesare at the eponymous winery since the founder—whose name was actually Cesare Pio—would be 150 years old were he alive today. Yet Pio Cesare's legacy has been passed down through subsequent generations of Pios and Cesares, and today his maternal great-grandson, Pio Boffa, is in charge of the iconic winery, assisted by his nephew Cesare Benvenuto.

Pio Cesare is the last of the area's seminal wineries to remain in Alba, once the undisputed capital of Barolo and Barbaresco production, where for generations all the major Barolo-making houses were located. Hidden from view by a high, nondescript wall in downtown Alba, the winery continues to make its complex, age-worthy wines in its ancient cellars, which were completely renovated and modernized a decade ago. The firm still has a wealth of old bottles, demonstrating that Pio Cesare was already bottling its wines early in the last century, albeit in small amounts at first, but this is still surprising given that the majority of wineries sold their Barolos and Barbarescos exclusively in demijohns and small barrels until the late 1950s and 1960s. By the time Cesare's son Giuseppe Pio took over in 1919, the firm was already exporting to Switzerland and Belgium. Giuseppe carried on in his father's footsteps, but when his only daughter married an engineer and moved away, Giuseppe Pio decided it was time to sell the firm.

FIGURE 31. Pio Boffa of Pio Cesare. Pio Boffa runs this historic estate, which was founded by his maternal great-grandfather. This is one of Barolo's longest-established wineries, and the firm also owns vineyards in key sites, including Ornato in Serralunga and Il Bricco in Treiso. Photograph by Paolo Tenti.

"But my father, Giuseppe Boffa, realized that my mother's family winery shouldn't be sold, and gave up his engineering career to come work at the firm. He trained under my grandfather, later taking over the business," recounts Boffa. Thanks to his entrepreneurial spirit, Giuseppe Boffa brought the winery into the modern age by purchasing vineyards, the same ones that for years had supplied grapes for the firm's award-winning Barolos and Barbarescos, including Il Bricco in Barbaresco in 1964, followed by Ornato in Serralunga in 1970.

These days the firm makes a classic Barolo and Barbaresco from different sites as well as two single-vineyard bottlings. Pio Boffa, who joined his father in 1972, is surprisingly protective of his more traditional bottlings, declaring: "These wines made Pio Cesare famous and are still our calling card, and have been for five generations. Blended Barolos and Barbarescos are the true expression of Nebbiolo in their respective territories and denominations." Despite Boffa's deference to the firm's storied wines, in 1985, Pio Cesare released a single-vineyard Barolo from Ornato, followed by Il Bricco Barbaresco in 1990, both of which quickly garnered critical acclaim.

However, Boffa is quick to note that "single-vineyard bottlings aren't necessarily better by definition than Barolos and Barbarescos made by blending different vineyards, they're just different interpretations."

Boffa ages 70 percent of his classic Barolo and Barbaresco in medium-capacity and large French casks, and 30 percent in barriques, while he does nearly the opposite for his single-vineyard selections: 20 percent casks and 80 percent barriques. Given that he uses both classic and international techniques, Boffa is adamant that he is neither an innovator nor a traditionalist and refuses to be pigeonholed into either category. "When the so-called modernists reigned, I was considered a traditionalist; now that the traditionalists have made a comeback, I'm labeled a modernist," laughs Boffa. "Until the late 1970s and 1980s, the technology and knowledge we have today weren't available. It would be ridiculous not to take advantage of today's better winemaking methods and skills in the name of tradition," he insists.

Boffa believes that while great Barolo and Barbaresco have to hold up to lengthy aging, they should also be approachable upon release. "If you buy my Barolo and have to wait ten years to drink it, then you should also be able to wait ten years to pay me," he states.

Production

Total surface area: 75 ha (185 acres)
Barolo/Barbaresco: About 40 ha (99 acres) combined, 123,000 bottles

Barolo.   Made from Barolo vineyards dispersed throughout the denomination that create a balance of fragrance, elegance, and structure, and aged predominantly in large casks, this represents the firm's ties to tradition. The 2007 boasts a classic Nebbiolo bouquet of rose petal, earth, and a hint of leather and slate. The palate shows delicious sour cherry flavors with hints of mineral. It's already complex, with great depth and nice balance. A hallmark Barolo and while already approachable, it should age well. Drink through 2022. The 1989, tasted in 2013, delivered rose, leather, underbrush, and tar— classic sensations of aged Nebbiolo—along with dark cherry supported by a still youthful tannic backbone. The 1978, also tasted in 2013, showed tar, truffle, flint, carob, dried cherry, and mineral. It's very earthy and still surprisingly young.

Barolo Ornato.   Made from Pio Cesare's cru in Serralunga, this a very structured Barolo destined to be aged, although I admit that I would love to see this wine made with less oak influence, which I feel muffles the great terroir behind this wine. The 2007 delivers concentrated black fruit and mocha with evident oak sensations. Round and opulent with aggressive tannins, but underneath the oak lurks a superb Barolo. Drink 2015 to 2022.

Barbaresco. Made from the firm's holdings in Treiso and aged predominantly in large French casks, this is Pio Cesare's classic Barbaresco. The 2007 offers intense rose petal and earthy aromas along with succulent raspberry and soothing licorice flavors. Supple tannins, lovely depth, and nice balance. Best through 2022.

Barbaresco Il Bricco. More of an internationally styled Barbaresco made entirely from the Il Bricco vineyard in Treiso, and aged 80 percent in barriques and the rest in French casks. The 2007 has loads of dark fruit with spice and espresso wrapped up in well-integrated oak. Powerful and robust with bracing tannins that need time to tame. Drink 2015 to 2022.

Prunotto

Corso Barolo 14
12051 Alba (Cuneo)
Tel. +39 0173 280017
www.prunotto.it
prunotto@prunotto.it

Prunotto is another one of Barolo and Barbaresco's most storied names. Even though the winery briefly followed the trend of producing oaky, extracted wines that muffled the *tipicità* and character of its Barolos and Barbarescos in the early 2000s, Prunotto is now back to making outstanding local wines full of personality and varietal authenticity.

In the 1920s a young Alfredo Prunotto purchased the struggling cooperative cellar known as Ai Vini delle Langhe, which had run into economic problems after the First World War. By all accounts, Prunotto and his wife, newlyweds at the time, poured their heart and soul into their new, eponymously named company, and began exporting their Barolo and Barbaresco to South America and later North America, helping place both wines on the map for connoisseurs around the globe. After decades of success, Prunotto decided to retire, and sold his winery to young Beppe Colla, a talented enologist who already had several years of experience at Bonardi—another successful Barolo house at the time.

In 1961, Colla, a big believer in the importance and identifiable traits and qualities of single vineyards, began separately vinifying and aging the best crus in the Langhe, including Bussia in Barolo, and he is credited as the first to release a single-vineyard bottling of Barolo Bussia from the 1961 vintage. In the late 1980s, Colla decided to look for investors after his longtime business partner passed away. Through a rather convoluted series of events, the new investors ceded their interests to Tuscan firm Marchesi Antinori, which started its involvement with Prunotto in 1989, taking full control in 1994. Beppe Colla, and by then his younger brother Tino, stayed on as consultants until 1994.

Once the Antinoris acquired Prunotto, guided by Colla, the firm purchased top vineyards, including prime property in Bussia in Monforte d'Alba and Bric Turot in Barbaresco, and the winery still sources grapes from top growers who have supplied the firm for decades. While I was a big fan of Prunotto for years, I noticed a change in style starting in the mid- to late 1990s that lasted for about a decade: the wines were darker, denser, and more forward with far more oak influence and less Nebbiolo backbone. However, starting around 2005 the firm has backtracked—in both the vineyards and the cellars—and is now making more elegant, classic, and terroir-driven Barolos and Barbarescos with less brawn and far less oak sensation.

Prunotto is even experimenting with whole-bunch fermentation with their single-vineyard Riserva, Vigna Colonnello, to be released in 2014. "Our Barolo Riserva Vigna Colonnello 2008 was fermented with the stems," says managing director Emanuele Baldi. "That year, the stems were perfectly ripe, and we decided to try whole-bunch fermentation. We are very pleased with the complexity of this wine, which had a long maceration period of thirty-five days." Baldi notes that "to get fine tannins, the stems have to be ripe, otherwise they can generate green tannins," and points out that stems do not always ripen well.

Production

Total surface area: 55 ha (136 acres)
Barolo: 7 ha (17 acres) of estate vineyard; 75,000 bottles
Barbaresco: 5.3 ha (13 acres) of estate vineyards; 50,000 bottles

Barolo. The firm's classic Barolo is a blend of Nebbiolo from Monforte d'Alba, Castiglione Falletto, and Serralunga, where average altitudes range between 350 and 400 meters (1,148 and 1,312 feet) above sea level. This undergoes straightforward vinification in temperature-controlled steel tanks, for about fifteen days, followed by two years in 50- and 75-hectoliter French casks and a small percentage of barriques used once before. The 2008 is an archetypical Barolo with cherry, underbrush, and mineral sensations alongside lovely depth and balance. Drink through 2028.

Barolo Bussia. This is Prunotto's signature wine, and the one that helped put the firm—and Barolo—on the map. Made from its parcel in Bussia, where vines average twenty-five years old and are situated at 350 meters (1.148 feet) above sea level and enjoy optimal southern as well as eastern and western exposures. This is fermented for fifteen days in Austrian oak vats, and then aged for two years in 50- to 75-hectoliter French casks and a small percentage of used barriques. The 2008 is stunning with a bright fragrance of rose, strawberry, and citrus peel. Its succulent strawberry and cherry palate shows great depth and layers of cinnamon and spice. Fantastic length. Still young and tannic and needs time to develop complexity. Drink 2015 to 2028. A classic.

In 2013, the firm opened up a number of older bottles of Bussia and Bussia Riserva:

Barolo Bussia 2004. This was holding up well, as you would expect from this great vintage. It was loaded with balsamic notes, dried cherry, and subtle oak balanced by fresh acidity and velvety tannins.

1985 Barolo Bussia Riserva. In great vintages the firm also makes a Bussia Riserva. Beppe Colla's Old School 1985 is compelling, with black cherry, tar, mineral, and pipe tobacco sensations alongside a still heroic structure.

1982 Barolo Bussia Riserva. This has layers of zabaglione, raspberry, tea, spice, and mineral notes. It is still very youthful with a nervous vein of acidity and supple, smoothed tannins. It delivers layers of complexity and continuously evolved in the glass. A gorgeous wine and still going strong.

1978 Barolo Bussia Riserva. This magnificent wine is a quintessential expression of Bussia. It has classic rose, tar, and leather aromas with a surprisingly intact core of black cherry, prune, carob, and mineral flavors. It's still tannic and youthful but with the depth and complexity that comes with age. Superb.

Barbaresco. Made from vineyards in Barbaresco and Treiso, this is vinified in steel and aged for one year—mostly in large French casks and a small percentage of seasoned barriques. The 2009 is intensely aromatic with floral notes and the earthy aromas you get while walking in a Barbaresco vineyard under the sun—"polvere della vigna" or vineyard dust, as the winemakers describe it—yet another reason to visit the area. The 2009 combines fleshy fruit and finesse. Delicious. Drink through 2024.

Barbaresco Bric Turot. Made from the eponymous vineyard located between Roncaglie and Tre Stelle in the village of Barbaresco. Until 2008 this was vinified in oak casks, but now only in steel, followed by twelve months aging in large French casks and a small amount of used barriques. The 2008 has a complex and layered bouquet of Alpine berries and forest floor that carry over to the palate with licorice and spice. Well-structured Barbaresco with a long finish. Drink through 2028.

1971 Barbaresco Riserva. Tried at the winery in 2013, this was the star of the tasting. While it was definitely mature, with tar, leather, rose, and tobacco sensations, it still has cherry fruit and freshness alongside smooth tannins. A majestic, gripping wine.

Ceretto

Strada Provinciale Alba/Barolo
Località San Cassiano 34
12051 Alba (CN)
Tel. +39 0173 282582
www.ceretto.com
ceretto@ceretto.com

With its numerous estate vineyards and four separate cellars—one in Alba, one in Castiglione Falletto, one in Barbaresco, and one in San Stefano Belbo for its sparkling whites—Ceretto is a major Barolo and Barbaresco player. Its story begins more modestly, when Riccardo Ceretto founded his eponymous firm in Alba in 1937. As was typical for the times, he was strictly a Barolo maker, purchasing his fruit from growers throughout the Langhe and selling wine in bulk and demijohns. In the 1960s, Riccardo's sons Bruno and Marcello brought the firm into the modern age, first by identifying the best vineyards in the Langhe and buying grapes from these chosen crus. Although they wanted to buy the vineyards, for years the owners wouldn't sell. In the meantime, the Cerettos began following and managing the vineyards as if they were their own. In the cellars, the brothers were soon separately vinifying the individual vineyards and bottling their wines.

Perhaps most importantly, with the financial backing of their somewhat skeptical father, who thought it best to buy the best grapes rather than own the vineyards, the two brothers acquired their own parcels throughout Barolo and Barbaresco, beginning in 1970 with their first purchase in Barbaresco, in Asili, where they later built a winery. Purchases in Serralunga in 1973 and in La Morra's Brunate in 1975 followed, and the firm was on its way to painstakingly acquiring 110 hectares (272 acres), 32 hectares (79 acres) of which are dedicated to Barolo and Barbaresco. In 1999, the brothers' children began working for the family firm, and today Marcello's son Alessandro is in charge of winemaking.

With the exception of a few excellent older bottlings from 1990 and 1985 and earlier, I have often found Ceretto's wines to be too oaked for my tastes, so I was surprised by the graceful, pure Nebbiolo aromas and elegance of the firm's 2008 Barbaresco Asij. The more graceful style, unfettered by obvious oak, was all the more surprising because in 2006 Alessandro Ceretto told me that he had no intention of trading in his 300-liter barriques for botti grandi, although he had just started pulling back on new oak, saying he was using "only 50 percent new barrels."

But that was then, this is now, he explains today. "When I began working at the winery it was all about concentration and new oak, not just in Piedmont, but everywhere," says Ceretto, noting that his palate has since evolved. "Now I want to make wines that express terroir, that taste like they could only be from here." To create such wines, starting in 2008 he began eliminating winemaking methods that influence taste, such as commercial yeasts, and has cut down on dominant new oak. He now ferments using indigenous yeasts and ages his red wines in a mix of barrels, 300-liter barriques and for some wines, French casks up to 25 hectoliters. However, his 2009 single-vineyard Barbaresco crus were still aged in 300-liter barriques only, half of which are new, and unsurprisingly, I find the oak still overwhelms these wines. But Alessandro tells me that starting with the 2012 vintage, he is aging all his Barolo and Barbarescos for six to eight months in 300-liter barrels, only 20 percent new, and fifteen months in large French casks. "My philosophy has definitely changed. Now I think using 100 percent new barriques is like buying a cut of fresh, excellent quality fish, and then dousing it in sauce. I can say this because here in Barolo and Barbaresco, we have great terroir, but winemakers who don't are forced to rely on invasive winemaking practices."

To better quality, Alessandro is methodically heading toward organic viticulture, although certification will take time, and each year he relies less on enology. Or as he puts it, "To make the wines I want to create, I have to pretty much do the opposite of everything I studied at enological school."

Production

Total surface area: 110 ha (272 acres)

Barolo and Barbaresco: 32 ha (79 acres), 88,000 bottles of Barolo, 40,000 bottles of Barbaresco

Barbaresco Asij.   This is a blend of their holdings in Barbaresco and Treiso, and is aged for two years in used 300-liter barriques. The 2008 has pretty Nebbiolo aromas of berry, underbrush, and porcini mushroom with berry and mineral flavors. Bright and elegant with a silky texture, and enjoyable. Drink through 2020.

Barolo Bricco Rocche Brunate.   Made from their holdings in La Morra's most-famed cru, where vines are situated between 276 and 342 meters (906 and 1,142 feet) above sea level and where thirty-five-year-old vines enjoy southeastern exposures. Aged in new and used barriques and 25-hectoliter French casks, the 2008 has toasted aromas with cherry, berry, and earthy notes. Still somewhat closed palate reveals fruit, spice, oak, and espresso. Still young and aggressive but fresh with nice length and finesse. 2015 to 2023.

Barolo Bricco Rocche.   Made from their holdings in Castiglione Falletto, aged partly in new and used barriques and French casks. The 2008 offers both Nebbiolo aromas and toasted, espresso notes. Drink through 2023.

Ascheri

Via G. Piumati 23
12042 Bra (CN)
Tel. +39 0172 412394
www.ascherivini.it
ascheri@ascherivini.it

This is yet another fine Barolo producer that I first discovered through Nebbiolo Prima, the annual five-day press tasting held in Alba to showcase the newest releases from Barolo, Barbaresco, and Roero. Ascheri's bottlings impress me for their sheer Baroloness. And even though that is not a word, it should be: the firm's Barolos possess all the earthiness, restrained cherry, and complexity of quintessential Nebbiolo—minus the fashion trends and flashiness.

Founded in 1880, the Ascheri family winery is the last of the Barolo houses that populated the town of Bra from the mid-nineteenth to the mid-twentieth century. Initially encouraged by the success of the royal family, who were producing Barolo at their estate and winery in the Bra district of Pollenzo, most of these large firms, which relied heavily on export markets, closed after the 1929 economic crash, while others ceased to exist after World War II, when global demand for quality wine plummeted. Ascheri—smaller and less reliant on exports—was the only one to survive the difficult period.

Ascheri's winemaking roots are in La Morra, in a microzone that is now officially noted as Ascheri in Barolo's list of geographic mentions. Here, before the family transferred to Bra to be closer to the key Turin market, "the late Dr. Matteo Ascheri developed a vine training system that is both antique yet modern," wrote Lorenzo Fantini in his late nineteenth-century monograph. Based on the sketches included with this brief description, it appears to have been a rather primitive precursor to the Guyot vine-training system, with a low wooden trellis to train one shoot and two high wires for other shoots.

Today the firm is managed by the doctor's namesake and descendant, Matteo Ascheri, who is turning out fine Barolos of the classic school from the family's estate vineyards in Sorano in Serralunga and Pisapola in Verduno. Ascheri adheres to integrated pest-management farming methods, drastically reducing vineyard treatments. In the cellars, Ascheri is straightforward with a traditional bent, fermenting in temperature-controlled steel vats with BRL 97—the specific Barolo yeast created by the University of Turin from select vineyards in Barolo. Aging takes place exclusively in Slavonian oak, for at least two years, followed by nearly a year bottle aging.

Production

Total surface area: 45 ha (111 acres)

Barolo: 15 ha (37 acres), 30,500 bottles

Barolo Sorano.   This is the firm's calling card, made from their holdings in Sorano in Serralunga. During fermentation, 60 percent of this wine undergoes fermentation and maceration under the customary submerged-cap technique, lasting for forty days. The 2008 delivers rather funky but pleasing aromas of leather, truffle, and tar with a hint of rose. Delicious Barolo palate of dense wild cherry, spice. Still young with a powerful structure. Best 2015 to 2033.

Barolo Sorano Coste & Bricco.   Made only in top vintages and produced from two of the highest vineyards in Sorano with full southern exposures. The 2008 shows quintessential Nebbiolo character with balsamic aromas, and rich cherry and spice palate. Still young, but already combines power and grace. Best 2016 to 2038.

Barolo Pisapola.   Made from the eponymous cru in Verduno where vines average 380 meters (1,247 feet) above sea level and benefit from warm southern and southeastern exposures. The 2008 is all about elegance, with rose, violet, leather, and sage aromas and bright cherry, cinnamon, and spice flavors. Still young with firm but fine tannins and nervous acidity. Best 2015 to 2028.

Vintage Guide to Barolo and Barbaresco

This vintage guide is based on a combination of my own tastings over the years and common local knowledge regarding the older vintages. For a look at Barolo vintages from 1868 to the present, you can check out Renato Ratti's vintage guide. I begin this guide with 1945, the first postwar vintage. Starting with 1978, I also suggest drink or hold; I add these suggestions, as well as any other comments, to exceptional older vintages only if relevant. Please note, however, that storage is a crucial factor in determining how a wine will age. Not even the greatest vintages, if they have not had ideal cellar conditions, will stand the test of time.

If you do find some of these aged Barolos, or have them already in your cellars, I'd suggest opening them three or four hours ahead of time as opposed to decanting, although this is generally impossible when ordering them from restaurant wine lists. I always try to avoid decanting old vintages, especially those that have been corked for decades, as I believe it can shock the wine. As Maria Teresa Mascarello, daughter of the late Bartolo, once told me, "Decanting an old or older vintage is traumatic for the wine. It's like going up to an eighty-five-year-old person and shaking him or her violently. It's harmful, perhaps even life threatening."

1945 ★★★★

1946 ★★

1947 ★★★★★   This was an exceptional vintage that old-timers still refer to on occasion.

1948 ★	1950 ★★	1952 ★★	1954 ★★★	1956 ★★★
1949 ★	1951 ★★★	1953 ★	1955 ★★★★	1957 ★★★★

1958 ★★★★★ I've tasted several Barolos from this vintage in the last decade and have found them to be mellowed with time and definitely on the decline but still impressive.

1959 ★★ While this is touted as a mediocre vintage, I had a few in the early years of this millennium and a Marchesi di Barolo 1959 in 2012 that had held up surprisingly well but were more memorable for the experience than because of the wines themselves.

1960 ★

1961 ★★★★★ This was a remarkable vintage that produced structured, tannic wines that needed years to come around. The best are still maintaining.

1962 ★★★

1963 ★

1964 ★★★★★ A super vintage that set a benchmark in the denominations. This produced long-lived wines with initially tough tannins that took years to come around.

1965 ★★★

1966 ★★

1967 ★★★★ This was a great vintage that made long-lived wines. Those I tried in 2012 and 2006 were still holding up well.

1968 ★★★

1969 ★★

1970 ★★★★★ An excellent vintage.

1971 ★★★★★ A superb vintage that produced age-worthy wines with complexity and finesse. Drink.

1972 ★ A very poor vintage.

1973 ★★ An unremarkable vintage.

1974 ★★★ A good vintage.

1975 ★★★ A normal vintage.

1976 ★★ A fair vintage that generated very few age-worthy wines.

1977 ★ Below average.

1978 ★★★★★ A superb vintage that produced monumental wines of extraordinary structure and longevity. The several 1978 Barolos I tried in 2013 were still shockingly youthful and nervous, but they also showed remarkable depth and complexity. They still have years to go. Drink or hold.

1979 ★★★   A good year that yielded better than average quality. These are on the downhill slide, so drink now.

1980 ★★★   A solid year that produced good wines.

1981 ★★   A mediocre year. Drink now.

1982 ★★★★★   A blockbuster vintage that produced gorgeous, richly textured, and structured wines. Tastings of several 1982 Barolos and Barbarescos in 2012 and 2013 demonstrated the depth and staying power of this fabulous vintage. Still growing strong. Drink or hold.

1983 ★   An unimpressive vintage that produced weak wines. Drink now.

1984 ★★   Uninspiring. Drink.

1985 ★★★★   This was perhaps the first vintage in the Langhe to receive hype even before the grapes got in the cellars. The quality of the fruit was superb, and made for delicious wines in Barolo and Barbaresco. While these were never as forward as the 1997s, the 1985s set the stage for a fruitier, more approachable style. They marked a departure from the quintessential austerity of other great vintages from the period—namely, the great 1982s and legendary 1978s. Drink.

1986 ★★★   This vintage was marked by hail in the Langhe, but those not affected made good wines. Drink.

1987 ★★   An uneven vintage with variable quality. Drink.

1988 ★★★★   Not an easy vintage due to rain in October, but many producers were able to make excellent wines. Drink.

1989 ★★★★★   This was an outstanding vintage in the Langhe (which was spared the rains that ruined vintages in much of Italy) and produced stunning wines destined for long cellaring. In 2013 I tried several 1989s and found them remarkably fresh, with bright fruit and silky tannins, but also with gripping sensations of leather, truffle, and tar. The ones I tried were still developing and had years left. Drink or hold.

1990 ★★★★   A very good but forward vintage that right away showed pedigree and class. However, when released it was believed this was superior to the 1989, but tastings of the two vintages over the years have convinced me that this has reached its peak, while the 1989 is still developing. Drink.

1991 **   After the excellent quality of the 1990, 1989, and 1988, this was a disappointment and the first in a string of average and below average vintages. Drink now.

1992 *   Cold, wet weather at harvesttime led to thin and diluted wines. Drink now.

1993 **   Although some producers made good wines, this was generally a middling and variable vintage that was recommended to drink early while waiting for the 1989s and 1990s to come around. If you have any, drink now.

1994 **   A mediocre vintage due to prolonged rain. Drink now.

1995 ****   Although hyped upon release as an outstanding vintage, probably because it was much better than the previous poor vintages, this is a very good vintage. It soon got left behind in the media hype over 1996 and 1997, which are superior. Drink.

1996 *****   This is a classic vintage that yielded austere, structured Barolos and Barbarescos with tough tannins and nervous acidity that recall old-school vintages like 1978. I think these will come around and develop gripping complexity and mesmerizing depth, but this year is one for the ages. Hold.

1997 ***   In general this is an extremely overrated vintage. This was a very warm year that yielded softer, rounder wines that were very friendly upon release, so much so that they caused a media frenzy when they hit the market because of their instant gratification appeal. However, with few exceptions, they don't possess enough acidity for moderate aging. Most are fading quickly as the fruit dries up. Drink.

1998 ****   A sleeper vintage. Austere when first released, many 1998s went through an extended mute period where they completely shut down between 2003 and 2008, after which they opened up and bloomed into classic bottlings showing leather, truffle, tar, and dried cherry, at least those that were not ruined by aggressive new oak. Drink or hold.

1999 *****   An excellent vintage that is starting to bloom now but can be aged for another decade or more. Already showing leather, tar, and dried rose petals but still has rich, dark fruit too. Drink or hold.

2000 ***   A very hot, dry year that produced warm, forward, and one-dimensional wines that in general lack intensity and have not developed complexity. A vintage for early pleasure but not aging. Drink.

2001 ★★★★★   This was an outstanding vintage that produced classic wines that needed time. Initially closed, they are bold, structured, and well balanced. They are drinking beautifully now (in 2014), but should continue to develop and maintain for another decade at least. Drink or hold.

2002 ★   A terrible vintage due to torrential rain at harvesttime and devastating hail in much of Barolo. Many producers in the latter did not even make Barolo in 2002, and those that did produced weak and diluted wines that should have already been consumed. On the other hand, Giacomo Conterno was not wiped out by hail and left his grapes to dry out in October and made a fabulous Riserva Monfortino, but this is most definitely an exception.

2003 ★★   One of the hottest, driest vintages ever recorded in all of Italy. Vineyards with full southern exposures and the lowest altitudes suffered the most. Both Barolo and Barbaresco show cooked fruit, evident alcohol, and green tannins because plants shut down before seeds ripened. Although there were a few good wines, this was an extreme vintage, and even the best of the lot won't develop or age well. If you have any in your cellars, drink now.

2004 ★★★★★   A fantastic vintage that yielded quality and quantity. Nebbiolo in Barolo and Barbaresco reached perfect maturation throughout the growing zones and produced gorgeous wines. They have rich black cherry flavors and big but fine tannins that made them enjoyable upon release, while bright acidity will allow them to age well and develop complexity. They are defined by impeccable balance and elegance. Drink or hold.

2005 ★★★   Rain during the harvest made this a difficult vintage for many, and quality depends on whether a producer picked before or after the rain. The best 2005s have bright fruit and elegant, silky tannins. These aren't the most complex or age-worthy Barolos and Barbarescos but are immensely enjoyable now. Drink.

2006 ★★★★★   This was a classic vintage for both Barolo and Barbaresco. They show bright red fruit, great depth, and gripping, chewy tannins along with nervous acidity. These are going to need time, but they should develop well for decades. The best already show a layer of complexity as of 2014. Hold.

2007 (*** Barolo, **** Barbaresco)   Another exceedingly hot, dry vintage that yielded forward wines. Barbaresco fared far better, and the wines have lovely dense fruit but should be consumed at the ten-year mark. Barolo on the other hand showed more signs of heat stress that shut down plants before reaching full phenolic maturation but at the same time accumulated high sugar levels. Thus many wines are unbalanced with cooked fruit, high alcohol, and green tannins. Drink soon.

2008 ****   Due to a cool, wet spring, followed by damaging winds (including hail in parts of Barolo) in August, this was a difficult vintage in both denominations, and quality greatly depends on whether or not vineyards were damaged during the summer storms. Those that survived the storms benefited from a warm, sunny September, and many are classic wines with very firm tannins that need time to develop. Barolos from La Morra showed very well. Drink or hold.

2009 (*** Barbaresco and most of Barolo, ** La Morra)   This is a buyer-beware vintage. Although I found some exceptional wines, they were few and far between compared to other recent vintages, and many estates profiled in this book made the best that I've tried from the vintage. The underlying problem was scathing heat that, according to the producers, created extremely uneven ripening, with plants weeks apart in terms of ripening, even within the same rows. The best wines are the result of multiple harvests. Some producers instead waited to pick when all grapes had reached full ripeness, which meant that many grapes in the same vineyard were overripe, and therefore resulted in a lot of cooked fruit and high alcohol levels. Other producers did a single harvest, combining both ripe and underripe grapes. In other cases, the vintage's bitter tannins were exasperated by the wood tannins imparted by new barriques, as in the case of many of La Morra Barolos. Barolo, Serralunga, and Castiglione Falletto performed the best. The vintage was more uniform in Barbaresco, but rather one-dimensional and ripe. Hold until ten-year mark.

2010 ★★★★★   The long, cool growing season generated classic, focused Barolos and Barbarescos with crunchy red fruit, racy acidity, and bracing but fine tannins. The vintage is hallmarked by elegance and impeccable balance. Many wines from both denominations were already surprisingly accessible upon release thanks to the noble quality of the tannins and ripe fruit, but they also deliver tremendous aging potential and should develop beautifully for decades. There are a number of gorgeous, vibrant wines across the board in both denominations. Hold for complexity.

Barolo and Barbaresco at a Glance

BAROLO

Became DOC in 1966.

Became DOCG in 1980.

Growing area covers eleven towns.

As of 2013, surface area under vine was 1,984 hectares (4,902 acres) with a potential bottle production of 13,902,404 bottles.

Key modifications to the 2010 revised production code:

a. Delimited "geographic mentions" (which are often referred to as subzones by producers), 170 subzones, and 11 village mentions.

b. Although the previous production codes have always stipulated that vineyards for Barolo must be located on hillsides, tighter restrictions on vineyard location in the modified version categorically exclude valley floors, humid and flat areas, areas without sufficient sunlight, and areas with full-on northern exposures. Minimum vineyard altitude must be between 170 meters and 540 meters.

c. Aging requirements (barrel aging) have also changed. Starting from November 1 after the harvest: thirty-eight months total aging, eighteen of which must be in wood. Previously, aging requirements called for three years total aging (starting from January after the harvest), two of which had to be in wood. It is generally believed the reduction in wood is to accommodate younger vines and the use of barriques. Most producers tell me, however, that they will continue to age a minimum of two years in wood.

Barolo Riserva must be aged for five years before release, eighteen months of which must be in wood.

Barolo's Geographic Mentions

(Italic indicates vineyards that are in more than one township. Bold indicates vineyard areas of particular merit. These areas are followed by star ratings, one to three, with three being the maximum in terms of quality.)

Barolo
Albarella, Bergeisa, Boschetti, Bricco delle Viole, Bricco San Giovanni, ***Brunate*** ★★★, ***Bussia***, **Cannubi** ★★★, **Cannubi Boschis** ★★★, Cannubi Muscatel, **Cannubi San Lorenzo** ★★, **Cannubi Valletta** ★, Castellero, *Cerequio*, Coste di Rose, Coste di Vergne, Crosia, Drucà, *Fossati*, La Volta, **Le Coste** ★, Liste, Monrobiolo di Bussia, Paiagallo, Preda, *Ravera*, Rivassi, Ruè, San Lorenzo, San Pietro, San Ponzio, **Sarmassa** ★★★, Terlo, Vignane, Zoccolaio, Zonchetta, Zuncai

Castiglione Falletto
Altenasso or Garblet Suè or Garbelletto Superiore, **Bricco Boschis** ★★★, Bricco Rocche, Brunella, Codana, **Fiasco** ★★, Mariondino or Monriondino or Rocche Moriondino, **Monprivato** ★★★, Montanello, Parussi, Pernanno, Piantà, **Pira** ★, Pugnane, ***Rocche di Castiglione*** ★★, Scarrone, Solanotto, Valentino, **Vignolo** ★, **Villero** ★★★

Cherasco
Mantoetto

Diano d'Alba
Gallaretto, La Vigna, *Sorano*

Grinzane Cavour
Bablino, Borzone, Canova, Castello, Garretti, Gustava, La Corte, Raviole

La Morra
Annunziata, **Arborina** ★, Ascheri, Berri, Bettolotti, Boiolo, Brandini, Bricco Chiesa, Bricco Cogni, Bricco Luciani, Bricco Manescotto, Bricco Manzoni, Bricco Rocca, Bricco San Biagio, ***Brunate*** ★★★, Capalot, Case Nere, Castagni, *Cerequio* ★★★, Ciocchini, Conca, *Fossati*, Galina, Gattera, Giachini, **La Serra** ★, Rive, **Rocche dell'Annunziata** ★★★, Rocchettevino, Roere di Santa Maria, Roggeri, Roncaglie, San Giacomo, Santa Maria, Sant'Anna, Serra dei Turchi, Serradenari, Silio, Torriglione

Monforte d'Alba
Bricco San Pietro, **Bussia [*** for the classic zones Bussia Sottana and Bussia Soprana, names that no longer exist but should]**, Castelletto, **Ginestra ****, **Gramolere ***, Le Coste di Monforte, Mosconi, Perno, Ravera di Monforte, *Rocche di Castiglione*, San Giovanni

Novello
Bergera-Pezzole, Cerviano-Merli, Ciocchini-Loschetto, Corini-Pallaretta, Panerole, *Ravera* ******, Sottocastello di Novello

Roddi
Bricco Ambrogio *

Serralunga d'Alba
Arione *, Badarina, Baudana, **Boscareto ***, Brea, Briccolina, Bricco Voghera, Broglio, Cappallotto, Carpegna, Cerrati, **Cerretta *****, Collaretto, Colombaro, Costabella, Damiano, **Falletto ****, Fontanafredda, **Francia *****, **Gabutti *****, Gianetto, **Lazzarito ****, Le Turne, Lirano, Manocino, Marenca, Margheria, Meriame, **Ornato ***, **Parafada ***, Prabon, **Prapò ****, Rivette, San Bernardo, San Rocco, Serra, *Sorano*, Teodoro, **Vignarionda *****

Verduno
Boscatto, Breri, Campasso, **Massara ****, **Monvigliero *****, Neirane, Pisapola, Riva Rocca, Rocche dell'Olmo, Rodasca, San Lorenzo di Verduno

In addition to these, there are eleven additional geographic mentions, one for each Barolo village.

BARBARESCO

Became DOC in 1966.

Became DOCG in 1980.

Growing area covers three towns and a sliver of a hamlet of Alba.

As of 2013, surface area under vine was 684 hectares (1,690 acres) with a potential bottle production of 4,681,737 bottles.

Important changes to the production code in 2007, with minor modifications added in 2010:

a. Sixty-six delimited "geographic mentions" (which are often referred to as subzones by producers).

b. Although the previous production codes have always stipulated that vineyards for Barbaresco must be located on hillsides, tighter restrictions on vineyard location in the latest production code categorically exclude valley floors, humid and flat areas, areas without sufficient sunlight, and areas with northern exposures. Vineyard altitude cannot surpass 550 meters.

c. Aging requirements (barrel aging) have also changed. Starting from November 1 after the harvest: twenty-six months total aging, nine of which must be in wood. Previously, aging requirements called for two years total aging (starting from January after the harvest), one of which had to be in wood. It is generally believed the reduction in wood is to accommodate younger vines and the use of barriques. Most producers tell me, however, that they will continue to age between one and two years in wood depending on the cru and the vintage.

Barbaresco Riserva must be aged for four years before release, nine months of which must be in wood. Most producers, however, are barrel aging their Riservas for far longer—usually about two years.

Barbaresco's Geographic Mentions

(Italic indicates vineyards that are in more than one township. Bold indicates vineyard areas of particular merit. These areas are followed by star ratings, one to three, with three being the maximum in terms of quality.)

Barbaresco
Asili ★★★, Cà Grossa, Cars, Cavanna, Cole, Faset, **Martinenga** ★★, Montaribaldi, **Montefico** ★★, **Montestefano** ★, Muncagöta, **Ovello** ★★, Pajè, **Pora** ★, **Rabajà** ★★★, Rabajà-Bas, **Rio Sordo** ★★★, Roccalini, **Roncaglie** ★★, **Roncagliette** ★★★, Ronchi, Secondine, **Tre Stelle** ★, Trifolera, Vicenziana

Neive
Albesani ★★★, Balluri, **Basarin** ★★, Bordini, Bricco di Neive, Bric Micca, Canova, **Cottà** ★, **Currà** ★, Fausoni, Gaia-Principe, **Gallina** ★★★, Marcorino, Rivetti, San Cristoforo, San Giuliano, Serraboella, Serracapelli, Serragrilli, Starderi

San Rocco Seno d'Elvio
Meruzzano, *Montersino*, *Rizzi*, Rocche Massalupo

Treiso

Ausario, Bernadot, Bricco di Treiso, Casot, Castellizzano, Ferrere, Garassino, Giacone, Giacosa, Manzola, Marcarini, *Meruzzano*, *Montersino*, **Nervo** ★★, **Pajorè** ★★★, **Rizzi** ★, Rombone, San Stunet, Valeirano, Vallegrande

VIGNA

In both Barolo and Barbaresco, this term can be applied only together with one of the official geographic mentions. To use Vigna on the labels, the vineyard must be within an approved geographic mention, and the resulting wine made from 10 percent lower yields for mature vineyards (at least seven years old), and lower for younger vineyards.

NOTES

CHAPTER 1. THE ANCIENT ORIGINS OF THE LANGHE HILLS

1. Cita, Chiesa, and Massiota, *Geologia dei vini italiani*, 36–37.
2. *Naturalia historia* 17.3. Alba Pompeia is the Roman name for Alba.
3. Vignolo-Lutati, "Sulla delimitazione delle zone a vini tipici."
4. Soster and Trevisan, *Barolo*, 26.
5. Cita, Chiesa, and Massiota, *Geologia dei vini italiani*, 45.
6. Soster and Trevisan, *Barolo*, 103.

CHAPTER 2. NOBLE NEBBIOLO

1. Fantini, *Monografia sulla viticoltura e enologia*, n.p.
2. Belfrage, *Barolo to Valpolicella*, 52.
3. Salaris, *La diffusione del vitigno Nebbiolo nel mondo*, with updates from statistics released in 2012 by the Consorzio of Barolo, Barbaresco, and Roero.
4. Rosso, *Barolo*, 18.
5. Vacchetto, *Le viti per il Barolo*, 12.
6. Molon, *Ampelografia*, 861.
7. Petrini et al., *Atlante delle vigne di Langa*, 13.

CHAPTER 3. THE KING OF WINES, THE WINE OF KINGS

1. Rosso, *Barolo*, 20.
2. Gabler, *Passions*, 97.
3. Ibid., 177 and 202.
4. Mainardi, *Il vino piemontese nell'Ottocento*, 178.

5. Ibid., 179.
6. Ibid., 183–84.
7. Ianniello, *Produttori del Barbaresco,* 11.

CHAPTER 6. BAROLO AND NOVELLO

1. Fantini, *Monografia sulla viticoltura ed enologia,* n.p.
2. Gallesio, *I giornali dei viaggi.*
3. Riccardi Candiani, *Louis Oudart e i vini nobili,* 47.
4. Massè, *Il paese di Barolo,* 48.
5. Ronco, *Giulio di Barolo,* 119–20.
6. Vacchetto, *Le viti per il Barolo,* 106.

CHAPTER 7. CASTIGLIONE FALLETTO

1. Based on statistics supplied by the Consorzio in 2012.
2. Vignolo-Lutati, "Sulla delimitazione delle zone a vini tipici."
3. Ibid., 12.
4. Ibid.

CHAPTER 9. LA MORRA AND CHERASCO

1. Ratti, "Barolo il Grande," 13.

CHAPTER 12. BARBARESCO: FROM DOMIZIO CAVAZZA TO SUBZONES

1. Production statistics for 2013 supplied by the Consorzio.
2. Cavazza, "Barbaresco e i suoi vini," 8.
3. Guattieri et al., *Barbaresco,* 71.
4. Fantini, *Monografia sulla viticoltura ed enologia,* n.p.
5. Ibid.
6. Ianniello, *Produttori del Barbaresco,* 28.

CHAPTER 13. (VILLAGE OF) BARBARESCO

1. Fantini, *Monografia sulla viticoltura ed enologia,* n.p.

CHAPTER 15. TREISO AND SAN ROCCO SENO D'ELVIO

1. Cavazza, "Barbaresco e i suoi vini."

CHAPTER 16. WINERIES IN ALBA AND OUTSIDE OF BAROLO/BARBARESCO VILLAGES

1. Tablino, "Un gioiello dell'enologia di nome Barolo."

ACKNOWLEDGMENTS

I'd like to thank the following people for the help and time they gave to me while I was writing this book: Emanuele Coraglia and Andrea Ferrero of the Consorzio for all the statistics on production and other material they provided; Moreno Soster and Stefano Dolzan, who shared their research and data from the Piedmont Region's Banca Dati Regionale dei Terreni Agrari—Laboratorio Agrochimico Regione Piemonte; Igor Boni of IPLA, Erminio Basso, Professor Francesca Lozar, Professor Eleonora Bonifacio, and Professor Marco Giardino of the University of Turin for their expertise on the area's soils, pedology, and geology. A special thanks to three more University of Turin academics: Professor Anna Schneider for her expertise on grapevines, Professor Silvia Guidoni for her expertise on viticulture, and Professor Vicenzo Gerbi for sharing his knowledge of enology, and in particular his knowledge of Nebbiolo. Thanks to Aldo Vacca and Alfio Cavallotto, who explained Nebbiolo vineyard management and vinification in great detail, and to Carlo Flamini of Unione Italiana Vini for statistical data and to all the local producers who spent hours on end walking me through their vineyards, answering my questions, and opening numerous bottles of Barolo and Barbaresco.

Most of all I want to thank my husband, Paolo Tenti, for his photography and for reading the manuscript, and my mother and best friend, Elinor O'Keefe, for encouraging me and lending endless moral support while I dedicated so much of the last three years to the writing of this book.

GLOSSARY

AGRITURISMO. Holiday apartments on a farming estate.

ANNATA. Vintage, or vintage wine that is not the Riserva bottling.

ARENARIA. Sandstone.

ARGILLA. Clay.

ASSEMBLAGGIO. Blending the different lots of wine, often made from grapes hailing from different vineyards.

AZIENDA, AZIENDE. Firm(s), estate(s).

BARRIQUE. 225-liter barrel, usually made with French oak, though is sometimes made with other oak, including American and Austrian. French wood is by far the most common in Italy.

BIOLOGICO. Organic farming.

BORGO. Hamlet.

BOTTI. Large barrels, the most traditional being made of Slavonian oak with capacities anywhere from 10 to 100 hectoliters. The most common used today are usually 20 to 50 hectoliters.

CA'. Abbreviation for *casa* often used in the Langhe as part of a winery's name.

CALCARE. Calcareous soil also called limestone.

CANTINA, CANTINE. Cellar, cellars.

CANTINA SOCIALE. Cooperative cellar.

CAPPELLO SOMMERSO. Submerged-cap method whereby the solids are kept submerged in the must during alcoholic fermentation.

CASTELLO. Castle.

CLASSICO. Term used to indicate the historical or original part of a growing zone.

CILIEGIA. Cherry, which is a typical aroma/flavor of Nebbiolo.

COLLINA. Hill.

COLTURA PROMISCUA. Mixed cultivation of crops prevalent in rural Italy that preceded specialized vineyards.

COMUNE. Commune or municipality. May incorporate several villages.

CONSORZIO. Consortium or growers' union.

CONSULENTE. In Italian wine terms, consulting enologist.

CORDONE SPERONATO. Spurred cordon vine-training system, prevalent in most of Tuscany for Sangiovese but not used in Piedmont for Nebbiolo.

CUOIO. Leather, an aroma/taste often found in aged Barolos and Barbarescos, although hints of this can be detected in younger, traditionally crafted wines.

CRU. A vineyard area. Sometimes used by producers to denote a single-vineyard bottling.

DÉLESTAGE. Also known as rack-and-return method of aerating fermenting wine by pumping it out of the fermenting vat and into awaiting receptacles (or another tank), and then back into the fermenting tank.

DIRADAMENTO. Thinning out of the bunches.

DISCIPLINARE. The legally binding regulations that govern a specific denomination.

DOC (DENOMINAZIONE DI ORIGINE CONTROLLATA). An appellation whose origin is controlled and regulated by the Italian government equivalent to France's A.O.C.

DOCG (DENOMINAZIONE DI ORIGINE CONTROLLATA E GARANTITA). The most rigidly controlled appellation, which is guaranteed by a tasting commission.

DOP (DENOMINAZIONE DI ORIGINE PROTETTA). The new European Union regulations that will eventually supplant Italy's current DOC and DOCG designations, though at press time how this will be implemented into Italy's current system, and how it will appear on labels, is not clear. Barolo, Barbaresco, and other DOCG wines will still be allowed to use the DOCG designation on labels.

ENOLOGO. Enologist.

ENOTECA. Wineshop.

EQUILIBRIO, EQUILIBRATO. Balance, balanced.

ETICHETTA. Label.

ETTARO, ETTARI. Hectare, hectares.

FATTORIA. Farm.

FECCE. Lees.

FOLLATURA. Punching down the cap during fermentation.

FORTEZZA. Fortress.

FRAZIONE. A small part of a commune.

FRIZZANTE. Sparkling.

GOUDRON. Tar aromas, a tertiary aroma sometimes found in aged red wine.

GUYOT. Vine-training system used for Nebbiolo.

IGT (INDICAZIONE GEOGRAFICA TIPICA). A more flexible designation that is not as strictly controlled as DOC and DOCG. Piedmont has no IGT designated wines. Recent European Union regulations will eventually transform IGT into IGP (Indicazione Geografica Protetta).

IMBOTTIGLIATO ALL'ORIGINE. When written on the label, this means the wine was made entirely by a single estate that grew the grapes, produced the wine, and bottled it. Equivalent to "estate bottled" on U.S. labels.

IN PUREZZA. In Italian winespeak signifies a wine made solely with 100 percent of a single varietal, as in "Barolo and Barbaresco are made with Nebbiolo *in purezza*."

INVECCHIAMENTO. Aging.

LIEVITI. Yeast used for fermentation.

MAESTRO. Master.

MARNA, MARNE. Marl, marls.

MASSAL SELECTION (SELEZIONE MASSALE). Propagation method whereby cuttings are taken from a number of the best-performing vines on an estate to propogate a new generation of vines. Unlike clonal selection, where vines are propogated from a single "mother vine" and have identical DNA, massal selection involves a number of vines. Hence, while the new vines are all from the same family with the same genes, individual plants are not identical.

MENZIONZIONI GEOGRAFICHE AGGIUNTIVE. Literally translated as "added geographic mentions." For Barolo and Barbaresco, the term refers to officially delimited vineyard areas, which many producers like to consider subzones.

MEZZADRIA. Sharecropping.

MEZZADRO. Sharecropper.

NORMALE. Usually used to describe a given wine in a firm's range that is not designated as a single vineyard or a Riserva.

PASSITO. Dried. In wine terms a wine made from dried grapes that have undergone *appassimento*.

PODERE. Small estate or farm.

POTARE. Pruning.

RESA. Yield.

RIMONTAGGIO. Pumping over of the wine or must during fermentation to break up the solid cap (*capello*) that forms on the top.

RIO. Brook.

RISERVA. A strictly controlled designation that means the wine has been aged longer than the Annata.

SABBIA. Sand.

SALASSO. Bleeding of the must whereby some of the must in a tank is siphoned off to concentrate the remaining wine, especially in terms of color. These days the siphoned-off wine is often bottled as a *rosato*.

SFUSO. Bulk. Used to describe bulk wine sales as opposed to sales of bottled wine.

SORÌ. In Langhe dialect this term refers to a hilltop vineyard with full southern exposure.

SOTTOZONA. Subzone.

SPUMANTE. Sparkling wine.

STECCATURA. This is the Langhe's traditional method of submerged-cap maceration, whereby planks of wood hold down the cap (a block of skins and other grape solids that forms during alcoholic fermentation). When this method is used, the cap stays submerged for an extended period postfermentation for slow, thorough extraction of Nebbiolo's nobile tannins and other substances.

SUOLO. Soil.

TENUTA, TENUTE. Large estate or holdings.

TERRENO. Land or soil.

TERRITORIO. Territory, but largely used in Italian as the term for "terroir."

TINO, TINI. Conical wooden vat(s) used for fermentation.

TIPICITÀ. Tipicity, or a wine that expresses its grape variety and terroir; a quintessential expression of a particular type of wine.

TONNEAU, TONNEAUX. 500-liter (sometimes 700-liter) French oak barrel(s).

TRACCIABILITÀ. Traceability. This system enables consumers to check on a series of data that help verify the wine's authenticity.

UVA, UVE. Grape, grapes.

VASCA. Tank.

VENDEMMIA. Harvest.

VIGNA/VIGNETO. Vineyard.

VITE. Grapevine.

ZONAZIONE. An in-depth analysis of soil, climate, sun exposure, and other considerations often undertaken before planting a vineyard.

BIBLIOGRAPHY

Accigliaro, Walter, Gianni Boffa, and Dario Destefanis. *Castiglione Falletto.* Cavallermaggiore: Gribaudo Editore-Comune di Castiglione Falletto, 1993.

Belfrage, Nicolas. *Barolo to Valpolicella.* London: Faber and Faber, 1999.

Boni, Igor. "La zonazione vitivinicola in Piemonte: Gli esempi del Barolo e del Barbera d'Asti." *Il Suolo* 3 (2006).

Botta R., A. Schneider, N. S. Scott, and M. R. Thomas. "Within Cultivar Grapevine Variability Studied by Morphometrical and Molecular Marker Based Techniques." *Acta Horticulturae* 528 (2000).

Cagnasso, Enzo, et al. "Il colore dei vini derivati dal Nebbiolo." *Quad. Vitic. Enol. Univ. Torino* 29 (2007).

Cavallo, Oreste, M. Macagno, and G. Pavia. *Fossili dell'Albese.* Savigliano: L'Artistica, 1986.

Cavallo, Oreste, and Alessandro Marengo. *Civico Museo Federico Eusebio di Alba: Sezione di Scienze Naturali.* Turin: Regione Piemonte, 2006.

Cavazza, Domenico. "Barbaresco e i suoi vini." *Almanacco dell'Italia Agricola,* 1907.

———. *I vigneti del Cav. Luigi Parà presso La Morra d'Alba.* 2nd ed. Alba: Luigi Vertamy, 1887.

———. "Le vendemmie del 1884." *Bollettino del Comizio Agrario,* 1885.

Chorti, Evaghelia, et al. "Ombreggiamento della fascia produttiva cv. Nebbiolo: Effetti sulla composizione polifenolica delle bacche." *Quad. Vitic. Enol. Univ. Torino* 29 (2007).

Cita, Maria Bianca, Sergio Chiesa, and Paolo Massiotta. *Geologia dei vini italiani: Italia settentrionale.* Milan: BE-MA editrice, 2001.

Comba, Rinaldo, ed. *Vigne e vini nel Piemonte moderno.* 2 vols. Cuneo: Famija Albèisa-L'Arciere, 1992.

Consorzio di Tutela Barolo, Barberesco, Alba Langhe e Roero. *Langhe e Roero.* Alba: L'Artigiana, 2012.

Costantini, Edoardo, ed. *Metodi di rilevazione e informatizzazione dei dati pedologici.* Florence: CRA-ABP, 2007.

de' Crescenzi, Pietro. *Ruralium Commodorum.* 1309.

Fantini, Lorenzo. *Monografia sulla viticoltura ed enologia nella provincia di Cuneo.* Monforte d'Alba: handwritten monograph, 1895. Reprinted by Ordine dei Cavalieri del Tartufo e dei Vini di Alba, 1973.

Forti, Cesare. "Guardiamoci dalla filossera: Istruzione popolare." *Ufficio Agrario Provinciale di Cuneo.* Supplement to *L'Agricoltura Subalpina,* 1898.

Gabler, James. *Passions—The Wines and Travels of Thomas Jefferson.* Baltimore: Bacchus Press, 1995.

Gallesio, Giorgio. *I giornali dei viaggi (1810–1839): Trascrizione e commento a cura di Enrico Baldini.* Florence: Atti dell'Accademia dei Gergofili, 1995.

Gazzetta della Associazione Agraria, November 2, 1943.

Gerbi, Vincenzo, et al. "La vinificazione del Nebbiolo." *Quad. Vitic. Enol. Univ. Torino* 28 (2006).

———. "Tradizione e innovazione nella produzione di vini a base Nebbiolo." *Proceedings Nebbiolo Grapes,* 2004.

Giardino, Marco. "Relazioni fra attività vitivinicola e dissesto idrogeologico: Esempi di studio dalle Terre del Barolo." *Boll. Soc. Geol. It.* 6 (2006).

Grab, Alexander. "The Napoleonic Legacy." In *Italy in Tosca's Prism: Three Moments of Western Cultural History,* ed. Deborah Burton, Susan Vandiver Nicassio, and Agostino Ziino, 3–18. Boston: Northeastern University Press, 2004.

Guattieri, Fabiano, Vincenzo Gerbi, Roberta Ferraris, and Gian Antonio Dall'Aglio. *Barbaresco: Il vino e il territorio.* Novara: De Agostini, 2003.

Guidoni, Silvia, and Alessandra Ferrandino. "La gestione agronomica del vigneto di Nebbiolo." *Quad. Vitic. Enol. Univ. Torino* 28 (2006).

Ianniello, Attilio. *Produttori del Barbaresco 1958–2008.* Revello: Tipolitografia Nuova Stampa, 2008.

Lanati, Donato. *De vino: Lezioni di enotecnologia.* 2nd ed. Brescia: Edizioni AEB, 2007.

Mainardi, Giusi, ed. *Il vino piemontese nell'Ottocento: Atti dei Convegni Storici OICEE 2002-2003-2004.* Alessandria: Edizioni dell'Orso, 2004.

Mannini, Franco. "Il vitigno Nebbiolo e il suo patrimonio clonale." *Quad. Vitic. Enol. Univ. Torino* 28 (2006).

Mannini, Franco, et al. "Rilievi a Barolo sull'interazione fra portinnesti e cloni di Nebbiolo." *Quad. Vitic. Enol. Univ. Torino* 28 (2006).

Marchese, Salvatore. *Le storie di un re di nome Barolo.* Verona: Franco Muzzio Editore, 1993.

Maresca, Tom. "Stop the Presses: 1978 Barolo Is Finally Drinkable." *Tom's Wine Line,* July 5, 2013.

Mariani, Mario. *Bruno e Marcello Ceretto: The Barolo Brothers.* Bergamo: Veronelli Editore, 2007.

Masnaghetti, Alessandro. *Le vigne e le cantine (Barolo, Monforte, Serralunga, La Morra, Castiglione Falletto, Verduno, Barbaresco).* Monza: Enogea, 2009–11.

Massè, Domenico. *Il paese del Barolo.* Alba: Pia Società San Paolo, 1928.

Mattivi, Fulvio, et al. "Il potenziale polifenolico delle uve Nebbiolo: Comparazione con le varietà internazionali ed italiane." *Proceedings Nebbiolo Grapes,* 2004.

———. "La struttura chimica dei tannini del Nebbiolo." *Quad. Vitic. Enol. Univ. Torino* 28 (2006).

Micheletto, Egle, Maria Cristina Preacco, and Marica Gambari. *Civico Museo Federico Eusebio di Alba: Sezione di Archeologia.* Turin: Regione Piemonte, 2006.

Ministero d'Agricoltura. *Ampelografia italiana.* Turin: Litografia Fratelli Doyen, 1879.

Molon, Girolamo. *Ampelografia.* Vol. 2. Milan: Hoepli Editore, 1906.

Mozzone, Marco. *Italia o Enotria: La vigna del Risorgimento.* Vezza d'Alba: Ambiente & Cultura, 2012.

O'Keefe, Kerin. "Aldo Conterno: 1931–2012." *World of Fine Wine,* 37 (2012).

———. "Amazing Grace: Barbaresco." *World of Fine Wine,* 20 (2008).

———. "Angelo Rocca (1948–2012): Barbaresco's Free Thinker." *World of Fine Wine* 38 (2012).

———. "Anti-Berlusconi Label Becomes Collector's Item." *decanter.com,* July 31, 2002.

———. "Barbaresco Breaks Ranks." *Wine News,* October–November 2006.

———. "Barbaresco's New Cru Class." *World of Fine Wine,* no. 18 (2007).

———. "Barolo 2001: 10 Years On." *Decanter,* Italy 2011 guide.

———. "Bartolo Mascarello." *wine-searcher.com,* October 11, 2013.

———. *Brunello di Montalcino: Understanding and Appreciating One of Italy's Greatest Wines.* Berkeley: University of California Press, 2012.

———. "Bruno Giacosa." *Decanter,* November 2011.

———. "Cavallotto: The Road Less Traveled." *World of Fine Wine,* 24 (2009).

———. "Cult Barolo Producer Teobaldo Cappellano Dies." *decanter.com,* February 24, 2009.

———. "Gaja Barbaresco over Four Decades." *World of Fine Wine,* 15 (2007).

———. "Italian Wine World Thrilled by Die-Hard Award." *decanter.com,* October 7, 2002.

———. "Italy and the American Palate: Debunking the Myth." *World of Fine Wine,* 37 (2012).

———. "Nebbiolo Is Voignier Cousin, Conference Hears." *decanter.com,* January 26, 2004.

———. "Pio Cesare." *Decanter,* April 2012.

———. "Safeguarding Barolo, the King of Soul." *Wine News,* October–November 2009.

———. "Shameful Ruling over Barolo Borders." *wine-searcher.com,* October 11, 2013.

———. "Tradition Underscores Celebrated Barolo." *wine-searcher.com,* January 4, 2013.

———. "Whole-Bunch Fermentation Spreads to Piedmont." *wine-searcher.com,* June 11, 2013.

Petrini, Carlo, et al. *Atlante delle vigne di Langa.* Bra: Slow Food Editore, 2000.

Pliny the Elder (Gaius Plinius Secundus). *Naturalis historia.* Latin text and English translation available at www.perseus.tufts.edu.

Ratti, Renato. "Barolo il Grande." *Civiltà del bere,* February 1985.

———. "Le fermentazioni in enologia." *Quaderni del Castello di Grinzane Cavour,* 1975.

Riccardi Candiani, Anna. *Louis Oudart e i vini nobili del Piemonte.* Bra: Slow Food Editore, 2011.

Rolle, Luca, et al. "Assessment of Physiochimical Differences in Nebbiolo Grape Berries from Different Production Areas." *American Journal of Viticulture and Enology,* February 2012.

———. "Studio delle proprietà meccaniche di uve Nebbiolo coltivate in ambienti diversi." *Quad. Vitic. Enol. Univ. Torino* 28 (2006).

Ronco, Simonetta. *Giulia di Barolo.* Turin: Edizioni del Capricorno, 2008.

Rosso, Maurizio. *Barolo, the Jewel of the Langa.* Turin: Omega Edizioni, 2009.

Rosso, Maurizio, and Chris Meier. *The Mystique of Barolo.* Turin: Omega Edizioni, 2002.

Salaris, Claudio. "La diffusione del vitigno Nebbiolo nel mondo." *Proceedings Nebbiolo Grapes,* 2004.

Santini, Deborah, et al. "Influence of Different Environments on Grape Phenolic and Aromatic Composition of Three Clones of Nebbiolo." *Quad. Vitic. Enol. Univ. Torino* 31 (2010).

———. "Modifications in Chemical, Physical and Mechanical Properties of Nebbiolo Grape Berries Induced by Mixed Virus Infection." *S. Afr. J. Enol. Vitic.* 32 (2011).

Schneider, Anna. "Apetti genetici nello studio dei vitigni del territorio." *Quad. Vitic. Enol. Univ. Torino* 28 (2006).

Schneider, Anna, Paolo Bocacci, Daniela Marinoni, Roberto Botta, Aziz Akkak, and José Vouillamoz. "Variabilità genetica e parentele inaspettate del Nebbiolo." *Proceedings Nebbiolo Grapes,* 2004.

Schneider, Anna, Daniela Marinoni, Paolo Boccacci, and Roberto Botta. "Relazioni genetiche del vitigno Nebbiolo." *Quad. Vitic. Enol. Univ. Torino* 28 (2006).

Silengo, Giovanni, ed. *Le lettere del fattore di Cavour da Grinzane 1847–1852.* Alba: Ordine dei Cavalieri del Tartufo e dei Vini di Alba, 1979.

Soldati, Mario. *Vino al vino: Terzo viaggio.* Milan: Mondadori, 1976.

Soster, Moreno, and Teodora Trevisan, eds. *Barolo: Studio per la caratterizzazione del territorio, delle uve, e dei vini dell'area di produzione.* Turin: Regione Piemonte, 2000.

Staglieno, Paolo Francesco. *Istruzione intorno al miglior modo di fare e conservare i vini in Piemonte.* Turin: Giuseppe Pomba, 1835. Reprinted by Edizioni dell'Orso in 2003.

Steinberg, Edward. *Sorì San Lorenzo: Angelo Gaja e la nascita di un grande vino.* Bra: Slow Food Editore, 1996.

Tablino, Lorenzo. "Un gioiello dell'enologia di nome Barolo." *Il Sommelier,* July–August 2003.

Tablino, Lorenzo, and Anna Sartorio. *Mirafiore & Fontanafredda.* Savigliano: L'Artistica, 2010.

Tegethoff, Wolfgang, ed. *Carbonate from the Cretaceous Period into the 21st Century.* Basel: Birkhauser, 2002.

Tenti, Paolo. "Barolo Patriarch Mascarello Dies." *decanter.com*, March 14, 2005.

———. "Pioneering Precision in Piedmont." *wine-searcher.com*, September 26, 2013.

Vacchetto, Pierangelo. *Le viti per il Barolo.* Guarene: Arti & Sapori, 2005.

Vignolo-Lutati, Ferdinando. *Le Langhe e la loro vegetazione.* Turin: Luigi Cecchini, 1929.

———. "Sulla delimitazione delle zone a vini tipici." *Annali della R. Accademia di Agricoltura di Torino,* November 1929.

Ziblatt, Daniel. *Structuring the State: The Formation of Italy and Germany and the Puzzle of Federalism.* Princeton, NJ: Princeton University Press, 2006.

Ziliani, Franco. "Castiglione Falletto." *World of Fine Wine,* 11 (2006).

INDEX